Getting It All Together In Daniel and Revelation

GETTING IT ALL TOGETHER by Marian Berry is a study of the Endtime significance of Daniel and Revelation. It is not an attempt to make a commentary on each verse but rather to focus on those aspects which are important to the last generation who will live to receive either the Seal of the Living God or the Mark of the Beast. It is intended to bring hope and courage to those who will live through the time of trouble.

This book is unique in that it is not an attempt to make an "interpretation" or to devise a new "application." Rather, it is an effort to permit the Bible to be its own expositor with unrelenting persistence in contrast to the many "opinions of men" which so often mislead us. It is an attempt to be consistent in permitting the Bible to furnish its own definitions, rationale, time frame, settings, and explanations. It permits the endtime prophet, Ellen G. White, to have first priority in providing the clues to understanding.

By
Marian Berry

TEACH Services, Inc.
PUBLISHING
www.TEACHServices.com • (800) 367-1844

World rights reserved. This book or any portion thereof may not be copied or reproduced in any form or manner whatever, except as provided by law, without the written permission of the publisher, except by a reviewer who may quote brief passages in a review.

The author assumes full responsibility for the accuracy of all facts and quotations as cited in this book. The opinions expressed in this book are the author's personal views and interpretations, and do not necessarily reflect those of the publisher.

This book is provided with the understanding that the publisher is not engaged in giving spiritual, legal, medical, or other professional advice. If authoritative advice is needed, the reader should seek the counsel of a competent professional.

Copyright © 1994, 2024 Marian Berry
Copyright © 1994, 2024 TEACH Services, Inc.
ISBN-13: 978-1-4796-1689-3 (Paperback)
Library of Congress Control Number: 93-61461

Published by

TEACH Services, Inc.
PUBLISHING
www.TEACHServices.com • (800) 367-1844

UPON COMPLETION OF THIS UNIQUE BOOK ON PROPHECY, YOU WILL KNOW THE VALUE OF:

1. prophetic studies to God's remnant people
2. permitting the Bible to be its own expositor
3. permitting the Bible to define its own terms
4. permitting the Bible to establish its own timeframes
5. establishing linkage between plagues, trumpets, and seals
6. knowing the Hermeneutic Rules of historicist interpretation
7. distinguishing the difference between applications and decoding of symbolism

KNOW THE IMPORTANCE OF:

1. Understanding the purpose of the seven last plagues
2. Knowing the linkage between plagues and trumpets
3. Linking the plagues, trumpets and seals all into one picture
4. Recognizing the "voices" of the seven thunders
5. Finding the "key" to understanding the 1260, 1290 and 1335
6. Locating the "warning" in Daniel 12
7. Recognizing the seven angels of Revelation 14 and 18

KNOW WHAT THESE ACTUALLY ARE:

1. Armageddon
2. The objective of the 2300 day-years
3. The Voice of God deliverance
4. Futurism
5. Preterism
6. Major Lines of Prophecy of Daniel and Revelation
7. Outlines of Daniel and Revelation
8. Timelines, how they begin and end

UNDERSTAND:

1. How the timelines of Daniel 12 furnish a framework for events mentioned in Revelation
2. How the timelines all are integrated and align with each other
3. How the "unrolling of the scroll" differs from speculation
4. How to count the "seven heads" of the dragon of Rev. 12
5. How to count the "seven heads" of the beast of Rev. 13
6. How to recognize the seven empires (heads) in Daniel 11
7. How to compute the "one hour" periods of Rev. 17:12 and 18:10, 17, 19
8. How the "daily taken away" establishes the abomination that maketh desolate
9. How to bring all this data into one rather simple picture and chain of events
10. How prophetic periods ended in 1844 and yet, "throw a flood of light" upon events to occur right down to the "eve of the great consummation." RH Sept. 25, 1889
11. The beast that was and is not, yet is—the eighth head

TABLE OF CONTENTS
DANIEL

	Preface	x
	Introduction	xiii
Chapter I	The Sanctified Life and Glorification	1
Chapter II	A Death Decree And the Deliverance	3
Chapter III	Deliverance By The "Faith of Jesus"	4
Chapter IV	Deliverance From the King of Babylon	8
Chapter V	The "Fall of Babylon" and the Seventh Plague	10
Chapter VI	Deliverance By the "Voice of God" Under The Seventh Plague	21
Chapter VII	Deliverance From the "Little Horn" Power	25
Chapter VIII	How Long Until the Deliverance?	29
Chapter IX	The Deliverance of Israel	30
Chapter X	Deliverance From Human Weakness	37
Chapter XI	Deliverance From the "king Of The North"	40
Chapter XII	Deliverance In the Timelines of Daniel 12	60

REVELATION

	Foreword From The Author	87
Chapter XIII	The Wrath of God	88
Chapter XIV	The First Five of The Seven Last Plagues	92
Chapter XV	The Sixth Plague Gathering Action	97
Chapter XVI	The Seventh Plague Deliverance	107
Chapter XVII	The Trumpets 1-4	120
Chapter XVIII	The Fifth Trumpet	132
Chapter XIX	The Sixth Trumpet	140
Chapter XX	The Seventh Trumpet	146
Chapter XXI	The Seven Seals	171
Chapter XXII	Revelation 17—Bible Symbolism	204
Chapter XXIII	The Web of Truth Summary	220
	Hermeneutics	222
	Appendix Note A The Triumph of John Paul II	228
	Appendix Note B The Great Red Dragon	229
	Appendix Note C The Composite Beast of Rev. 13	235
	Appendix Note D 317 Helpful Questions	244
	Appendix Note E Equating 1260 Days, 42 Months, & 3½ Times	261
	Appendix Note F Revelation 11	266
	Appendix Note G Comments On Symposium On Revelation Bk I & II	276
	Appendix Note H Letter to John Barrows	280
	Appendix Note I Some Thoughts On Timesetting	285
	Appendix Note J The Hewit Statement	288
	Appendix Note K The "One Hour" Period of Rev. 17:12	290
	Index	293

FROM THE AUTHOR

> Of what value is a study of prophecy? What good is it? After continuing research, the author has concluded that prophecy is the luminous torch in the hands of the faithful, which will lead them through earth's darkest hour. It is a "light that shineth in a dark place." II Pet. 1:19. It is the "clock" which will tell them where they are in the stream of time. It is the author's conviction that the people of God will know where they are all the way through closing events, final crisis and deliverance; year by year, month by month, day by day, and at last, hour by hour.

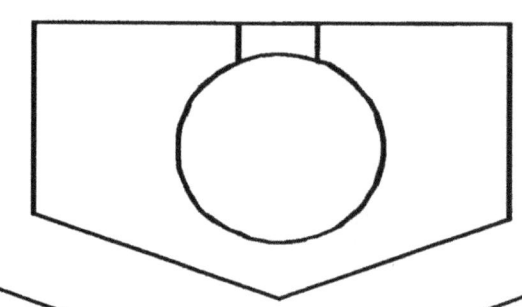

THE PROPHETIC CLOCK

CHARTS, DIAGRAMS, AND TABLES

1.	Getting It All Together In Daniel and Revelation 1994	i
2.	TEACH Services	ii
3.	Upon Completion of this Unique Book of Prophecy You . . .	iii
4.	Table of Contents: Daniel I-XII, Revelation XIII-XXIII	iv
5.	From the Author	v
6.	The Prophetic Clock	vi
7.	Charts, Diagrams, and Tables	vii
8.	Preface	x
9.	Picture of a Bible	xi
10.	Acknowledgments	xii
11.	Introduction: Daniel and Final Deliverance	xiii
12.	The Structure of Daniel: One Major Line of Prophecy	xvii
13.	Three Frogs	14
14.	Snake	15
15.	Dragon, Beast, False Prophet, and Three Frogs	17
16.	Chart: Consider the Vision . . . To make an end of sins	35
17.	Diagram: Forward Progressive Movement . . . of datable time in Daniel	40
18.	Map of Israel, Syria, Egypt	42
19.	Correlation of Daniel 11 and Revelation 13	49
20.	The Composite Beast of Revelation 13—7 Heads	57
21.	Chart: Sequence . . . of Daniel 11 Seven Empires	58
22.	Review and Herald Quotation, Sept 25, 1883	60
23.	The Literal Approach	62
24.	The Second Papal Supremacy (No. 2)	65
25.	The Voice of God Deliverance	67
26.	The Ascending and Descending Action of Final Crisis and Deliverance	68
27.	The 1335 Day Wait for the Blessing	69
28.	The National Sunday Law	70
29.	The Final Timeliness of Daniel 12. (a "grid" on which to place the events of Revelation)	73
30.	The Final Timeliness of Daniel 12 With Added Detail	74
31.	The Seven Thunders "Voices" of Revelation are Identified	78
32.	Thunder Sequence, Timeline, Event, Scripture Chart	79
33.	Warning Poem	80
34.	The Aligning, Interlocking, Structure of Prophecy	85
35.	The Gathering Action Culminating in the Sixth Plague of Revelation 16-18	105
36.	Psalm 91	106
37.	Three Deliverances	110

38.	One "day" vs. one "hour"	116
39.	Two "one hour" Periods	118
40.	Battle of Armageddon Battle Alignment	119
41.	Trumpets 1-4	123
42.	Table of Comparisons of the Seven Last Plagues with the Seven Trumpets	125
43.	Plagues WHAT, WHO, WHEN, WHERE, WHY, and HOW	126
44.	Trumpet Timeframe Sandwich	128
45.	Trumpets and Plagues After Close of Probation	128
46.	Sequence and Alignment of Plagues and Trumpets	131
47.	Her Plagues Come in one "day" (year) Rev. 18:8	137
48.	A Lion-King	139
49.	A Correlation of Plagues and Trumpets	154-155
50.	A Chart of the Alignment of the Three Major Lines of Prophecy of Daniel and Revelation	157
51.	The Chronological Order of the Major Line of Prophecy in Revelation 1-11	159
52.	The Chronological Order of the Major Line of Prophecy in Revelation 12-22	160
53.	An Alignment of the Chronological Order of the Major Lines of Prophecy in Revelation 1-11 and 12-22	161
54.	A Diagram Which Reveals the Sequential and Chronological Arrangement of the Two Aligning Major Lines of Prophecy in Revelation	162-163
55.	An Alignment of the Two Major Lines of Prophecy in Revelation	164
56.	Diagram 2. Paralleling Structures in Revelation's Eight Major Visions	166
57.	Diagram Paralleling Structures in Revelation's Eight Major Visions . . . Rev. 1-11	168
58.	Diagram Paralleling Structures in Revelation's Eight Major Visions . . . Rev. 12-22	169
59.	A Chart of Comparisons of Daniel 7:9-14 with Revelation 4 and 5	173
60.	The Order and Relationship of the First and Second Seals	176
61.	The Fifth Seal Leads Into Plagues and Trumpets	180
62.	The First Five Seals Leading into the Plagues and Trumpets	181
63.	Sequence and continuity in a Correlation of Plagues, Trumpets and Seals	182
64.	The Sixth Seal	183
65.	A Correlation of Seal 6, Plague 7 and Trumpet 7	184
66.	The Sixth Seal Earthquake and Signs Began and Conclude "The Time of the End"	184
67.	A Correlation of Seals, Trumpets, and Plagues	186-187
68.	Feast days . . . time pointed out . . .	188
69.	Fall Feast Days	189
70.	Fall Feast Days and Daniel 12 and Revelation 17	190
71.	The Last Year of Earth's History	194
72.	A Correlation of Seals, Trumpets, and Plagues	196-197
73.	Daniel 12 Timelines are the Framework for Events Described in Revelation	198
74.	Getting It All Together: Daniel 12 Timelines, Plagues, Trumpets, Seals, Revelation 17, Thunders, Fall Feasts	199

75. A Circular Correlation Chart of Interacting Endtime Events as Revealed by Plagues, Trumpets, Seals, Daniel 12 Timelines, and Major Lines of Bible Prophecy   201
76. A Sequential Outline of Endtime Events from 1844 to the Second Coming   202-203

APPENDIX

77. Jerusalem and Babylon   206
78. Jerusalem and Babylon Table of Comparisons   207
79. Seven Heads and Seven Horns   209
80. Babylon Sitting on the Scarlet Beast—Dragon   210
81. A Correlation Chart of an Alignment of Revelation 17:10-18 With Plagues and Trumpets   213
82. Satan's Seven Attempts to Establish His Kingdom   214
83. The Great Red Dragon   215
84. The Eight Heads of Revelation 17   216
85. Cartoon: The Bible Its Own Interpreter   221
86. The "Literal Approach"   223
87. The Triumph of John Paul II   228
88. The Great Red Dragon   229
89. The Composite Beast of Revelation 13   235
90. A Correlation of Daniel and Revelation on the Beast—Daniel 7, Revelation 13   236
91. Sequence and Continuity of the Seven Heads of the Beast of Revelation 13   238
92. The Three and an Half Days of Revelation 11 and "Fall of Babylon" of Revelation 18   273
93. Basic Differences in *Getting It All Together* and *Symposium on Revelation*   277, 278, 279

PREFACE
by the Author

The human eye has the ability to form an instantaneous view of a **panorama**. From a good perspective, one may take in the entire expanse of azure sky, clouds and contrails, hills and mountains, ships at bay and little inlets, the bridges, boats and fishermen, some houses, red roofs, as well as the flowers and birds nearby. There the whole scene lies before us in an interrelated view, each object as a part making the whole. That particular view will ever be identified as to its unique and specific location, whether on postcard, in movie or return visit.

This book, ***GETTING IT ALL TOGETHER IN DANIEL AND REVELATION***, is a unique effort, not so much to ferret out all the details of each verse of Scripture, but rather to discover the **linkage** between verses, or passages, and the **relationships** which exist between the books of Daniel and Revelation. It is an attempt to **align** the visions of the two books, tying them all into one unified panorama, significant to those of us who live in the "endtime" of earth's history. This is an effort to permit the Bible to be its own interpreter, to lay aside the varied and fragmented opinions of men, in order to get one cohesive view of endtime events. The entire Bible has one Source and is unified. This book, ***GETTING IT ALL TOGETHER*** gathers many details into **one** meaningful picture.

For this reason there is a **correlation** of plagues, trumpets, and seals presenting a **sequential** story of events from 1844 to the end of time. There are **interlocking** timelines which interpret each other and **bind** themselves into meaningful **units** of explanation. There is an emphasis on **sequence and continuity** of events and **linkage** between concepts as revealed in each of the visions.

There will always be those who "cannot see the forest for the trees," but there are many more who are longing to get it all together into one clear picture, into one great panorama with each predicted event falling into its proper place in time and sequence.

Not until this is accomplished can God's last generation have the surety and understanding to enable them to give the third angel's warning message and Loud Cry, or to be in perfect unity with each other, ready to receive the Latter Rain of the Holy Spirit to enable them to gather in the final harvest.

Therefore, this book is unique in its endtime perspective. Both Daniel and Revelation are searched for endtime application. These do not conflict with old truths long cherished on which the Sabbatarian church was founded. It contains many illustrated charts and interrelated timelines. It is relentless in its war against human opinions as they conflict with plain statements of the prophets, of Scripture and of Ellen G. White. It is almost tiresome as it repeats and never lets up on the insistence that the Bible is its own expositor, and that it furnishes its own definitions and **time frames** for the visions. Please be patient with these repetitions. They are an attempt to break out of the manmade errors that have fettered our thinking on prophecy.

"What says the Bible, the blessed Bible?
This should my only question be;
Teachings of men so often mislead us,
But what says the Book of God to me?"
—F.E. Belden

ACKNOWLEDGMENTS

The author expresses praise to God, who, through His providence, has made it possible to complete this book, ***GETTING IT ALL TOGETHER IN DANIEL AND REVELATION.*** Many prayers have been answered for wisdom and understanding, insight and skill to accomplish this work. All the praise, honor, and glory must be directed to God.

Special gratitude is expressed for the writings of Ellen G. White. Her inspired comments have furnished many clues to the linkage between Daniel and Revelation. Appreciation should be given to all who have gone before: historians, expositors, prophets, pioneers and others who have contributed through the ages to the process of "unrolling the Scroll." My appreciation also goes to those who have endeavored to develop the hermeneutic principles from Scripture to guide the expositor, in his endeavors to bring forth treasures from the prophetic Word.

Gratitude is expressed to my husband, who has given his support through the long processes of writing and publication, as well as in travel and presentation. Our son, Dr. Daniel Berry and his wife have contributed much to the entire project. Those who have contributed to the production of this book are beyond complete listing. Some have given hundreds of hours of their precious time proof reading the manuscript and to the committee which refined it. Others have given precious talents to the work of illustrations, charts, tables, graphs, and other items. Special mention should be given to Teach Services and their staff who make publication possible. Some who have contributed the most in consistent support have requested that their names be anonymous. It seems unfair to give some credit without naming all. But to all of them, I extend my utmost gratitude.

The author makes no claim to "Inspiration Revelation," as given to the prophets. In exactly the same way that the minister who will stand in the pulpit, or the Christian who prays before opening the Scripture; the author has sought illumination from the Holy Spirit or insight into Truth. It is intended that whatever may be helpful to others in their search for understanding of prophetic Scripture, may be shared in this book. It is the great satisfaction and happiness of finding the gems of Truth and the beauty of the Word that has been enough reward.

To all who have contributed toward the success and completion of this publication, I express my deepest pleasure and appreciation. May it help us through the stressful times ahead.

Marian G. Berry
The Author

INTRODUCTION

DANIEL AND THE FINAL DELIVERANCE

The book of Daniel, written more than 500 years before Christ's birth, contains specific parallels and references to the final deliverance of God's people. Incidents from the first to the last chapter repeatedly focus on confrontation over the worship of the true God, threat of extinction or a death decree, providential deliverance, and final triumph for the people of God. Thus the book of Daniel has a specific application to the last generation—those who will be involved in the climactic confrontation of the ages, face a death decree, and rejoice in that final deliverance at the voice of God and the second coming of Jesus.

Biblical interpretation needs to proceed by a careful observance of hermeneutic principles applied in an orderly fashion. Nowhere is this rule more valid than in dealing with apocalyptic material such as Daniel. Uriah Smith in his verse-by-verse exposition of the book, used a literal approach, in which he identified the historical settings of Daniel and made historical applications from the prophecies.

After such a base is established, the preacher, with homiletic freedom, may draw parallels, make comparisons, and note general principles and consistencies in God's dealings with man, thereby making the texts significant to the contemporary generation, specifically relating the prophecies to the final conflict and deliverance of the people of God.

Without a basic literal-historical exposition, analogy is unreliable. On the other hand, the mere linkage of history to prophecy is barren unless made spiritually pertinent to the contemporary generation. The prophecies of Daniel take on meaning for us today when the literal-historical approach merges with analogy in reference to the final crisis and deliverance.

Seven specific accounts of deliverance occur in Daniel's book, beginning with the personal experiences of Daniel and his friends, expanding to embrace the Jewish nation, the Gentile Christian Church, and at last the grand theme of worldwide deliverance from sin and the grave. These seven deliverances are: (1) Daniel's deliverance from Nebuchadnezzar's death decree for the wise men (Chap. 2:18-46); (2) the three Hebrews' deliverance from the fiery furnace (Chap. 3:24-30); (3) Daniel's deliverance from the lion's den (Chap. 6:22, 27); (4) deliverance of the Jews from Babylonian captivity (Chap. 9:25); (5) deliverance of the Gentile Christian church from the "little horn" power (Chap. 7:26, 27); (6) deliverance of God's people from sin (Chap. 9:24); (7) deliverance from the grave (Chap. 12:1-3).

Seven chronological lines in the book of Daniel culminate either in the deliverance of God's people or in the establishment of the kingdom of everlasting righteousness. When placed in context, these prophetic outlines will reveal a common focus—the deliverance of God's people from persecution, oppression, and sin. The seven are:

1. **The metallic image and the establishment of the "stone" kingdom** (Chap. 2). Through the ages, various governments have persecuted and martyred God's saints, but the great stone shall break in pieces and consume all these persecuting powers.

2. **The four beasts and the "little horn" persecution ending in judgment** (Chap. 7). The prophecy pictures the little horn making war with the saints, (A.D. 538-1798) but concludes with the assurance that "the judgment shall sit, and they shall take away his dominion, to consume and to destroy it unto the end." (Verse 26)

3. **The ram and the goat, the fierce king, and the cleansing of the sanctuary** (Chap. 8). A heavenly inhabitant questions, "How long shall be the . . . desolation?" (verse 13) The answer returns that the persecuting power will be "broken without hand" following a 2300-year period (verses 14, 25). The angelic tutor gives the general and specific objectives of the Investigative Judgment—"to finish the transgression, and to make an end of sins, . . . to make reconciliation for iniquity, and to bring in everlasting righteousness." (Dan. 9:24). In regard to final persecution and deliverance, the angel concludes by saying, "For the overspreading of abominations he shall make it desolate, even until the consummation." (Verse 27)

4. **The succession of kings continuing to the reign of the King of Kings** (Chapters 11, and 12:1-4). The reiteration of the rise and fall of kings and the struggle of nations builds to a climax when the "king of the north" goes forth "with great fury to destroy" (Chap. 11:40,44). However, the drama comes to a thrilling conclusion with the magnificent deliverance of the living righteous and the resurrection of the sleeping saints.

5. **The 1260 days of the persecution of God's people.** (Dan. 12:7)

6. **The 1290 days of the "abomination that maketh desolate"** (Chap. 12:11). This time period, given in reference to a persecuting power, must be viewed in connection with Revelation 13:16; 14:9, 16-18.

7. **The 1335 days until the pronouncement of blessing.** "Blessed is he that waiteth, and cometh to the thousand three hundred and five and thirty days." (Dan. 12:12) Ellen White writes: "The voice of God is heard from heaven . . . delivering the everlasting covenant to His people. . . . And when the **blessing** is pronounced on those who have honored God by keeping His Sabbath holy, there is a mighty shout of victory." *The Great Controversy*, p. 640.

Note: The last three timelines (5, 6, and 7), describe the final persecution, the reign of the persecutors, and the final deliverance. They form one picture of final crisis and deliverance.

In addition to prophetic lines dealing with deliverance for God's people, many parallels significant to the last generation may be found throughout Daniel's book.

Chapter 1 points out the striking contrast between the faces of those in Daniel's band who followed the counsel of God and the faces of those who ate the food of Babylon. This experience may be seen as a parallel to the contrast between the faces of the wicked, which "gather blackness" (Nahum 2:10), and the glorified shining faces of God's triumphant people.

> Jesus rides forth as a mighty conqueror. . . . Before His presence "all faces are turned into paleness;" upon the rejecters of God's mercy falls the terror of eternal despair. ". . . and the faces of them all gather blackness." Jeremiah 30:6; Nahum 2:10. The righteous cry with trembling: "Who shall be able to stand?" . . . Then the voice of Jesus is heard, saying: "My grace is sufficient for you." The faces of the righteous are lighted up, and joy fills every heart. *The Great Controversy*, p. 641.

When king Nebuchadnezzar acknowledged the supernatural revelation of his dream and the manner in which the God of heaven had delivered Daniel from the death decree pronounced upon the wise men, he "fell upon his face, and worshipped Daniel." (Dan. 2:46) In parallel, during the final conflict, the wicked will see the deliverance of God's people, and they, as Nebuchadnezzar, will fall down and worship at the saints' feet.

> Then it was that the synagogue of Satan knew that God had loved us who could wash one another's feet and salute the brethren with a holy kiss, and they worshipped at our feet. *Early Writings*, p. 15.

Nebuchadnezzar's gathering of "the princes, the governors, and captains, the judges, the treasurers, the counsellors, the sheriffs, and all the rulers of [Babylon]" (Dan. 3:3) finds a parallel in the gathering of "the kings of the earth and of the whole world" (Rev. 16:14) to the final confrontation.

Other parallels between events in Daniel and the experience of God's people at the end of time include: (1) the death decree on the plain of Dura (Dan. 3) and the final death decree (Rev. 13:15); (2) the interpretation of the words, mene, tekel, and upharsin of Daniel 5:25-28 ("God hath numbered thy kingdom. . . . Thou art weighed . . . and . . . found wanting. . . . Thy kingdom is divided") and the three angels' messages of Revelation 14:6-12 ("Judgment is come. . . . Babylon is fallen." God's wrath is come); (3) Darius' diversion of the Euphrates River to accomplish the fall of Babylon (Dan. 5:30, 31; Isa. 44:27-45:1) and the drying up of the Euphrates to prepare the way for the kings of the east (Rev. 16: 12, 19). Many other such parallels may be found.

The Book of Daniel remains a precious message from God thousands of years after it was written, giving courage to those who face the final confrontation between good and evil. The student of Daniel's prophecies will find its pages an exhaustless mine of truth filled with timely applications and parallels to his own day.

THE ENDTIME SIGNIFICANCE OF THE BOOK OF DANIEL

The book of Daniel bears a peculiar parallel and reference to the final deliverance of God's people. From the first to the last chapter, various incidents focus on the theme of confrontation and providential deliverance.

Daniel, the prophet, was one of the remnant of ancient Israel who was taken captive by Babylon and he prefigured that final remnant "which keep the commandments of God and have the testimony of Jesus Christ." (Rev. 12:17) His prophetic insight and prophetic visions are typical of that final remnant whose "testimony of Jesus Christ"—"is the spirit of prophecy." (Rev. 19:10) Daniel was a commandment-keeper and kept the Seventh-day Sabbath. He was also an "Adventist" in that he was intently anticipating the advent of the Messiah (See Daniel 9:26).

Daniel and his faithful friends composed that small "remnant" which found themselves in the midst of Babylon, in confrontation over their mode of worship of the true God. Their experiences parallel those of that final remnant who, in the midst of spiritual Babylon, will face a confrontation or "final test," a death decree, and a joyful final deliverance.

Not until the Bible student has mastered the book of Daniel, is he ready to understand the book of Revelation.

THE STRUCTURE OF DANIEL

THE MAJOR LINE OF PROPHECY IN DANIEL

The book of Daniel not only contains four outlines and numerical timelines, but it is also evident that the book is framed upon one **"Major Line of Prophecy."** That major line of prophecy extends from 606 B.C. to the stone kingdom-Second Coming of Christ. The four outlines and the timelines are all contained within that **"Major Line of Prophecy."**

THE ONE MAJOR LINE OF PROPHECY IN BOOK OF DANIEL

THE ONE MAJOR LINE OF PROPHECY IN THE BOOK OF DANIEL		
606 B.C.		Second Coming
	(Four Vision Outlines)	
606 B.C.		
606 B.C.	First Vision —	Outline of Daniel 2
538 B.C.	Second Vision —	Outline of Daniel 7
538 B.C.	Third Vision —	Outline of Daniel 8
	Fourth Vision —	Outline of Daniel 11

A **"Major Line of Prophecy"** represents the stream of time as it passes from one point of history to the end in **SEQUENCE, CONTINUITY, AND PERFECT ORDER.** Various details may be added to enhance its comprehensive forward movement as they are revealed in prophetic outlines and timelines.

There is only one "Major Line of Prophecy" in the structure of the book of Daniel.

The book of Revelation is more complicated. It contains **TWO MAJOR LINES OF PROPHECY,** which move in sequence, continuity, and order, from a point of beginning to the end.

To sum it all up:

1. Daniel has one **"Major Line of PROPHECY."**
2. Revelation has two **"Major Lines of PROPHECY."**
3. **Daniel's Line extends from 606 B.C. to the Second Coming**
4. **Revelation's Line, Chapters 12-22 extend from Lucifer's Fall to the New Earth.**
5. **Revelation's Line, Chapters 1-11 extend from A.D. 100 to The Second Coming.**

These lines of prophecy in both books overlap and cover some of the same historical time. Therefore the books should be studied together to enlighten and confirm, to supplement, to compliment, each other. This is why Ellen G. White wrote:

The study of the Revelation directs the mind to the prophecies of Daniel, and both present most important instruction, given of God to men, concerning events to take place, at the close of this world's history. *The Great Controversy,* p. 341.

When the Bible is permitted to be its own expositor; when the symbols are decoded by the Bible itself, when one timeline is aligned with another so that they are locked together, when the fragments are gathered up and placed in their correct sequence and continuity, and given Biblical timeframes; then the prophecies become clear and connected. They become so distinct that the theories, conjectures, and assumptions of various ones are revealed in all their disorder and confusion.

CHAPTER I

THE SANCTIFIED LIFE AND FINAL GLORIFICATION

The first chapter of Daniel gives insight into the kind of spiritual maturity and character development which will identify that final generation who will be glorified in the sight of the wicked. It portrays the justified, sanctified life which ever prepares for final crisis.

Like today's supermarkets and elegant restaurants, King Nebuchadnezzar's table displayed every food and drink in the most attractive manner to stimulate the appetite. Refined foods, pastries and sweets, unclean meats and seafoods, and alcoholic drinks were served. But Daniel and his friends adhered strictly to that undeviating principle of abstemious habits, which, in every age, is a glory to God. That principle is stated:

> Whether therefore ye eat, or drink, or whatsoever ye do, do all to the glory of God. I Cor. 10:31.

"Daniel **purposed** in his heart that he would not defile himself." (Dan. 1:8) A sanctified life requires a will and purpose to overcome the lusts of the flesh and to conquer and bring the appetite under the control of reason. Only in this way is God glorified. The Hebrew worthies guarded their bodies as the temple of the Holy Spirit that they might retain a clear mind and bring glory to their Creator.

For ten days they were allowed to test a simple diet of "pulse" (vegetarian diet) and water. "And at the end of the ten days **their countenances appeared fairer**." (Dan. 1:15) This striking contrast between these healthful, lighted countenances and those who participated in the fare of Babylon points toward that great contrast at the end of time, wherein the faces of the people of God who have lived to glorify Him, will themselves be glorified in contrast to the darkening faces of the wicked.

> Jesus rides forth as a mighty conqueror. . . . Before His presence, "all faces are turned into paleness;" upon the rejecters of God's mercy falls the terror of eternal despair. . . . and the faces of them all gather blackness. . . . (Nahum 2:10). . . . The faces of the righteous are lighted up, and joy fills every heart. *The Great Controversy*, p. 641.

> Soon I heard the voice of God, which shook the heaven and the earth. . . . Their captivity was turned. A glorious light shone upon them. How **beautiful** they then looked! All marks of care and weariness were gone, and **health and beauty were seen in every countenance**. Their enemies, and the heathen around them, fell like dead men; and they could not endure the light that shone upon the **delivered**, holy ones. This light and glory remained upon them, until Jesus was seen in the clouds of heaven, and the faithful, . . . were changed . . . from glory to glory. *Early Writings*, p. 272, 273.

Their **countenances are lighted up with His glory**, and shine as did the face of Moses when he came down from Mt. Sinai. The wicked cannot look upon them. *The Great Controversy*, p. 640.

This light and glory remained upon them, until Jesus was seen in the clouds of heaven, and the faithful, . . . were changed . . . from glory to glory. *Early Writings*, p. 273.

CHAPTER II

A DEATH DECREE AND THE DELIVERANCE

The second chapter of Daniel presents a prophetic outline which extends from Daniel's time to the establishment of Christ's kingdom. The great image of Nebuchadnezzar's dream reiterates the sequential rise and fall of nations and focuses upon "what shall be in the latter days." Dan. 2:28.

In Chapter 2 the prophet, Daniel, like those who shall live in "the latter days," was confronted with a death decree! Nebuchadnezzar declared, ". . . there is but one decree for you: . . . and commanded to destroy all the wise men of Babylon." Dan. 2:9, 12. Daniel was classed as a "wise man" and therefore was included in the death decree. Daniel defines the "wise" men of the latter days: "And they that be **wise** shall shine as the brightness of the firmament; and they that turn many to righteousness as the stars . . ." Dan. 12:3. The "wise men" or righteous in that final confrontation will face a death decree as did Daniel in the midst of Babylon. As the seven last plagues fall on spiritual Babylon, God's people will find themselves under accusation and death penalty.

> These plagues enraged the wicked against the righteous; they thought that we had brought the judgments of God upon them, and that if they could rid the earth of us, the plagues would then be stayed. A **decree** went forth to slay the saints, which caused them to cry day and night for deliverance. *Early Writings*, p. 36, 37.

"Then Daniel . . . Hananiah, Mishael and Azariah . . . would desire mercies of the God of heaven . . . that Daniel and his followers should not perish." Dan. 2:17, 18. In like manner, the saints will "cry day and night for deliverance." Prayer is the only resource in extremity.

When king Nebuchadnezzar acknowledged the supernatural revelation of this dream and the signal deliverance wrought for Daniel by the God of Israel, he "fell upon his face, and worshipped Daniel." Dan. 2:46.

When the wicked observe the deliverance of the people of God; when by the voice of God the righteous are delivered from the death decree; they, like Nebuchadnezzar, will "fall down and worship at the saints' feet."

> Then it was that the synagogue of Satan knew that God had loved us who could wash one another's feet and salute the brethren with a holy kiss, and they worshipped at our feet. *Early Writings*, p. 15.

CHAPTER III

DELIVERANCE BY THE "FAITH OF JESUS"

Nebuchadnezzar was not pleased with the idea that his kingdom of Babylon should soon come to an end. Satan is not pleased that his kingdom of spiritual Babylon also must soon come to an end—this is the parallel of Daniel 3. It is also a parallel of the third angel's warning against the **image** of the beast.

Nebuchadnezzar had seen in his dream an **image** composed of different metals, representing the succession of kingdoms. The head of gold, which represented Babylon, was to be succeeded by the silver breast and arms which portrayed the soon coming conqueror—Medo-Persia. Nebuchadnezzar determined to override this prophecy by setting up an image to portray the never-ending glory of Babylon. He therefore constructed a great image over 100 feet tall, entirely of gold. Instead of acknowledging the fact that Babylon would soon be followed by another kingdom, he was proclaiming that great Babylon would never fall.

Nebuchadnezzar determined to gather all his forces to proclaim and establish the concept that Babylon should remain a world kingdom forever. He gathered together the government administrators of the entire then-known civilized world.

> Then the princes, the governors, and captains, the judges, the treasurers, the counsellors, the sheriffs, and all the rulers of the provinces were gathered together unto the dedication of the image that Nebuchadnezzar the king had set up. . . . Dan. 3:3.

This gathering of world rulers was similar to that which is described and shall occur at the end of time under the sixth plague:

> And the sixth angel poured out his vial upon the great river, Euphrates; [Babylon] and the water thereof was dried up, that the way of the kings of the east might be prepared . . . the spirits of devils . . . go forth unto the kings of the earth and of the whole world, to gather them to the battle of that great day of God Almighty. Rev. 16:12-14.

As Nebuchadnezzar called together all administrators to the plain of Dura, so also Satan will gather all the "kings of the earth" to Armageddon. It was and will be a confrontation between Babylon and the people of God.

At the sound of patriotic music, all were required by Nebuchadnezzar to "fall down and worship" the image. Although it was an affair of state, its character was of specific religious significance. It required "worship" and was an example of a church-state union.

Three Hebrews, Shadrack, Meshack and Abednego, had come, seemingly unnoticed to the dedication service. It is evident that they had not come to worship, but as is often the case with God's people, Providence places them at the scene of confrontation. And as it often appears, the people of God seem insignificant among the assembly of the great men of the world. Not until confrontation, is attention directed to them.

Nebuchadnezzar intended that all eyes and minds should be focused on the image and every knee bow down before it. But when the three Hebrews, true to the God of heaven alone, did not bow down, they stood out in bold contrast to the kneeling throng. The attention of those who were supposed to be worshipping the image, was irresistibly drawn to those worshippers of Jehovah. God's people, instead of the image, became the focus of attention.

The situation will be similar in the final confrontation of the great controversy between good and evil. Although the people of God, "which keep the commandments"—observing the true Sabbath, are now relatively obscure in the world of a people whose attentions are focused on other interests; in the final confrontation between the laws of a world government and the laws of God, a "final test" of the people of God will become the center of attention, and all eyes will be focused on them.

> Men will surely set up their laws to counterwork the laws of God. They will seek to compel the conscience of others, and in their zeal to enforce these laws they will oppress their fellow men. The warfare against God's law, which was begun in heaven, will be continued until the end of time. Every man will be tested. Obedience or disobedience is the question to be decided by the whole world. All will be called to choose between the law of God and the laws of men. Here the dividing line will be drawn. There will be but two classes. Every character will be fully developed; and all will show whether they have chosen the side of loyalty or that of rebellion. Then the end will come. God will vindicate His law and **deliver** His people. *The Desire of Ages*, p. 763.

> Those who honor the Bible Sabbath will be denounced as enemies of law and order, as breaking down the moral restraints of society, causing anarchy and corruption, and calling down the judgments of God upon the earth. Their conscientious scruples will be pronounced obstinacy, stubbornness, and contempt of authority. They will be accused of disaffection toward the government. . . . The dignitaries of church and state will unite to bribe, persuade, or compel all classes to honor the Sunday. The lack of divine authority will be supplied by oppressive enactments. . . . Liberty of conscience, which has cost so great a sacrifice, will no longer be respected. In the soon-coming conflict we shall see exemplified the prophet's words: "The dragon was wroth with the woman, and went to make war with the remnant of her seed, which keep the commandments of God, and have the testimony of Jesus Christ." *The Great Controversy*, p. 592.

> Fearful is the issue to which the world is to be brought. The powers of earth, uniting to war against the commandments of God, will decree that "all, both small and great, rich and poor, free and bond," shall conform to the customs of the church by the observance of the false sabbath. All who refuse compliance will be visited with civil penalties, and it will be finally declared that they are deserving of **death**. *The Great Controversy*, p. 604.

Nebuchadnezzar's frustration and anger at seeing his great efforts, cherished plans and great expense, go awry, is a parallel of that resentment which will be displayed by the whole world and the "antichrist" against those who resist universal Sunday legislation and refuse the "mark of the beast."

The penalty for resistance against Nebuchadnezzar's politico-religious world government was a "burning, fiery furnace" stoked to highest heat for all dissenters.

> Important are the lessons to be learned from the experience of the Hebrew youth on the plain of Dura.... Especially will the wrath of man be aroused against those who hallow the Sabbath of the fourth commandment; and at last a **universal decree** will denounce these as deserving of **death**. *Prophets and Kings*, p. 512.

The fire of that furnace was heated to maximum so that the "flame of the fire slew those men that took them up" to cast them in. But the Hebrews themselves suffered "no hurt . . . upon whose bodies the fire had no power, nor was an hair of their heads singed, neither were their coats changed, nor the smell of fire had passed upon them." Dan. 3:22-27.

At the end of time, the righteous will be preserved, but of the wicked, the Bible states: "fire came down from God out of heaven, and devoured them." Rev. 20:9. The last great warning which God's people will give to the inhabitants of spiritual Babylon is known as the "third angel's message," and it is a warning of fire:

> And the third angel followed them, saying with a loud voice, If any man worship the . . . image . . . the same . . . shall be tormented with fire. . . . Rev. 14:9, 10.

The fire will not devour those who have the "seal of God," but like those men who picked up the Hebrew worthies to toss them into the furnace, the wicked themselves will perish in the fire.

The Hebrew worthies were a type of the final remnant "that keep the commandments of God, and **the faith of Jesus**." Faith **in** Jesus is not the same as "faith **of** Jesus." Faith **of** Jesus," is a faith **like** the faith Jesus had. What kind of faith did Jesus display?

> The Savior could not see through the portals of the tomb. Hope did not present to Him His coming forth from the grave a conqueror, or tell Him of the Father's acceptance of the sacrifice. He feared that sin was so offensive to God that Their separation was to be eternal . . . [this] broke the heart of the Son of God.
>
> Amid the awful darkness, apparently forsaken of God, Christ had drained the last dregs in the cup of human woe. In those dreadful hours He had relied upon the evidence of His Father's acceptance heretofore given Him. He was acquainted with the character of His Father; He understood His justice, His mercy, and His great love. . . . By **FAITH**, Christ was victor. *The Desire of Ages*, p. 753, 756.

The Hebrew worthies could not see through the "portals" of the fiery furnace. They said, "If it be so, our God . . . is able to deliver us from the burning fiery furnace . . . but **if not** . . ." Dan. 3:17, 18. They did not know the outcome, but they knew the character of God, "his justice, mercy and love" and in submission committed themselves to Him. By this faith, similar to that of Jesus, they were victors. They had the "faith of Jesus."

So, at the end of time, those who face the death decree will seek deliverance in the same manner—by the "faith of Jesus," and finally hold in their hands the "palm of victory." Rev. 7:9.

By their integrity, the Hebrew worthies, in their mode of worship of the Creator, were able to reveal the glory of God so that even Nebuchadnezzar saw in their midst, the Son of God.

> Then Nebuchadnezzar the king was astonished, and rose up in haste, and spake, and said unto his counsellors, Did not we cast three men bound into the midst of the fire? . . . Lo, I see four men loose, walking in the midst of the fire, and they have no hurt; and the form of the fourth is like the Son of God. Dan. 3:24, 25.

In like manner, the integrity of the final remnant will portray to the world and to the universe, One walking among them, in the midst of them, in glorious display of courage and truth. They will see the glory of the Deliverer.

> I saw another angel come down from heaven, having great power: and the earth was lightened with his glory. Rev. 18:1.

The Hebrews introduced the DELIVERER; saying "our God whom we serve is able to deliver us . . . and he will DELIVER us." Dan. 3:17. "Then the king promoted Shadrack, Meshach, and Abednego." Dan. 3:30. After the deliverance from the death decree, by the voice of God, the people of God will be glorified.

> All who have died in the faith of the third angel's message come forth from the tomb **glorified**. . . . *The Great Controversy*, p. 637.

> The voice of God is heard from heaven . . . the Israel of God stand listening. . . . Their countenances are **lighted up with his glory**, and shine as did Moses when he came down from Sinai. The wicked cannot look upon them. *The Great Controversy*, p. 640.

> Blessed and holy is he that hath part in the first resurrection: on such the second death hath no power, but they shall be priests of God . . . and shall **reign** with him a thousand years. Rev. 20:6.

CHAPTER IV

DELIVERANCE FROM THE KING OF BABYLON

Nebuchadnezzar, as an individual may be saved. However, in his role and office as "king of Babylon," he is a type of Satan, king of spiritual Babylon. Chapter 4 of Daniel portrays the final humiliation of Satan. Nebuchadnezzar boasted, "Is not this great Babylon, that I have built for the house of the kingdom by the might of my power, and for the honor of my majesty?" Dan. 4:30.

Revelation 17 is a description of Satan's kingdom, entitled, "BABYLON THE GREAT . . ." Rev. 17:5. It is composed of "peoples, and multitudes, and nations, and tongues" (Rev. 17:15), and will include "all nations." Rev. 18:3. Finally, the "kings of the earth and of the whole world" will be gathered together, (Rev. 16:14), united, to carry out the will of its great king, Satan himself.

However, just as Nebuchadnezzar was boasting that he had finally brought his entire dominion under his personal control, the voice of God declared: "Thy kingdom is departed from thee." Dan. 4:31.

> . . . they shall drive thee from men . . . seven times shall pass over thee . . . Dan. 4:25.

Nebuchadnezzar was driven away from men into a desolate field for "seven times." Seven, representing completeness, shows the full period required to accomplish his full humiliation. In type, this represents the full millennium, that complete period in which Satan shall be separated from all men, and left in solitary confinement to think over the results of his rebellion, his attitudes and evil work.

> And I saw an angel come down from heaven, having the key to the bottomless pit and a great chain in his hand. And he laid hold on the dragon, that old serpent, which is the Devil, and Satan, and bound him a thousand years, And cast him into the bottomless pit, and shut him up, and set a seal upon him, that he should deceive the nations no more, till the thousand years shall be fulfilled: and after that he must be loosed a little season. Rev. 20:1-3.

In Chapter 4 of Daniel, Nebuchadnezzar had a dream of a huge tree. Daniel the prophet interpreted the dream, telling the king, "The tree that thou sawest, which grew, and was strong . . . It is thou, O king." Dan. 4:20, 22. The tree was cut down in the dream, but the "stump of the tree **roots**" were allowed to remain until the period of the humiliation was over, after which time, the kingdom was returned to him for a little season.

In the same manner, after the millennium of humiliation has passed for Satan, his kingdom will be restored to him for a little season:

> But the rest of the dead lived not again until the thousand years were finished. . . .
> And when the thousand years are expired, Satan shall be loosed out of his prison.
> And shall go out to deceive the nations which are in the four quarters of the earth,

Gog and Magog, to gather them together to battle: the number of whom is as the sand of the sea. And they went up on the breadth of the earth, and compassed the camp of the saints about, and the beloved city: and fire came down from God out of heaven, and devoured them. Rev. 20:5, 7-9.

CHAPTER V

THE FALL OF BABYLON AND THE SEVENTH PLAGUE

The fifth chapter of the book of Daniel is a description of the fall of Babylon, and the transition of world dominion as it was wrested from Babylon and given to Medo-Persia. It presents a picture of Babylon's characteristic indifference to the sacred trusts and the obedience required in the worship of the true God. Chapter 5 dramatically announces the message of doom and immediate judgment of Babylon.

This chapter is a parallel to final events in which Satan's kingdom of spiritual Babylon will fall under the judgments of God.

Daniel 5:1-4 introduces the scene with Belshazzar's banquet in which he, as king, initiates the ultimate disregard for the sacred holy vessels, which had come from Jerusalem's temple. The entire dissolute company performed its debauchery, drinking wine from these sacred vessels.

The Scriptures often liken a person to a "vessel." (Acts 9:15; Rom. 9:22, 23; I Thess. 4:4; II Tim. 2:21; I Pet. 3:7). God's people are referred to as "holy vessels" of the Lord's temple. The persecution of God's people, the misuse of these "holy vessels" and the cruelty of spiritual Babylon to them is described in Revelation:

> BABYLON THE GREAT . . . drunken with the blood of the saints, and with . . . the martyrs of Jesus . . . Rev. 17:5, 6.

> And in her was found the blood of prophets, and of saints, and of all that were slain upon the earth. Rev. 18:24.

Spiritual Babylon will be judged and its fall will come in direct retribution for its determined cruelty to **the people of God** and their total disregard for **these "holy vessels."** Judgment will fall immediately at the time of the implementation of Babylon's universal death decree.

> Reward her even as she has rewarded you, and double . . . according to her works: in the cup which she hath filled, fill to her double. Rev. 18:6.

The last great wicked banquet of spiritual Babylon is described as follows:

> . . . Babylon the great is fallen . . . **For all nations have drunk** of the wine of the wrath of her fornication . . . and the merchants of the earth are waxed rich through the abundance of her delicacies. Rev. 18:2, 3.

Modern spiritual Babylon is making preparations for its final celebration banquet. Its clergy is sending out its ecumenical invitations and "all nations" and all churches are invited to come to drink from one table. Belshazzar, king of Babylon, portrays Satan who shall "gather together" all nations to that scene of final confrontation.

The handwriting on the wall was the equivalent of the three angels' messages of Revelation 14. Consider them:

MENE, MENE, TEKEL, UPHARSIN (PERES)

Daniel's interpretation of these words begins in Daniel 5:18. He said to king Belshazzar: ". . . and the God in whose hand thy breath is . . . hast thou NOT GLORIFIED." Dan. 5:23. The first angel's message is: "Fear God, and GIVE GLORY to Him . . . worship Him that made heaven, and earth, and the sea, and the fountains of waters." Rev. 14:7. Belshazzar's judgment came as a result of his rejection of the first angel's warning—which he had viewed in the humiliation of his grandfather, Nebuchadnezzar.

The first angel's message also states: ". . . the hour of his judgment is come . . ." Rev. 14:7. Daniel interpreted the handwriting on the wall: "TEKEL; Thou are weighed in the balances, and art found wanting." Dan. 5:27. TEKEL—was an announcement of the beginning and end of an investigative judgment for Belshazzar.

The second angel's message of Revelation 14 declares: ". . . Babylon is fallen, is fallen . . ." Rev. 14:8. Daniel said to Belshazzar, "This is the interpretation of the thing: MENE; God hath numbered thy kingdom, and finished it. . . . In that night was Belshazzar the king of the Chaldeans slain." Dan. 5:26, 30. MENE—announced the fall of Babylon.

The fall of the ancient capital city of Babylon was a brilliant execution of military strategy. The broad walls of the city appeared impregnable. The city was self-supporting and apparently eternally secure from attack. The Euphrates River ran through the city, supplying water for gardens and produce—a "river of life."

Darius, the Mede, a sixty-two year old military genius, brought his troops to Babylon. He commanded them to dig a lake bed beside the city and then channeled the water away from the city of Babylon into the lake bed, causing the river to dry up. Then at midnight, as Belshazzar desecrated the holy vessels at his banquet, Darius' troops entered through the dried up river bed, opened the gates and took the city. The "drying up" of the river, Euphrates, brought about the final fall of ancient Babylon.

The military strategy of Darius is a type and parallel of the strategy of the Son of God in executing the final fall of spiritual Babylon. This specific technique is described under the sixth plague of Revelation 16.

> And the sixth angel poured out his vial upon the great river Euphrates; and the water thereof was dried up . . . and great Babylon came in remembrance before God, to give unto her the cup of the wine of the fierceness of his wrath. Rev. 16:12, 19.

The sixth and seventh plagues are a description of the strategy and fall of Babylon. Therefore, it is pertinent at this point, to investigate the parallel of Daniel 5—in the fall of ancient Babylon, as it relates to the last plagues which describe the fall of spiritual Babylon.

> And the sixth angel poured out his vial upon the great river Euphrates [not a "sea"]; and the water thereof was dried up . . . Rev. 16:12.

A symbolic "river" in Scriptures represents the Holy Spirit.

> He that believeth on me, as the Scripture hath said, out of his belly shall flow **Rivers** of living water. (But this spake he of the **Spirit**, which they that believe on him should receive, for the **Holy Ghost** was not yet given . . .) John 7:38, 39.

It is rain which makes a river swell and overflow its banks. It is lack of rain which dries up a river. ("The great river Euphrates . . . was dried up.") As the remnant people of God give the third angel's warning message they will receive the outpouring of the "Latter Rain" of the Holy Spirit.

This will enable them to give the message in power and glory that will lighten the whole earth in the "Loud Cry." As the great rivers flood in rain season, bringing life and nourishment to desert lands, so the "Latter Rain" of the Holy Spirit will bring one last call to Babylon, saying, "Come out of her, my people, that ye be not partakers of her sins, and that ye receive not of her plagues." Rev. 18:4. The outpouring of the Latter Rain is the last chance for the inhabitants of Babylon to be nourished by the great river of life.

But as the Investigative Judgment of the living closes, the Latter Rain will cease, "and the water thereof was dried up."

> When He [Jesus] leaves the sanctuary . . . **the Spirit of God, persistently resisted, has been at last withdrawn.** Unsheltered by divine grace, they have no protection from the wicked one. Satan will then plunge the inhabitants of the earth into one great, final trouble. *The Great Controversy, p. 614.*

Some will question, "Does the withdrawal of the Holy Spirit not precede the first five plagues?" Why is it mentioned here in the sixth plague? The mention of the withdrawal of the Holy Spirit under the figure of a river being dried up, is not intended to break the sequence of events. Rather, it is given as a very important setting for the dramatic action portrayed in the sixth plague. The sixth plague describes the work of evil spirits, which would not have complete freedom to accomplish their purposes except for the fact that the Holy Spirit has been withdrawn and the previous restraints have been taken away. This concept is very important to the understanding of this plague and is therefore inserted at this point.

THE DRAMA OF THE SIXTH PLAGUE

The sixth plague is written in the form of a drama. We need to understand that although the Greeks and Romans developed play-acting to a fine art, that form of entertainment was rejected by the Hebrew people. To them, the only acceptable drama was the action of God leading His people through the history of crisis and deliverance. Not for the purpose of entertainment, but to reiterate the providences of God and His interactions with Israel, was drama used. It should be the same with the people of God today. The form of drama that is brought to view in the sixth plague is described as follows:

> The world is a **theater; the actors,** its inhabitants, are preparing to act their part in **THE LAST GREAT DRAMA** . . . A power from beneath is working to bring about **THE LAST GREAT SCENES IN THE DRAMA** . . . Testimonies 8, p. 27, 28.
>
> For I think that God hath set forth us the apostles last, as it were appointed to death: for we are made a spectacle unto the world, and to angels, and to men. I Cor. 4:9.

The sixth plague, written in the form of a drama portrays a number of characters who take the stage.

The Characters of the Sixth Plague Drama:

- The kings of the east
- Three unclean spirits. (They are the spirits of devils who appear as frogs.)
- The dragon
- The beast
- The false prophet
- The kings of the earth, and of the whole world
- One who comes as a thief

Before a Biblical drama begins, characters need to be identified, particularly the main characters who take the leading roles. Others are introduced as the action continues. True to form, the main character, Christ, is introduced first, as the King of kings and His armies—referred to as the "kings of the east." Christ will come from the "east," "And I saw another angel ascending from the *east,* [heaven] having the seal of the living God:" Rev. 7:2. "And, behold, the glory of the God of Israel came from the way of the *east* . . ." Eze. 43:2. Christ is the KING OF KINGS AND LORD OF LORDS. It is He who shall ascend from the east. John saw, ". . . heaven opened, and behold a white horse; and He that sat upon him was called Faithful and True, and in righteousness he doth judge and make war . . . And the armies which were in heaven followed him. . . ." Rev. 19:11-14. Christ and "His armies" are these "kings of the east."

> The Battle of Armageddon is soon to be fought. He on whose vesture is written the name, King of kings, and Lord of lords, is soon to lead forth the armies of heaven. *Testimonies*, Vol. 6, p. 406.

Preparing the Way.

In what way does the "drying up of the river Euphrates" (the withdrawing of the Holy Spirit) "prepare the way" for the coming of Jesus? The answer lies in the concept that the Holy Spirit must be withdrawn from the earth to give Satan "complete control of the wicked," that it may be demonstrated to the universe, the utter destruction which he would have brought upon all creation, had he not been quarantined to this earth and constantly restrained by the Holy Spirit. Like spectators at a theater, the intelligences of other worlds view the full malignity of his spirit of rebellion. Only after this demonstration, is the "way prepared" for the "kings of the east" to ride forth in the glorious Second Coming of Jesus.

The Action of the Drama of the Sixth Plague.

> And I saw three unclean spirits like frogs come out of the mouth of the dragon, and out of the mouth of the beast, and out of the mouth of the false prophet. For they are the spirits of devils, working miracles, which go forth unto the kings of the earth and of the whole world, to gather them to the battle of that great day of God Almighty. Rev. 16:13, 14.

Who Are the "Three Unclean Spirits?"

The number "three," when referring to spiritual Babylon, indicates it as a **whole entity**. For example: ". . . the great city was divided into three parts . . . and great Babylon came into remembrance before God, to give unto her the cup of the wine of the fierceness of His wrath." Rev. 16:19. Again, there are "three" in the whole entity of the Godhead. The reference to "three" unclean spirits would appear to indicate that the "whole" entity of evil apostate religions is unleashed.

These Evil Spirits Appear Like Frogs . . .

Step out in the summer night when the frogs are croaking. Their sounds are all about you, croaking and echoing, single and in chorus, but to see them or find them is difficult. Their deep voices carry over the night air in vibrating tones, but you do not see them. This is a good description of the work of evil spirits, invisible, but altogether too audible as they speak out of the "mouth of" those agencies in counterfeit religion—in Babylon, under the sixth plague. These are the voices of the clergy, urging for action. The first five plagues have already fallen, devastating the earth. The clergy are seeking, through the prodding of the evil spirits, to lay the blame for these calamities upon a specific cause—upon the people of God, who keep the commandments, and the true Sabbath. These evil spirits speak out:

> out of the mouth of the dragon,
> out of the mouth of the beast,
> out of the mouth of the false prophet.

"Out of the mouth of" indicates **verbal** action. It infers agitation. Who are these three agencies, the "dragon," the "beast," and the "false prophet" who agitate at the instigation of evil spirits?

The Dragon.

The "dragon" is identified in Scripture:

> And there appeared another wonder in heaven; and behold a great red dragon . . . And the great dragon was cast out, that old serpent, called the devil, and Satan, which deceiveth the whole world. . . . Rev. 12:3, 9.

Satan is represented in this world by those agencies which directly worship him in all kinds and various forms of spiritism. These include Spiritist "Christian" bodies, the Satan worshipers, those engaged in witchcraft, the New Age Movement, oriental religions which worship the serpent, and devil worshippers in primitive lands.

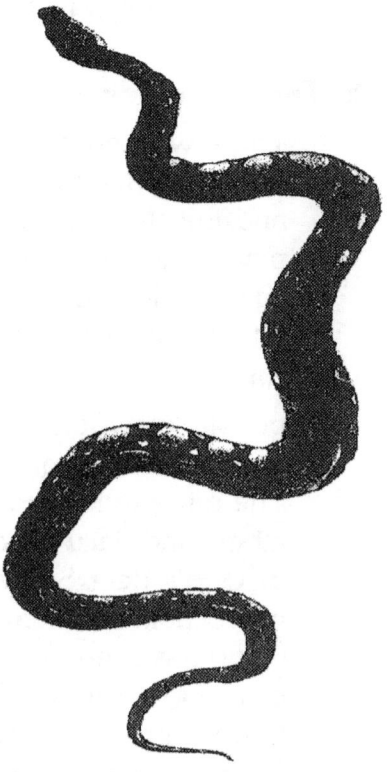

"And out of the mouth of the beast." Who is the beast?

The beast is also identified in Scripture:

> And I stood upon the sand of the sea, and saw a beast rise up out of the sea, having seven heads and ten horns . . . like unto a leopard, a bear . . . a lion . . . and the dragon gave him his power, and his seat and great authority. Rev. 13:1, 2.

This is the same beast against which the third angel's warning message is given in Revelation 14:9-11. This "beast" and his "mark"—with its false sabbath projects a symbol of rebellion against God's government and law. These identify with the Roman Catholic structure throughout the whole earth.

Under the sixth plague, spiritism and Roman Catholicism will unite and agitate together to accomplish one purpose.

The False Prophet.

The "false prophet" is the "false preacher." This is apostate Protestantism which also rebels against the law of God, supporting the false sabbath in place of God's holy Sabbath enjoined in the Ten Commandments. It is Protestantism with its many denominations which are the great "preachers." Their programs are seen by millions each Sunday on television.

The Three-Fold Union.

> When Protestantism shall stretch her hand across the gulf to grasp the hand of the Roman power, when she shall reach over the abyss to clasp hands with spiritualism, when, under the influence of this threefold union . . . then we may know that the time has come for the marvelous working of Satan and that the end is near. *Testimonies*, Vol. 5, p. 451.

Before the plagues begin this threefold union is formed to promote the observance of the false sabbath. After the calamities of the first five plagues have fallen, this three-fold union advances with new emphasis to agitate for the false sabbath, with more strict enforcement, developing into a death decree.

The evil spirits (like croaking frogs everywhere from all directions) through the concerted agencies of spiritual Babylon, agitate, agitate for a death decree.

The Death Decree.

> Those who honor the law of God have been accused of bringing judgments upon the world, and they will be regarded as the cause of the fearful convulsions of nature and the strife and bloodshed among men that are filling the earth with woe. The power attending the last warning has enraged the wicked; their anger is kindled against all who have received the message, and Satan will excite to still greater intensity the spirit of hatred and persecution.
>
> When God's presence was finally withdrawn from the Jewish nation, priests and people knew it not. Though under the control of Satan, and swayed by the most horrible and malignant passions, they still regarded themselves as the chosen of God. The ministration in the temple continued; sacrifices were offered upon its polluted altars, and daily the divine blessing was invoked upon a people guilty of the blood of God's dear Son and seeking to slay His ministers and apostles. So when the irrevocable decision of the sanctuary has been pronounced and the destiny of the world has been forever fixed, the inhabitants of the earth will know it not. The forms of religion will be continued by a people from whom the Spirit of God has been finally withdrawn; and the satanic zeal with which the prince of evil will inspire them for the accomplishment of his malignant designs, will bear the semblance of zeal for God.
>
> As the Sabbath has become the special point of controversy throughout Christendom, and religious and secular authorities have combined to enforce the observance of the Sunday, the persistent refusal of a small minority to yield to the popular demand will make them the objects of **universal** execration. It will be urged that the few who stand in opposition to an institution of the church and a law of the state, ought not to be tolerated; that it is better for them to suffer than for whole nations to be thrown into confusion and lawlessness. The same argument eighteen hundred years ago was brought against Christ by "the rulers of the people." "It is expedient for us," said the wily Caiaphas, "that one man should die for the people, and that the whole nation perish not." This argument will appear conclusive; and A **DECREE** WILL FINALLY be issued against those who hallow the Sabbath of the fourth commandment, denouncing them as deserving of the severest punishment and giving the people liberty, after a certain time, **TO PUT THEM TO DEATH**. Romanism in the Old World and apostate Protestantism in the New will pursue a similar course toward those who honor all the divine precepts. *The Great Controversy*, p. 614-616.

Romanism, Apostate Protestantism and Spiritism make up that "three-fold union" of counterfeit religion called "Babylon," which will, under the sixth plague, agitate all over the world to set up a UNIVERSAL DEATH DECREE.

> And I saw three unclean spirits like frogs come out of the mouth of the dragon, and out of the mouth of the beast, and out of the mouth of the false prophet. Rev. 16:13.

DRAGON
"Spiritism"

BEAST
Roman Catholicism

FALSE PROPHET
Apostate Protestantism

Note: "Out of the mouth of" infers **verbal agitation!** It is verbal agitation which will "gather the Kings of the earth and the whole world" into unified action to legislate a Universal Death Decree against God's saints.

Three frogs—(unclean spirits)
"gather the kings of the earth." Rev. 16

The Union of Church and State.

In the days of Christ, religious agencies could not execute a death sentence without the support of the state. This need for unification of church and state to carry out a death decree brings about the next act of the drama described in the sixth plague.

> For they are the spirits of devils, working miracles, which go forth unto the kings of the earth and of the whole world, to gather them to the battle of that great day of God Almighty. Rev. 16:14.

The "spirits of devils" work miracles through the agencies of "Babylon," in a "three-fold union" to influence the "kings of the earth" and the population of the "whole world" into one concerted action to bring about the death decree. This movement is described as follows:

Fearful sights of a supernatural character will soon be revealed in the heavens, in token of the power of miracle working demons. The spirits of devils will go forth to the kings of the earth and the whole world (Rev. 16:14), to fasten them in deception, and urge them on to unite with Satan in his last struggle against the government of heaven. By these agencies, rulers and subjects will be alike deceived . . . They will perform wonderful miracles of healing, and will profess to have revelations from heaven contradicting the testimony of the Scriptures.

As the crowning act in the great drama of deception, Satan himself will personate Christ. . . . This is the strong, almost overmastering delusion. *The Great Controversy*, p. 624.

The Kings of the Earth and of the Whole World.

Belshazzar's feast was made to a "thousand of his lords" and included even his wives and concubines. It was a gathering of administrators from his whole empire. In like manner, under the sixth plague, there is a gathering of the "kings of the earth" and "of the whole world."

There was a period of prophetic exposition when it was presumed that the "kings of the east" represented the countries of the Orient, and that the Battle of Armageddon would be fought between the Orient and western nations. However, the statement of Scripture which describes those who are in opposition to the "kings of the east," does not refer to them as the "kings of the west," but rather as the "kings of the earth," and more specifically "of the **whole world**."

And He Gathered Them Together.

The action described in Revelation 16:16 is not a "dividing" of the kings of the earth, to attack each other, but rather a "gathering—a unifying movement" in which the "whole world" (verse 14) is concerted against "God Almighty." The attack on "God Almighty" will be waged against His representatives who stand firmly for His government and authority by keeping His law and the true Sabbath of the fourth commandment. The attack by the wicked will culminate in a **UNIVERSAL DEATH DECREE**.

"These Kings" and the Beast.

These "kings of the earth and of the whole world," are also mentioned in the 17th chapter of Revelation, where their collusion with Babylon is symbolized as "fornication." It describes their support of the Papacy in which they unite fully for a specific period of time to set up, and attempt to carry out the **UNIVERSAL DEATH DECREE**.

> And the ten horns which thou sawest are ten kings,[1] which have received no kingdom as yet; but receive power as kings "one hour" or fifteen days of literal time with the beast. These have one mind, and shall give their power and strength unto the beast. These shall make war with the Lamb . . . Rev. 17:12-14.

When the true issues of the Great Controversy are considered, there is no indication that the Battle of Armageddon is involved with politics and wars between nations, but rather it is a war between

---

[1] "Ten," a symbolic number, used by Jesus in the Matt. 25 parable of the "ten" virgins represents **ALL** believers. Therefore, "ten" kings refer to **ALL** the kings of the "whole world" See Rev. 16:14.

Christ and Satan; between those who are attempting to put aside the law of God in rebellion against Him, and those who are sealed with the Sabbath sign of loyalty and allegiance.

Armageddon.

> And He gathered them together into a place called in the Hebrew tongue Armageddon. Rev. 16:16.

The "Hebrew tongue" gives evidence that "Armageddon," rather than being a specific place, is a term meaning: "mount—of confrontation." As ancient Babylon suddenly slipped into the hands of the Medo-Persians, so also modern spiritual Babylon, will fall as its kingdom submits to the King of kings in the battle of Armageddon.

The sixth and seventh plagues are one continuous action describing the fall of spiritual Babylon. Whereas the sixth plague describes the military strategy and gathering of the opposing forces, the seventh plague describes the final stroke which defeats Babylon. As the controversy mounts between the religious forces of spiritual Babylon and the people of God, the Battle of Armageddon comes to its climax in the implementation of the death decree:

> These plagues enraged the wicked against the righteous; they thought that we had brought the judgments of God upon them, and that if they could rid the earth of us, the plagues would then be stayed. A **decree** went forth to slay the saints, which caused them to cry day and night for deliverance. *Early Writings*, p. 36, 37.

> As Satan influenced Esau to march against Jacob, so he will stir up the wicked **to destroy God's people** in the time of trouble. And as he accused Jacob, he will urge his accusations against the people of God. *The Great Controversy*, p. 618.

> My attention was turned to the wicked . . . they were all astir . . . I saw measures taken against the company who had the power of God. I heard them crying unto God earnestly. Day and night their cry ceased not. . . . Deliver us from the heathen . . . *Early Writings*, p. 272.

> I saw the saints leaving the cities and villages, and associating together in companies, and living in the most solitary places. Angels provided them food and water, while the wicked were suffering from hunger and thirst. Then I saw the leading men of the earth consulting together, and Satan and his angels busy around them. I saw a **writing**, copies of which were scattered in different parts of the land, giving orders that unless the saints should yield their peculiar faith, give up the Sabbath, and observe the first day of the week, the people were at liberty after a certain time **to put them to death**. . . . It was an hour of fearful, terrible agony unto the saints. Day and night they cried for deliverance. *Early Writings*, p. 282, 283.

The ancient Babylonians saw the handwriting on the wall and "that same night" Babylon fell. Likewise the **UNIVERSAL DEATH DECREE** goes into effect at a "**certain time**." Dates are reckoned from "midnight" and it would be understood that the death decree would go into effect at **MIDNIGHT** at a "certain time" or date. It is also at midnight that God "delivers His people," by uttering His voice from heaven.

> And the seventh angel poured out his vial into the air; and there CAME A **GREAT VOICE** OUT OF THE TEMPLE OF HEAVEN . . . Rev. 16:17.

> A decree went forth to slay the saints, which caused them to cry day and night for deliverance. . . . Then all the saints of God cried out with anguish of spirit, and were **delivered by the voice of God**. *Early Writings*, p. 36, 37.
>
> Soon I heard the **voice of God** which shook the heavens and the earth. . . . Their captivity was turned. *Early Writings*, p. 272.

It is not the immediate coming of Jesus which delivers His people. It is the "voice of God" which delivers them from the death decree. It is the voice of God which brings about the fall of Babylon which is described under the seventh plague. It says:

> And the seventh angel poured out his vial into the air; and there came a great voice out of the temple of heaven, from the throne, saying, It is done . . . and great Babylon came in remembrance before God, to give unto her the cup of the wine of the fierceness of his wrath. Rev. 16:17, 19.

At the voice of God, the saints are glorified. They are fully identified as the people of God. The wicked cannot approach nor harm them. At this point Babylon is exposed as the counterfeit. As the wicked fall upon each other, the great earthquake destroys the cities of the world and Babylon is left desolate.

The fall of ancient Babylon was a type of the future fall of spiritual Babylon described in the drama of the sixth and seventh plagues of Revelation 16:14-21.

CHAPTER VI

DELIVERANCE BY THE VOICE OF GOD UNDER THE SEVENTH PLAGUE

The setting of Chapter VI of Daniel is that of Medo-Persia, the second of the four consecutive "world kingdoms," which finds a parallel in its universal government to that future coalition which will unite the entire world to set up a universal false sabbath and death decree. Darius, king of Medo-Persia set up "an hundred and twenty princes" (Dan. 6:1) and over them three presidents (Dan. 6:2). These were the representatives of the entire kingdom and formed the highest council of government. This "cabinet" of administrators was in some aspects a parallel of that government council described in Revelation 17, composed of the "kings of the earth . . ." ten kings (who shall) receive power as kings "one hour" or fifteen days of literal time, with the beast (Papacy). "They shall have one mind, and shall give their power and strength unto the beast. . . . These shall make war" and set up a death decree against the people of God who represent the Lamb—Christ.

These princes of Persia were of "one mind" and "sought to find occasion against Daniel" (Dan. 6:4). Unitedly, they sought to find a method to condemn Daniel legally and put him to death. This appears to be a parallel or type of the action taken under the sixth plague, when the "kings of the earth and of the whole world" will be "gathered together" against God's representatives on earth. They will legislate a **UNIVERSAL DEATH DECREE**.

However, there was "neither—any fault found in" Daniel. In parallel, the 144,000 who will face a final death decree, will already have passed through the judgment of the living, the "blotting out of sins" and there will be neither error or fault found in them. It will be said of them, "We shall not find any occasion against . . . [them] except we find it against . . . [them] concerning the law of . . . God." (Dan. 6:5). There will be no fault in the 144,000 for it is written:

> And in their mouth was found no guile; for they are without fault before the throne of God. Rev. 14:5.

The Investigative Judgment or "blotting out of sins" will have accomplished its work for them. The purpose of that "day of atonement"—(judgment) was stated by Daniel—to accomplish the following (Dan. 9:24):

> to finish the transgression [of God's people],
> to make an end of sins [in the lives of His people],
> to make reconciliation for the iniquity [of His people],
> to bring everlasting righteousness [to His people].
> Dan. 9:24

It is God's purpose in the final battle between the forces of good and evil, to reveal the utter malignity of sin. The wicked will seek to destroy the people of God, not because there is fault in them, but because of their own evil motives.

In Medo-Persia, "these presidents and princes assembled together," as the kings of the earth will "gather together" to the battle of Armageddon against the people of God. ". . . all the presidents of the kingdom, the governors, and the princes, the counsellors, and the captains . . . consulted together to establish a . . . statute, and make a firm decree," (Dan. 6:6, 7) by which Daniel could be put to death.

"Wherefore king Darius signed the writing and the decree." Dan. 6:9. Again the parallel holds for the people of God under the sixth plague:

> I saw the saints leaving the cities and villages, and associating together in companies, and living in the most solitary places. Angels provided them food and water, while the wicked were suffering from hunger and thirst. Then I saw the leading men of the earth consulting together, and Satan and his angels busy around them, I saw a **writing, copies of which were scattered in different parts of the land**, giving orders that unless the saints should yield up their peculiar faith, give up the Sabbath, and observe the first day of the week, the people were at liberty after a certain time to put them to death. *Early Writings*, p. 282, 283.

Daniel's action was not one of panic:

> Now when Daniel knew that the writing was signed, he went into his house; and his windows being open in his chamber toward Jerusalem, he kneeled upon his knees three times a day, and **prayed, and gave thanks** before his God, as he did aforetime. Dan. 6:10.

The reaction of the 144,000 will be similar:

> But in this hour of trial the saints were calm and composed, trusting in God and leaning upon His promise that a way of escape would be made for them. *Early Writings*, p. 283.

". . . Thy God whom thou servest continually, He will deliver thee." Dan. 6:16.

Then Daniel was cast into the den of lions. Satan is likened to "a roaring lion" who seeks to devour God's people.

> Humble yourselves therefore under the mighty hand of God, that he may exalt you in due time: Casting all your care upon him; for he careth for you. Be sober, be vigilant; because your adversary the devil, as a roaring lion, walketh about, seeking whom he may devour. I Peter 5:6-8.

It is the Lord Jesus who delivers His people. He is known as "the angel" of the covenant. Deliverance from sin and sinners is a special part of the covenant promise. Daniel said: "My God hath sent his angel, and hath shut the lions' mouths . . ." (Dan. 6:22) Darius, the king, perceived the identity of Daniel's Deliverer as Nebuchadnezzar had seen the "Son of God" in the fiery furnace. Darius declared of Him: ". . . He is the living God . . . He delivereth and rescueth . . . who hath delivered Daniel from the power of the lions." Dan. 6:26, 27.

Again, the fate of those who had set up the death decree against Daniel is a parallel to that which shall befall those who attempt to set up such a decree against the people of God at the end of time. Under the seventh plague they will meet their judgment.

> And the king commanded, and they brought those men which had accused Daniel, and they cast them into the den of lions, them, their children, and their wives; and

the lions had the mastery of them, and brake all their bones in pieces or ever they came at the bottom of the den. Dan. 6:24.

"And the king commanded." At the king's command, the (voice of the king) executive judgment began to fall. This parallels the "voice of God" by which His people are delivered and the judgment of the wicked begins. This parallel is found in the seventh plague:

> And the seventh angel poured out his vial into the air; and there came a **great voice** out of the temple of heaven, from the throne, saying, It is done. Rev. 16:17.

> And there were voices . . . and the cities of the nations fell. Rev. 16:18, 19.

In the sixth plague, the wicked "gather together" against the government of heaven—the people of God. But in the seventh plague, deliverance begins with the voice of God. The description follows:

> In the time of trouble we all fled from the cities and villages, but were pursued by the wicked, who entered the houses of the saints with a sword. . . . Then we all cried day and night for deliverance, and the cry came up, before God. The sun came up and the moon stood still. The streams ceased to flow. Dark, heavy clouds came up and clashed against each other. But there was one clear place of settled glory, whence came the **voice of God**. . . . And as God spoke the day and the hour of Jesus' coming and delivered the everlasting covenant to His people . . . The Israel of God stood . . . listening . . . Their countenances were lighted up with the glory of God. . . . The wicked could not look upon them for the glory. Early Writings, p. 34.

> (Also)
> After the saints had been **delivered by the voice of God**, the wicked multitude turned their rage upon one another. The earth seemed to be deluged with blood, and dead bodies were from one end of it to the other. Early Writings, p. 290.

Those who planned to destroy Daniel, were themselves destroyed at the voice of the king. In parallel, those who plan the death decree and attempt to carry it out, will be destroyed instead.

Chapter 6 concludes by stating "So this Daniel prospered . . . " As soon as he was delivered from the lion's den, he was exalted to a position of honor. After the saints are delivered, their prosperity is described as follows:

> Then the living saints and the risen ones raised their voices in a long, transporting shout of victory. Those bodies that had gone down into the grave bearing the marks of disease and death come up in immortal health and vigor. The living saints are changed in a moment, in the twinkling of an eye, and caught up with the risen ones, and together they meet the Lord in the air. Oh, what a glorious meeting! Friends whom death had separated were united, never more to part. . . . And the chariot rolled upward to the Holy City. Early Writings, p. 287, 288.

THE SAINT'S REWARD

> Then I saw a very great number of angels bring from the city glorious crowns—a crown for every saint, with his name written thereon . . . [and] harps . . . Then I saw Jesus lead the redeemed company to the gate of the city. . . . Within the city there was everything to feast the eye. Rich glory they beheld everywhere. . . . [Jesus] said ". . . Your sorrows are ended. There shall be no more death, neither sorrow nor crying, neither shall there be any more pain."

I then saw Jesus leading His people to the tree of life . . . Upon the tree of life was most beautiful fruit, of which the saints could partake freely. . . . Language is altogether too feeble to attempt a description of heaven. *Early Writings*, p. 288, 289.

CHAPTER VII

DELIVERANCE FROM THE LITTLE HORN POWER

The theme of DELIVERANCE runs, like a thread, through the entire book of Daniel. Persecution or a death decree and Providential deliverance are found seven times as follows:

1. **Nebuchadnezzar's Death Decree for the Wisemen.**

    And the decree went forth that the wise men should be slain; and they sought Daniel and his fellows to be slain. Dan. 2:13.

    Daniel and his fellows desired "mercies" (verse 18) of the God of heaven. The secret of the dream was revealed and God's people were **delivered**.

2. **Nebuchadnezzar's Death Decree in the Fiery Furnace.**

    Thou, O king, hast made a decree, that every man . . . shall fall down and worship the golden image . . . And whoso falleth not down and worshippeth . . . he should be cast into the midst of a burning fiery furnace. Dan. 3:10, 11.

    When the three Hebrew worthies proved their allegiance to the God of heaven and were thrown into the furnace, the king looked into the furnace and said, "Lo, I see four men loose . . . and the form of the fourth is like the Son of God." Dan. 3:25. It was God who brought **deliverance**.

3. **Darius' Death Decree in the Lion's Den.**

    "Wherefore king Darius signed the writing and the decree . . . Then the king commanded, and they brought Daniel, and cast him into the den of lions." (Dan. 6:9, 16). The great question was: "O Daniel, servant of the living God, is thy God, whom thou servest continually, able to deliver thee?" (Dan. 6:20). After Daniel's deliverance, Darius wrote . . . "the living God . . . He **delivereth** and **rescueth**." Dan. 6:26, 27.

4. **Babylonian captivity of the Jews and Deliverance.** 457 B.C.

Whereas the first three deliverances concerned specific individuals, the fourth example concerned the entire nation of Israel. Taken captive by Babylon, the entire nation was doomed to slavery and extinction by absorption—comparable to a death decree for an individual. Daniel prayed for the deliverance of the nation. Dan. 9:3-20.

Although the prince of Persia withstood the Lord's messengers, deliverance was finally secured by none other than Michael (Jesus Christ Himself). The decree was passed in 457 B.C. that the Jews should return to the holy land to restore and rebuild the holy city. God delivered the entire nation from a situation of hopeless doom. Dan. 10:13.

5. **Papal Captivity of the Christian Church and Deliverance in A.D. 1798.**

In prophetic vision, Daniel foresaw the oppression of the Christian church in the rise of the "little horn" power. (Dan. 7:8, 21, 25). Death decrees were multiplied through the 1260 years of papal supremacy. "His power shall be mighty . . . he shall destroy wonderfully . . . and shall destroy the mighty and the holy people." (Dan. 8:24). Yet that period of oppression was to last only 1260 years and at its end, *deliverance* would come.

> And the earth helped the woman, and the earth opened her mouth, and swallowed up the flood. . . . Rev. 12:16.

The pope was taken prisoner by Napoleon of France in 1798. Providentially, the Lord cut short persecution before the end of the 1260 day-year period. Deliverance was granted to the emerging remnant.

6. **Deliverance from the Power of Sin.**

The next concept of deliverance broadens to a wider scope—encompassing the people of God of all ages. The entire human race is under the death penalty decree! "For all have sinned, and come short of the glory of God. . . . the wages of sin is *death*." Rom. 3:23; 6:23.

Daniel was given a vision of the legal procedure by which men can be delivered from that universal death decree. He saw " . . . the judgment was set, and the books were opened"—a court room scene in which every sinner was condemned to a death penalty. Dan. 7:10.

But " . . . in the night visions . . . behold, one like the Son of man [Jesus Christ] came to the [judgment scene] before the Ancient of Days" to deliver His people. None other than Michael—that great prince which standeth for His people—that High Priest and Advocate—the greatest lawyer of all the time, comes to the *rescue* and *delivers* His people.

As each name or each case is brought up, it is the Son of man (Jesus Christ) who delivers from the death sentence and legally bestows eternal life with a guarantee of resurrection perfection—*perfect and complete deliverance from the power and grip of sin and the penalty of sin*. He performs this service in fulfillment of the everlasting covenant (contract) which is the legal binder of final deliverance.

Those who are living, when their names come up in the judgment will experience deliverance from all aspects of sin involving the character and conscience. The seal of God will be placed upon them making them eternally secure. Rev. 14:1-5; Rev. 7.

7. **Deliverance from the Grave—Immortality.**

> And at that time shall Michael stand up . . . and at that time thy people shall BE DELIVERED, every one that shall be found written in the book. And many of them that sleep in the dust of the earth shall awake . . . to everlasting life . . . [to] shine as the brightness of the firmament . . . as the stars for ever and ever. Dan. 12:1-3.

In Chapter VII, Daniel's vision portrays the history of the world in broad outline from his own day to the establishment of Christ's kingdom. Using "beasts" as symbols of nations, the vision describes the consecutive rise and fall of four great world empires—Babylon, Medo-Persia, Greece and Rome. Using the beast's horns also as symbols, the vision shows the division of the Roman Empire into the countries of Europe. Out of this European setting, and specifically out of Rome, Daniel predicted the emergence of a "little horn" politico-religious organization, easily identified as the Roman Papacy.

Daniel observed in his vision that this "little horn" papal system would set up a counterfeit religion, persecute God's true saints and attempt to change God's Ten Commandment law.

The "little horn" is identified as the Papacy by the following characteristics:

1. It would arise from among the ten horns (Europe), as its location.
2. It would be a continuation of the fourth beast—Rome.
3. It would uproot "three horns" (the Heruli, Ostrogoths, and Vandals).
4. It would be a "seer" or have prophetic or religious character with "eyes."
5. It would have a "mouth" or be a spokesman for Christendom.
6. It would be a blasphemous power—taking the place of God on earth.
7. It would be a persecuting power. (The Papacy set up the Inquisition and condemned to death heretics.)
8. It would think to change times and laws (the seventh day Sabbath to Sunday).
9. It would rule in Europe 1260 years (time, times and dividing of times).

> I considered the . . . little horn . . . a mouth speaking great things. Dan. 7:8.
>
> And he shall speak great words against the most High, and shall wear out the saints of the most High, and think to change times and laws . . . Dan. 7:25.

Daniel also saw that this Roman Papal system would reign supreme in Europe for a period of 1260 years. Dan. 7:25.

John, the revelator, predicted in vision (Rev. 13) that a beast power would arise, and that Roman tyranny in Papal form would continue until the end of time, making war against the remnant people of God. (Rev. 12:17). John also prophesied that the last great message of warning to the world would identify this Papacy as the final persecuting power on earth, using the Sunday (false sabbath), as a "mark" of its authority and an excuse for final persecution.

> And the third angel followed them, saying with a loud voice, If any man worship the beast and his image, and receive his mark in his forehead, or in his hand, The same shall drink of the wine of the wrath of God, which is poured out without mixture into the cup of his indignation; and he shall be tormented with fire and brimstone in the presence of the holy angels, and in the presence of the Lamb: And the smoke of their torment ascendeth up for ever and ever: and they have no rest day nor night, who worship the beast and his image, and whosoever receiveth the mark of his name. Rev. 14:9-11.

Daniel's primary concern was a question as to when and how the power of the Papacy would be broken. Daniel and John both saw that its influence would be universal and would practice and prosper until the end of time. Daniel's great question was: "What will bring the Papacy to its end and finally deliver the people of God from its persecutions?" The answer was given in the vision:

> ... the **judgment** shall sit, and they shall take away his dominion, to consume and destroy it unto the end. Dan. 7:26.

> ... the **judgment** was set, and the books were opened ... I beheld even till the beast [Papacy] was slain, and his body destroyed, and given to the burning flame. Dan. 7:10, 11.

The judgment is further described by John, the Revelator:

> And I saw the dead, small and great, stand before God; and the books were opened ... and the dead were judged out of those things which were written in the books, according to their works. Rev. 20:12.

The judgment in which "the books were opened" is an investigation of the records of mens' lives, and is therefore spoken of as the "Investigative Judgment." As soon as the Investigative Judgment of the righteous should be completed, the beast power was to meet the beginning of its punishment or "executive judgment."

The effects of the Investigative Judgment would not only bring the Papacy and counterfeit religions to their end, but it would also establish Christ's kingdom. As each individual's record is investigated, with his confession of sin and his belief in the Savior, he is accepted as a member of Christ's kingdom. Christ's kingdom continues to grow, and will do so, until it is complete. Daniel saw this taking place:

> ... the judgment was set, and the books were opened. ... I saw ... the Son of man [Christ] ... And there was given him ... a kingdom. Dan. 7:10, 13, 14.

It is important to understand that the Investigative Judgment was to be a main factor in the deliverance of God's people. By it, the powers of evil would be legally condemned in the court of heaven, and by it the righteous would be legally admitted to Christ's kingdom. Not until this important work for the righteous is completed will it be possible to make the final deliverance of God's people.

Therefore, Daniel's great desire was to know **when** this great Investigative Judgment would begin. He was not to have this information until the next vision. It is given in Chapters 8 and 9.

Note: Daniel describes the beginning of the Investigative Judgment of the saints whereas John describes the Investigative Judgment of the wicked; (Rev. 20) but the process is similar. One is simply a continuation of the other. Jesus judges and delivers His people first, to get them out of this world as soon as possible. Only after they are safe and happy, does He take time to judge the wicked.

CHAPTER VIII

HOW LONG UNTIL THE DELIVERANCE?

Again in Chapter VIII, Daniel sees in vision the rise and fall of world empires but quickly his attention is turned to the "little horn" Papacy. He notes:

> . . . a little horn, which waxed exceeding great . . . and it cast down the truth to the ground; and it practiced and prospered. Dan. 8:9, 12.

Daniel said, ". . . I heard one saint speaking . . . " (Dan. 8:13). He was questioning how long this "little horn" Papal power should continue its persecutions and "desolations" of God's people. He asked:

> . . . How long shall be the vision concerning . . . the transgression of desolation . . . ? Dan. 8:13.

Daniel overheard the answer! The reply came clearly saying:

> . . . two thousand and three hundred days . . . Dan. 8:14.

These were two thousand three hundred **symbolic** days. The Scriptures clearly state that one "symbolic day" represents one year of literal time. (See Num. 14:34 and Eze. 4:6.) Therefore Daniel knew the vision stated that it would be two thousand three hundred years until the judgment would begin, which would finally bring the "little horn" "beast" power to its end.

> At **the time of the end**, shall be [the fulfillment of] the vision . . . at the time appointed **the end shall be**. Dan. 8:17, 19.

Daniel saw this "little horn" as "a king of fierce countenance" who would "prosper and practice . . . and shall destroy the mighty and the holy people . . ." (Dan. 8:23, 24). But he also saw that this power would be ". . . broken without [human] hand." Dan. 8:25. **The Lord Himself would deliver**.

It is important to understand that Daniel saw the Papacy "little horn" as the main persecuting power from which God's people would seek their final deliverance. John saw it persecuting the "remnant" and its persecuting work is not yet fully accomplished. The people of God will yet have to deal with this power in the final crisis. No human force can bring it to judgment. Only God, in the court of heaven before the jury of the universe, can finally overcome this counterfeit system and deliver His people for eternity.

As Daniel viewed the work of the "little horn," he fainted. He was "sick certain days." Daniel was "worried sick" over many things—some of which will be reviewed in the next chapter.

CHAPTER IX

THE DELIVERANCE OF THE NATION OF ISRAEL AND THE DELIVERANCE OF SPIRITUAL ISRAEL FROM SIN.

Chapter IX of Daniel deals with two specific deliverances: The deliverance of the nation of Israel from Babylon (Medo-Persia), and the deliverance of universal "Israel" or the people of God from spiritual Babylon, a symbol of sin.

Daniel's visions of the "little horn" persecuting power caused extreme anxiety:

And I Daniel fainted, and was sick certain days . . . " Dan. 8:27.

He was distressed for the following reasons:

1. In all the visions of the future Daniel lost sight of the Jewish nation! In the visions of the "little horn," he saw the saints of God, but they were not the nation of Israel. What had happened to his people, the chosen ones?

2. The promise of a Messiah had been given to the descendants of Abraham and the Messiah was to be born to the Jews. If the nation of Israel were to disappear from the religious scene, to whom would the Savior be born?

3. Was the work of the Messiah not to deliver Israel from her oppressors? Would Israel never return to Jerusalem to build and restore the city and the temple?

4. Daniel understood by the book of Jeremiah that the Jews were to be in Babylon seventy years. Dan. 9:2. The time was nearly up, but no sign of deliverance could be seen.

5. The nation of Israel was steadily merging into Babylonian society. Was it to be dissolved among the heathen and lose its identity?

6. The king of Persia was a "man of the world" with no interest in the future of the nation of Israel. He was an absolute monarch, under whom Israel was held in bondage. He had not the slightest inclination to release the Jews to return to rebuild Jerusalem.

7. The "little horn" persecution stretched out before the people of God for more than a millennium (one thousand two hundred sixty years), and the prospect of waiting for two millenniums (two thousand three hundred years) of struggle until the judgment would even begin, presented a discouraging expanse of time and delay in the establishment of the kingdom of God.

8. Solomon's temple, the sanctuary, had been destroyed by Nebuchadnezzar. Its symbolic services which prefigured the Messiah's death and priesthood had ceased! The yearly service, the "Day of Atonement" or Day of Judgment had ceased! Was the plan of salvation in jeopardy?

Daniel did not stand from our vantage point in history, and he, like the rest of us, was subject to the concerns of an unknown future. His consternation for the future of his nation and for the plan of salvation was poured out to God in prayer. See Dan. 9:3-20.

In some aspects, the concerns of Daniel were similar to the concerns of the remnant today:

1. The Investigative Judgment began about one hundred fifty years ago and we might "have been in the kingdom long ere this." Why the delay? How much longer will we be here in the bondage of sin?

2. Although the coming of Jesus might have occurred long ago, to all appearances the people of God are becoming ever more comfortable and settled in spiritual ease, enjoying the prosperity of Babylon. Ignorance and apathy in modern Israel foretell no exodus from Babylon in the near future.

3. It is self-evident that the king of this world has no intention of releasing his prisoners that they may go to the holy city.

It is appropriate that modern Israel turn to God with prayer, as did Daniel; that the **Lord**, Himself, should begin to work for the deliverance of His people. The angel, Gabriel, came to bring comfort and understanding, to answer the questions which were troubling Daniel. See Dan. 9:24-27. For simplicity, Daniel's questions are listed, and the answers, in the vision given as follows:

DANIEL'S QUESTIONS	GABRIEL'S ANSWERS
Q: What is to happen to the nation of Israel?	A: "Seventy weeks are determined upon thy people . . ." Dan. 9:24. (Thy people—the Jews—are to be the "chosen" people for "seventy weeks" or 490 literal years. After that, God's people will become the Christian church.) "And he [the Messiah] shall confirm the covenant with many . . . [Jews]. Dan. 9:27.
Q: When does one begin to count the "seventy weeks" (490 years)?	A: "Know therefore and understand, that **from** the going forth of the commandment to restore and to build Jerusalem . . . shall be . . ." Dan. 9:25. Yes, the Jews will return to build Jerusalem, and you shall start counting the time **from** the date when the king of Persia makes the final command that the Jews return to do this work (457 B.C.).
Q: How long will it take for the Jews to rebuild the holy city?	A: ". . . from the going forth of the commandment to restore and build Jerusalem . . . shall be seven weeks [49 literal years] . . . the street shall be built again, and the wall . . ." 408 B.C. (Dan. 9:25).
Q: Will the Messiah be born to the Jews and when will He come?	A: ". . . from the going forth of the commandment to restore and to build Jerusalem unto the Messiah the Prince shall be seven weeks, and threescore and two weeks . . ." [sixty-nine weeks or 483 years] ". . . to anoint the most Holy" [to His anointing at His baptism, A.D. 27].
Q: Will the Messiah die for the sins of the people?	A: "Messiah shall be cut off, but not for himself." (Not for any fault in him.) Dan 9:26.
Q: When Messiah dies, what will happen to the ceremonial sacrificial system?	A: ". . . he shall cause the sacrifice and the oblation to cease . . ." Dan. 9:27.
Q: Why will the Jews be no longer the chosen people, just as the Messiah has come to them?	A: (Because they themselves will reject Him.) Matt. 23:37.

Q: Will God reject them?

A: It will be the Jews who reject God and bring their covenant with Him to an end. He, the Messiah, "... shall **confirm** the covenant with many for one week: and in the midst of the week he shall cause the sacrifice ... to cease ..." (Dan. 9:27). A "symbolic week" is seven literal years.[1] Even after His death, He will confirm or carry out the old covenant relationship with the Jews for three and a half years. Not until they, as a nation, take action in their Sanhedrin to put His missionaries to death, will they bring the covenant to an end. They were a "chosen nation" to be missionaries—but in persecuting them, they will nullify the covenant completely.

Q: After Jerusalem and the sanctuary are rebuilt will they stand forever?

A: "... the people of the prince [of Rome] that shall come ... shall destroy the city and the sanctuary ..." Dan. 9:26.

Q: Is this power from the "prince" (Pagan Rome) to continue as the Papal Rome "little horn"? Is this the same "beast" power and its horns the persecuting power which will continue to the end of time?

A: Yes, "... and the people of the prince [of Pagan Rome] that shall come shall destroy the city and the sanctuary; **and** the end [of time] ... shall be with a flood [of persecutions], and unto the end of the war [Armageddon] desolations [persecutions] are determined. Dan. 9:26. (This is the "beast" power mentioned in the third angel's message of Rev. 14:9, 13). God's people will continue to suffer persecutions of the powers from Rome until the very end of time.

Q: Is there no way to avoid this terrible conflict?

A: "... the overspreading of abominations [overspreading the whole earth] he [the little horn Papal power] shall make it [God's church] desolate [persecute it] even until the consummation—[the end of time], and that determined [prophetic history] shall be poured upon the desolate [church]." Dan. 9:27.

Q: What will finally bring this power of the "little horn" to its end?

A: "... the judgment shall sit, and they shall take away his dominion ..." Dan. 7:26.

Q: When will the judgment begin?

A: "Unto two thousand and three hundred days [literal years] ..." Dan. 8:14.

---

1 Num. 14:34 and Eze. 4:6: "I have given you a [symbolic] day for a [literal] year."

Q: When do I begin to count this period of time?

A: "Know therefore and understand, that ***from*** the going forth of the commandment to restore and to build Jerusalem . . ." Dan. 9:25.

Q: If I begin to count from that date, 457 B.C., and count forward 2300 years, that will bring me to the date A.D. 1844 I understand therefore that the judgment will begin in 1844. Where will this judgment take place?

A: ". . . behold, one like the Son of man came with the clouds of **heaven**, and came to the Ancient of days . . ." Dan. 7:13. ". . . the judgment was set." Dan. 7:10. ". . . We have such an high priest . . . ***in the heavens***: A minister of the ***sanctuary*** . . . which the Lord pitched . . . not man." Heb. 8:1, 2.

Q: How will this judgment in heaven, bring the reign of sin and the "little horn" to an end?

A: ". . . Unto two thousand and three hundred days; then shall the [heavenly] sanctuary be cleansed." (from all records of sin of God's people.) Dan. 8:14.

Q: How does this "cleansing of the sanctuary" bring the records and sin itself to an end in the lives of God's people?

A: ". . . consider the vision . . . [its purpose is to] **FINISH THE TRANSGRESSION . . . MAKE AN END OF SINS . . . AND TO BRING IN EVERLASTING RIGHTEOUSNESS** . . ." Dan. 9:23, 24

Q: What is the "cleansing of the sanctuary?" Can the records of sin be removed from heaven without a corresponding work in the hearts of God's people?

A: The "cleansing of the sanctuary" is a complete work. It is a "Day of AT-ONE-MENT," a day of complete reconciliation between God and His people. It is a day of "blotting out of sins" both in heaven's records and ***in the minds of God's people***. It is the purpose of this judgment to "bring in everlasting righteousness" into the lives of God's people. Dan. 9:24. See: *The Great Controversy*, p. 620, 425; *Patriarchs and Prophets*, p. 202, 356; *III Selected Messages*, p. 135; *Testimonies*, Vol. 5, p. 472-475.

Q: How does an "end of sins" in the lives of God's people, bring the "little horn" power to its end?

A: After God's people experience the blotting out of sins in the judgment of the living, they will be "sealed" in righteousness. They will reflect the image of Jesus fully, thus vindicating the Law of God and condemning the "little horn" kingdom. They will live without a Mediator while the plagues are poured out on the beast. (See Rev. 7:1-4; 14:1-5, 23, 24.)

Q: Does this cleansing of the sanctuary, with its message of final judgment and reign of righteousness, bring the history of the world to its close?

A: Yes. ". . . consider the vision . . . seal up the vision, and prophecy . . ." (Dan. 9:23, 24). The concept of the closing work of the Investigative Judgment (Day of Atonement, the blotting out of sins, and the cleansing of the sanctuary), brings earth's history to its close—it initiates God's kingdom and brings the reign of evil to its end.

Q: Is this vision sure of fulfillment?

A: ". . . the thing was true, but the time appointed was long . . ." Dan. 10:1.

Daniel ". . . understood the thing, and had understanding of the vision." (Dan. 10:1). It is important that the people of God today also have understanding of the vision. Not only should they understand its prophetic outline of events, the destiny of the Jewish nation, the coming of the Messiah, his death, and the date for the beginning of the Investigative Judgment; but they should understand **primarily the purpose** of the Investigative Judgment, which is so clearly specified in the prophecy itself ". . . to make an end of sins . . . to bring in everlasting righteousness . . ." in direct application to their own lives. They should take courage that the fulfillment brings the reign of sin to its close and marks the end of the papal "beast" power, against whom all are warned in the third angel's message of Revelation 14.

Until these concepts are understood by those who shall enter into the experiences of the judgment of the living, the pertinence of this prophecy is lost to this generation. Prophecy is not given merely to outline history, but more specifically, so that the people of God can meet coming crises with understanding of the issues and purposes of God in their own lives. This prophecy has been preserved in Holy Scripture so that the last generation may understand that the final deliverance from sin will come to the Israel of God: first in a **deliverance from sin** in their lives through the blessings of the judgment, and secondly that **deliverance from the papal "beast"** power will come after the saints are "sealed" and complete in Christ's kingdom. Only in this way can they live through the time of the plagues without a Mediator. See Rev. 15:8.

> **. . . CONSIDER THE VISION . . . TO MAKE AN END OF SINS . . . AND TO BRING IN EVERLASTING RIGHTEOUSNESS . . . Dan. 9:23, 24.**

It was Daniel's prayer that brought him into favor with God and gave him understanding of the vision. If God's people would pray the kind of prayer, which Daniel prayed, their understanding would increase. The main points of Daniel's prayer were:

1. **"We** have sinned . . . committed iniquity . . . done wickedly" Dan. 9:5.

2. "Neither have **we** hearkened unto thy servants the prophets . . ." Dan. 9:6, 10. [**We** have not listened to the Spirit of Prophecy—hated new light].

3. ". . . have rebelled . . ." Dan. 9:5.

4. ". . . to **us** belongeth confusion . . ." Dan. 9:8.

5. ". . . all Israel [the whole church] have transgressed . . ." Dan. 9:11.

6. "... Yet made *we* not our prayer before the Lord [We were proud] ..." Dan. 9:13.

7. "... Because of *our* sins, and for the iniquities of our fathers ..." Dan. 9:16.

It is time that we, as did Daniel, confess that our generation also has committed all these sins, going far from the "blueprint." It is time we confess that we too have hated new light and rejected every emphasis which has come repeatedly to us, which had to do with the "blotting out of sins" in the lives of God's people, a "Day of Atonement" or complete reconciliation with God; that we have been sleeping virgins, unready for the "marriage-judgment," a flirtatious and coy bride, unwilling to meet the Bridegroom in the "cleansing of the sanctuary," in a full repudiation of sin.

It is time for the church to recognize her absolute rebellion against being led out of sin—"Babylon"—and away from the king of this world. It is time for the church to confess that she is confused and ashamed in that she has rejected numerous counsels in regard to almost every phase of the work she has attempted to do. She has attempted to conduct her campaigns on the spirit of competition, has followed the world in practice of medicine, education and evangelism. She is merging into Babylon and has lost, in many ways, her distinctive character. She has shown indifference to the typology and symbolism of prophetic messages, making her "blind, miserable, poor and naked."

When the church confesses her sins, her proud and boastful character, and seeks wisdom from the Holy Word, she will be in a better position to understand the vision of Daniel 8:14 to enter into the final judgment of the living and endure the final conflict. If she does not do this, the great bulk of the church will remain captive to "Babylon" as they did in the days of Daniel, where only a few names and families were registered in that exodus. Ezra 2 gives the list. How few today would return to the holy city!

It is the responsibility of church leadership to lead such public confession, to proclaim such a fast and prayer and then wait for the Lord to lead us. It is the responsibility of each individual to prepare his own life "in fear and trembling" for it is a fearful thing to fall into the hands of the living God in judgment.

Conclusion

The 2300 day-year prophecy declares a message of DELIVERANCE. It not only foretold the deliverance of the nation of Israel from ancient Babylon, but it is a message of DELIVERANCE from sin, and final DELIVERANCE from the persecuting "beast" power at the end of time.

It is a joyful prophecy which proclaims the "Day of At-one-ment," when the Messiah will be fully united to all His people, and it will be the "... day of the gladness of his heart." Song of Solomon 3:11. It will be the "day of His espousals"—or the day of His **marriage**. His bride must be ready for the ceremony, when it will take place in the Most Holy Place where she will have entered by faith.

> God calls upon us to awake, for the end is near. Every passing hour is one of activity in the heavenly courts to make ready a people upon the earth to act a part in the great scenes that are soon to open upon us. These passing moments, that seem of so little value to us, are weighty with eternal interests. ... The time that so many are now allowing to go to waste should be devoted to the charge that God has given us of preparing for the approaching crisis. *Testimonies*, Vol. 5, p. 716-717.

CHAPTER X

DELIVERANCE FROM HUMAN WEAKNESS

"In those days I Daniel was mourning three full weeks." Dan. 10:2. Daniel mourned because the deliverance of the Jews from ancient Babylon was not evident. Although the prophecy of Jeremiah indicated that Jerusalem should lie desolate only seventy years, and the time had come for them to return to rebuild the city; Cyrus, king of Persia, would not release his captives. Neither was Israel, as a whole, particularly interested or desirous to return, because they had settled and prospered in Babylon. But Daniel was zealous for the cause and glory of God and the plan of salvation. In his distress, he fasted and prayed twenty-one days.

> It is our duty, as we see the signs of approaching peril, to arouse to action. Let none sit in calm expectation of the evil, comforting themselves with the belief that this work must go on because prophecy has foretold it, and that the Lord will shelter his people. *Testimonies*, Vol. 5, p. 713-714.

Daniel was aroused to action, but it was not the action of his own righteous works. Much human effort will "spin the wheels" while the chariot of Truth barely moves. The action which Daniel took was that of ***fasting and prayer!*** When God's people today understand our similar dilemma, and enter the conflict with fasting and prayer, then the Lord, Himself, will accomplish the final deliverance.

The angel explained to Daniel the powerful effects of such prayer:

> Then he said unto me, Fear not, Daniel: for ***from the first day*** that thou didst set thine heart to understand, and to chasten thyself before thy God, thy words were heard, and I am come for thy words.

> But the prince of the kingdom of Persia withstood me one and twenty days: but lo, Michael [Christ], one of the chief princes, came to help me; and I remained there with the kings of Persia. Daniel 10:12, 13.

When the people of God seek the glory of God and chasten themselves with fasting and prayer, the great forces of heaven begin action! As the final test and the judgment of the living draws on, God's people are called to fast and pray for deliverance:

> . . . for the day of the Lord is great and very terrible; and who can abide it? Therefore also now, saith the Lord, turn ye even to me with all your heart, and with fasting, and with weeping, and with mourning: And rend your heart . . . Blow the trumpet in Zion, sanctify a fast, call a solemn assembly: Gather the people, sanctify the congregation, assemble the elders, gather the children, and those that suck the breasts . . . Let the priests, the ministers of the Lord, weep between the porch and the altar, and let them say, Spare thy people, O Lord, and give not thine heritage to reproach, that the heathen should rule over them: wherefore should they say among the people, Where is their

God? Then will the Lord be jealous for his land, and pity his people. . . . Be glad then, ye children of Zion, and rejoice in the Lord your God: for he hath given you the former rain moderately, and he will cause to come down for you the rain, the former rain, and **THE LATTER RAIN** . . . Joel 2:11-18, 23.

It is the responsibility of the church administration, the "priests, the ministers of the Lord" to call such a fast of mourning and weeping, to "gather the entire congregation" to prayer for deliverance. Then the Lord will send the LATTER RAIN.

As Daniel entered into such fasting and prayer, he was taken off in vision into the presence of heaven. As modern Israel enters such fasting and prayer, they too will be taken into the presence of God in the Most Holy place of the heavenly sanctuary in the judgment of the living. Will they be ready to stand before the Lord in judgment? Let Daniel tell of his experience.

At this point, Daniel mentions again and again his weakness and human deficiency in trying to stand before the Lord in this vision. This inadequacy in the godly Daniel, is an example of every godly saint as he shall be brought into the presence of the Lord in the Investigative Judgment of the living. Daniel exclaimed:

> . . . there remained no strength in me for my comeliness was turned in me into corruption, and I retained no strength. Dan. 10:8
>
> . . . I stood trembling. Dan. 10:11.
>
> . . . I set my face toward the ground, and I became dumb. Dan. 10:15.
>
> . . . I . . . said unto him that stood before me, O my lord . . . my sorrows are turned upon me, and I have retained no strength. For how can [I] talk with . . . my lord? . . . there remained no strength in me, neither is there breath left in me. Dan. 10:16, 17.

As Daniel declared "there is [no] breath left in me"—he was as a dead man from whom breath had departed. In the judgment, all will stand in their own weakness, trembling, as dead men with no breath, and no strength to plead their own case before God.

But again and again, as Daniel acknowledged his own weakness and insufficiency he was strengthened and made ready. He said:

> And, behold, an hand touched me, which set me [up] . . . Dan. 10:10.
>
> Then said he unto me, Fear not . . . thy words were heard . . . Dan. 10:12.
>
> And, behold, one like the similitude of the sons of men touched my lips: then I opened my mouth, [and confessed my weakness] . . . Dan. 10:16.
>
> Then there came again and touched me one like the appearance of a man, and he strengthened me . . . Dan. 10:18.

The people of God, as they come into the judgment of the living have only one responsibility—to confess their own weakness and sinfulness.[1] It is Christ, the High Priest, who will plead their case and make them ready to meet the Bridegroom. It is Christ who will apply the Final Atonement and bring them into full harmony with the perfection required.

Daniel finally declared:

> . . . he strengthened me, And said, . . . ***fear not: peace*** be unto thee, **be strong**, yea, be strong . . . I was strengthened . . . ***thou hast strengthened me***. Dan. 10:18, 19.

---

1 "Sinfulness" (not sinning) . . . a state of incompleteness, imperfection, or immaturity. See Song of Solomon 8:8.

This transformation from weakness to strength in the closing up of the judgment was also described in similar fashion by Zechariah:

> Zechariah's vision of Joshua and the Angel applies with peculiar force to the experience of God's people ***in the closing up of the great day of atonement***. The remnant church will be brought into great trial and distress . . . Satan . . . has gained control of the apostate churches; but here is a little company that are resisting his supremacy. If he could blot them from the earth, his triumph would be complete.
>
> Their only hope is in the mercy of God; ***their only defense will be prayer***. As Joshua was pleading before the Angel, so the remnant church, with brokenness of heart and earnest faith, will plead for pardon and deliverance through Jesus their Advocate. They are fully conscious of the sinfulness of their lives, ***they see their weakness and unworthiness***, and as they look upon themselves they are ready to despair. The tempter . . . points to their . . . defective characters. He presents their ***weakness*** and folly, their sins of ingratitude, their unlikeness to Christ, which has dishonored their Redeemer. . . . But while the followers of Christ have sinned, they have not given themselves to the control of evil. They have put away their sins, and have sought the Lord in humility and contrition . . .
>
> As the people of God ***afflict their souls*** before Him . . . the command is given, "Take away the filthy garments" from them . . . "Behold, I have caused thine iniquity to pass from thee, and I will clothe thee with change of raiment." The spotless robe of Christ's righteousness is placed upon the tried, tempted, yet faithful children of God. The despised remnant are clothed in glorious apparel, ***nevermore to be defiled*** by the corruptions of the world. Their names are retained in the Lamb's book of life, enrolled among the faithful of all ages. . . . Now they are ***eternally secure*** from the tempter's devices. Their sins are transferred to the originator of sin . . . "A fair miter" is set upon their heads. They are to be as kings and priests unto God. While Satan was urging his accusations and seeking to destroy this company, holy angels, unseen, were passing to and fro, placing upon them ***the seal of the living God***. These are they that stand upon Mount Zion with the Lamb, having the Father's name written in their foreheads . . . the hundred and forty and four thousand . . .
>
> **CHRIST IS REVEALED AS THE REDEEMER AND DELIVERER OF HIS PEOPLE**. *Testimonies*, Vol. 5, p. 472-476.

The book of Daniel, with its many points of deliverance would be incomplete if it did not focus upon that ***final atonement of the living,*** in which the seal of God reveals Christ as the **DELIVERER** of His people.

Take courage therefore, as the final test comes upon modern Israel. Fast and pray for the glory of God to be revealed. Christ, Himself will DELIVER His people from their human weaknesses, deficiencies, and corruption.[1]

---

[1] "Corruption" of heart is not be confused with corruption of body. This corruptible (body) will be changed to incorruptible at the Second Coming of Jesus.

CHAPTER XI

DANIEL 11

DELIVERANCE FROM THE KING OF THE NORTH

INTRODUCTION

Four times in the book of Daniel, a prophetic outline is presented. They are found in Daniel, Chapters 2, 7, 8, and 11. Chapter 11 aligns with Daniel 2, 7, and 8. At the time Daniel wrote this vision, Babylon had already passed off the scene. Chapter 11 begins with Medo-Persia, continues with the reign of the third kingdom, Greece, and then Rome. In each succeeding prophetic outline, more details are given which focus more clearly on endtime events. While chapters 2, 7, and 8 reiterate the rise and fall of great **empires,** Chapter 11 deals with the succession of **kings** as they sat on the throne of those empires.

A DIAGRAM OF THE FORWARD PROGRESSIVE MOVEMENT OF DATABLE TIME, AND THE ALIGNMENT, SEQUENCE, AND CONTINUITY OF THE OUTLINES OF THE BOOK OF DANIEL

Daniel 2	Babylon	Medo-Persia	Grecia	Rome	Europe		Stone Kingdom
				476 A.D.			
Daniel 7	Babylon	Medo-Persia	Grecia	Rome	Europe	Papal Rome	
					1798 A.D.		
Daniel 8		Medo-Persia	Grecia	Rome		Investigative Judgment Begins	
						1844 A.D.	
Daniel 11		Medo-Persia	Grecia	Rome	Papal Rome		
						"the time of the end"[1]	

Daniel, Chapter 11 (and 12:1-4) is called the "fourth vision" and is the fourth prophetic outline. Chapter 11 **aligns** with the first three visions which outline the rise and fall of empires. Chapter 11 begins with Medo-Persia because, at the time the vision was given, Babylon had already fallen. Whereas the first three outlines cover the rise and fall of empires, Chapter 11 reiterates the rise and fall of the kings who sat on the thrones of those empires. All four visions cover the same major line of prophecy. All four visions are given in historical sequence and continuity. Each additional outline adds more detail and with great specificity focuses on endtime events.

---

1 "time of the end" refers in Dan. 11:40, not to 1798, but to **the end of time.** Ellen G. White used it both ways. See Ltr. 161, 1903.

In the same way that each empire followed the one before it so that the **sequence** is intact, so also in Daniel 11, the kings follow in sequence and with continuity. It is this very continuity which gives credibility to the entire application of the prophetic outlines to historical events, and also makes it possible to understand the outline straight through to the end of time.

Uriah Smith, prophetic expositor in the eighteen hundreds, was a conservative student of the "School of Historicist" thought. He was an excellent historian and usually dealt with Daniel 11 in a methodical and logical manner. His comprehension of Daniel 11 was often excellent in matching the elements of the prophecy to the historical past. He was able to gather together the exposition of the centuries by great men of the Reformation and produced his book, ***Thoughts on Daniel and the Revelation***. Except for minor concerns, his views on Daniel 11 up to his own day are valid. There is no need to "reinvent the wheel." We may therefore review his materials from verses 1 to 22. But at verse 35, the prophecy ran ahead of his time in historical events and he was at a disadvantage. We may pick up the threads where he could not see into the future, but we can now easily discern the meaning of verses 35-45.

It should be understood that the timeline of Daniel 11 extends on into Daniel 12:1-4. (Most students of prophecy are agreed on this matter.)

It should also be understood that this line of kings brought to view in Daniel 11 are all reiterated **in their order**, moving forward to the end of time when the last king will sit on the throne as predicted in Revelation 13:18.

I. TIME AND SETTING

Prophetic outlines are of no value unless they have a time and setting with which to begin. The Bible always ***provides its own timeframe*** and this is true of Daniel 11.

> Also I, **in the first year of Darius the Mede,** even I, stood to confirm and to strengthen him. And now will I show thee the truth. Behold, there shall stand up yet three kings **in Persia**; and the fourth shall be far richer than they all: and by his strength through his riches he shall stir up all against the realm of **Grecia**. Dan. 11:1, 2.

In Dan. 2, Medo-Persia was illustrated by the arms and breast of silver. In Daniel 7, it was illustrated by the bear. This same conflict between Medo-Persia and Grecia is spoken of in the outline of Daniel 8. These empires are symbolized by a ram and a he-goat. (See Dan. 2:32, 39; 7:5-7; 8:3, 4.) This vision in Daniel 8:2-8 of the ram and the he-goat struggle revealed the fall of Medo-Persia and the rise of Grecia. Again in Daniel 8:8 the power of Grecia is broken and divided into four.

The alignment of the four visions makes it possible for the Bible student to "get his feet on the ground"—to establish the time and setting and the point of beginning of the outline. He must know time and setting before he can proceed to add details and focus correctly on the endtime message at the end of the prophecy.

II. THE STRUGGLE FOR WORLD DOMINATION

When Grecia fell, it was many years before the fourth kingdom came on the scene. The big question was: "Who will become the fourth great world empire?" Egypt desired to become the fourth kingdom. But Syria also determined to have the prize. These two battled each other and that is the subject of Dan. 11:5-14.

III. AN INTRODUCTION TO THE KING OF THE NORTH AND THE KING OF THE SOUTH

Dan. 11:5-14 introduces two titles: "The king of the south" and "The king of the north." Not until we get a correct perspective on these titles in verses 5-14, can we apply these same titles with understanding in verses 36-45 which apply to the end of time and to our own day.

It is generally understood that the "king of the south" referred to Egypt and the "king of the north" to Syria, but where does this information come from and how is it derived?

IV. PROPHECY REVOLVES AROUND GOD'S PEOPLE

In the days of Medo-Persia, Grecia and Pagan Rome, God's people lived in the Holy Land. All prophecy revolved around them. They were the ***geographical*** center of prophetic utterance in Old Testament times.

To the south of Israel, was Egypt. To the north was Syria. It is always in reference to God's people that prophecy must be understood. Therefore, the "king of the south" referred to Egypt to the south and the "king of the north" was Syria to the north.

Prophecy is given to enable God's people to know where they are in the stream of time. By a study of Dan. 11:5-13, Israel was able to discern the progress of prophetic application. Each time that Egypt marched up across Israel to attack Syria, God's people could trace that prophetic fulfillment. In the same way, as Syria marched back down to counter-attack, God's people could watch that fulfillment also.

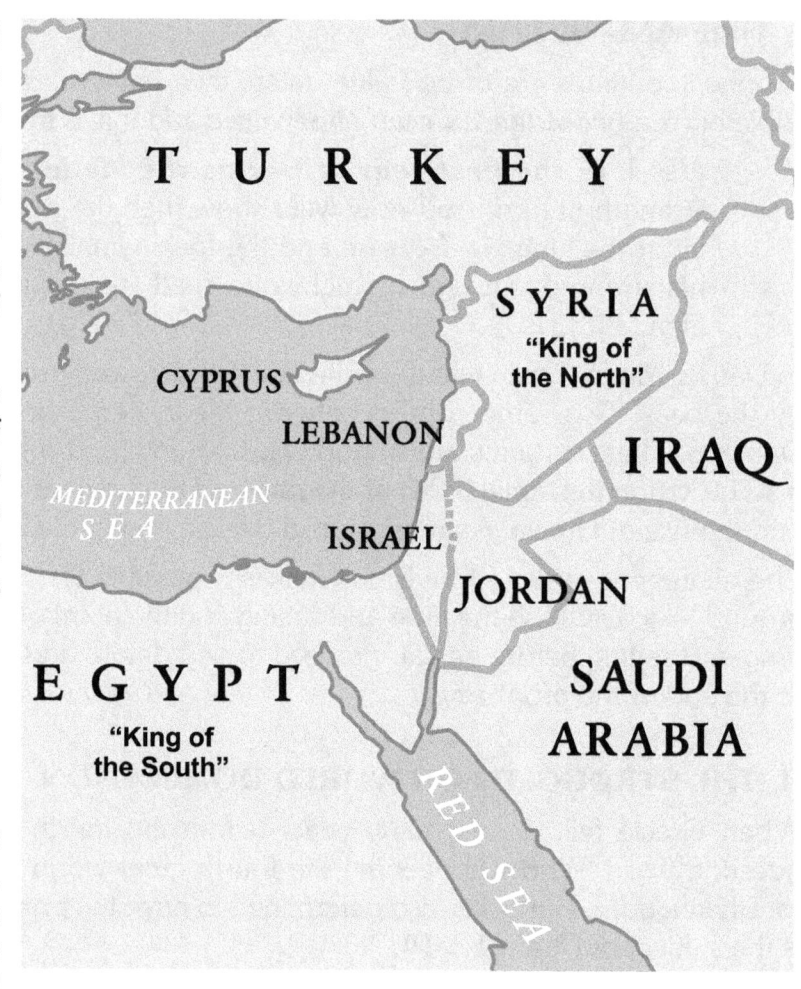

Egypt, "king of the south," struggled against Syria, "king of the north," to become THE FOURTH WORLD EMPIRE. Dan. 11:5-14. In like manner, "the king of the north" and the "king of the south" (Dan. 11:36-40.) struggle to become the ***LAST GREAT WORLD EMPIRE (a New World-Order.)***

It is for this reason that the Bible student should review the actions of Egypt and Syria, because their titles as "king of the north" and "king of the south," in struggle, are not used again until verse 40—the close of earth's history.

V. ROME (PAGAN ROME) BECAME THE FOURTH WORLD EMPIRE

Neither Egypt nor Syria became the fourth great empire. It was Rome, rising from the west which fulfilled the prophecy. Daniel 11 describes the various methods by which Egypt and

Syria fought, made alliances, entered into leagues, intermarried, by intrigue and other ways sought to become the fourth great kingdom. These are interesting stories and they can be traced in Uriah Smith's book and by historical accounts. King after king "stood up" or took the place of the one before him, so that the account is **continuous** and in **perfect sequence**.

VI. THE TIME OF CHRIST IS ESTABLISHED IN THE PROPHETIC OUTLINE

> Then shall stand up . . . a raiser of taxes [Caesar Augustus] . . . they [shall] be overflown . . . **ALSO THE PRINCE OF THE COVENANT**." Dan. 11:20, 22. See Luke 2:1-6.

VII. THE RISE OF THE PAPACY ESTABLISHED IN THE PROPHETIC OUTLINE

The prophet has established at what point the outline speaks of the rise of the Roman Papal Supremacy as follows (Dan. 11:30):

> The world is stirred with the spirit of war. The prophecy of the eleventh chapter of Daniel has nearly reached its complete fulfillment. Soon the scenes of trouble spoken of in the prophecies will take place . . . 9T 14.

> The prophecy in the eleventh (chapter) of Daniel has nearly reached its complete fulfillment. . . . In the **THIRTIETH VERSE** A POWER [Papal Rome] IS SPOKEN OF . . . THAT SHALL TAKE AWAY THE DAILY . . . and they shall place the abomination that maketh desolate. *Manuscript Releases* Vol. 13, p. 394 taken from Letter 103, 1904, p. 5, 6. Quoted in *Review & Herald* July 8, 1976.

If any should have a problem as to when each verse applies, the above statement should serve as an anchor. Verse 30 places the outline right at the beginning (A.D. 538) of Papal Supremacy No. 1 when it reigned over Europe. We may therefore understand verses 31-36 to refer to that reign which brings the action to 1798. This was the understanding of Adventist pioneers. It was a part of the Scripture which identified Papal Rome as the "beast" of Rev. 13 which reigned from 538-1798 and will reign again in the near future. It was a "plank" in the platform of the third angel's warning message.

Daniel 11:32-34 describe the medieval Papal Reign and its persecutions. It also describes the European Reformation and exploits done by the Reformers as they translated the Bible into the languages of the common people and raised up Protestantism.

VIII. DANIEL 11:35 BRINGS THE OUTLINE TO 1798

> And some of them of understanding [European Reformers] shall fall, to try them, and to purge, and to make them white, EVEN TO **THE TIME OF THE END** . . . [1798] Dan. 11:35.

1798 was the end of a timeline prophecy, predicted in Dan. 7:25; and Rev. 12:6, 14. It was also a Jubilee year—the dating which ties in with the anchor dates of the 2300 day prophecy: 457 B.C., 408 B.C. and A.D. 34. The thirty-fifth verse of Daniel 11 therefore declares 1798 to be **"a time appointed,"** as follows:

> . . . even to the time of the end: because it is yet for a time appointed . . . for that [which] is determined [predicted by prophetic timelines] shall be done. Dan. 11:35,36.

IX. THE END OF PAPAL SUPREMACY NO. 1

Scripture declares that The Papal power would be "wounded."

> And I saw one of his heads as it were wounded to death . . . Rev. 13:3

In these four visions of Daniel's outlines (Dan. 2, 7, 8, and 11) there is a **continuity** which cannot be ignored. As each power fell, another followed in **continuous action**.[1] The power which won in battle became the next great world empire. This understanding of outlines must be applied at this point in Daniel 11. We have no right to presumptuous conjecture that one may bypass or violate the forward movement, sequence, and continuity in the rise and fall of great empires surrounding God's people.

Therefore, we must look closely at what power inflicted the wound to the Papacy in 1798 and follow its rise and fall in our own day.

History advises that in 1798, there was an **ATHEISTIC** power in France. It was the governing body of France, and its ruler, Napoleon Bonapart, which inflicted the deadly wound on the Papacy and took the Pope prisoner.

We need to keep our eye, not on France as such, but on **ATHEISTIC IDEOLOGY** which spread from France into Russia. From Russia, atheistic Communism spread to more than half the world and endangered the entire Western civilization, persecuting God's people wherever they were. It warred against all forms of Christianity. If it had succeeded in becoming a world empire, the work of God would have been wiped out. How many millions suffered and were martyrs under atheistic Communism! Only time will tell.

X. DAN. 11:35-39 DESCRIBES THE CONQUEST OF ATHEISTIC-COMMUNISM.

THE IDEOLOGY OF ATHEISM

> And the king [France's ruling power] shall do according to his will; and he shall exalt [not God, but] himself, and magnify himself above every god, and shall speak marvelous things against the God of gods, and shall prosper till the indignation [regime] be accomplished: for that that [which] is determined [predicted in prophecy] shall be done. Dan. 11:36.

Uriah Smith and the pioneers were not able to see the rise and spread of Communism in their day. We cannot expect them to have understood those events predicted from verse 35 onward. Only the course of history could unveil the meaning of these verses.

COMMUNISM RECOGNIZED NEITHER GOD NOR CHRIST

> Neither shall he regard the God of his fathers, [or traditions of the church] nor the desire of women [The Messiah-Christ], nor regard any god: for he shall magnify himself above all. Dan. 11:37.

---

1. Each additional vision adds information to that which went before it. The fourth vision of Daniel 11 supplies details which were missing in the visions before it, so that there is continuity in the story of the rise and fall of nations. Chapter 11 supplies the details of events which transpired between the fall of Grecia and the rise of Rome. It also adds details which enable us to identify the entire seven empires down to the end of time.

THE MILITARY SPREAD OF COMMUNISM

> But in his estate shall he honor the God of forces [armed power of the military to make its conquests]: and a god whom his fathers knew not [humanism] shall he honor with gold, and silver, and with precious stones, and pleasant things. Dan. 11:38.

Communism spent itself into bankruptcy among the nations in its attempt to master the whole world. Communism with its atheistic ideology was not formerly known. It was a new experiment in a godless society. God permitted Satan to demonstrate what he—the god of forces—could do when power was granted to continue for a time.

THE TEMPORARY SUCCESS OF COMMUNISM

> Thus shall he do [Satan primarily, working through Communism] in the most strongholds [communistic centers of government] with a strange god [humanism—man himself, in the socialist state] whom he shall acknowledge and increase with glory: and he shall cause them to rule over many [over half the world spanning 11 timezones came under communistic rule], and shall divide the land for gain. Dan. 11:39.

It must be remembered that under Communism the "land" was not the property of the people but for the "gain" of the state itself. The land was therefore apportioned as the state directed.

From 1798 the seeds of atheism were growing in the Communistic empire. Had it not been for the strong forces of the United States and Europe, we would all be under Communist rule today. Such power is recognized by prophecy and described very well in Daniel 11:35-40. God has not "skipped" over the last century without mention! Those, whose eyes are blinded to a correct application of prophecy, cannot see the meaning of rather plain statements of Scripture.

XI. THE "KING OF THE NORTH" REPRESENTS PAPAL ROME

> And at the time of the end shall the king of the south push at him: and THE KING OF THE NORTH shall come against him like a whirlwind, with chariots, and with horsemen, and with many ships; and he shall enter into the countries, and shall overflow and pass over. Dan. 11:40.

Before correct application can be made of Daniel 11:40-45, it is necessary to identify the "king of the north" and the "king of the south." Let it be understood that prophecy is "history written before it happens," and history always has a geographical location. God's people, Israel, lived in the Holy Land, originally the center of prophetic fulfillment. Anything "north" was north of Israel and anything "south" was south of Israel.

To the north was Syria, and in Daniel 11:5-15 the "king of the north" referred to Syria. When the fourth kingdom, Rome, came into power, Syria was swallowed up by Pagan Rome. At that point in time, ***the "king of the north" became Rome***. Its armies invaded Israel from the north. Later, when pagan Rome gave way to PAPAL ROME, ***the title "king of the north" shifted to the Papacy***.

Today, the covenant people are no longer the nation of Israel. (Their covenant ended in A.D. 34.) The people of God "at the time of the end" (Dan. 11:40) are now all over the world. The "king of the north" now applies to a figure which is of worldwide importance in political power. The greatest figure in the world today is the Pope of Rome whose political moves affect every country in the world.

The pioneers of Adventism did not always agree on the identity of the "king of the north." James White, who benefited from his close association with the prophetess, was also at advantage as he gave due attention to the hermeneutic principle of the **alignment of the four outline visions** of Daniel, and he thereby identified the "king of the north" as the Papacy. Time and current events validate his views as follows:

> Let us take a brief view of the line of prophecy four times spanned in the book of Daniel. It will be admitted that the same ground is passed over in Chapters two, seven, eight, and eleven. We first pass down the great image of Chapter 2, where Babylon, Persia, Greece and Rome are represented by the gold, the silver, the brass, and the iron. All agree that these feet are not Turkish, but Roman. And as we pass down to the lion, the bear, the leopard, and the beast with ten horns, again all will agree that it is not Turkey that is cast into the burning flame, but the Roman beast. So of Chapter 8, all will agree that the little horn that stood up against the Prince of princes is not Turkey but Rome. In all these thus far, Rome is the last form of government mentioned.[1]
>
> Now comes the point in the argument upon which very much depends. Does the eleventh chapter of the prophecy of Daniel cover the ground measured by chapters two, seven, and eight. If so, then **the last power mentioned in that chapter is Rome**. *Review and Herald,* Nov. 29, 1877, James White.

This conclusion bears up under close scrutiny. Not only is the Papacy the "last power mentioned" in the former visions, but the conclusion of these visions is all the same:

> . . . the beast was slain . . . and given to the burning flames. Dan. 7:11.
>
> . . . he shall be broken without hand. Dan. 8:25
>
> . . . he shall come to his end, and none shall help him. Dan. 11:45.

The conclusion that the "king of the north" refers to Papal Rome is also in harmony with the third angel's message as presented in Revelation 13 and 14.

XII. THE TIMEFRAME FOR DANIEL 11:40

> AND AT THE TIME OF THE END shall the king of the south push at him . . . Dan. 11:40.

The "time of the end" **WAS** mentioned in verse 35, as it applied to 1798 or the "time appointed" by the 1260 year timeline-vision of Dan. 7:25.

The Bible student should give attention to the fact that, in these timelines, there is continually a **FORWARD PROGRESSION**, with *each verse moving forward in time* as history is chronologically revealed in the prophetic outline. From 1798 in verse 35 the historical progression has moved forward beyond 1798, with continuity of action right to verse 40.

---

1 Note: Uriah Smith concluded that it would be Turkey—not the Roman Papacy which would "come to his end." Dan. 11:45. To this James White took issue.

Whereas, Dan. 11:35 "time of the end" refers to 1798, five verses later, the chronological progression of time points to events beyond that of 1798—to a later date in context of endtime events. Verses 35-42 reveal the last great struggle between two great powers, so that one of them was to become the head of the final "New World-Order." This endtime setting places Dan. 11:40 into our very recent past, present and future fulfillment—The fall of Communism and rise of Papal power.

XIII. THE KING OF THE SOUTH [King of the South Identified]

Who is the "king of the south"? In Old Testament times, as spoken of in Dan. 11:5-14, the geographical "king of the south" was Egypt. In the same way that the "king of the north" in New Testament times becomes a worldwide figure, so in the time of the end, the "king of the south" also represents a worldwide influence, battling for world dominion.

Whoever that is, it must somehow be connected with "Egypt." It is at this point that we are assisted by the prophet to understand in what way "Egypt" could fit into this outline. She has made a comment which will give light on this subject.

In Dan. 11:35 there is the description of the 1798 wounding of the beast head. That prophecy was understood to be supplemented in Rev. 11:7-8. The description of France, as it wounded "the beast's head," is described as follows:

> These [the Scriptures] have power to shut heaven, that it rain not in the days of their prophecy: and have power over waters to turn them to blood, and to smite the earth with all plagues, as often as they will. And when they shall have finished their testimony, the beast that ascendeth out of the bottomless pit . . . shall overcome them, and kill them.
>
> And their dead bodies shall lie . . . in the great city, which **spiritually is called** Sodom and **EGYPT**, where also our Lord was crucified. Rev. 11:6-8.

In commenting on this passage, Ellen G. White stated:

> "The great city" in whose streets the witnesses are slain, and where their dead bodies lie [Rev. 11:8], is **"SPIRITUALLY" EGYPT** ["the king of the south"]. Of all nations presented in Bible history, Egypt most boldly denied the existence of the living God and resisted His commands. No monarch ever ventured upon more open and highhanded rebellion against the authority of Heaven than did the king of Egypt. When the message was brought him by Moses, in the name of the Lord, Pharaoh proudly answered: "Who is Jehovah, that I should hearken unto His voice to let Israel go? I know not Jehovah, and moreover I will not let Israel go." Exodus 5:2, A.R.V. **THIS IS ATHEISM** . . . *The Great Controversy*, p. 269.

The prophet interpreted the symbolism of Egypt or the "king of the south" to be representative of **ATHEISM**—the ideology of COMMUNISM. *It is Atheistic Communism which has been represented by the "king of the south."*

This concept, that the "king of the south" as it represents Atheistic Communism preserves a perfect SEQUENCE from verse 35-45.

In verse 35, the atheistic-ideology, currently seen in Communism, began its work of enmity against the Roman Papacy by taking the Pope prisoner. From 1798, the Papacy has conducted a great struggle against this power to the present time. There is no break in the SEQUENCE of the rise and spread of Atheistic Communism from verse 35 right on to verse 43. Verses 40-43 reveal this struggle for world dominion between the Papacy, "king of the north" and Communism, "king of the south." The USSR, spanning Eleven Time Zones of the Old World—half the world surface—is described in Dan. 11:36-42.

The PAPACY HAS USED THE WESTERN NATIONS (the democracies) to fight its battles for it. For decades this struggle, or "pushing" has been going on. A description of the military efforts used by the Papacy working through the western nations, especially the United States of America, is described as follows:

> And at the time of the end [endtime—last few decades] shall the king of the south [Communism] push at him [the Papacy]: and the king of the north [the Papacy working through the Western Democracies] shall come against him [Communism] like a whirlwind, with chariots [army], and with horsemen, and with many ships [navy and air ships]; and he [the Papacy] shall enter into the countries [of Eastern Europe, etc.], and shall overflow and pass over. Dan. 11:40.

Thus we saw the "fall of the Berlin wall" and "the fall of Communism," 1989 through the early nineties. LIFE, TIME, and other publications, gave all credit to the Pope of Rome. See Appendix Note A.

DANIEL 11:40 HAS ALREADY BEEN FULFILLED

Further conquest by the Papacy is described in verses 41 and 42.

XIV. THE PAPACY WILL ALSO TAKE POSSESSION OF THE HOLY LAND

> He shall enter also into the glorious land . . . Dan. 11:41.

The Arab-Israeli conflict will be resolved shortly:

> . . . and many [countries] shall be overthrown . . . He shall stretch forth his hand upon the [Arab] countries. Dan. 11:41, 42.

XV. PAPAL SUPREMACY NO. 2 TO BE ESTABLISHED—A "New World-Order"

> . . . and the land of Egypt shall not escape. Dan. 11:42.

If Egypt represents atheistic ideology, then this statement is a clear declaration that nothing of atheistic ideology will remain out of the grasp and control of the Papacy. Not only China, which seems so remote, but also every government, regardless of origin or philosophical bent will not escape, in fulfillment of Rev. 13:3-8.

> And I saw one of his heads as it were wounded to death [1798 by atheistic ideology in France]; and his deadly wound was healed [still healing]: and **ALL** the world wondered after the beast, saying . . . who is able to make war with him.
>
> And it was given unto him to make war with the saints, and overcome them: and power was given him over **ALL** kindreds, and tongues and nations.
>
> And **ALL** that dwell upon the earth shall worship him, whose names are not written in the book of life of the Lamb slain from the foundation of the world. Rev. 13:3-8.

Again, the Bible is its own expositor—and Revelation 13 is complimentary to Daniel 11. It is also easier to identify the seven heads of the Beast of Rev. 13:1-3, when Daniel 11 is understood. They are as follows:

Head	Empire	Reference	Dates	Symbol	Reference
\multicolumn{6}{c}{A CORRELATION OF DANIEL 7-11 AND REVELATION 13}
1	Babylon	Dan. 7	606 B.C.	Lion's Mouth	Rev. 13:2
2	Medo-Persia	Dan. 7, 8	538 B.C.	Bear's Feet	Rev. 13:2
3	Grecia	Dan. 8	331 B.C.	Leopard's Body	Rev. 13:2
4	Roman Empire	Dan. 7	168 B.C.-476	4th Head,	
5	Papal Rome No. 1	Dan. 7, 8	A.D. 538-1798	Wounded Head	Rev. 13:3
6	Atheistic Communism	Dan. 11:36-43	1918-1989	6th Head	
7	Papal Rome No. 2	Dan. 12:7-12	Future	Healed Head	Rev. 13:3-10

Not until the seventh head emerged victor over Communism was it possible to identify the seven heads of the composite beast of Rev. 13. Recognition of prophecy is ever **contemporary with fulfillment**.

THE COMPOSITE BEAST OF REVELATION 13

THE NAME OF THE BEAST.

While it is true that John saw this beast rise up out of the sea, it should not be called the "sea beast", but rather the **COMPOSITE BEAST** because it is **composed** of the **components** introduced in Dan. 7. Daniel saw four great beasts rise up out of the sea (Dan. 7:3). These beasts were a lion, a bear, a leopard, and another beast "dreadful and terrible". These beasts represented four great empires which surrounded the people of God. They were Babylon, Medo-Persia, Grecia and Rome. Revelation 13 names the first three of these **same** beasts, thus giving sufficient information to know that a succession of empires is brought to view.

THE SEVEN HEADS OF THE BEAST.

A prophetic outline always gives sufficient information to allow the expositor to know where and how to begin the sequential outline. This information is provided by naming the lion, the bear, and the leopard as follows:

> And I stood upon the sand of the sea, and saw a beast rise up out of the sea, having seven heads and ten horns, and upon his horns ten crowns, and upon his heads the name of blasphemy.
> And the beast which I saw was like unto a **leopard,** and his feet as the feet of a **bear,** and his mouth as the mouth of a **lion**: Rev. 13:1, 2.

The lion, bear, and leopard are clues as to the identity of the first empires which begin this series of seven.

SEVEN HEADS REPRESENT SEVEN EMPIRES.

A lion's mouth will always be found in a lion's head. Therefore one of the seven heads of the beast should be a lion's head. Bear's feet belong on a beast with a bear's head. Therefore, one of the seven heads of the beast should be a bear's head. A beast with a leopard's body certainly will have a leopard's head. Therefore, one of the heads of the beast will be a leopard's head. These first three heads begin the line of empires as follows:

Babylon	606-538 B.C.
Medo-Persia	538-331 B.C.
Grecia	331-168 B.C.

The fourth head can easily be identified by anyone who has had a course in Modern History or World History. The fourth head, "dreadful and terrible" represented Rome.

THE FIFTH HEAD REPRESENTED THE FIFTH EMPIRE, PAPAL ROME.

As barbarian invasions sacked Rome, the emperors moved out and placed the scepter in the hands of the Popes. Thus making the Papacy ruler over all Europe in a dominion which began in 538 and ended only by the capture of the Pope by Napoleon's general, Berthier, in 1798.

THE SEVEN HEADS REPRESENT A SEQUENCE OF SEVEN EMPIRES.

It is important that the prophetic expositor understand that the beast wears only **one head at a time!** Only one empire prevailed at a time. As one empire fell, the next took its position as a head on the beast. It is difficult to picture this beast on a sheet of paper because only one head should appear at a time. A moving picture would illustrate it better.

Artists have had difficulty illustrating the beast of Revelation for several reasons. First, they did not know the identity of all seven empires and could not picture them correctly. In the second place, they seemed unaware of the fact that this is a sequence of one head at a time. Last of all, they were not using the Biblical clues to identify the heads as Babylon, Medo-Persia, Grecia, Rome and Papal

Rome, and produced monsters which had a variety of efforts exhibited, such as a beast with seven dragon heads, or maybe seven leopard heads, or even seven lion heads. Sometimes a combination of various monster heads took their place on the beast. A review of various publications illustrates this confusion. But the time has come to clarify this picture.

THE SIXTH HEAD REPRESENTED ATHEISTIC COMMUNISM. 1798-1989

It is necessary to be consistent, not only with sequence, but also in the matter of continuity. One of the heads (the fifth) was "wounded" in 1798 by an atheistic government of France. Since that time, atheism has been the great enemy of the Papacy. As the Papacy, slowly at first, recuperated and "healed", atheism was growing and expanding. Slowly at first, but growing in momentum, it spread eastward until in 1918 Russia espoused it and set up an atheistic-Communistic USSR empire which encompassed eleven time zones. It knocked on the very door of the Vatican in Rome, expanded its ideology across China, absorbed Cuba, crept into South and Central America, and even threatened the Alaskan borders!

From 1945 onward it "pushed" (Dan. 11:40) against the west and the Papacy to gain world dominion. Millions of Christians suffered under its iron curtain cold-war oppression. It was a "Holy Alliance" between the Papacy and western powers which finally brought that great empire to its end in 1989. We saw the fall of the Berlin wall and the general fall of Communism.

We have seen the 6th head of the beast removed and the seventh head moving into place. Now we know where we stand in the stream of time. We wait only to see the inauguration of the seventh head world empire to find the beast spoken of in Revelation 13 actively engaged in its reign wherein "all the world wondered after the beast" and receive its "mark" of authority.

THE SEVENTH HEAD REPRESENTS A "ONE WORLD GOVERNMENT" UNDER PAPAL CONTROL.

The seventh head or last empire is described in Revelation 13:

> . . . and **ALL** THE WORLD WONDERED AFTER THE BEAST. And they worshipped the dragon which gave power unto the beast: and they worshipped the beast saying, Who is like unto the beast? who is able to make war with him? And there was given unto him a mouth speaking great things and blasphemies; and power was given him to continue forty and two months. (See Dan. 12:7, 11)
> And he opened his mouth in blasphemy against God, to blaspheme his name, and his tabernacle, and them that dwell in heaven.
> And it was given unto him to make war with the saints, and to overcome them: (See Dan. 12:7) and power was given him over all kindreds, and tongues, and nations. And all that dwell upon the earth shall worship him, whose names are not written in the book of the Lamb slain from the foundation of the world. Rev. 13:4-8

> And he had power to give life unto the image of the beast, that the image of the beast should both speak, and cause that as many as would not worship the image of the beast should be killed.
> And he causeth all, both small and great, rich and poor, free and bond, to receive a mark in their right hand, or in their foreheads;
> And that no man might buy or sell, save he that had the mark, or the name of the beast, or the number of his name. Here is wisdom. Let him that hath understanding

count the number of the beast: for it is the number of a man; and his number is Six hundred threescore and six. Rev. 13:15-18

Malachi Martin knows who he will be. The number is already on many documents. Governmental agencies are working to bring in the "New World Order." Do God's people know where they are in the stream of time?

DANIEL 11 AND REVELATION 13 INTERPRET EACH OTHER.

It is the "unrolling of the scroll"—the events of history which unlock the mysteries of prophetic Scripture. It is the fall of Communism that has amazed everyone, broken the seal on Daniel 11, and identified all seven heads of the beast. It is when these two are viewed together that they interlock and assure the scholar that the applications are correct.

XVI. GOD'S PEOPLE ESCAPE THE MARK OF THE BEAST

> . . . but these shall escape out of his hand, even Edom, and Moab, and the chief of the children of Ammon. Dan. 11:41.

These obscure peoples were "cave-dwellers" and "rock-dwellers." God's people have been told to FLEE the cities and they will go to the most solitary and desolate parts of the earth. Look at this description:

> I saw the nominal church and nominal Adventists, like Judas, would betray us to the Catholics to obtain their influence to come against the truth. The saints then **will be an obscure people, little known to the Catholics**; but the churches and nominal Adventists who know of our faith and customs (for they hated us on account of the Sabbath, for they could not refute it) will betray the saints and report them to the Catholics as those who disregard the institutions of the people; that is, that they keep the Sabbath and disregard Sunday. Then the Catholics bid the Protestants to go forward, and issue a decree that all who will not observe the first day of the week, instead of the seventh day, shall be slain. And the Catholics, whose numbers are large, will stand by the Protestants. The Catholics will give their power to the image of the beast, And the Protestants will work as their mother worked before them to destroy the saints. But before their decree bring or bear fruit, the saints will be delivered by the Voice of God. *The Spalding and Magan Collection*, Document 101 of 112, p. 1, 2.

God's saints will not be able to carry on business as usual. They will be an obscure, little known people. Rural fugitives, "rock and cave dwellers" in abject poverty.

XVII. THE BUYING-SELLING DECREE OF REV. 13 ESTABLISHED

Dan. 11:43 and Revelation 13 bear the same testimony as follows:

> But he [the Papacy] shall have power over the treasures of gold and of silver, and over all the precious things of Egypt: and the Libyans and the Ethiopians shall be at his steps. [follow after him]. Dan. 11:43.

> And he causeth all, both small and great, rich and poor, free and bond, to receive a mark in their right hand, or in their foreheads:

> And that no man might buy or sell, save he that had the mark, or the name of the beast, or the number of his name. Rev. 13:16, 17.

"ALL" the world shall enter into this "New World-Order" and financial plan—even those of "heathen nations," such as Africa, and the Moslem world. None shall escape. All will receive his mark except the people of God.

Just as the great "king of the north," Papal Supremacy No. 2, will bring the whole world under his dominion, God interferes by sending the Loud Cry!

XVIII. THE SEALING AND THE LOUD CRY

> But tidings out of the EAST and out of the north shall trouble him . . . Dan. 11:44.
>
> And I saw another angel ascending from the EAST, having the seal of the living God . . . Rev. 7:2.

It is the angel "ascending from the east having the seal of the living God," who will come with the third angel's warning message against the "beast," his "mark," his "name," and the number of his name. That message will come in the power of the Latter Rain of the Holy Spirit and will be called the LOUD CRY. Revelation 18:1-4. It will be this message which will trouble him. In desperation he will then take action as follows:

> . . . therefore he shall go forth with great fury to destroy, and utterly to make away many. Dan. 11:44. See Rev. 13:15.

XIX. THE SPURIOUS "PRINCE OF PEACE" IN THE "CITY OF PEACE"

> And he shall plant the tabernacles of his palace between the seas in the glorious holy mountain; yet he shall come to his end, and none shall help him. Dan. 11:45.

Negotiations are being made so that the Papacy may have "the tabernacles of his palace"—embassy, not in Tel Aviv, but in **Jerusalem, the "city of peace**."

The day will come when he will not only have his tabernacles or embassy in Jerusalem, but as head of the New World-Order the Pope will reign from that seat as the **prince of peace.** This is one more blasphemous title which belongs to Christ. And it is there that the Pope of Rome will usher in Satan himself to personate Christ as King of kings. There the king, Satan, and the Papal prince will reign together.

XX. THE END OF PAPAL SUPREMACY NO. 2

> "YET HE SHALL COME TO HIS END
> AND NONE SHALL HELP HIM" Dan. 11:45

THE DANIEL 11:45 AND CHAPTER 12:1-4 CONNECTION

The fourth vision of Daniel 11 extends beyond the last verse (45), and includes the first four verses of Chapter 12. If the translators had not divided the book of Daniel into chapters and verses or had done it differently, they could have given chapter 11, 49 verses! That would have completed the fourth vision.

The Bible supplies its own timeframe which connects the last verse (45) of chapter 11, with the first verse of chapter 12 as follows:

> . . . he shall come to his end, and none shall help him [chapter 11:45, **AND AT THAT TIME** shall Michael stand up . . . [chapter 12:1]

The words, **AND AT THAT TIME (12:1), refers to that which is spoken right before it (11:45), which** says, "he shall come to his end, and none shall help him."

Exactly WHEN does Papal Supremacy No. 2 come to his end? His "end" is described in Revelation 18:6-24 and is known as "THE FALL OF BABYLON." The fall of Babylon occurs in "one hour" symbolic time which represents 15 literal days. The FALL of Babylon begins at the Voice of God.

Therefore, it is self-evident that the Bible places the standing up of Michael, Dan. 12:1 at the very time of the Fall of Babylon and that which brings about that fall—the Voice of God.

It has been generally understood that Michael is to "stand up" at the close of probation. Daniel 7:10 declares that the judgment did **SIT,** and when that judgment is completed Christ **stands up.** It is good to remember that when Christ presides in a particular work, He "sits" and when that work is finished He "stands up." He presides over and accomplishes several different kinds of work. First, he wears His priestly robes as He sits in the Investigative Judgment. When He stands up, having completed that work, he changes from His priestly robes and puts on the garments of vengeance, for the pouring out of the seven last plagues. There again, he presides or "sits" in that office as the Commander of the armies of heaven, and earth. As the crisis emerges into the legislation of a Universal Death Decree, Michael again "stands up" and puts on His kingly garments making ready to deliver His people at the Voice of God.

> And he was clothed with a vesture dipped in blood . . . on his vesture and on his thigh a name written **KING OF KINGS, AND LORD OF LORDS.** Rev. 19:13, 16.

DANIEL 11:45 AND 12:1-4 PARAPHRASED

And he [*Papal Supremacy, No. 2*] shall plant [*or establish*] his tabernacle [*or place of worship*] between the seas [*The Black Sea to the north, The Persian Gulf to the east, The Dead Sea to the southeast, The Red Sea to the south, The Caspian Sea to the northeast, And The Mediterranean Sea on the west, and Sea of Galilee to the North.*]

[*He will move the Vatican Palace from Rome*] to the glorious holy mountain [*which is Mount Zion or Jerusalem*]. Yet he, [*Papal Supremacy No. 2*] shall come to his end [*which is the "fall of Babylon" under plague no. 7*], and none shall help him. Dan. 11:45.

And at that time [*when the Voice of God initiates the fall of Babylon*], shall Michael stand up [*to put on his kingly robes in which to deliver his people. He is*] the great prince which standeth for the children of thy people: and there shall be a time of trouble, such as never was since, there was a nation, even to that same time: [*under the sixth trumpet—woe 2 holocaust of Rev. 9:14-20, and the seventh plague when the cities fall. Rev. 16:18, 19.*]

And at that time thy people shall be delivered [*at the Voice Of God*], everyone that shall be found written in the book. Dan. 12:1.

And many of them that sleep in the dust of the earth shall awake, some to everlasting life, and some, [*those who pierced Him and persecutors of God's people shall awake*] to everlasting contempt. Dan. 12:2.

And they that be wise shall shine as the brightness of the firmament; and they that turn many to righteousness as the stars for ever and ever. Daniel 12:3.

But thou, O Daniel, shut up the word, and seal the book, even to the time of the end [*to endtime*]: many shall run to and fro [*cross reference the scripture finding linkage*], and knowledge [*of endtime application of prophecy*] shall be increased. Daniel 12:4.

This is the end of the fourth vision.

XXIII A SUMMARY OF DANIEL 11

A brief outline of Daniel 11 is presented to enable the reader to view the sequence of historical action in this chapter. The Bible verses are listed in sequence and the dates are at the right side. A glance at the dates reveals the fact that the story begins about 538 B.C. and continues chronologically to the end of earth's history. See p. 58.

Verses 1-22 are outlined in the same manner as done by Uriah Smith in the book, *Daniel and the Revelation*. These verses follow the history of the rise and fall of nations (empires) from 538 B.C. to the crucifixion of "the prince of the covenant"—Jesus Christ.

At that point, Uriah Smith abandoned a sequential application of verses 23-29. He went back in time to 161 B.C. He sought to link these verses to events in the rise and progress of Rome. He was probably not aware that breaking the sequential nature of a prophetic outline destroys the entire premise on which a logical application is built. If the prophetic expositor takes verses out of their order, he ignores the fact that prophecy is simply history written before it happens—in the order of which it occurred.

Prophecy deals only with nations or events which affect the people of God. Verse 22 describes the crucifixion of Christ. Observing sequence and continuity, verse 23 to the end of the prophetic vision should outline events which affect the Christian Church—the people of God. Verses 23-29 should correspond to early church history, the struggle for primacy among the bishops of the church, their interaction with the emperors of Rome, and the formation of the Papal power. Verse 23 introduces "deception" or apostasy. Paul declared that in his day, that ". . . the mystery of iniquity doth already work. . . ." II Thess. 2:7.

Verse 24 speaks of a "scattering," or persecution, of the early church. Verse 25 describes warfare and battle. This may refer to the struggle between the bishops of Rome and Arianism—"king of the south." Arius was a priest in Alexandria, Egypt, A.D. 270. This struggle aligns with Dan. 7:8. Verse 26 describes the fall of Arianism which permitted the bishops of Rome to increase their religious and political power.

Verses 27-29 will find a better application in reference to the increase of power of the Roman bishops and the fading political power of the emperors of Pagan Rome. A correct application of these verses should reveal that the way was clear for the emperor of Rome to hand over the scepter of power to the popes and establish Papal Supremacy No. 1: 538-1798.

Verses 30 and 31 are clearly tied to the emergence of Papal Supremacy No. 1.

Verses 30-35 describe Papal Supremacy, No. 1 (539-1798) and its struggle against Protestantism.

Verse 36 brings to view Papal Rome as it was "wounded" (Rev. 13) and the Pope taken prisoner by atheistic France.

Verses 37-40 reveal the emergence of atheistic Communism as it crept from France eastward in the "Old World" until it conquered over half the world's surface. It ruled as a formidable power, threatening the whole free world, persecuting Christians and fulfilling the prophecy of the sixth head of the beast of Revelation 13.

Verses 40-42 describe the "pushing," aggressive action and struggle between Communism and Papal Rome. We have now viewed the triumph of popery and the fall of Communism in 1989.

Verses 42-44 describe the expanding power of Rome today and in the near future.

Verse 45 is a prophecy of the final triumph of Papal Supremacy No. 2 (future) when it will "plant the tabernacle of his palace between the seas in the glorious holy mountain—Jerusalem. At that time the pope will assume the title, "Prince of peace" which belongs to Christ. There, that political "Prince of peace" will demand worship as he sits on His throne in the "City of peace"—Jerusalem. At that time the "Holy Father" will reign in the "Holy City."

This has been viewed as the "crowning act" of Papal dominion for centuries. The crusades were efforts, long sustained by the popes of Rome, to secure Jerusalem that they might reign there. But the fulfillment of Daniel 11:45 was not to occur back then. This act in the drama is yet to occur to be viewed by the last generation.

When this last and seventh kingdom (empire) is fully established, "he will come to his end and none shall help him." Dan. 11:45.

THE COMPOSITE BEAST OF REVELATION 13 WITH ITS SEVEN HEADS

The seven heads of the composite beast of Revelation 13 interpret Daniel 11 and in turn; the kings listed in Daniel 11, (as they reign over seven great empires which affect God's people) decode the seven heads of the Revelation 13 beast. Daniel and Revelation are one.

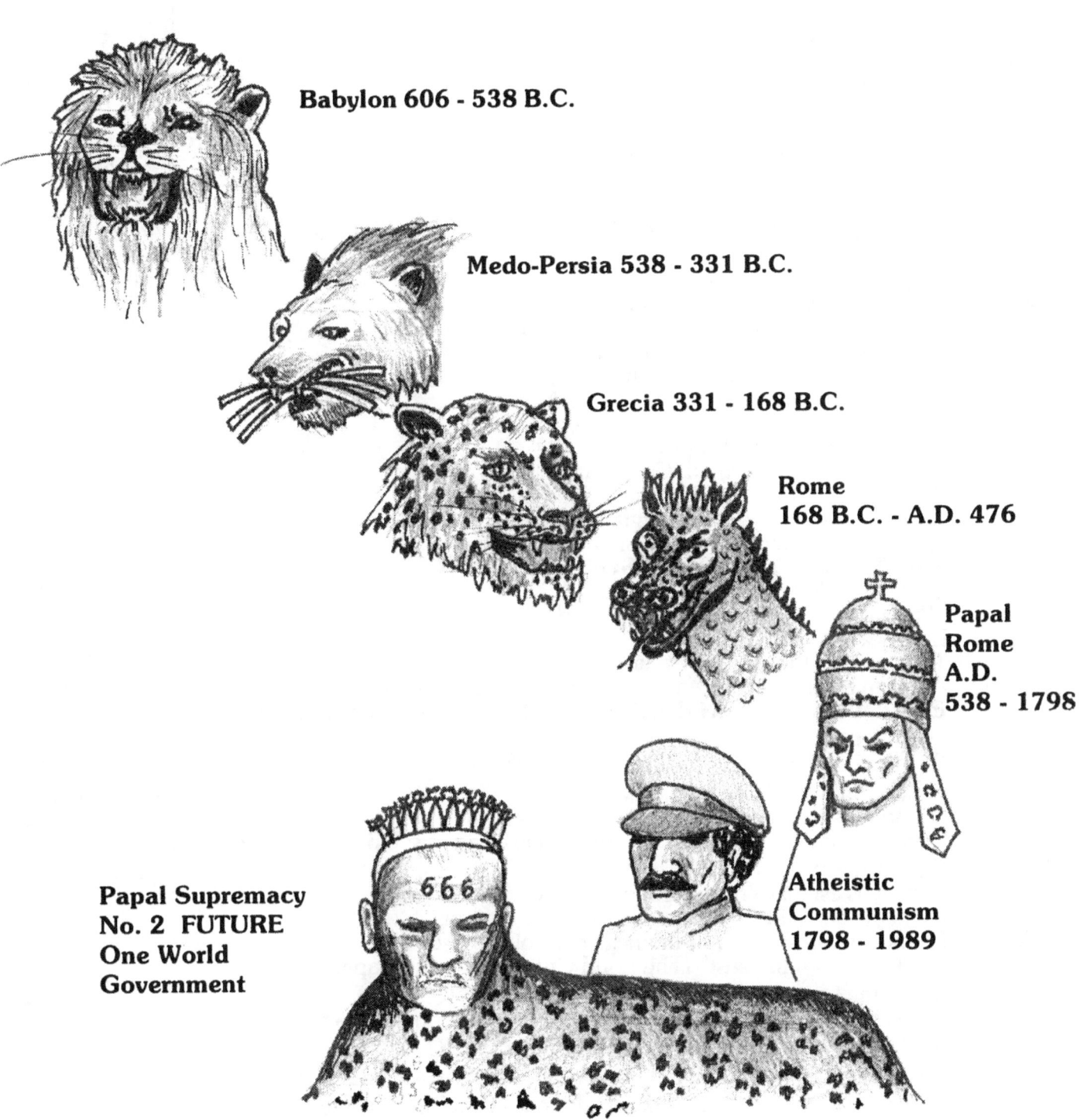

THE SEQUENCE AND CONTINUITY OF DANIEL 11 HISTORICAL FULFILLMENT		
Verse	Empire	Date
1	**EMPIRE NO. 1 — BABYLON.** (already fallen), **EMPIRE NO. 2 — MEDO-PERSIA.** Daniel begins with Medes and Persians	538 B.C.
2	Persia battles with Grecia,	
3	**EMPIRE NO. 3 — GRECIA.** Conquers Medo-Persia.,	
4	Grecia falls — divides into four,	
5	Egypt aspires to become Empire No. 4,	
6	Egypt and Syria form alliance, aspiring to be Empire No. 4,	
7	Egypt and Syria at war,	
8	Egypt punishes Syria	221 B.C.
9-13	Egypt and Syria continue to struggle,	
14-15	Rome emerges (200 B.C.) and conquers Syria	65 B.C.
16	Rome conquers Palestine,	
17	Rome conquers Egypt	47 B.C.
18	**EMPIRE NO. 4 — PAGAN ROME;** established under Julius Caesar	44 B.C.
19	Julius Caesar falls,	
20	Augustus Caesar, "raiser of taxes" (Luke 2:1; Jesus born)	4 B.C.
21	Tiberius Caesar, "a vile person",	
22	Crucifixion of "The Prince of the Covenant" — Christ	A.D. 31
23	Deception — Apostasy enters Christianity	A.D. 100
24	Persecution of the early church,	
25	Struggle of Roman bishops with Arianism	A.D. 270
26	The fall of Arianism (See Daniel 7:8),	
27	Intrigue and struggle for power,	
28	Church hierarchy formed; Constantine corrupts	A.D. 323
29	Fading power of pagan Roman emperors,	
30	Barbarian invasions cause the fall of Rome	A.D. 476
31	"Daily taken away" — Paganism absorbed and exalted **EMPIRE NO. 5 — PAPAL SUPREMACY NO. 1** (538-1798)	A.D. 508 A.D. 538
32	God's people enter the Dark Ages	A.D. 538
33	1260 years of papal persecution,	
34	European Reformation	A.D. 1500
35	The "time of the end" — "a time appointed"	A.D. 1798
36	Atheism arises in France and wounds the Papal "head"	A.D. 1798
37	**EMPIRE NO. 6 — ATHEISTIC COMMUNISM,** atheism expands into Communism	A.D. 1918
38	Communism conquers half the world — threatens all armed forces and seeks world dominion	A.D. 1940
39	Communism spreads; persecutes and rules,	
40	Communism "pushes" and Papacy struggles against USSR; the fall of Communism	A.D. 1989
41	Papacy is establishing control over the world and Israel,	
42	Moslems and Africans come under Papal control,	
43	Papacy establishes world-financial control (Rev. 13:17),	
44	"Seal . . . from the east" (The Loud Cry) enrages the Papacy, brings about the Universal Death Decree (UDD) Rev. 13:15,	
45	Papal control over Jerusalem—New World Order headquarters; **EMPIRE NO. 7 — PAPAL SUPREMACY NO. 2** Papacy comes to its end and none shall help him. Michael stands up and delivers His people from the UDD. Plagues fall. The resurrection. (See Daniel 12:1-3).	
NOTE: Daniel chapter 11 is the story of the rise and fall of empires surrounding the people of God.		

CONCLUSION

Of what value is a study of Daniel 11?

1. The additional details supplied in the outline of Daniel 11 closes the gap between the fall of Grecia and the rise of Rome. The four outlines align with each other, each supplying additional detail making the picture complete.

2. The additional details supplied in the outline of Daniel 11 trace the rise and fall of all seven empires which have persecuted or affected the people of God. These empires are listed in sequence.

    Daniel 2 presents **four** great empires, Daniel 7 reveals the **5th** empire. Daniel 11 presents all **seven**.

3. The sequence and continuity of Chapter 11 pinpoints the sixth empire to be that of atheistic Communism and the seventh to be that Papal Supremacy No. 2—yet future, as described in Revelation 13.

4. The seven empires of Daniel 11 enable us to name with ease the seven heads of the beast of Revelation 13.

CHAPTER XII

DELIVERANCE IN THE TIMELINES OF DANIEL 12

> ### THE PROPHETIC PERIODS OF DANIEL
>
> In the Scripture are **PRESENT TRUTHS** that relate especially to our own time.
>
> > To the period ***just prior to the appearing of the Son of man, the prophecies of Scripture point***, and their warnings and threatenings preeminently apply.
>
> **THE PROPHETIC PERIODS OF DANIEL, EXTENDING TO THE VERY EVE OF THE GREAT CONSUMMATION, THROW A FLOOD OF LIGHT UPON EVENTS THEN TO TRANSPIRE.**
>
> > The book of Revelation is also replete with warnings and instruction for the **LAST GENERATION**…
>
> None need remain in ignorance, none need be unprepared for the coming of the day of God.
>
> *Review and Herald*, Sept. 25, 1883

DELIVERANCE IN THE FINAL TIMELINES OF DANIEL 12:5-13

The thesis of this chapter proposes that the timelines of Daniel 12:5-13 find fulfillment in future confrontation and final deliverance of the people of God.[1]

THE INTRODUCTION

Reliable hermeneutics require, not merely attention to specific details, but also a greater perspective: to view the book of Daniel as a whole unit, giving attention to structure, pattern, movement and theme focus. Viewing the book as a whole, it is apparent that it contains a

---

1 A thesis is valid only as it conforms to the Scriptural hermeneutic principle stated in Isa. 28:10-13, which describes a system of research using a method of Biblical cross-reference. This book presents an interlocking reference to texts in Daniel, Revelation and Matthew 24. Reinforcement is made by the use of quotations from the inspired writings of Ellen G. White.

succession of prophetic outlines—***repeating*** and ***reinforcing***; in each succeeding prophecy ***adding details*** which steadily draw toward the grand climax of earth's history, confrontation, and final deliverance of the people of God.[1] The following 24 Biblically based premises develop a logical understanding of Daniel 12:5-13.

BIBLICAL PREMISE NO. 1—Daniel 12:5-13 is an Epilogue.[2]

The grand climax of the prophecies of the book of Daniel is reached in Daniel 12:1-3, where it describes the great resurrection. Immediately after that, in verse 4, those prophetic outlines are brought to a conclusion. It says: ". . . SHUT UP THE WORDS, AND SEAL THE BOOK . . ." These words, "shut up the words" complete those outlines which have outlined the history of the ages. At first view the remaining verses 5-13 appear simply to be tacked on as a needless repetition. Closer investigation leads to a conclusion that this passage is an epilogue, pointing to the final confrontation of the great controversy and final deliverance of the people of God.[3]

PREMISE NO. 2—Daniel 12:5-13 Uses Literal Language. It Contains No Symbolic Time.

Reliable hermeneutic principle demands that texts and time units be viewed in context. Symbolic time is computed by the Year-Day Principle when nestled in symbolic or figurative context. The Daniel 12 timelines are given without figurative symbolism,[4] and are literal statements of three specific time periods.

---

1 The Outlines and Timelines of Daniel
   1. The Image of Dan. 2 outline.
   2. The Beasts of Dan. 7 outline, with its 1260 day-years timeline.
   3. The Beasts and Horns of Dan. 8 outline, and the 2300 year timeline.
   4. The outline of Kings in Dan. 11:1-45.
   5. The Computation of the 1260 day prophetic timeline of Dan. 12:7.
   6. The Computation of the 1290 day prophetic timeline of Dan. 12:11.
   7. The Computation of the 1335 day prophetic timeline of Dan. 12:12.

   The Seven Death-Decrees and Deliverance of Daniel
   1. The Death Decree of the Wisemen. Dan. 2.
   2. The Death Decree of the Hebrews and Fiery Furnace. Dan. 3.
   3. The Death Decree and the Lion's Den Deliverance. Dan. 6.
   4. Deliverance from multiple Death Decrees of the "Little Horn" Persecution of Dan. 7; and Dan. 11:45; 12:11.
   5. Deliverance from sin in the judgment. Dan. 9:24.
   6. Deliverance from the universal death decree by the voice of God. Dan. 12:7-11.
   7. Deliverance from the grave. Dan. 12:2.

2 Definition: "Epilogue." "A speech . . . spoken after the conclusion of a play." "Concluding section . . . serving to complete the plan of the work." *Webster's Dictionary.*

3 Note: The death decree and deliverances begin with the personal experiences of Daniel and his friends, then expand to the entire nation in danger of extinction in Babylonian captivity. Death decrees were multiplied in the Papal Supremacy persecutions. All mankind is on "death row" in the judgment, but the righteous are delivered by the High Priest. The final death decree and final deliverance are the subjects of Dan. 12:5-13.

4 Daniel 12:5-13 presents no symbolism such as the image, the beast, the horns, as found in previous outlines. It is simply the recording of a conversation. Therefore, the year-day principle of figurative symbolic time should not be used to compute the timelines of Dan. 12:5-13. It should be viewed as literal time, in its literal context.

> ## THE LITERAL APPROACH
> Every declaration of Scripture is to be taken in the most obvious and literal sense, except where context and the well-known laws of language show that the terms are figurative, and not literal, and whatever is figurative must be explained by other portions of the Bible which are literal. G. M. Hyde, Ed.: *A Symposium on Biblical Hermeneutics*. (Washington, D.C.: Review and Herald Publishing Association, 1979), Statement by Don Neufeld. (See also GC 599).

The above quotation defines one of the most important hermeneutic rules to be used in a study of the Bible. This is called "the literal approach" and it applies to **all** parts of the books of the Bible. It is the **only** approach approved by Seventh-day Adventists. By this literal approach, all foundations were laid for Adventism, the doctrines held by the church, as well as its valid expositions of prophecy. This means that Daniel 12 must **also** be subjected to this literal approach and guarded by this hermeneutic principle. Daniel 12:5-13 uses no symbols; the language is literal. Therefore the "days" are **literal** days.

PREMISE NO. 3 — No Timeline Will Ever Establish A Date; Day and Hour for the Coming of Jesus. (See Appendix Notes H and I.)

The angel of Revelation 10:6 declared "there should be time no longer." This meant that the 2300 day-year prophetic time***line*** ended in 1844. Prophetic computation of time will never again be a test to the people of God.[1] Never again shall prophecy be used to establish a date for the coming of Jesus. He said, "Of that day and hour knoweth no man." Matt. 24:36. The Dan. 12:5-13 timelines may not be used to establish a date for the coming of Jesus.[2]

PREMISE NO. 4 — The Daniel 12:5-13 Timelines do not Establish Dates, but Rather Outline a Sequence of Events Dealing with the Final Crisis and Deliverance, and *"throws a flood of light upon events then to transpire [FUTURE]."* Review and Herald, Sept. 25, 1883.

Jesus said, "Of that day and hour knoweth no man . . . [but] when you see all these things, know that it is near, even at the doors." Matt. 24:33. Although Ellen G. White has set no date for the Second Coming of Jesus, she has written much in regard to future events and their sequence.[3] The final timelines of Dan. 12:5-13 should be viewed in the same way. Since there is no symbolism in Dan. 12, the timelines of Dan. 12:5-13 should not be computed by the year-day principle. It should be viewed merely as literal time periods outlining or establishing a **sequence of events** connected with the closing crisis and deliverance.[2]

---

1   *Spiritual Gifts*, Vol. I. p. 148; *Early Writings*, p. 75.

2   "The repeated efforts to find new **dates** for the beginning and close of the prophetic periods, [of the 2300 day-year prophecy] and the unsound reasoning necessary to sustain these positions . . . lead minds away from the present truth . . . Those who persist in this error will at last fix upon a **date** too far in the future for the coming of Christ." ***The Great Controversy***, p. 457.

3   See *The Great Controversy*, Chapters 38-42, on sequence of future events.

PREMISE NO. 5 — The Final Timelines of Dan. 12:5-13 Contain Three Time Periods.

The following time periods are given: 1260 days ("A time, times and a half") in verse 7; 1290 days in verse 11; and 1335 days in verse 12. Although these appear to be three different time periods, a close investigation of content, leads to the conclusion that they are all interlocking parts of one unit. This thesis is developed in this book in its progressive premises. Each period will be examined point by point, contributing to an understanding of a sequence of events connected with the final confrontation and deliverance of God's people. All the other outlines in the book of Daniel conclude with the establishment of Christ's kingdom and the destruction of the antichrist power. It is appropriate that these final timelines should be consistent, ending with the same subjects as the grand climax of prophetic focus.

PREMISE No. 6 — The Dan. 12:5-13 Timelines Refer to the Very End of Time.

The timelines are introduced by two questions: 1. "How long shall it be **to the end** of these wonders?" (verse 6). 2. "[W]hat shall be **the end** of these things?" (verse 8). The answer given states that "when [the timelines are finished] . . . **all** these things shall be *finished*" (verse 7). Verse 13 also mentions the "**end** of the days." If understood in a literal sense, there is no question but that these timelines refer to the very **end** of time.[1]

PREMISE NO. 7 — The 1260 Final Timeline Refers to the Persecution by the Second Papal Supremacy of Revelation 13.

> . . . it shall be for a time, times and a half [1260 days]; and when **he** shall have accomplished to scatter the power of the holy people, all these things shall be finished. Dan. 12:7.

Who is "he" that will "scatter," or persecute, God's people at the very end of time? The answer is found in Revelation 13, which declares plainly that there are two Papal supremacies.[2] The apostle John describes the second Papal Supremacy as follows:

> . . . the beast which I saw . . . one of his heads as it were wounded to death [1798]; and his deadly wound was healed [in progress now]: and **all** the world wondered after the beast [future] **and** power was given unto him **to continue** forty and two months [1260 days]. . . . And it was given unto him to make war with the saints, and to overcome them: and power was given him over **all** kindreds, and tongues, and nations. And all that dwell on the earth shall worship him . . . no man might buy or sell [future], save he that had the mark, or the name of the beast, or the number of his name. See Rev. 13:2, 3, 5, 7, 8, 17.

---

1. The "end of time" should not be confused with "the time of the end."
   Definition: "End" as used in Dan. 12:4, 6, 9, 13 Word 7093 קֵץ **qêts** pronounced *kates;* an extremity, (utmost) border [utmost end]. *Strong's Exhaustive Analytical Concordance Hebrew and Chaldee Dictionary.*

2. The first Papal Supremacy extended from A.D. 538 to 1798 wherein the Pope was known as "The Corrector of Heretics" and reigned over Europe. That reign came to an end in 1798 with a "deadly wound." Revelation 13 refers to a Papal Supremacy which occurs after the "wound was healed"—a **second** reign at the very end of time over **ALL** the world.

PREMISE NO. 8 — The Final Timelines of Dan. 12 Refer to the Third Angel's Message.

Revelation 13 declares that the "beast" (Roman Power) with the healed head will persecute God's people for "forty and two months"—"make war with the saints," which corresponds to the final timeline in which Daniel declares that "he" will **"scatter"** God's people for a "time, times and a half" (forty-two months or 1260 days). This beast power of Revelation 13 is the very "beast" against which the third angel warns in Revelation 14:9-12. It is a fact that these prophecies were computed in the symbolic context of a "beast" in symbolic time to apply to Papal Supremacy No. 1. But now the literal context of the plain statements of a series of events—the 1798 wound, the current healing and future worship must be applied to Papal Supremacy No. 2, and a literal forty-two months.

PREMISE NO. 9 — The Papal Supremacy No. 2 Will be Established When There is a Universal Sunday Law.

> . . . when Sunday observation shall be enforced by law [a union of church and state] . . . **the world** . . . will thereby honor popery above God . . . As men then reject the institution which God has declared to be the sign of His authority, [the Seventh-day Sabbath], and honor in its stead that which Rome has chosen as the token of her supremacy, they will thereby accept the sign of allegiance to Rome—[Sunday sacredness], "the mark of the beast." *The Great Controversy*, p. 449.

> The powers of earth, **uniting** to war against the commandments of God will decree that **all** . . . shall conform to . . . the false sabbath. *The Great Controversy*, p. 604.

Therefore, the 1260 days of the final timeline of Daniel 12:5-13 should begin at the time of a "world" law, or enforcement of Sunday. Papal Supremacy No. 2 will be a worldwide force ". . . over all kindreds, and tongues, and nations." Rev. 13:7. "When Sunday observation shall be enforced by law . . . the world . . ." will have set up the second Papal Supremacy, and the 1260 days of Dan. 12:7 should begin.

PREMISE NO. 10 — Papal Supremacy No. 2 Cannot be Set Up Until Religious Liberties Provided by Governments are Suspended.

> And from the time the daily (sacrifice) shall be taken away, and the abomination that maketh desolate set up, there shall be a thousand, two hundred and ninety days. Dan. 12:11.

What is this "daily (sacrifice)" which must be taken away, before the "abomination which maketh desolate" is set up?[1] The following comment is helpful:

> Then I saw in relation to the "daily" (Dan. 8:12)[2] that the word "sacrifice" was supplied by man's wisdom, and **does not belong** to the text, and that the Lord gave the correct view of it to those who gave the judgment hour cry. When union existed, before 1844, nearly all were united on the correct view of the "daily"; but in the confusion since 1844, other views have been embraced, and darkness and confusion have followed. *Early Writings*, p. 74, 75.

---

1 "The abomination which maketh desolate" refers to Rome. See Matt. 24:15.

2 The same word "daily" is used both in Dan. 8:12 and Dan. 12:11.

Early pioneers understood the "daily" to refer to state government, or as Uriah Smith applied it, to "pagan Rome"—the Roman Empire. The "daily" translated from the Hebrew language has a meaning of "continual" or that which continueth.[1] In our day, we could refer to it as the **power, seat,** and **authority** of state governments "that which continueth"—to guarantee religious freedom. Today in the United States especially, the government "continueth daily" to grant freedom of worship according to conscience, and protects from religious persecution. But the day will come when these freedoms will be suspended. The final timeline of Daniel 12 says, "the daily shall be taken away" and Revelation says: "As many as would not worship the beast should be killed." Rev. 13:15.

PREMISE NO. 11 — The 1260 Days and the 1290 Days Both Refer to the Second Papal Supremacy in (A) Its Persecution; and (B) Its Establishment. Therefore Both Periods Run Simultaneously.

. . . *all* the world wondered after the beast. Rev. 13:3. . . . over *all* kindreds and tongues and nations Rev. 13:7 . . . to receive a MARK [A worldwide Sunday law] . . . Rev. 13:16, 17.

THE SECOND PAPAL SUPREMACY (No. 2)
Dan. 12:7 Persecution for 1260 days
Dan. 12:11 Established (to reign) for 1290 days

Civil and Religious Liberties are Taken Away.[2]
The "daily" is Taken Away. Dan. 12:11.

PREMISE NO. 12 — The Thirty Day Difference Between the 1260 Days and the 1290 Days is Explained in Revelation 17 and 18.

Daniel and Revelation are interlocking and explain each other. In Revelation 17:12, it states that ". . . ten kings . . . receive power as kings one hour with the beast." Revelation 18:10, 17, and 19 state that ". . . in one hour is thy [Babylon's] judgment come." These two periods are not "indefinite" but a very specific "one hour" of symbolic time.[3] When "one hour" of symbolic time is converted to literal time, it represents 15 literal days. When these two "one hour" periods are added together, they total 30 literal days. The two "one hour" periods of *Revelation 17 and 18 correspond to the 30 days difference in the Daniel 12:5-13 Final Timeline.* This is relevant to the final confrontation and deliverance of the people of God.

---

1 (A simplfied explanation) *Seventh-day Adventist Commentary*, Vol. 4, p. 843.

2 Note: It is when secular power or the "scepter of power," seat and authority is taken away from the kings of the earth and placed in the hand of the Papal "king" that the "daily" is "taken away" in order to "set up the abomination" that makes desolate. (The Papacy that persecutes) Dan. 12:11.

3 The "one hour" periods in Revelation are couched in prophetic symbolism of "ten horns," "the beast," and spiritual "Babylon," and are therefore symbolic time. If they are to correspond to the final timelines of Daniel 12:5-13, they must be converted to literal time by the day-year principle. Since one symbolic day equals one literal year, then "one hour" of symbolic time equals 15 literal days.

PREMISE NO. 13 — The Two "One Hour" Periods of Revelation 17 and 18 Reveal the Ascending and Descending Action in the Great Drama of the Final Confrontation and Deliverance.

The "one hour" period of Revelation 17 refers to a triumphant **reign**, but the "one hour" period of Revelation 18 refers to a "fall" or judgment. The false sabbath issue culminates in a final death decree and deliverance of God's people. The "beast" reigns triumphant in a union of church and state when the "ten kings" of Rev. 17 unite with him in his final act of persecution to annihilate all the people of God. But God delivers His people and then in "one hour" Babylon falls.

PREMISE NO. 14 — The Final Confrontation Climaxes in a Universal Death Decree.

> Then I saw the leading men of the earth consulting together, and Satan and his angels busy around them. I saw a ***writing***, copies of which were scattered in different parts of the land, giving orders that unless the saints should yield their peculiar faith, give up the Sabbath, and observe the first day of the week, the people were at liberty after a certain time to put them to death. *Early Writings*, p. 282, 283.

PREMISE NO. 15 — The Death Decree Will Go Into Effect at Midnight.

> It will be determined in one night to strike a decisive blow. *The Great Controversy*, p. 635.

> . . . after ***a certain time*** to put them to death. *Early Writings*, p. 283.

> Haman said . . . let it be written . . . that they may be destroyed . . . in one day . . . for a prey . . . The copy of the writing . . . in every providence was published unto the people. Esther 3:6-14.

First a law is passed by a legislative body. Then, when it is mandated, it goes into effect on a certain date at midnight. The kings of the earth and the beast in a union of church and state, "reign" together from the date the death decree is mandated until it goes into effect at midnight. See Rev. 17:12.

PREMISE NO. 16 — God Delivers His People From the Death Decree at Midnight by the "Voice of God."

> It is at ***midnight*** that God manifests His power for the deliverance of His people. . . . In the midst of the angry heavens is one clear space of indescribable glory, whence comes the voice of God like the sound of many waters, saying, "It is done."[1] *The Great Controversy*, p. 636.

PREMISE NO. 17 — The Midnight "Voice of God" Deliverance From the Death Decree is NOT the Same Event as the Second Coming of Jesus.

> The voice of God is heard from heaven, declaring the day and hour of Jesus' coming . . . *The Great Controversy*, p. 640.

---

[1] "It is done"—Ellen White quotes from Rev. 16:17, a description of the 7th plague. It is the "Voice of God" that says, "It is done," which begins the last plague. The seventh plague describes the "Fall of Babylon."

PREMISE NO. 18 — Between the "Voice of God" Deliverance, and the Second Coming of Jesus, There Occurs the "One Hour" Fall of Babylon.

> The voice of God is heard from heaven. . . . The Israel of God stand listening, with their eyes fixed upward. Their countenances are lighted up with His glory, and shine as did the face of Moses when he came down from Sinai. The wicked cannot look upon them. . . . At the voice of God they were glorified . . . *The Great Controversy*, p. 640, 645.

> When the voice of God turns the captivity of His people, there is a terrible awakening of those who have lost all in the great conflict of life . . . The people see that they have been deluded . . . heaping their bitterest condemnation upon the ministers. . . . The multitudes are filled with fury. . . . they turn upon the false shepherds. . . . The swords which were to slay God's people are now employed to destroy their enemies. . . . Now the angel of death goes forth. . . . The false watchmen are the first to fall. *The Great Controversy*, p. 654-656.

The "false watchmen" are the representatives of spiritual "Babylon" which falls in "one hour." This one hour period (15 days) occurs between the "Voice of God" and the Second Coming of Jesus.

PREMISE NO. 19 — The Sixth and Seventh Plagues Portray the Final Climax of Confrontation and Final Deliverance.

Under the sixth plague, evil spirits working through the false ministers of spiritual Babylon "go forth unto the kings of the earth and of the whole world, to gather them **together**" to legislate a death decree. From the time the death decree is mandated, until it goes into effect, is "one hour." During this "one hour" these kings and the beast reign together. But at midnight under the seventh plague, under the "seventh angel," "there came a great voice out of the temple of heaven, from the throne, saying, 'It is done.' " The "Voice of God" which glorifies the righteous, is the great deliverance of God's people from their enemies. Then under the seventh plague, in "one hour," wicked Babylon falls. The sixth and seventh plagues reveal the **ascending** and **descending drama** of the final confrontation and deliverance.

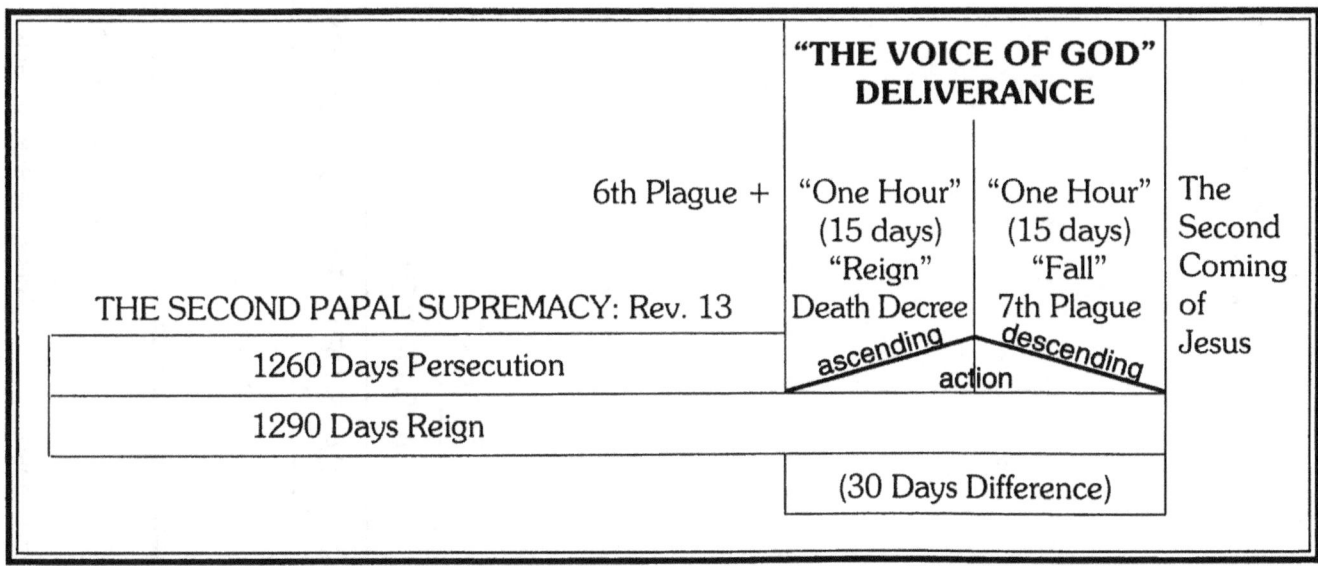

The Daniel 12:5-13 Final Timeline and the two "one hour" periods of Revelation 17 and 18 are not superfluous repetition, nor given as a mere enigma to the people of God. They are intended—

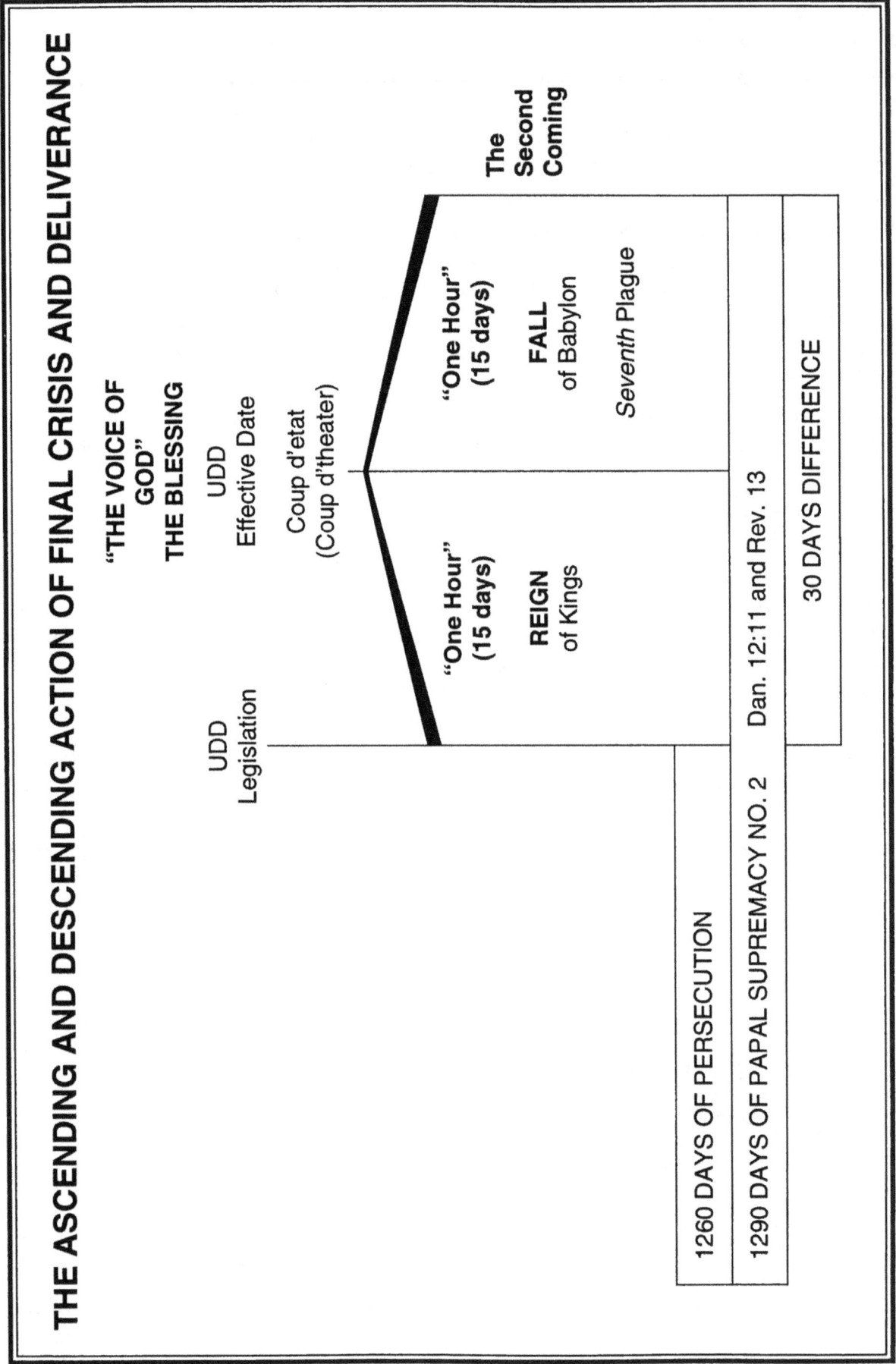

as is all prophecy—to clarify in bold sequence the specific events connected with the drama of the ages. Comprehension of their meanings signifies that their fulfillment is imminent.

PREMISE NO. 20. The "Voice of God" Pronounces the BLESSING

The "Voice of God" proclaims several things: It gives the day and hour for the coming of Jesus. It says, "It is done"—that is, the trials of God's people are done. He "delivers the everlasting covenant" which is the pronouncement of THE BLESSING.

> The voice of God is heard from heaven . . . delivering the everlasting covenant to His people . . . And when the BLESSING is pronounced on those who have honored God by keeping His Sabbath holy, there is a mighty shout of victory. *The Great Controversy*, p. 640.

This "blessing" is a key to understanding the last time period of 1335 days in the Daniel 12:5-13 Timeline. It marks the end of that period.

PREMISE NO. 21 — The 1335 Days of the Daniel 12:5-13 Timeline End with the Voice of God Pronouncement of the BLESSING.

> **BLESSED** is he that waiteth, and cometh to the thousand three hundred and five and thirty days. Dan. 12:12.

If the 1335 days ends at the Voice of God, it runs simultaneously with the 1260 and 1290 day periods. The 1335 days is longer than the 1260 or 1290 days and precedes them both. The question is this: what event begins the 1335 day period?

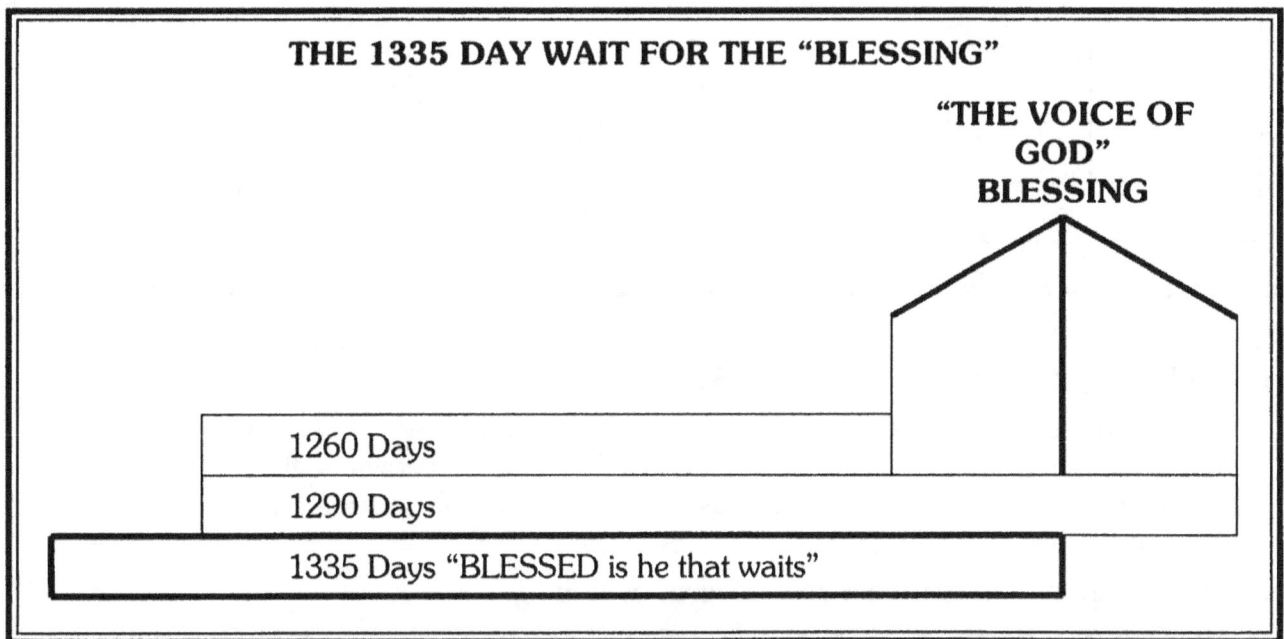

PREMISE NO. 22 — A National Sunday Law in the United States of America is the Event which Begins the Final Confrontation.

The United States is so significant to the final confrontation that it is the particular and last "beast" mentioned in Revelation 13. It arose with lamb-like horns which represented civil and religious liberty, but finally "spake as a dragon." It is "he" who "causeth all . . . to receive a mark"—the mark of the beast. The United States, out of all the countries of the world, is the only one mentioned at the end of time in Rev. 13, except for the beast himself. When the religious liberty in the United States is suspended and there is Sunday legislation as a **national** law, the Daniel 12:5-13 Final Confrontation and Deliverance scenario will begin.

> The prophecy of Revelation 13 declares that the power represented by the beast with the lamblike horns shall cause "the earth and them which dwell therein" to worship the papacy—there symbolized by the beast "like unto a leopard . . . to command all . . . to receive the mark of the beast. . . ." This prophecy will be fulfilled **when the United States shall enforce Sunday observance** . . . The Great Controversy, p. 578, 579.

First, the United States will enforce the mark of the beast—Sunday observance—and then shortly this will be imitated by the rest of the world, so that the Second Papal Supremacy, No. 2 will become a worldwide dominion.

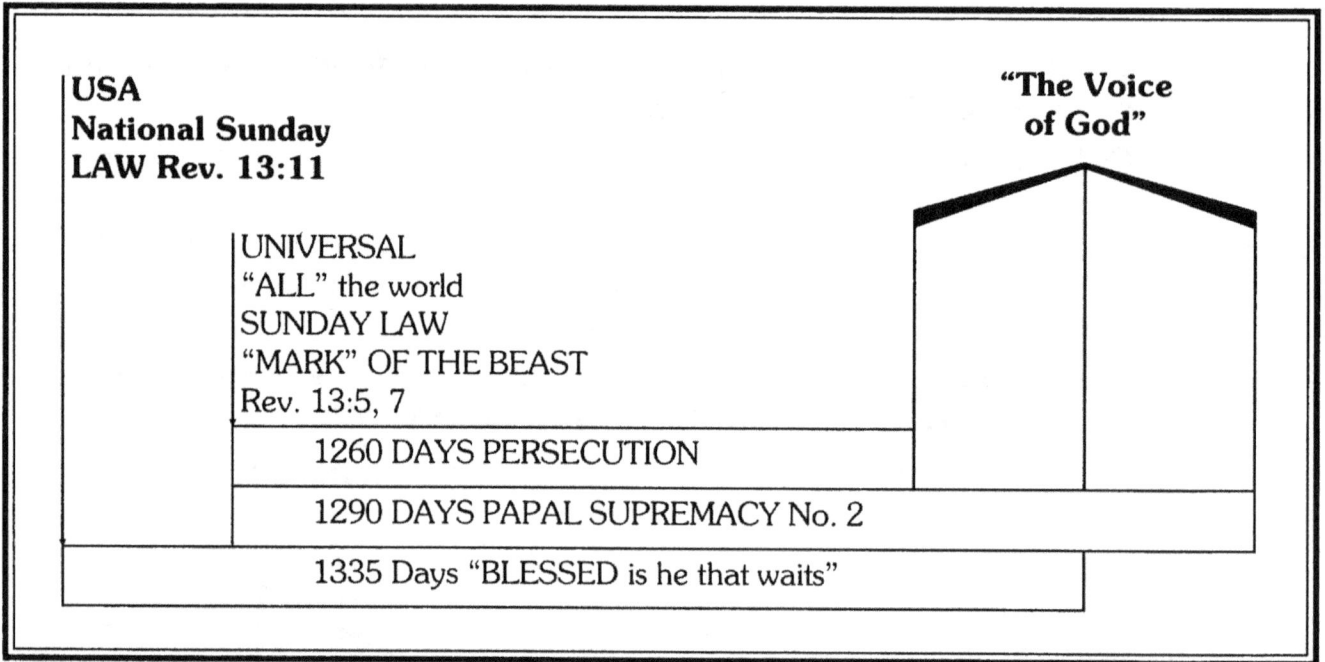

PREMISE NO. 23 — A National Sunday Law in the United States of America is the Sign of Warning to Leave the Large Cities.

> . . . the assumption of power on the part of our nation in the decree enforcing the papal sabbath will be A WARNING to us. It will then be time to leave the large cities, preparatory to leaving the smaller ones, for retired homes in secluded places among the mountains. Testimonies, Vol. 5, p. 464, 465.

This inspired warning is a comment on the words of Jesus:

> When ye therefore shall see the abomination of desolation, spoken of by Daniel the prophet, stand in the holy place [stand where it ought not] . . . Then let them . . . flee unto the mountains.[1] Matt. 24:15, 16.

---

1   Jesus mingled the signs pertaining to the destruction of Jerusalem and those which pertained to the destruction of the last days. Only those who believed prophecy in the days of Jerusalem's destruction escaped. Likewise, those who study prophecy and move in accordance with its warning may escape the perils foretold.

PREMISE NO. 24 — The Significance of the Daniel 12:5-13 Timeline is a Warning We Shall All Need to Understand, that the Final Confrontation has Begun and to Flee the Large Cities.

The Daniel 12:5-13 Final Timelines do not indicate a date for the Second Coming of Jesus. Not even after the United States Sunday Law has begun, will the people of God dare to set a date. Not until the "Voice of God," which gives the day and hour of His coming, will the date be known. The Final Timelines of Daniel 12 "throw a flood of light on *events then to transpire*." See *Review and Herald*, Sept. 25, 1883.

Note: It is often asserted that the "one hour" periods of Revelation 17 and 18 are not "one hour" but simply a "brief space of time." It is crucial to find the truth regarding this matter because it is upon the correct understanding of this "one hour" that the key is given to unlock the three timelines of Daniel 12, to comprehend the interlocking action of plagues, trumpets, seals, Revelation 11, 17, and 18. Upon a correct understanding of these "one hour" periods hangs the ascending and descending action of the final crisis and deliverance of God's people. For a study of the "one hour" in Greek and Hebrew see Appendix K.

A LIST OF PREMISES PERTAINING TO THE
FINAL TIMELINE OF DANIEL 12:5-13

1. Daniel 12:5-13 is an Epilogue.
2. Daniel 12:5-13 uses Literal language. It contains no Symbolic Time.
3. No Timeline will ever establish or set a date for the day and hour of the Coming of Jesus.
4. The Daniel 12:5-13 timelines do not Establish Dates, but Rather Outline a Sequence of Events Dealing with Final Crisis and Deliverance, and "throw a flood of Light upon Events then to transpire."
5. The Daniel 12:5-13 Timelines Contain Three Time Periods.
6. The Daniel 12:5-13 Timelines Refer to the Very End of Time.
7. The Daniel 1260 Final Timeline Refers to the Persecution by the Second Papal Supremacy of Rev. 13.
8. The Daniel Timelines Involve the Third Angel's Message and Loud Cry. Rev. 14:9-12; 18:1-4.
9. The Second Papal Supremacy will begin when there is a Universal Sunday Law—Sunday Observance and Legislation is enforced on a Universal Scope, Over the Whole World.
10. The Second Papal Supremacy Cannot be Established Until Religious Liberty, Provided by State Governments is Suspended.
11. The 1260 Days and the 1290 Days Both Refer to the Second Papal Supremacy in: (A) Its Persecuting role, and (B) Its Establishment. Therefore Both Periods Run Simultaneously.
12. The Thirty day Difference Between the 1260 Days and the 1290 Days is Explained in Revelation 17 and 18.
13. The Two "One Hour" Periods in Revelation 17 and 18 Reveal the Ascending and Descending Action in the Great Drama of the Final Confrontation and Deliverance.
14. The Final Confrontation Climaxes in a Universal Death Decree.
15. The Universal Death Decree will go Into Effect at Midnight.
16. God Delivers His People from the Universal Death Decree at Midnight by "The Voice of God."
17. The Midnight "Voice of God" Deliverance from the Universal Death Decree is Not the Same Event as the Second Coming of Jesus.
18. Between the "Voice of God" Deliverance, and the Second Coming of Jesus, There Occurs the "One Hour" Fall of Babylon.
19. The Sixth and Seventh Plagues Portray the Final Climax of Confrontation and Final Deliverance.
20. The "Voice of God" Pronounces the BLESSING.
21. The 1335 Days of the Daniel 12:5-13 Timeline Ends With the "Voice of God" Pronouncement of the BLESSING.
22. A National Sunday Law in the United States of America is the Event Which Begins the Final Confrontation.
23. A National Sunday Law in the United States of America is the Sign of Warning to Leave the Large Cities.
24. The Significance of the Daniel 12:5-13 Final Timeline is the Warning that " . . . we shall all need to understand before the [end of time] . . ." Ltr. 161, July 30, 1903.

THE FINAL TIMELINES OF DANIEL 12:5-13

A "grid" on which to place the events of Revelation

- REV. 13:11 VOICE OF USA-NSL
- 1335 DAY "WAIT"
- REV. 16:17 VOICE OF GOD
- REV. 13:5 VOICE "ALL" USL
- REV. 13.15 VOICES "ALL" UDD
- 1260 DAYS — "He shall . . . scatter the holy people." DAN. 12:7
- 1290 DAYS — "The Abomination that Maketh Desolate" DAN. 12:11
- REV. 16:18 VOICES OF DOOM
- REIGN OF KINGS REV. 17:12 "1 HOUR" or 15 DAYS
- FALL OF BABYLON REV. 18:10 "1 HOUR" or 15 DAYS
- 30 DAYS

THE FINAL TIMELINES OF DANIEL 12 WITH ADDED DETAIL

"[which] throw a flood of light upon events then to transpire." *Review and Herald* Sept. 25, 1883.

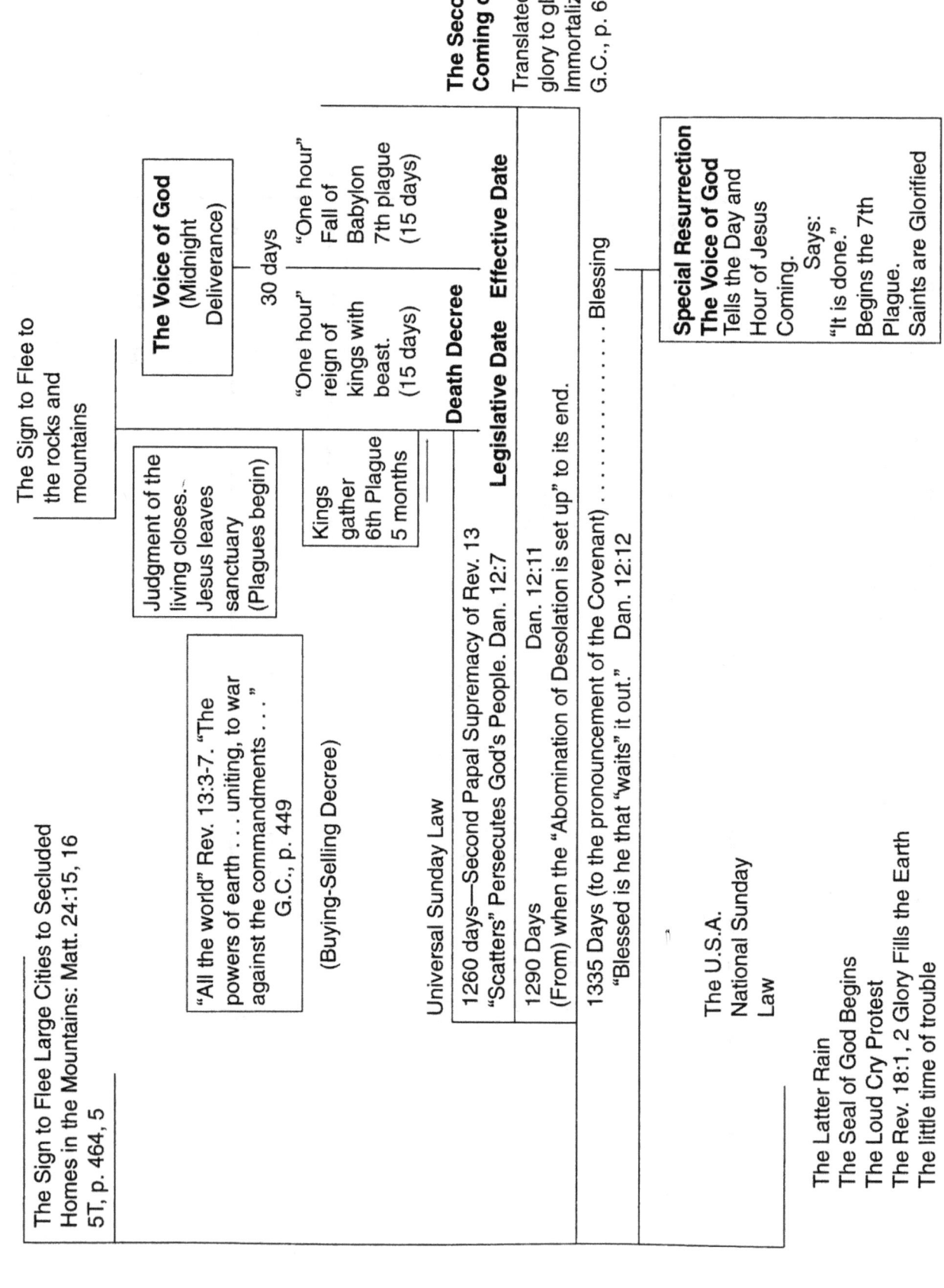

A CONCLUSION TO DAN. 12:5-12

Heathen nations were not mentioned in Bible prophecy, regardless of their attainments, unless they had something to do with God's people. Great civilizations, such as those of the orient or Central America, rose and fell without Biblical mention. The Bible is a Judeo-Christian book, tracing a sequential history (past, present and future) of those who shall be heirs of salvation.

The prophet Daniel saw in four visions (Dan. 2, 7, 8, and 11) a prophecy of the rise and fall of great world empires which affect God's people. But as he wrote Dan. 12, he still did not understand how the rise and fall of the last endtime great world empire would bring the great controversy between good and evil to its end. He wished to know in **greater detail** what would happen to God's people at that time and how they would be delivered from that iron rule. Therefore, Daniel asked the question:

"O my Lord, what shall be the **end** of these things?" Dan. 12:8.

Over the last two centuries, since 1798, God's people have struggled with the same question. Bewildered by political struggles and upheaval of nations, God's people have found it difficult to focus on that which is really significant to them—a true fulfillment of Bible prophecy.

Daniel 12:5-13, with its three timelines were not understood by Daniel, nor our pioneers, with its specific application to the LAST generation when they will experience "the END of all these things." (Verse 8) This passage was given to assist the last generation to get their bearings and to focus on the rise and fall of the last great world empire, when ". . . **ALL** the world will wonder after the beast," Rev. 13. The timelines of Daniel 12 describe the reign of that beast power. In Revelation the last great world empire is called the "beast," but in Daniel 12 it is called the "abomination that maketh desolate." These three timelines of Daniel 12 not only limit the reign of the beast power, but also describe the persecution of God's people during that time. The 1335 day timeline describes the final reward of the righteous who wait it all out and are delivered by the voice of God.

Therefore, we need to understand that the three timelines of Daniel 12 are simply three statements, written in literal language regarding future events. These timelines simply state as follows:

1. There are 1290 literal days of the reign of the beast. Dan. 12:11.

2. There are 1260 literal days of persecution of the people of God under that reign. Dan. 12:7.

3. There are 1335 literal days of the time from the beginning of that final crisis until deliverance by the Voice of God.

Although these timelines are time spans, they do not tell us the day and hour of the coming of Jesus, but enable us to know when it is near, even at the door.

When studied carefully in correlation with the book of Revelation, Chapters 12 through 20, they ". . . throw a flood of light upon **events then to transpire**." *Review and Herald*, Sept. 25, 1883.

Because of the fact that these timelines have not yet begun, nor does the beast power yet have all the world under its control, it is not possible to know when to begin counting the timelines or to know when they will end. Not until events pertinent to the timelines occur, can God's people begin to count them. Although God's people have long been in the "waiting and watching time," a time will come, under the out-pouring of the Latter Rain, that God's people will have the power to proclaim these time periods:

Note: Not any dates are set for the Second Coming.

> And he said unto them, It is not for you to know the **TIMES OR THE SEASONS [NOW]**, which the Father hath put in his own **POWER**.
> **BUT** [things will change] **YE SHALL RECEIVE POWER [TO KNOW TIMES AND SEASONS] AFTER** that the Holy Ghost is come upon you [in the Latter Rain]: and ye shall be witnesses unto me [explaining times and seasons] both in Jerusalem [in the church] . . . and in Samaria [related Christian bodies], and unto the uttermost part of the earth [to all of Babylon to reap the final harvest]. Acts 1:7, 8.

The great message of the angel of Rev. 14:15 says, ". . . the *time* is come . . ." These *timed* messages may be stated clearly as follows:

1. The holy people of the last generation will be scattered or persecuted for 1260 literal days. See Dan. 12:7.

2. The last great world empire—"New World-Order"—which is the "beast" power of Rev. 13, who does the persecution, will rise and fall within 1290 literal days.

3. God's people will wait it out 1335 literal days, until they are delivered and receive the **BLESSING**. (the pronouncement of the everlasting covenant) Rev. 16:17.

This will be **GOOD NEWS!**

When these timeline messages go forth in the power of the Latter Rain, it will be the proclamation of the mystic "seven thunders" of Revelation 10. The Prophetess wrote that the seven thunders

> relate to **FUTURE EVENTS WHICH WILL BE DISCLOSED IN THEIR ORDER** . . . then Daniel's prophecies have their proper place in the first, second, and third angel's messages *TO BE GIVEN* [future] to the world. **7BC 971.**

> After these seven THUNDERS uttered their voices, their injunction comes to John as to Daniel in regard to the little book: "Seal up those things which the seven thunders uttered." These relate to future events which **WILL BE** disclosed in **THEIR ORDER**. Daniel shall stand in his lot at the end of the days. John sees the little book unsealed. **Then Daniel's** prophecies have their proper place in the first, second, and third angels' messages **TO BE GIVEN** to the world. The unsealing of the little book was the message **IN RELATION TO TIME**. 7BC 971

7 THUNDERS MESSAGES IN RELATION TO TIME[1]

> . . . when the seven thunders had uttered their **VOICES,** I was about to write: and I heard a voice from heaven saying unto me, Seal up those things which the seven thunders uttered, and write them not. Rev. 10:4

---

[1] The angel which announces the seven thunders has been linked to the "man clothed in linen" of Daniel 12:6,7 timelines by use of the Hebrew verb "peribeblemeno" The oath sworn in Rev. 10:6-7 reflects Dan. 12:7-9 where the angel clothed in linen swears with his right and left hands toward heaven that there will be "a time, two times, and a half time" before the end of the wonders. " . . . 'the angel's oath is an echo of Daniel 12:7' "
See SYMPOSIUM ON REVELATION Book I, p. 280-325.
Although this information is presented to support the application of the Daniel 12 timelines as related to the medieval era, and an argument therefore against its endtime application; the data, when objectively assessed; bears equal evidence that the seven thunders are indeed the "Voices" of the Daniel 12 timelines yet to be sounded.

The seven thunders uttered their **VOICES**. These are the same **VOICES which begin and end the timelines!** By examining the timelines which begin and end with "speaking **VOICES**" we can easily identify the seven thunders.

These seven thunders pertain to future events in relation to time:

> ... these seven thunders uttered their voices ... these relate to **FUTURE EVENTS,** which will be disclosed in their order ... in relation to **TIME.** *The Seventh-day Adventist Commentary,* Vol. 7, p. 971

These "future events" are specified in the Word of God. They are identified in the timelines of Daniel 12 and Revelation. That which has been sealed "even to the time of the end" (See Dan. 12:4) will be opened by the thunderous voices of the timelines as they are brought forth in the Loud Cry. These events are brought to view in the three angels' messages:

> Daniel shall stand in his lot at the **END OF THE DAYS.** John sees the little book unsealed. Then Daniel's prophecies have their proper place in the first, second, and third angels' messages **TO BE GIVEN** [future tense] to the world. The unsealing of the little book was the message **IN RELATION TO TIME.** *The Seventh-day Adventist Commentary,* Vol. 1, p. 971

The Loud Cry of the Three Angels Messages will be given before probation closes. However, the events foretold occur before and after the close of probation. These events will continue to fulfill prophecy all the way through final crisis and deliverance.

The following chart outlines these **VOICES** of the seven thunders in connection with the "speaking voices" of the timelines of Daniel 12.

Note: Timelines begin and end with "speaking" voices. The "speaking" of a nation is the legislative and judicial action of its governing authorities. *The Great Controversy,* p. 438. It is Legislative decrees which begin and end timelines. Examples are: the 2300 days began with the decree of 457 BC, and the 1260 days began with the decretal letter of Justinian AD 538. The three timelines of Daniel 12 follow that precedent.

THE SEVEN THUNDERS' "VOICES" OF REVELATION ARE IDENTIFIED
by the "Voices" which begin and end the timelines of Daniel 12:5-13*

THUNDER NO.1
2300 DAY-YEAR PROPHECY ENDS—A.D. 1844—THE INVESTIGATIVE JUDGMENT OF DEAD BEGINS
DAN. 8:14

THUNDER NO. 2
REV. 13:11
VOICE OF USA-NSL

THUNDER NO. 6
REV. 16:17
VOICE OF GOD

THUNDER NO. 7
REV. 16:18
VOICES OF DOOM

1335 DAY "WAIT"

THUNDER NO. 5
REV. 13.15
VOICES "ALL" UDD

REV. 13:5
VOICE "ALL" USL

THUNDER NO. 3 1260 DAYS
"He shall . . . scatter the holy people." DAN. 12:7

THUNDER NO. 4 1290 DAYS
"The Abomination that Maketh Desolate" DAN. 12:11

REIGN OF KINGS
REV. 17:12
"1 HOUR"
or
15 DAYS

FALL OF BABYLON
REV. 18:10
"1 HOUR"
or
15 DAYS

30 DAYS

---

*"The 'speaking' of the nation is the action of its legislative and judicial authorities."
Great Controversy, p. 442:1

THUNDER SEQUENCE, TIMELINE DEFINITION, EVENT AND SCRIPTURE REFERENCE

THUNDER SEQUENCE	DEFINED BY TIMELINE	EVENT	SCRIPTURE
1	2300 Day-Years Ended	Investigative Judgment Began for the dead	Dan. 8:14 Rev. 4, 5 GC 483:1, 2
2	1335 Days Begin	National Sunday Law Legislation In the USA	Dan. 12:12 Rev. 13:11
3	1260 Days Begin	Universal Sunday Law Legislation	Dan. 12:7 Rev. 13:5-7
		Persecution Begins	
4	1290 Days Begin Note: the 1260 and the 1290 begin at the same time	Papal Supremacy No. 2 Begins. Its sign of authority is "The Mark of the Beast."	Dan. 12:11 Rev. 13:5-7 Rev. 13:16-18
		(The Seal of God)	Rev. 14:1-5
		The Final Test—Investigative Judgement Begins for the living	Rev. 14:15-19
5	1260 Days End	Universal Death Decree Legislation Date	Dan. 12:7 Rev. 13:15
		Reign of Kings "one hour" Begins (15 days)	Rev. 17:12, 13
		Time of Jacob's Trouble	Jer. 30:7
6	1335 Days End	Voice of God Effective Date for the Universal Death Decree	Dan. 12:11 Rev. 13:15 Rev. 9:13; 16:17
7	1290 Days End	Voices of Doom	Dan. 12:11
		Fall of Babylon "one hour" (15 days) Ends	Rev. 18:10, 17, 19
		Papal Supremacy No. 2 Ends	Rev. 16:18

CONCLUSION

The timelines of Daniel 12 provide a **framework** of endtime events which define the final crisis and deliverance of the people of God. Not until this is understood, will the major events spoken of in plagues, trumpets, seals, and other areas of Revelation come into focus to take their proper places in the stream of time.

There is but one God, one Source of prophecy, and one historical "stream of time." All the events spoken of in Daniel and Revelation are but one continuous panorama of history written in advance. Daniel and Revelation must be studied together. The book of Daniel comes first and the entire book must be understood before plagues, trumpets and seals events can fit into their proper slot of the endtime framework of Daniel 12 and the sequence of history—past, present and future.

The objective of this book, ***GETTING IT ALL TOGETHER,*** is to integrate the final events of Daniel and Revelation into one concerted, harmonious whole.

Past history is important. Prophecy already fulfilled should be understood. Chapters 1-10 of Daniel should be mastered in regard to the rise and fall of empires, including that of Papal Supremacy No. 1 A.D. 538-1798. Without it, we cannot recognize the identity of the future Papal Supremacy No. 2! However, prophetic fulfillment does not stop with the past. Major portions of Revelation and Daniel 11 and 12, deal with endtime events of final crisis and deliverance. It is imperative that our feet not be cemented into the past so that we cannot move into our own times and into the future which God has outlined for us in Daniel and the Revelation.

𝔚𝔄ℜ𝔑𝔍𝔑𝔊

1260, 1290, and 1335 are, you see,
A warning for ALL . . . that includes you and me.

Prophetic periods of Daniel, extending to the end of time,
Whose meaning all must have stored deep in their mind.

Futurism, Preterism, or date setting, we do not aspire,
But only to have a flood of light on events then to transpire.

Why the reluctance to study this sacred writ?
Could it be a Jesuit trick of 'Ole Nick?

To keep God's people in ignorance isn't fair,
Until the books are closed and they die in despair.

Carol Lee Hardin

Getting It All Together In Revelation

Getting It All Together In Daniel and Revelation

The Structure of Revelation
(The Nature and Purpose of the Book of Revelation)
Eight Visions in Two Major Lines of Prophecy
From the First Advent to the Second Advent of Jesus

Directions: First, Let the Bible be its own interpreter of Figurative Language
Keep every verse in its chronological order, and
Then, match each verse to its historical event in sequential order.

Vision 1	**Vision 2**	**Vision 3**	**Vision 4**	**Vision 5**	**Vision 6**	**Vision 7**	**Vision 8**
Rev. 1	Rev. 4,5	Rev. 8:5	Rev. 11:1	Rev. 12, 13	Rev. 15:8	Rev. 19,20	Rev. 21, 22
Holy Place	Most Holy	Censer	Measuring	The Dragon	Smoke fills	2nd Advent	New
High Priest's	The Invest-	Thrown down	Assessment	The Woman	the temple	of Jesus	Jerusalem
Ministry	igative	Judgment	of "Temple"	The Manchild	No Mediator	Executive	New
Began	Began..........Ends		of "Altar"	The "Beast"		Judgment	Heaven
		Close of	of "Worship-	"Another	Close of	-------------	New
A.D. 31	A.D. 1844	Probation	pers"	"Beast"	Probation	1000 yrs.	Earth
			Ready?			Begin	
High Priest	**Sacrificial Lamb**			**The Manchild**		**King of kings**	
	(opens the books)	closes them.	Lord, God		King of		
			Almighty Rev. 11:17.		Saints Rev. 15:3		

Note: The vision above dictates when to begin the first item of the following prophetic outline.

Prophetic Outline 1	**Prophetic Outline 2**	**Prophetic Outline 3**	**Prophetic Outline 4**	**Prophetic Outline 5**	**Prophetic Outline 6**	**Prophetic Outline 7**	**Prophetic Description**
Rev. 2,3	Rev. 4,5	Rev. 8-11	Rev. 11:3-11	Rev. 12,13	Rev. 16,17	Rev. 20	Rev. 21-22
Seven	Seven	Seven	1260 days	1260 years	Seven	1000 years	
Letters	Seals	Trumpets	Two Witnesses	Persecution	Plagues	"Surely, I	God's Throne
To the	1-6	1-6		& Persecutors	1-6	Come Quickly"	on earth.
Seven							
Churches							

Note: "Who shall be able to stand?" Seal 6 Rev. 6:17

Interlude	**Interlude**	**Interlude**	**Interlude**	**Interlude**	**Interlude**
Rev. 7	Rev. 10	Rev. 11:12	Rev. 14:1-5	Rev. 18:1-5	Rev. 20:4-6
144,000	144,000	144,000	144,000	144,000	144,000
Sealed	Witness	Vindicated	Sealed	Witness	Vindicated
	"Time no	Law Displayed		"Loud Cry"	Reign
	Longer"				

Endtime Event	**Endtime Event**	**Endtime Event**	**Endtime Event**	**Endtime Event**	**Endtime Event**
Rev. 8:1	Rev. 10:4-11	Rev. 11;15-19	Rev. 14:15-19	Rev. 18:5-24	Rev. 21:2
Seal 7	7 Thunders	Trumpet 7	3 Harvests	Plague 7	The 3rd
	Fulfilled	2nd Coming	Completed	Fall of Babylon	Coming
	(Dan. 12:5-12	Of Jesus			of Jesus
	Timeliness)				

HERMENEUTIC PRINCIPLES AND THE STRUCTURE OF REVELATION

The book of Revelation is an enigma to many persons in that it is made up of what appears to be many fragments—Letters, Seals, Trumpets, Plagues, Angels' Messages, Beasts, Symbolism, Judgments, and many other things. It seems impossible to get it all together. There are some basic concepts however, which will help the Bible student to see the relationship of all these parts, and to recognize within the structure of the book a great picture of the controversy between good and evil, and to know the final outcome of it all.

The Bible student needs to look at both books, Daniel and Revelation, from the point of view of the "Historicist School of Prophetic Interpretation." This "school" provides guidance and guards against error by furnishing some Hermeneutic Principles (Rules of Bible study) as presented in the following premises.[1]

1. Prophecy is simply history written before it happens.

2. The "Stream of time always moves forward." Just as history happens in a SEQUENCE of events, so also, prophecy is given in outlines written with its verses in SEQUENCE or chronological order.

This SEQUENCE and orderly progression must be observed and applied in the process of prophetic exposition.

> For God is not the author of confusion . . . I Cor. 14:33.

God is the Source of the books of Daniel and Revelation and although they are a challenge, they are constructed in the same orderly and logical manner, as the nature of the God from whom they come. They are constructed in such a way that their outlines contain events which are enumerated in perfect sequence, and are fulfilled in the same logical sequential progression. The expositor should be very careful to remember to keep the events within an outline in orderly sequence, not removing beginnings or ignoring timeframes, not inserting, and not placing anything after its stated sequential placement. This is common sense, but is often violated by those who should know better.

3. The orderly structure of Revelation is a Key to its meaning.

In examining the structure of Revelation, it is necessary to observe the structure of Daniel to apply the same principles in its exposition. The orderly structure of Daniel's outlines, and especially the sequence, is proven by an examination of its four timelines. All four timelines cover approximately the same major line of historical time: 606 B.C. to the Second Coming of Jesus, and are aligned to each other and interlocking. Note the sequence as follows:

---

[1] Appendix Note on **Hermeneutics**. p. 222.

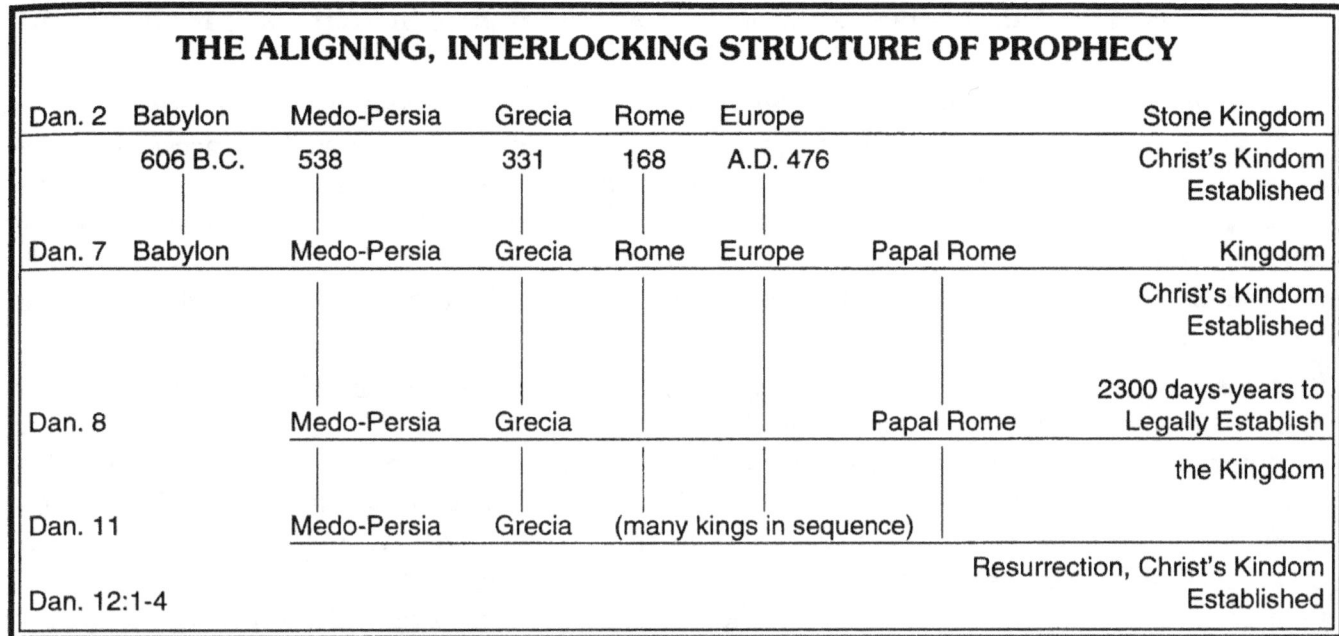

The above outline reveals several things:

1. The verses and events predicted are sequential.
2. All four outlines, reiterating the same historical, prophetic line of history are aligned.
3. Each successive outline gives additional information.
4. The additional information in each succeeding outline moves toward the end of time or focuses more and more on ENDTIME EVENTS.

These four observable factors in the book of Daniel give insight as to how outlines of Revelation function. This is further explained in "The Structure of the book of Revelation," complete with illustrations, p. 159.

It should also be recognized that the objective of prophecy is to reiterate the past, identify the present, and focus on future events which usher in the kingdom of God. By this characteristic of prophecy God's people have been able to know exactly where they stand in the stream of time. It does the same for God's people today. The outlines found in Revelation: Plagues, Trumpets, and Seals will, when correctly understood, enable God's people to recognize each event in its sequence and know where they are in the stream of time.

But again, to accomplish this, it is imperative that the Bible be permitted to be its own expositor. This is stated in Scripture as follows:

4. "Knowing this first [This is the first rule of prophetic exposition] that no prophecy of the scripture is of any private interpretation." II Peter 1:20

This verse, II Peter 1:20, does not forbid you to have your own personal convictions regarding prophecy or that you may not teach it. It does **not** mean that prophecy must be interpreted by a committee, by theologians, or by the "church." It means that prophetic **symbolism** must be **decoded** by **Biblical** key verses. It is the Bible which explains prophetic symbols, and no man has any right to interpret or decode them, independent of Scripture.

After they are decoded, it is possible to find an **application to match the prophecy with historical events.**

It is imperative that we understand the difference between "interpretation" or decoding of symbolism and the various **applications** made after decoding is done. Even the process of making an application is specified. The Bible is to be thoroughly researched because it plainly states that ". . . precept must be upon precept [one concept built upon another] . . . line upon line [cross reference study], line upon line [or **OUTLINE UPON OUTLINE**]; here a little, and there a little . . ." Isa. 28:10. Prophetic exposition is done best by astute Bible students, who pay attention to the hermeneutic rules.

It is also very important that we recognize that the Historicist **"SCHOOL"** of Prophetic Interpretation proffers hermeneutic principles to guide and guard the expositor. We also need to recognize that there were expositors, who endorsed that school, while seeking historical applications, but did not always follow carefully **ALL** the rules. Many expositors through the centuries, called themselves "historicists" and did the best they knew how, but were not aware of emerging historicist hermeneutics and therefore had only partial sight. This was not entirely their fault because it is a fact that prophecy usually opens up at the time of fulfillment. Those who lived a century ago could not be expected to know what we may see self-evident today. See Appendix Note Hermeneutics.

Prophetic expositors are not usually prophets. Uriah Smith was not a prophet. He did not have the advantage of visions or dreams but was simply an excellent student of history and Biblical studies. He gathered up the gems of past expositors and added insights on the Seventh-day Sabbath and sanctuary message. He was a student like you and me. He was not infallible.

Although Uriah Smith endorsed the Historicist "school" in his approaches to prophecy, he did not know or follow all the hermeneutic principles we understand today. We have advantages he did not have both in scholarly research and advancing historical events. We are in a position to advance far beyond his day. While we acknowledge much excellence in his work, it is now in some cases obsolete—excellent for his day, and for the church at that time,—but we "ought to know far more today than we do know."

In the outlines of Revelation we need to expect to advance beyond the day of Uriah Smith, in an "unrolling of the scroll."

FOREWORD FROM THE AUTHOR

Dear Reader:

We all nod our heads to the statement, **"THE BIBLE IS ITS OWN EXPOSITOR," but** in reality we are more likely to say, "Yes, I know the Bible says . . . , but ***in my opinion***. . . ." We do the same with the writings of E.G. White. It seems to be the order of the day to lay aside the plain statements of Scripture and the explanations of a prophet, and substitute the opinions of man and our own personal conclusions! As long as we continue these practices, we will never unlock the secrets of the prophetic books of Daniel and Revelation, nor find unity among prophetic expositors of end-time prophecy. Not until we permit the **BIBLE** to define its own terms, enlighten us on the unchanging character of God, provide a rationale for the plagues, trumpets, and seals; and permit the inspired statements of Ellen G. White to enlarge and enrich these descriptions of end-time events, will we ever "get it all together."

Only as we permit the books of Daniel and Revelation to interpret each other as supplementary and complementary information, align the outlines of Daniel with each other in their interlocking nature, and do the same with the outlines of Revelation (plagues, trumpets and seals), will these books begin to present one unified clear picture of history—past, present, and future.

The study of Scripture is a "science"—a body of knowledge. There are rules, as in the collection of data for any other branch of science, which, when applied to Scripture, are called **HERMENEUTIC PRINCIPLES**.[1] (You can't even play a game of marbles without some rules. When each player makes up his own rules the game falls apart and usually ends in dispute and anger.) Our Creator God is a Being of **LAW and ORDER**. The Bible is of the same character and we must look for and observe the laws of study—hermeneutic principles.

The most basic of these rules is that **"THE BIBLE IS ITS OWN EXPOSITOR," therefore,** we must permit Bible terminology to be understood by a Bible definition. The term, "The Wrath of God," which refers to the seven last plagues (Rev. 15 and 16), must be given ***Biblical definition***. (Romans 1). The Bible definition of "The Wrath of God" sheds light on the character of God, not only in the seven last plagues, but also to the other endtime events brought to view in Revelation. Therefore, the first task to be accomplished in this book is to examine the wrath of God and to find within it a rationale for the seven last plagues, and a comprehension of God's character as He finishes the great controversy between good and evil in endtime events. This is the subject of Chapter XIII.

---

1   See Appendix Note Hermeneutics.

CHAPTER XIII

THE WRATH OF GOD

1. "THE WRATH OF GOD" IS A *BIBLE* TERM

John the Revelator, wrote:

> And I saw another sign in heaven . . . seven angels having the **seven last plagues** for in them is filled up **the wrath of God**. Rev. 15:1.

The **"wrath of God"**—seven last plagues—is the subject of the **third angel's warning message**, and it is imperative for the last generation who give that **warning** to understand it.

> And the **third angel** followed them, saying with a loud voice, If any man worship the beast and his image . . . The same shall drink of the wine of the **wrath of God**, which is poured out without mixture . . ." Rev. 14:9, 10.

2. "THE WRATH OF GOD" IS FALSELY DEFINED BY HUMAN CONJECTURE

There are some who view the seven last plagues—wrath of God—as a change in the character of God. They see a patient God suddenly lose his patience. They see the love of God and His mercy turn to rage as He takes His final revenge. They see a final generation suffering the accumulated wrath of the ages, poured out as punishment for all that their ancestors have committed. They assume that this "strange act" is an exception to God's character. This concept of the "wrath of God" presents His character similar to that of a god whose delight is an ever burning hell.

It is the privilege of God's people to reveal the true character of God in which the Bible is permitted to be its own interpreter. John declared, ". . . God is love . . ." I John 4:8. James wrote;

> Every good gift and every perfect gift is from above, and cometh down from the Father of lights, with whom is **no variableness, neither shadow of turning**. James 1:17.

What is the Bible definition of the "wrath of God" that is consistent with the statements of John and James?

3. THE BIBLE DEFINES THE "WRATH OF GOD"

> For the **wrath of God** is revealed from heaven against all ungodliness . . . Because that, when they knew God, they glorified him not as God, neither were thankful; but became vain in their imaginations, and their foolish heart was darkened. . . . wherefore God also **gave them up** to uncleanness . . . For this cause, **God gave them up** unto vile affections . . . God **gave them over** to a reprobate mind . . . " Romans 1:18, 21, 24, 26, 28.

The Bible definition of the "wrath of God" is that action in which **God gives the sinner up and over to sin and its results.** God does not force the will. At the close of probation, when every soul has made his final choice, when Christ no longer ministers in the sanctuary as Mediator for the fallen race, and when the wicked have fully chosen to follow Satan and to reject the grace of God; then the Holy Spirit will be fully withdrawn from the wicked, and God will **give them over** to those forces which they have chosen.

> As Jesus moved out of the most holy place, I heard the tinkling of the bells upon His garment; and as He left, a cloud of darkness covered the inhabitants of the earth. There was then no mediator between guilty man and an offended God. While Jesus had been standing between God and guilty man, **A RESTRAINT** was upon the people; but when He stepped out from between man and the Father, **THE RESTRAINT was removed and Satan had entire control of the finally impenitent.** It was impossible for the plagues to be poured out while Jesus officiated in the sanctuary; but as His work there is finished, and His intercession closes, there is nothing to stay the **wrath of God**, and it breaks with fury upon the shelterless head of the guilty sinner . . . *Early Writings*, p. 280.

4. GOD CONTROLS THE SITUATION; SATAN CONTROLS THE WICKED

The seven last plagues are called the wrath of **GOD**, because God has **entire control of the situation**. **GOD** is putting on the "demonstration." **GOD** is in control of the timing. **GOD** is removing the restraints as it pleases Him. **GOD** is in complete control of the safety of the righteous and fully protects His own. But it is Satan who has "entire control of the **wicked**" and is permitted to do the work of a destroyer. It is **GOD** who *permits* this to occur.

Those who give the third angel's warning message, as it swells to the Loud Cry, must understand clearly that the "wrath of God," is this warning which will reap the final harvest.

> And another angel came out from the altar, which had power over fire; and cried with a **loud cry** to him that had the sharp sickle, saying, Thrust in thy sharp sickle, and gather the clusters of the vine of the earth; for her grapes are fully ripe. And the angel thrust in his sickle into the earth . . . and cast it into the winepress of the **wrath of God**. Rev. 14:18, 19.

Those who give the loud cry warning against the coming wrath of God (seven last plagues) must know that God is in control of the entire demonstration, but that Satan will be permitted to control the wicked. The loud cry is an appeal for all to receive the Seal of God and accept salvation to escape that time of complete Satanic control!

5. THE RATIONALE BEHIND THE SEVEN LAST PLAGUES—*WRATH OF GOD*

Why does God remove restraints to give Satan "entire control" of the wicked? What is God's objective?

The Bible is its own expositor. The book of Job pulls back the curtain between the visible and invisible world, giving insight into the great controversy between Christ and Satan. In the book of Job we can view a scene in which God is being accused of placing **RESTRAINTS** in Satan's way.

> Now there was a day when the sons of God came to present themselves before the Lord, and Satan came also among them. And the Lord said unto Satan, Whence

comest thou? Then Satan answered the Lord, and said, From going to and fro in the earth, and from walking up and down in it. And the Lord said unto Satan, Hast thou considered my servant Job, that there is none like him in the earth, a perfect and an upright man, one that feareth God, and escheweth evil?

Then Satan answered the Lord, and said . . . Doth Job fear God for naught? **Hast thou not made an hedge [RESTRAINT] about him**, and about his house, and about all that he hath on every side? thou hast blessed the work of his hands, and his substance is increased in the land. But put forth thine hand now, and touch all that he hath, and he will curse thee to thy face. Job 1:6-11.

6. SATAN'S ARGUMENT AND ACCUSATIONS CONCERN FREEDOM FROM RESTRAINTS

It is necessary to understand that Satan had rebelled against God's law and government in heaven before the creation of this earth and was cast out of heaven (Rev. 12:7-9). He portrayed the laws of God to be a violation of freedom and unnecessary **RESTRAINT**. He claimed that created beings should be freed from the "yoke of bondage" of law. He claimed that if intelligent beings could be freed from God's laws, the whole universe could be elevated to a higher, happier state. When Satan was cast out of heaven, he desired a place to serve as a "proving ground" where he could demonstrate his claims. The first chapters of Genesis tell how God created Adam and gave him dominion over everything on this earth. Gen. 1:26. When Adam sinned, he "sold out" his dominion to Satan; therefore, Satan boastfully declared his right to go "to and fro in the earth" and walk "up and down" in it. Job 1:7. When Adam became obedient to Satan he sold out his rulership, and Satan immediately claimed a "legal right" to it as his own "proving ground" on which he could demonstrate his claim that his system of government would be an improvement over that of God and His laws. This planet earth became the "demonstration laboratory" to reveal and settle forever before the entire universe and all heaven, the true nature of good and evil, of law and lawlessness, the true character of God and Satan, and the destructive nature of sin and its results.

Although Adam relinquished his dominion, God has continued to protect the original human right to freedom of choice. God does not force the will, neither does He permit Satan to force the will. These restraints and restrictions on Satan's activities by the Holy Spirit, ever promoting the plan of salvation, have resulted in constant complaint and accusation by Satan, as he did in the heavenly council (Job 1 and 2), charging God with interference and infringement on his territory.

Every charge and accusation, every argument propounded by Satan, must be demonstrated to be false in the great controversy. It is therefore necessary, before Jesus comes, to withdraw restraints, one by one, plague by plague, to "give them [the wicked] over" to Satan, so that the entire universe can see what Satan would have done to them and to their worlds if no restraints had been imposed. The plagues are one last object lesson in the destructiveness of sin.

> It [is] impossible for the plagues to be poured out while Jesus officiates in the sanctuary; but as His work there is finished, and His intercession closes, there is nothing to stay the wrath of God, and it breaks with fury upon the shelterless head of the guilty sinner . . . *Early Writings*, p. 280.

When Jesus leaves the sanctuary, probation will have closed in that the decree will be uttered:

> He that is unjust, let him be unjust still: and he which is filthy, let him be filthy still: and he that is righteous, let him be righteous still: and he that is holy, let him be holy still. Rev. 22:11.

The wicked will be given over to the depth of evil in their hearts. Evil men and evil angels unrestrained, will combine to bring about the seven last plagues. The universe will get a new revelation of the malignity and evil of wicked angels and evil men. God is not indifferent to their sufferings but this demonstration must be accomplished for the full picture to appear in the great controversy and for the security of all the universe throughout all eternity.

7. SAFETY IN THE SEAL OF THE LIVING GOD

As the wicked are given over to the "entire control" of Satan, it is the Seal of the Living God which protects God's people.

> . . . I saw four angels standing on the four corners of the earth, holding the four winds of the earth, that the wind should not blow on the earth, nor on the sea, nor on any tree. And I saw another angel ascending from the east, having the **seal of the living God:** and he cried with a loud voice to the four angels, to whom it was given to hurt the earth and the sea, Saying, Hurt not the earth, neither the sea, nor the trees, till we have sealed the servants of our God in their foreheads. Rev. 7:1-3.

Not only will Satan demonstrate what he will do to man when the restraints are removed, but what he will do to the **planet**. It is "given to **hurt**" the **earth, sea,** and **trees**. The last generation will see the final ruin of this fair world as they ride upward in the cloudy chariot!

Whereas the Holy Spirit will be withdrawn from the wicked, it will be poured out in full measure upon the people of God in the Latter Rain as they give the Loud Cry of the third angel's warning against the wrath of God. In the fullness of the Holy Spirit, God's people will be sealed to "reflect the image of Jesus fully" while the wicked are completely possessed with evil demons.

There are "prerequisites" to an understanding of Revelation and its relevance to endtimes. The Bible student must first permit the Bible to define the wrath of God, he must allow the book of Job to provide the rationale of the great controversy struggle. He must comprehend the nature of the final demonstration of which God has complete control, but in which Satan has complete control of the wicked. He must understand that the character of God is unchanging and that He is love, working for the good of the entire universe for all time and permitting sin to destroy itself.

Only then is the Bible student ready to discuss plagues, trumpets, and seals and the rest of the endtime prophecies, and blend them into one unified picture. Only then can he answer these puzzling questions:

1. Are the plagues God's plagues or Satan's?
2. Why would God permit such terrible things to happen?
3. What do the plagues accomplish?
4. Is God venting anger?
5. Are they God's plagues but Satan doing God's work?
6. Are God and Satan cooperating in the work of destruction?

It is imperative that we understand the rationale before making further study.

CHAPTER XIV

THE FIRST FIVE OF THE SEVEN LAST PLAGUES

And I heard a great voice out of the temple saying to the seven angels, Go your ways, and pour out the vials of the wrath of God upon the earth. Rev. 16:1

The first five plagues are described in this Chapter, in brief sequence. The sixth plague is described in a different literary manner and will be dealt with separately in the next chapter.

1. *THE TIMEFRAME:* THE SEVEN LAST PLAGUES OCCUR *AFTER* THE CLOSE OF PROBATION

> . . . I saw that Jesus would not leave the most holy place UNTIL every case was decided either for salvation or destruction, and that the wrath of God could not come UNTIL Jesus had finished His work in the most holy place . . . WHEN our High Priest has finished His work in the sanctuary, He will stand up, put on the garments of vengeance, and THEN the seven last plagues will be poured out. . . . I saw that the four angels would hold the four winds UNTIL Jesus' work was done in the sanctuary, and THEN will come the seven last plagues. *Early Writings*, p. 36.

In 1844, Jesus began the Investigative Judgment for the dead and continues to the judgment of the living. In this judgment, called the "Day of Atonement," Christ makes atonement for the righteous and blots out their sins, placing upon them the Seal of the Living God, retaining their names in the Lamb's Book of Life. Thus His kingdom is made up. They are eternally secure. Then as Jesus moves out from the most holy place, there is no longer a Mediator in the heavenly sanctuary to plead, and the Holy Spirit is withdrawn on earth from the wicked. It is then that the wicked are given over to the complete control of Satan and he brings upon them the seven last plagues.

> Every case had been decided for life or death. While Jesus had been ministering in the sanctuary, the judgment had been going on for the righteous dead, and then for the righteous living. Christ had received His kingdom, having made the atonement for His people and blotted out their sins. The subjects of the kingdom were made up. The marriage of the Lamb was consummated . . . As Jesus moved out of the most holy place, I heard the tinkling of the bells upon His garment; and as He left, a cloud of darkness covered the inhabitants of the earth. There was then no mediator between guilty man and an offended God. *Story of Redemption*, p. 402, 403.

See Rev. 15:8; 8:5—Close of probation.

2. THE SCOPE OF ACTION OF THE FIVE PLAGUES—NOT UNIVERSAL

The first five plagues are not universal. The sixth plague is different in that it affects the kings of "the whole world." Rev. 16:14. The seventh plague also affects "every island." The first five plagues are ". . . not universal, or the inhabitants of the earth would be wholly cut off."

> "There fell a noisome and grievous sore upon the men which had the mark of the beast, and upon them which worshiped his image [first plague]." The sea "became as the blood of a dead man: and every living soul died in the sea [second plague]." And "the rivers and fountains of waters . . . became blood [third plague]." . . . In the plague that follows, power is given to the sun "to scorch men with fire. [fourth plague]." . . . These plagues are **NOT UNIVERSAL** or the inhabitants of the earth would be wholly cut off. *The Great Controversy*, p. 628.

Apparently then, these FIRST FIVE PLAGUES are literal. This is literal language involving the inhabitants of the earth with literal or real happenings. Will any of them affect the United States of America?

> The nation with which He bears long, and which He will not smite until it has filled up the measure of its iniquity in God's account, will finally drink the cup of wrath unmixed with mercy. *The Great Controversy*, p. 627.

Just as Egypt hosted the people of God in the days of Moses, so also the United States has been the home base for the remnant people of God for over a century. Eventually Egypt took God's people into bondage; so also in the United States oppressive laws will be enacted against the commandment keepers. As the plagues fell on Egypt, they will also fall on the United States of America.

> When Christ ceases His intercession in the sanctuary, the unmingled wrath threatened against those who worship the beast and his image and receive his mark (Revelation 14:9, 10), will be poured out. The plagues upon Egypt when God was about to deliver Israel were similar in character to those more terrible and extensive judgments which are about to fall upon the world just before the final deliverance . . . *The Great Controversy*, p. 627, 628.

> God's hand at that time will be stretched out still in wrath and justice and will not be brought to Himself again until His purposes are fully accomplished . . . until all the unrighteous ones are destroyed from the earth. *Early Writings*, p. 124.

3. GOD CONTROLS THE PLAGUES ACCORDING TO THE GUILT OF THE WICKED

> I saw that the priests who are leading on their flock to death are soon to be arrested in their dreadful career. The plagues of God are coming, but it will not be sufficient for the false shepherds to be tormented with one or two of these plagues. God's hand at that time will be stretched out still in wrath and justice and will not be brought to Himself again until His purposes are fully accomplished, and the hireling priests are led to worship at the feet of the saints, and to acknowledge that God has loved them because they held fast the truth and kept God's commandments, and until all the unrighteous ones are destroyed from the earth. *Early Writings*, p. 124.

The last quotation indicates that some will suffer only one or two plagues and that there are varying degrees of guilt. Those religious teachers who have promoted the false sabbath and have been active against the true Sabbath, who fought against the law and government of heaven, who have received the mark of the beast, will experience as much as the full seven plagues. Again this view of the equity of God's judgments is commented on as follows:

> The wrath of God in the seven last plagues had been visited upon the inhabitants of the earth, causing them to gnaw their tongues in pain and to curse God. The false shepherds had been the signal objects of Jehovah's wrath. Their eyes had consumed away in their holes, and their tongues in their mouths, while they stood upon their feet. *Story of Redemption*, p. 415.

> Many of the wicked were greatly enraged as they suffered the effects of the plagues. . . . The people turned upon their ministers with bitter hate and reproached them, saying, "You have not warned us . . ." I saw that the ministers did not escape the wrath of God. Their suffering was tenfold greater than that of their people. *Early Writings*, p. 282.

4. SEQUENCE OF THE PLAGUES

PLAGUE NO. 1. "A STINKING AND PAINFUL SORE"

> And I heard a great voice out of the temple saying to the seven angels, Go your ways, and pour out the vials of the wrath of God upon the earth. And the first went, and poured out his vial upon the earth; and there fell a noisome and grievous sore upon the men which had the mark of the beast, and upon them which worshipped his image. Rev. 16: 1, 2.

As soon as God removed the "hedge" from about Job, Satan destroyed his property and attacked him physically. "So went Satan forth from the presence of the Lord, and smote Job with sore boils from the sole of his foot unto his crown." Job 2:7. As soon as the restraints of the Spirit of God shall begin to be withdrawn from the earth, Satan will smite the wicked inhabitants with sores. These continue through the fifth plague:

> And the fifth angel poured out his vial upon the seat of the beast; and his kingdom was full of darkness; and they gnawed their tongues for pain, And blasphemed the God of heaven because of their pains and their **sores** . . . Rev. 16:10, 11.

5. THE SECOND AND THIRD PLAGUES AFFECT EARTH'S WATER SYSTEMS

> And the second angel poured out his vial upon the sea; and it became as the blood of a dead man: and every living soul died in the sea. And the third angel poured out his vial upon the rivers and fountains of waters; and they became blood. Rev. 16:3, 4.

It is the water on planet Earth, which makes it habitable. Man has already polluted his water supplies until there is almost no pure water. How shall God's people prepare for this emergency?

> The Lord has shown me repeatedly that it is contrary to the Bible to make any provision for our temporal wants in the time of trouble. I saw that if the saints had food laid up by them or in the field in the time of trouble, when sword, famine, and pestilence are in the land, it would be taken from them by violent hands and strangers would reap their fields. Then will be the time for us to trust wholly in God,

and He will sustain us. I saw that **our bread and water will be sure** at that time, and that we shall not lack or suffer hunger; for God is able to spread a table for us in the wilderness. If necessary He would send ravens to feed us, as He did to feed Elijah, or rain manna from heaven, as He did for the Israelites." *Early Writings*, p. 56.

6. THE FOURTH PLAGUE AFFECTS EARTH'S WEATHER SYSTEM

And the fourth angel poured out his vial upon the sun; and power was given unto him to scorch men with fire. And men were scorched with a great heat, and blasphemed the name of God . . . Rev. 16:8, 9.

It is the water systems of this planet that create the weather system with its cooling rains and evaporation vapors. When the oceans and rivers are affected, great drought and heat are the result. The planet will appear as a barren waste land. In these plagues, it will be Satan's main objective to destroy God's people, but the real damage falls instead upon the wicked and the planet itself. All of this time, Satan's destructive nature is demonstrated:

Satan's hatred against God leads him to hate every object of the Savior's care. He seeks to mar the handiwork of God, and he delights in destroying even the dumb creatures. It is only through God's protecting care that the birds are preserved to gladden us with their songs of joy. *Desire of Ages*, p. 356, 357.

7. THE FIFTH PLAGUE IS THAT OF SUPERNATURAL DARKNESS

And the fifth angel poured out his vial upon the **seat** of the beast; and his **kingdom** was full of darkness; and they gnawed their tongues for pain, . . . Rev. 16:10.

CONCLUSION:

During the first five plagues the wicked will be in anguish: suffering from painful sores, parched for water, scorched with heat, and groping about in thick darkness. These calamities will bring those in governmental positions to a place where they are determined to find the cause of these plagues and do whatever is necessary to stop them. They cannot understand why their New World-Order is not bringing peace and happiness and the blessings of God to the earth. The false ministers in Babylon lay the blame for the first five plagues on those who do not conform to the false sabbath, which is the mark of authority of the new one-world system. They advise that those who keep the commandments of God rather than the laws of men must be forced into subjection or receive the death penalty.

Satan will be unable to destroy the people of God in the first five plagues. He will be restrained from inflicting these sores, and their bread and water will be sure.

SUMMARY OF PREMISES IN CHAPTERS XIII AND XIV

1. The Bible is its own interpreter and definer of terms.
2. The Bible defines the wrath of God.
3. The wrath of God is defined as a point in time when God gives the sinner over to the master he has chosen, to sin and its results.
4. The wrath of God is not a change in God's character.
5. The wrath of God is revealed when restraints are removed from Satan.
6. The wrath of God reveals that GOD is in control of the entire demonstration.
7. Satan will have entire control of the wicked.
8. God will remove restraints from Satan plague by plague.
9. The third angel's message is a warning against the plagues.
10. The third angel's message pleads with men to accept the Seal of God as a protection against the plagues.
11. The book of Job reveals the rationale of the plagues.
12. The plagues are the final demonstration of what Satan would do to this planet and to men when restraint is removed.
13. The entire universe needs this demonstration to secure them against sin.
14. God is vindicated against Satan's accusations by this demonstration of the plagues.
15. The plagues begin AFTER probation is closed.
16. The first five plagues are not universal in scope.
17. The United States will suffer the plagues also.
18. God controls the plagues according to the guilt of the wicked.
19. False ministers suffer the greatest.
20. The sores of the first plague are like those of Job's boils.
21. The second and third plagues affect the ocean, water sources, and planet earth's weather systems.
22. The bread and water for God's people will be sure.
23. The fourth plague will scorch men with heat.
24. Satan's hatred of God and His creatures is revealed.
25. The fifth plague is that of darkness.
26. Men seek for the cause of the plagues.
27. The New World-Order will not have brought expected peace and happiness.
28. The New World-Order will have a seal of authority—the false sabbath.
29. Babylon declares the cause of the plagues to be those people who will not conform to the false sabbath.
30. The first five plagues are written in literal language.

CHAPTER XV

THE SIXTH PLAGUE GATHERING ACTION TO ARMAGEDDON

> And the sixth angel poured out his vial upon the great river Euphrates; and the water thereof was dried up, that the way of the kings of the east might be prepared. And I saw three unclean spirits like frogs come out of the mouth of the dragon, and out of the mouth of the beast, and out of the mouth of the false prophet. For they are the spirits of devils, working miracles, which go forth unto the kings of the earth and of the whole world, to gather them to the battle of that great day of God Almighty. . . . And he gathered them together into a place called in the Hebrew tongue Armageddon. Rev. 16:12-14, 16.

The sixth plague is not merely another of a sequence, but is written in a different literary style and changes to the use of symbolic language. Biblical drama in which there is dramatic **action**, has all the elements of a drama: characters, setting, and action which builds toward a climax.

1. THE SETTING

> And the sixth angel poured out his vial upon the great river Euphrates . . . Rev. 16:12.

Prophecy and prophetic symbolism are rooted in historical backgrounds. The Euphrates river ran right through the city of ancient Babylon. Verse 19 immediately refers to that "great city"—"great Babylon"—as the place where the plague is poured out. Since the nation of ancient Babylon no longer exists, it is obviously a reference to **spiritual** Babylon or apostate Christendom, and in a larger sense a conglomerate of **ALL** false religions and forms of worship. The original meaning of the word "Babylon" or Babel was that of "confusion" or false teaching.

The setting of the sixth plague, which immediately calls attention to the symbolic "river Euphrates," sets the stage and draws attention to spiritual Babylon. (Chapter 17 continues to explain more fully the judgment of Babylon—the "great whore"—and Chapter 18 describes its fall.)

2. THE SYMBOLISM OF A RIVER

> **And the sixth angel poured out his vial upon the great *RIVER* Euphrates; and the water thereof was dried up . . .** Rev. 16:12.

The Euphrates is a **RIVER,** not a sea. Whereas a symbolic "sea," as mentioned in Rev. 13:1 and 17:15 (waters) represents peoples, multitudes, and nations, and tongues; a "river" symbol is quite different and represents the Holy Spirit.

Let the *Bible* be its own expositor and let Jesus, who gave the symbol, interpret it. Let us remember this most basic hermeneutic principle. The greatest prophetic expositor who ever lived was Jesus. Only when we permit **Him** to interpret the symbolic **RIVER** correctly, can we understand the meaning of the sixth plague setting. What did Jesus say?

Jesus explained the symbol of a **RIVER** as follows:

> He that believeth on me, as the scripture hath said, out of his belly shall flow **RIVERS** of living water (But this he spake of the **SPIRIT** . . .) John 7:38, 39.

In the lands of the Middle East, such as Egypt and Babylon, a river is literally a "river of life," in that its irrigation systems bring water to the gardens to furnish food for these nations. Their food and water depends on these rivers and in turn the rivers depend on the outpouring of rain, and dry up when the rains diminish. In symbolism, it is the outpouring of the Holy Spirit, (often spoken of in Scripture as the early or latter **rain**), which brings life and blessings and the opportunity for eternal life to those who accept it. As long as the Holy Spirit is poured out to attend the Loud Cry, the river of Life is extended to those in Babylon. But when probation closes, the Holy Spirit is withdrawn and the ***river begins to dry up***.

It is rain that makes a river swell and overflow its banks. It is a lack of rain which dries up a river. As the remnant people of God give the third angel's message warning, the residents of Babylon will live under the outpouring of the "Latter Rain." That one last call to Babylon will say, ". . . Come out of her, my people, that ye be not partakers of her sins, and that ye receive not of her plagues." Rev. 18:4. The outpouring of the latter rain is the last chance for Babylon to be nourished by the great river of life. But as the Investigative Judgment of the living closes, the Latter Rain will cease, and the water of the symbolic river begins to dry up.

> When He leaves the sanctuary . . . the Spirit of God, persistently resisted, has been at last withdrawn. Unsheltered by divine grace, they have no protection from the wicked one. Satan will then plunge the inhabitants of the earth into one great, final trouble. *The Great Controversy*, p. 614.

Some will question: "If the Holy Spirit is withdrawn at the close of probation, why is it not mentioned before the first plague rather than at the beginning of the sixth plague?" The Holy Spirit does more than one kind of work. He does woo the sinner to Christ before the close of probation. But His work encompasses more than that. He restrains evil. The seven last plagues reveal the fact that as restraints are removed, one by one, the plagues are poured out, one by one, accordingly. The particular restraint which has held back the work of evil spirits as described in the sixth plague, is removed so that the action of evil spirits may take place.

The drying up of the Euphrates River—the withdrawal of the Holy Spirit and His restraining action removed—is a very important setting for the dramatic action brought to view in the sixth plague. The sixth plague describes the work of evil spirits, drawing—gathering—the kings of the earth together, to destroy the people of God.

The sixth plague is that of a drama building toward a grand climax—"coup d' etat," or a "coup d' theater," which ***does not happen until the seventh plague***.

A correct understanding of the symbolic **RIVER**, is imperative to the rationale of the plagues in that the entire demonstration is that in which the universe is permitted to view the destructive work of Satan when the Holy Spirit is removed—the restraints are removed and Satan is permitted to have free reign over the wicked. Whereas the first five plagues demonstrate Satan's destructive power against the natural world—oceans, weather systems, and the bodies of men—the sixth plague demonstrates the action of evil spirits on the kings of the earth as they are gathered together to legislate a universal death decree against the people of God.

3. THE PLAN OF ACTION—TO UNIFY BABYLON FOR ARMAGEDDON

The action described in the sixth plague is that of *gathering—unifying—assembling—preparing* for a battle. In 538 B.C. the city of Babylon appeared invincible. But Darius, the Mede, diverted the flow of water of the Euphrates so that the river which ran through the city was dried up. The soldiers entered the city on the riverbed and caused the fall of Babylon (See Dan. 5). The sixth plague describes the unification of Babylon made possible by the withdrawal of the Holy Spirit and resultant action of evil spirits. The seventh plague describes the fall of spiritual Babylon.

4. THE CHARACTERS OF THE SIXTH PLAGUE DRAMA

> The world is a theatre; the actors, its inhabitants, are preparing to act their part in the last great drama . . . *Testimonies* 8, p. 27, 28

The sixth plague, written in the form of a dramatic allegory portrays a number of characters who take the stage. They are:

The kings of the east
Unclean spirits, (they are the spirits of devils who appear as frogs)
The dragon
The beast
The false prophet
The kings of the earth, and of the whole world
One who comes as a thief (Christ)

Before the drama begins, the characters need to be identified, especially the main characters who take the leading roles. Others are introduced as the action continues. The sixth plague begins with an introduction to the main character: Jesus Christ, the King of kings, and His armies.

> And the sixth angel poured out his vial upon the river great Euphrates; and the water thereof was dried up, that the way of the **kings of the east** might be prepared. Rev. 16:12.

The Bible is its own expositor. The "east" represents heaven.

> And I saw another angel ascending from the **east** [heaven] having the seal of the living God . . . Rev. 7:2.

> And, behold, the glory of the God of Israel came from the way of the **east** . . . Eze. 43:2.

Christ is the KING OF KINGS AND LORD OF LORDS and He comes from the "**east**." John saw ". . . heaven opened, and behold a white horse; and he that sat upon him was called Faithful and True, and in righteousness he doth judge and make war . . . And the armies which were in heaven followed him . . . Rev. 19:11, 14.

> The battle of Armageddon is soon to be fought. He on whose vesture is written the name, King of kings, and Lord of lords, is soon to lead forth the armies of heaven." *Testimonies* 6, p. 406.

5. PREPARING THE WAY FOR THE KINGS OF THE EAST

In what way does the "drying up of the river, Euphrates" (the withdrawal of the Holy Spirit) **"prepare the way" for the coming of Jesus?** The answer lies in an understanding of the rationale of the seven last plagues. The premise is that the Holy Spirit and His restraints must be withdrawn to give Satan "complete control" of the wicked, so that it can be demonstrated to the entire universe the utter destruction which Satan would have brought to all creation, had he not been "quarantined" to this earth and constantly restrained by the power of God. As spectators, the other worlds view the full malignity of his spirit of rebellion. Only after this demonstration is completed, and after every accusation and complaint is met, is the **"way prepared"** for the kings of the east to ride forth in the glorious Second Coming of Jesus.

Chapter 16, Verse 12, which introduces the sixth plague, gives this setting to show that the action is in spiritual Babylon. The timing is after the Holy Spirit's restraints have been withdrawn from evil angels; only then is the stage set,—so that the action can begin.

6. THE GATHERING ACTION OF THE SIXTH PLAGUE

> And I saw three unclean spirits like frogs come out of the mouth of the dragon, and out of the mouth of the beast, and out of the mouth of the false prophet. For they are the spirits of devils, **working miracles**, which go forth unto the kings of the earth and of the whole world, **to gather them** to the battle of that great day of God Almighty. Rev. 16:13, 14.

The sixth plague does not describe the battle itself. That is described in the seventh plague. The sixth plague describes **only the gathering, unifying** action drawing the kings of the earth into unity, getting ready for the battle.

7. THREE EVIL SPIRITS IN ACTION

How is the gathering action accomplished? Why **three?** Because there are three main characters in Babylon who do the gathering work. They are spoken of as "the dragon," "the beast," and the "false prophet." Under the seventh plague these three are defeated and fall apart:

> . . . the great city [Babylon] was divided into **three** parts . . . **and** great Babylon came into remembrance before God, to give unto her the cup of the wine of the fierceness of His wrath. Rev. 16:19.

Who exactly are these three? They are the "dragon," the "beast," and the "false prophet."

8. THE DRAGON REPRESENTS SPIRITISM

The "dragon" is identified by the Bible itself:

> . . . a great red dragon . . . that old serpent, called the Devil, and Satan, which deceiveth the whole world . . . Rev. 12: 3,9.

Yes, the dragon is primarily Satan.

Satan works in this world through agencies which repeat his first lie: the immortality of the soul and this deception is found in all forms of spiritism. These included Spiritist "Christian" bodies, apostate "Christians" who teach the immortality of the soul, Satan worshipers, New Age adherents, oriental mystics, serpent worshipers and devil worshipers of foreign lands.

> Among the most successful agencies of the great deceiver are the delusive teachings and lying wonders of spiritualism. *The Great Controversy*, p. 524

9. THE BEAST REPRESENTS THE PAPACY

> And I . . . saw a beast rise up out of the sea, having seven heads and ten horns . . . and the dragon gave him his power, and his seat, and great authority." Rev. 13:1, 2.

Satan works through all false religions. This composite "beast" of Revelation 13:2 and its parts as described in Daniel 7, can be identified as Papal Rome. It is identified by its "mark" of authority which is the false sabbath. This beast is mentioned in the sixth plague because it will be so effective in the **gathering** action of drawing the kings of the earth together in what is currently referred to as the "New World-Order." It will play a key role in establishing the universal death decree legislation.

10. THE FALSE PROPHET REPRESENTS APOSTATE PROTESTANTISM

The "false prophet" is the "false preacher." Apostate Protestantism is that great body in the new world which has rebelled against the law of God, and supports the false Sabbath of Papal origin. It is apostate Protestantism with its many denominations in an ecumenical union, which are in full sympathy with Rome. It will also work great miracles to **gather** the kings of earth to legislate against the people of God who keep the Seventh-day Sabbath of the fourth commandment.

> When Protestantism shall stretch her hand across the gulf to grasp the hand of the Roman power, when she shall reach over the abyss to clasp hands with spiritualism, when, under the influence of this threefold union . . . we may know that the time has come for the marvelous working of Satan and that the end is near." *Testimonies* 5, p. 451.

The sixth plague does not describe the initial unification of these three. That ecumenical work is already in progress and they are now, nearly unified. The sixth plague describes the gathering action of kings, in which these three urge the legislation of a **Universal Death Decree**. The three-fold union advances with new emphasis to agitate more strongly for the false sabbath, with more strict enforcement, developing into a **Universal Death Decree**.

By what kind of action do these three gather the kings of the earth together? How do these three religious groups gain the support of the kings of the earth to back them up in legislation of a universal death decree against the people of God?

11. "OUT OF THE MOUTH OF" SIGNIFIES VERBAL AGITATION

> And I saw three unclean spirits like frogs come **out of the mouth** of the dragon, and **out of the mouth of** the beast, and **out of the mouth** of the false prophet Rev. 16:13.

"Out of the mouth of" indicates **verbal action**. It infers agitation. Why like "frogs?"

Step out in the summer night when the frogs are croaking. Their sounds are all about you, croaking and echoing, single and in chorus, but to see or find them is difficult. Their deep voices carry over the night air in vibrating tones, but you do not see them. This is a good description of the work of evil spirits; invisible, but very audible as they speak **"OUT OF THE MOUTH OF"** agencies in false religion (Babylon at the time of the sixth plague). The first five plagues have devastated the earth and placed men in great agony. The clergy of Babylon, through the prodding of evil spirits will lay the blame of these calamities upon those who will not conform to their New World-Order—who still keep the true Sabbath of God. The wicked believe that if only the whole world would come under one mode of worship, God would be appeased, and the plagues would stop. Under this argument it is believed that it would be better if the commandment keepers were put to death than for the whole world to perish.

12. THE UNIVERSAL DEATH DECREE

The "battle of Armageddon" is the "mount of confrontation" between the kings of the earth and the Lord—in the person of His people. It has nothing to do with political skirmish. It is not battle nor war over territory, nor oil, nor any such thing. It is a battle over the Law of God and the laws of men in conflict. This is made abundantly clear in the closing chapters of the *Great Controversy*. The Bible does not deal with trivia nor generally concern itself about civilizations or the rise and fall of empires, unless it has to do with the welfare of the people of God.

There was a time when it was presumed that the kings of the east represented the kings of the orient who would fight against the western nations. Today there are those who assume that the nations will direct their atomic weapons upon Jesus as He comes in the clouds of heaven, and that will be Armageddon. None of this is correct in setting, timing, nor focus. Listen to the prophetess as she described the final confrontation:

> Fearful sights of a supernatural character will soon be revealed in the heavens, in token of the power of miracle-working demons. **The spirits of devils will go forth to the kings of the earth and to the whole world** [Rev. 16:14], to fasten them in deception, and urge them on to unite with Satan in his last struggle against the government of heaven. By these agencies, rulers and subjects will be alike deceived. . . . They will perform wonderful miracles of healing and will profess to have revelations from heaven contradicting the testimony of the Scriptures.

> As the crowning act in the great drama of deception, Satan himself will personate Christ. The church has long professed to look to the Saviour's advent as the consummation of her hopes. Now the great deceiver will make it appear that Christ has come. In different parts of the earth, Satan will manifest himself among men as a majestic being of dazzling brightness, resembling the description of the Son of God given by John in the Revelation. . . . he heals the diseases of the people . . . This is the strong, almost overmastering delusion. *The Great Controversy*, p. 624.

> When God's presence was finally withdrawn from the Jewish nation, priests and people knew it not. Though under the control of Satan, and swayed by the most horrible and malignant passions, they still regarded themselves as the chosen of God. The ministration in the temple continued; sacrifices were offered upon its polluted altars, and daily the divine blessing was invoked upon a people guilty of the blood of God's dear Son and **seeking to slay His ministers and apostles**. So when the irrevocable decision of the sanctuary has been pronounced and the destiny of the world has been forever fixed, the inhabitants of the earth will know it not. The forms of religion will be continued by a people from whom the Spirit of God has been finally withdrawn; and the satanic zeal with which the prince of evil will inspire them for the accomplishment of his malignant designs, will bear the semblance of zeal for God.

As the Sabbath has become the special point of controversy throughout Christendom, and religious and secular authorities have combined to enforce the observance of the Sunday, the persistent refusal of a small minority to yield to the popular demand will make them objects of universal execration. It will be urged that the few who stand in opposition to an institution of the church and a law of the state ought not to be tolerated; that it is better for them to suffer than for whole nations to be thrown into confusion and lawlessness. The same argument eighteen hundred years ago was brought against Christ by the "rulers of the people." "It is expedient for us," said the wily Caiaphas, "that one man should die for the people, and that the whole nation perish not." This argument will appear conclusive; and **A DECREE** will finally be issued against those who hallow the Sabbath of the fourth commandment, denouncing them as deserving of the severest punishment and giving the people liberty, after a certain time, **TO PUT THEM TO DEATH.** Romanism in the Old World and apostate Protestantism in the New will pursue a similar course toward those who honor all the divine precepts. *The Great Controversy*, p. 615-616.

13. GOD'S PEOPLE

> Behold, I come as a thief. Blessed is he that watcheth, and keepeth his garments, lest he walk naked, and they see his shame. Rev. 16:15.

The sixth plague describes the wicked as they gather together to legislate a Universal Death Decree against God's people. But in verse 15, the scene changes to that of God's people. What are they to be doing during this time of confrontation?

They are to be "watching." Watching what? Watching the fulfillment of prophecy and understanding what is going on! They are to be **keeping** their garments. The "garments" are those "robes" of ". . . fine linen, clean and white . . . the righteousness of the saints." Rev. 19:8. They have received the Seal of the Living God before the close of probation. They cannot obtain robes after probation closes. They can only **keep** them and watch with prayer for deliverance.

14. CONCLUSIONS ON ARMAGEDDON

There is no specific mention in the Old Testament of a *place* called "Armageddon." But Rev. 16:16 gives a clue to understanding, in that the term "Armageddon" is to be found "in the Hebrew tongue." The language itself gives meaning. "Armageddon" is made up of two Hebrew words, "Har" meaning "mount" and "Megedden" meaning a "place of troops." Rather simply, the word, "Armageddon," means a mountain on which is gathered troops—that is, a place of confrontation. The final confrontation will be worldwide for that is where God's people will be—all over the world.

Yes, it will be a **spiritual conflict** because it involves the Law of God versus the laws of man—issues of right and wrong. It will also be **literal** because the universal death decree will be a literal legislative action and will bring the real threat of death to all concerned. It is **political** in that it involves the unification of the governmental "kings of the whole world" but it will not concern itself with the usual conflicts over territory or the things wars are usually fought over.

Armageddon is not a war, it is a battle. The war is the great controversy conflict of the ages. The battle of Armageddon is fought **before** Jesus comes. The battle of Gog and Magog is fought at the end of the millennium. They are not the same battle. See Rev. 20:8.

The battle of Armageddon is called a **plague** because it involves the work of unrestrained evil angels. Those who have dabbled in spiritism have often testified of the cruelty and torment of evil spirits. The sixth plague is further described in Rev. 9 and it there reveals the physical and mental torture of evil spirits as they perform the gathering action.

The sixth plague is merely the gathering of forces. It is the gathering to battle. It is the dramatic action building toward the climax of the drama. The battle itself does not occur until the seventh plague. The sixth and seventh plagues are one continuous action. The drama reaches its climax at the Voice of God which begins the seventh plague.

15. A PRECIOUS PROMISE

The Holy Spirit ever abides with him who is seeking for perfection of Christian character. The Holy Spirit furnishes the pure motive, the living, active principle, that sustains striving, wrestling, believing souls in every emergency and under every temptation.

The Holy Spirit sustains the believer amid the world's hatred, amid the unfriendliness of relatives, amid disappointment, amid the realization of imperfection, and amid the mistakes of life. Depending upon the matchless purity and perfection of Christ, the victory is sure to him who looks unto the Author and Finisher of our faith. Ellen G. White, *Review and Herald*, Nov. 30, 1897.

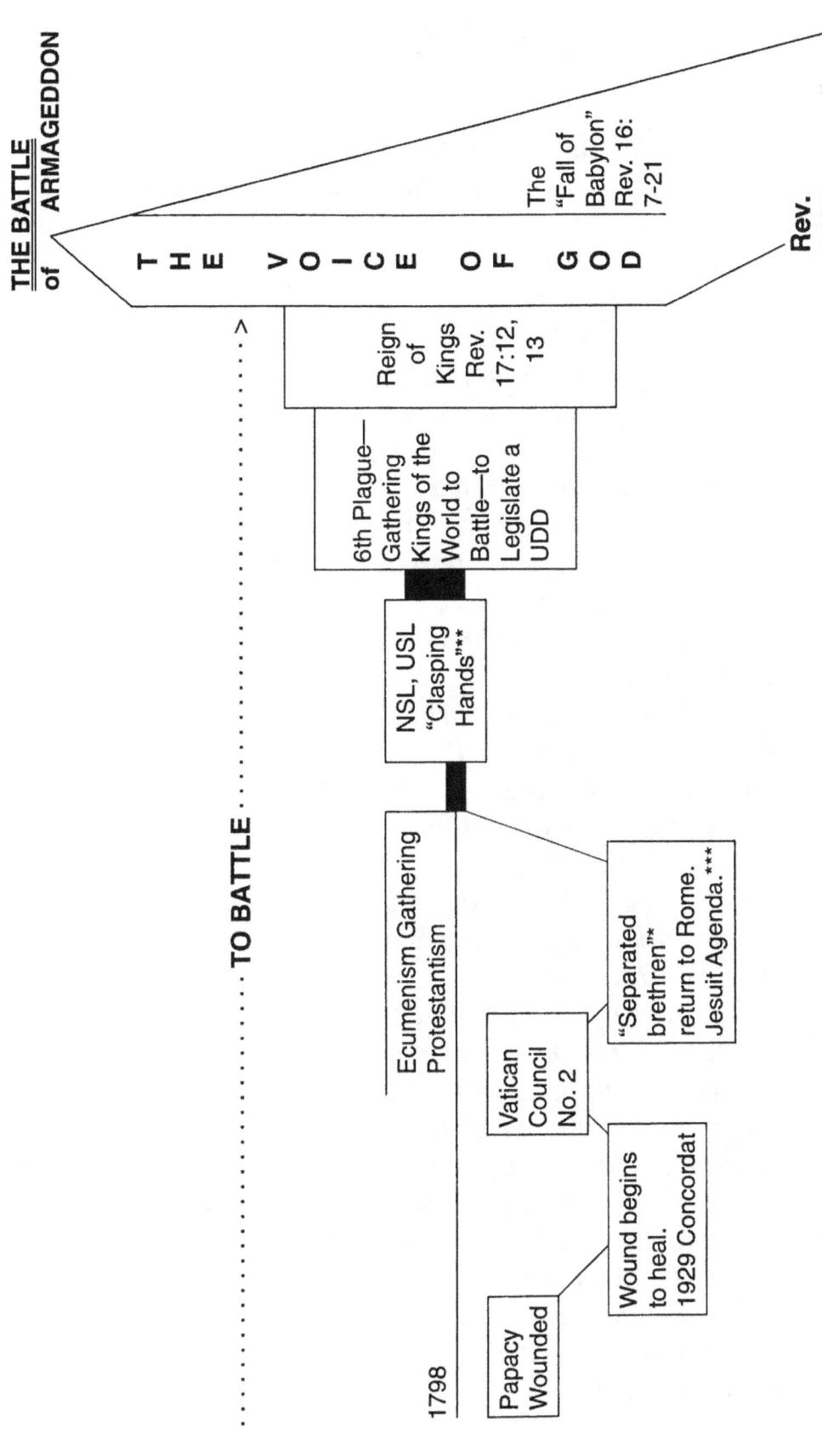

Psalm 91

He that dwelleth in the secret place of the Most High
shall abide under the shadow of the Almighty.
I will say of the Lord, He is my refuge and my fortress:
my God; in him will I trust.
Surely he shall deliver thee from the snare of the fowler,
and from the noisome pestilence.
He shall cover thee with his feathers,
and under his wings shalt thou trust:
his truth shall be thy shield and buckler.
Thou shalt not be afraid for the terror by night;
nor for the arrow that flieth by day;
Nor for the pestilence that walketh in darkness,
nor for the destruction that wasteth at noonday.
A thousand shall fall at thy side,
and ten thousand at thy right hand;
but it shall not come nigh thee.
Only with thine eyes shalt thou behold
and see the reward of the wicked.
Because thou hast made the Lord, which is my refuge,
even the Most High, thy habitation;
there shall no evil befall thee,
neither shall ANY PLAGUE come nigh thy dwelling.
For he shall give his angels charge over thee,
to keep thee in all thy ways.
They shall bear thee up in their hands,
lest thou dash thy foot against a stone.
Thou shalt tread upon the lion and adder:
the young lion and the dragon shalt thou trample under feet.
Because he hath set his love upon me, therefore will I deliver him:
I will set him on high, because he hath known my name.
He shall call upon me, and I will answer him:
I will be with him in trouble;
I will deliver him, and honour him.
With long life will I satisfy him,
and shew him my salvation.

CHAPTER XVI

THE SEVENTH PLAGUE DELIVERANCE

INTRODUCTION: THE STRUCTURE OF THE DRAMA[1]

The curtain closes on the last scene of the sixth plague at a point of high interest. The religious forces of Babylon, united with the kings or governments of the "whole world" stand ready for battle. A good playwright builds the cast and accelerates the action, scene after scene, until the drama reaches high tension. In the last act, in one master stroke, called the "coup d' etat," or "coup d' theater," it reaches a climax and the tension breaks. Mysteries are solved, each character is plainly identified, the hero and heroine are united, the villain exposed and the future obviously settled. The seventh plague begins with the Voice of God, which is the "coup d' etat," or "coup d' theater," and this begins the last act in this great drama.

1. THE SETTING FOR THE SEVENTH PLAGUE: LEGISLATION OF A UNIVERSAL DEATH DECREE

> These plagues [the first five] enraged the wicked against the righteous; they thought that we had brought the judgments of God upon them, and that if they could rid the earth of us, the plagues would then be stayed. A **decree** went forth **to slay the saints**, which caused them to cry day and night for deliverance. *Early Writings*, p. 36, 37.

> As Satan influenced Esau to march against Jacob, so he will stir up the wicked to **destroy God's people** in the time of trouble. As he accused Jacob, he will urge his accusations against the people of God. *The Great Controversy*, p. 618.

> My attention was turned to the wicked . . . They were all astir. . . . I saw measures taken against the company who had the light and power of God. I heard them crying unto God earnestly. Day and night their cry ceased not . . . Deliver us from the heathen . . . *Early Writings*, p. 272.

> I saw the saints leaving the cities and villages, and associating together in companies, and living in the most solitary places. Angels provided them food and water, while the wicked were suffering from hunger and thirst. Then I saw the leading men of the earth consulting together, and Satan and his angels busy around them. I saw *a writing*, copies of which were scattered in different parts of the land, giving orders that unless the saints should yield their peculiar faith, give up the Sabbath, and observe the first day of the week, the people were at liberty after a certain time **to**

---

[1] The decisive action, known in literature and drama as the "coup d' theater" is called historically a "coup d' etat," pronounced Koo d' Tah.

> ***put them to death***. . . . Day and night they cried unto God for deliverance. *Early Writings*, p. 282, 283.

The sixth plague is a description of the wicked gathering for the battle of Armageddon. This action comes to the great climax when they pass a **UNIVERSAL DEATH DECREE** causing the saints to cry for deliverance. As the day comes for this legislative decree to go **into effect**, suddenly God delivers His people. The seventh plague begins with this mighty deliverance at the **VOICE OF GOD**.

2. THE VOICE OF GOD DELIVERANCE FROM THE UNIVERSAL DEATH DECREE

> And the seventh angel poured out his vial into the air; and there came **A GREAT VOICE** out of the temple of heaven, from the throne, saying, ***It is done***. Rev. 16:17.

> A decree went forth to slay the saints, which caused them to cry day and night for deliverance. . . . Then all the saints cried out with anguish of spirit, and ***were delivered by the VOICE OF GOD***. *Early Writings*, p. 36, 37.

> Soon I heard the **VOICE OF GOD**, which shook the heavens and the earth. . . . Their ***captivity was turned***. *Early Writings*, p. 272.

The "voice of God" is the master stroke ("coup d' theater," or "coup d' etat")[1] which breaks the tension of the drama. From this point onward, the action turns, descending, with one concluding event following another in swift succession. Let us turn our attention to this voice of God. What exactly does it say?

3. THE VOICE OF GOD DECLARES THE DAY AND HOUR OF CHRIST'S COMING

In Rev. 16:17 the Bible itself declares that the voice says, **"IT IS DONE."** This declaration is similar to Christ's triumphant cry: **"IT IS FINISHED."** When Jesus spoke these words upon the cross, He referred to the fact that the specific segment of the plan of salvation, which involved His life on earth in the battle against Satan had been completed. In the seventh plague this similar voice announces that the segment of the plan of salvation which involved His people on earth in their battle against Satan, has been completed. Their life and witnessing has been complete and sufficient through the time of trouble to vindicate the righteousness and power of Christ in providing salvation against Satan's accusations. From this point forward, their struggle and anguish is over. There is yet much to occur under the seventh plague, but the people of God have been delivered by the voice of God and their sufferings are over.

The prophet also adds the following information:

> The voice of God is heard from heaven, ***declaring the day and hour of Jesus' coming*** . . . *The Great Controversy*, p. 640.

The fact that the Voice of God declares the day and hour of Jesus' coming **proves** that the Voice of God is **not** the same event as the Second Coming of Jesus; and that the two events are not simultaneous. The Voice of God **precedes** His coming.

---

[1] Definition: "coup d' etat" the violent overthrow . . . of an existing government. Literally—"coup" is a blow of force.

Great confusion has reigned for many years among God's people because they have assumed that the events connected with the voice of God will occur at the Second Coming. There are a "number of days" difference between the two. Although we cannot know the "day and hour" of His coming until it is announced by the Voice of God, we can eliminate much confusion regarding endtime events by a thorough study of the plagues and prophecy of Scripture, supplemented by the comments of Ellen G. White.

4. THE VOICE OF GOD DELIVERS (DECLARES) THE EVERLASTING COVENANT

> The voice of God is heard from heaven, declaring the day and hour of Jesus' coming, and delivering THE EVERLASTING COVENANT to His people. Like peals of loudest thunder His words roll through the earth. *The Great Controversy*, p. 640.

The "words" of the everlasting covenant are the **"reading of the will."** These words declare the reward of the righteous. What will they get? Eternal life! Eden restored—a home in the new earth—a mansion in the Holy City and a country home. God's people will receive a new body free from pain and illness. They will travel to worlds afar. They will enjoy the company of angels and sinless beings and, best of all, the companionship of God and His dear Son for all eternity, with the Holy Spirit dwelling within them.

Those who have died in the faith of the third angel's message will come up in a special resurrection to hear the voice of God deliver the words of the everlasting covenant. That voice accomplishes the special resurrection and glorifies the living righteous:

> A decree went forth to slay the saints, which caused them to cry day and night for deliverance. This was the time of Jacob's trouble. Then all the saints cried out with anguish of spirit, and were delivered by the voice of God. The 144,000 triumphed. ***Their faces were lighted up with the glory of God***. *Early Writings*, p. 36, 37.

5. THE VOICE OF GOD GLORIFIES THE FACES OF THE RIGHTEOUS

> The voice of God is heard from heaven, declaring the day and hour of Jesus' coming, and delivering the everlasting covenant to His people. Like peals of loudest thunder His words roll through the earth. The Israel of God stand listening, with their eyes fixed upward. Their ***countenances are lighted up with His glory, and shine as did the face of Moses when he came down from Sinai. The wicked cannot look upon them***. *The Great Controversy*, p. 640.

> Soon I heard the voice of God, which shook the heavens and the earth. . . . Their captivity was turned. A glorious light shone upon them. How **beautiful** they then looked! All marks of care and weariness were gone, and **health** and **beauty** were seen in every countenance. Their enemies, the heathen around them, fell like dead men; and they could not endure **the light that shone upon the delivered**, holy ones. This **light and glory remained upon them,** until Jesus was seen in the clouds of heaven, and [they were] **changed . . . from glory to glory**. *Early Writings*, p. 272, 273.

God's people are "glorified" at the Voice of God. But they are translated at the Second Coming of Jesus. Thus they are changed "from glory to glory." At the close of probation, or before, in the process of the sealing and final atonement in the Investigative Judgment, God's people are delivered from **SIN**. At the voice of God they are delivered from their **ENEMIES**. At the Second

Coming of Jesus and the resurrection or translation they are delivered from this body of **DEATH** and given immortality.

These three deliverances occur at three different times and should be clearly understood.

> 1. Sin, at the Investigative Judgment Sealing.
> 2. Enemies, at the Voice of God
> 3. This body of death by resurrection or translation, at the second coming of Jesus

6. GOD'S PEOPLE ARE HOLY, HARMLESS, AND UNDEFILED AT THE VOICE OF GOD

> By the people of God a voice, clear and melodious, is heard, saying, "Look up," and lifting their eyes to the heavens, they . . . see the glory of God and the Son of man seated upon His throne . . . and . . . hear the request . . . "I will that they also, whom Thou hast given Me, be with Me where I am." John 17:24. Again a voice, musical and triumphant, is heard, saying: **"They come! they come! holy, harmless, and undefiled**. They have kept the word of My patience; they shall walk among the angels . . . *The Great Controversy*, p. 636.

In the battle of Armageddon, God's people do not fight. They are not in a fighting mood! They are **"holy, harmless, undefiled."** The battle is set in array by the wicked who are determined to put them all to death, but it is God who makes their deliverance sure.

Neither wicked men nor evil angels will be able to face the glorified army of the 144,000 who reflect the image of Jesus fully. "Glorious will be the deliverance of those who have patiently waited for His coming . . ." *The Great Controversy*, p. 634. The decisive blow of the battle of Armageddon is delivered at the Voice of God. But the battle is not yet over. The long standing controversy must be brought to its bitter end and the foe completely vanquished. More information is available regarding the timing of the voice of God and its implications in regard to those events, which are listed in Rev. 16:18-21.

7. THE TIME FOR THE VOICE OF GOD DELIVERANCE

We are given information even as to **the time of day** when the voice of God will take place!

> . . . there will be, in different lands, a simultaneous movement for their destruction. As **the time appointed** in the decree draws near, the people will conspire to root out the hated sect. It will be determined to strike **in one night** a decisive blow . . . It is now, in the hour of utmost extremity, that the God of Israel will interpose for the deliverance of His chosen. *The Great Controversy*, p. 635.

8. The UNIVERSAL DEATH DECREE WILL SPECIFY A *DATE* WHEN IT SHALL GO INTO EFFECT. LAWS GO INTO EFFECT AT *MIDNIGHT*.

> It was at **midnight** that God chose to deliver His people. . . . there was one clear place of settled glory, whence came the voice of God like many waters, shaking the heavens and the earth. *Early Writings*, p. 285.

The enemies of God's people will anticipate the effective date to occur, and will surround the people of God.

With shouts of triumph, jeering, and imprecation [cursing], throngs of evil men are about to rush upon their prey, when, lo, a dense blackness, deeper than the darkness of the night, falls upon the earth. Then a rainbow, shining with the glory from the throne of God, spans the heavens and seems to encircle each praying company. The angry multitudes are suddenly arrested. Their mocking cries die away. The objects of their murderous rage are forgotten. *The Great Controversy*, p. 635, 636.

9. A LIST OF VOICE OF GOD EVENTS
From *The Great Controversy*

1. It occurs at midnight .... GC 636
2. The sun appears
3. The streams cease to flow
4. Dark heavy clouds clash against each other
5. One clear space of indescribable glory is seen in the heavens
6. The **Voice of God** shakes the heavens and the earth
7. There is a mighty earthquake .... GC 637
8. The firmament appears to open and shut
9. Glory from God's throne flashes through
10. Mountains shake like a reed in the wind
11. Ragged rocks are scattered on every side
12. There is a roar of coming tempest
13. The shriek of a hurricane sounds like demon voices on a mission of destruction
14. Earth's surface heaves and swells
15. Earth's surface is breaking up
16. Earth's foundations are giving way
17. Mountain chains are sinking
18. Inhabited islands disappear
19. Seaports are swallowed up by water
20. Babylon (false religion) is identified
21. Hailstones destroy great cities
22. Beautiful palaces and homes are destroyed
23. Prison walls break open (God's people are set free)
24. Graves are opened in a special resurrection
25. All who died in faith in the 3rd angel's message come forth, glorified to hear the covenant blessing on those who kept His law
26. Those who pierced Jesus are resurrected
27. Persecutors of God's people of all ages are resurrected to see God's people glorified
28. Fierce lightning envelopes the earth in a sheet of flame .... GC 638
29. Voices declare the doom of the wicked (understood by false shepherds)
30. The wails of the wicked are heard above the sound of the elements
31. Demons acknowledge the deity of Christ
32. Men grovel in terror and cry for mercy
33. The wicked seek to enter the caves, casting away gold and silver
34. A star, four-fold in brilliance, brings hope and joy from heaven (The same star terrorizes the wicked)
35. The righteous are delivered from their enemies .... GC 639
36. The faces of the righteous are aglow with wonder, faith and love
37. God's people quote Psalm 46:1-3

38. The glory of the holy city, with gates ajar, streams from heaven
39. Two tables of stone (The Ten Commandments) appear in the sky folded together
40. A hand opens the tables of stone
41. The Ten Commandments—are seen in the heavens as traced with a pen of fire
42. All men view the Ten Commandments—the standard of judgment (All superstition and heresy is swept away from their minds)
43. The wicked are in horror and despair
44. The wicked are condemned by The Ten Commandment Law
45. It is too late for repentance and change .... GC 640
46. The **Voice of God** declares the day and hour of Jesus' coming
47. The **Voice of God** delivers the everlasting covenant to his people
48. The covenant words are like peals of thunder
49. The covenant words, sentence after sentence, roll around the earth
50. God's people stand listening, eyes fixed upward
51. Their faces light up with glory (as did Moses as he came down from Mt. Sinai)
52. The wicked cannot look upon the glory of the righteous
53. The righteous give a mighty shout of victory
54. Soon after the Voice of God a sign is given of the coming of Jesus—a small black cloud in the East

From *Early Writings* additional concepts are given:
55. The **Voice of God** sounds like many waters .... EW 15
56. The living saints, 144,000 in number, knew and understood the voice
57. The wicked thought the voice was an earthquake
58. The **Voice of God** declares the day and hour of Jesus' coming; God pours out the Holy Ghost so that the faces of the righteous light up and shine like Moses' as he came down from Mt. Sinai
59. The 144,000 will have been sealed and perfectly united
60. The wicked rush violently to lay hands on God's people to thrust them into prison
61. The righteous stretch forth the hand in the name of the Lord and the wicked fall helpless to the ground
62. The wicked fall helpless to the ground and worship at the saint's feet

From *Testimonies*, Vol. 1, additional concepts emerge:
63. At the **Voice of God** buildings were shaken down .... 1 T 184
64. Their (God's people) captivity was turned
65. A glorious light shone upon them
66. How beautiful they then looked
67. All weariness and marks of care were gone
68. Health and beauty were seen in every face
69. Their enemies fell like dead men

70. The wicked could not endure to look upon their glory
71. The light and glory shining on the delivered ones remain on them until Jesus is seen coming in the clouds of heaven
72. Buildings totter and fall with a terrible crash .... 1 T 354
73. The sea boils like a pot
74. The captivity of the righteous is turned
75. With sweet and solemn whisperings the righteous say to one another "We are delivered. It is the Voice of God."
76. The wicked fear and tremble while the saints rejoice
77. Satan and his angels and wicked men witness the glory conferred on God's people who have kept His Law and Sabbath
78. The faces of the righteous reflect the image of Jesus
79. Satan and his angels flee from the glorified saints
80. Their power to annoy them is gone forever
81. Those who died in faith of the third angel's message rise in a special resurrection ... SR 409

10. THE SEVENTH PLAGUE—"FALL OF BABYLON"

> And there were voices, and thunders, and lightnings; and there was a great earthquake, such as was not since men were upon the earth, so mighty an earthquake, and so great. And ***the great city was divided into three parts,*** and the cities of the nations fell: and ***great Babylon came in remembrance before God, to give unto her the cup of the wine of the fierceness of his wrath***. Rev. 16:18, 19.

11. TIMEFRAME: BABYLON FALLS *AFTER* THE VOICE OF GOD

The **sixth** plague describes the gathering unifying action of Babylon as having three parts—the dragon, the beast, and the false prophet. They work together to unify the kings of the earth and the whole world, surging toward the legislation of a universal death decree. It is the **seventh** plague which describes the Voice of God which causes the collapse and fall of Babylon.

It is imperative that the events enumerated in a prophetic outline be kept in **SEQUENCE**. History has occurred in a sequence of events in the past and will continue to do so in the future. Prophecy, which is history written before it happens, occurs in the same way—in **SEQUENCE**, one event following another. There is also **CONTINUITY**, especially in a case where there is cause-and-effect relationship. It is the Voice of God which is the **cause**, and the fall of Babylon is the **effect**.

This orderliness also is evident in the sequence of chapters as follows: Revelation 16:17 describes the Voice of God. Chapters 17 and 18 describe events connected with the fall of Babylon.

It is the Voice of God which makes evident who are the real people of God, and also makes apparent the deceptive nature of the false-apostate religion of Babylon. At that point the religious leaders lose all credibility and influence in the eyes of the "kings of the earth." This "waking up" of the kings of the earth is described below:

> And the ten horns which thou sawest upon the beast, these shall hate the whore, and shall make her desolate and naked, and shall eat her flesh, and burn her with fire. For God hath put in their hearts to fulfill his will, and to agree, and give their kingdom unto the beast, until the words of God shall be fulfilled. Rev. 17:16, 17.

The fact that the fall of Babylon is **AFTER** the Voice of God and follows it in sequence, is verified by the prophet:

> Such are the judgments that fall upon Babylon in the day . . . of God's wrath. She has filled up the measure of her iniquity; her time has come; she is ripe for destruction. **WHEN THE VOICE OF GOD** turns the captivity of His people, there is a terrible awakening of those who have lost all in the great conflict of life. . . . The wicked are filled with regret . . . Ministers and people see that they have not sustained the right relation to God. . . . The people see that they have been deluded. They accuse one another of having led them to destruction; but all unite in heaping their bitterest condemnation upon the **ministers** . . . these **teachers** confess before the world their work of deception. The multitudes are filled with fury . . . they turn upon their **false shepherds** . . . The swords which were to slay God's people are now employed to destroy their enemies. Everywhere there is strife and bloodshed . . . He [the Lord] will give them that are wicked to the sword . . . Now the angel of death

goes forth, represented in Ezekiel's vision by the men with the slaughtering weapons . . .

> In the mad strife of their own fierce passions, and by the awful outpouring of God's unmingled wrath, fall the wicked inhabitants of the earth—**priests**, rulers, and people, rich and poor, high and low. "And the slain of the Lord shall be at that day from one end of the earth even unto the other . . . *The Great Controversy*, p. 653-657.

It is the **ministers, priests, teachers, and false shepherds** which make up the "fabric" of Babylon—false religion. When these leaders confess and lose their influence, *that* is the fall of Babylon. Neither the people nor the kings of the earth follow them any longer. *False religion collapses at the Voice of God*. It is at the Voice of God, not before, that the support of the people will be withdrawn from Babylon.

12. THE *BIBLE* PROVIDES THE *TIMEFRAME* FOR THE FALL OF BABYLON

The Bible is its own expositor. The Bible provides the necessary timeframe for us to understand clearly *the timing of the plagues*, and *the fall of Babylon*. The Bible tells us clearly the time that will be required for the seven last *plagues* to fall and it also states the time required for *Babylon* to fall: they are *NOT one and the same*.

> The plagues fall in one *day*. Rev. 18:8
> Babylon falls in one *hour*. Rev. 18:10, 17, 19.

> **. . . her plagues shall come in ONE DAY** . . . Rev. 18:8.

> Alas, alas, that great city Babylon, that mighty city! for **in ONE HOUR** is thy judgment come. . . . For in **ONE HOUR** so great riches is come to nought. . . . for in **ONE HOUR** is she made desolate. Rev. 18:10, 17, 19.

Whereas the seven last plagues come in **ONE DAY**, the fall of Babylon which occurs under the seventh plague requires **ONLY ONE HOUR**.

What is the hermeneutic principle by which this information is to be understood? If God has given such specifics, how can the Bible student put it to good use? A "day" and an "hour" are very **specific** units of time. They are *measurable*. How shall they be regarded to take on important meaning?

13. BIBLE STATEMENTS MUST BE KEPT IN CONTEXT

It is generally understood that any Scripture taken out of context is abused. When applied to prophecy we may know that if the context is written in **literal language**, the **TIME** mentioned therein should be understood as literal time. But if the **TIME** is couched in **symbolic language**, then it should remain within that context and be understood as symbolic time and computed by the year-day principle.

Although there are some who assume that the Year-day principle was destroyed in 1844, there is no Biblical foundation, nor any words of the prophet to indicate such a thing! The Year-day principle is the only reliable tool by which a conversion from symbolic time can be computed into literal time.

Revelation 18 is written in symbolism, and is a description of "Babylon" which is a **symbol** of apostate religion. Therefore, any time, mentioned within that chapter, is also kept in the context of symbolic time. The *one hour* and *one day* periods are symbolic time and must be computed by the Year-day principle.

> ... her plagues shall come in **ONE DAY**. Rev. 18:8.

This becomes a plain statement that the seven last plagues shall come in **ONE YEAR**.

But then how long is the **"one hour"** which describes the fall of Babylon, that occurs after the Voice of God? Using the Year-day principle let us compute it as follows:

One prophetic day represents one literal year.[1,2]

- Step 1: One hour is one-twenty-fourth of a day.
- Step 2: One-twenty-fourth of a year is half a month.
- Step 3: Half a month of thirty days is fifteen days.
- Conclusion: **"ONE HOUR" of symbolic time represents FIFTEEN DAYS of literal time.**

Therefore: The "fall of Babylon," which occurs after the Voice of God, will occur in fifteen literal days.

A knowledge of the fact that the seven last plagues will require one year of time does not give the day and hour of the coming of Jesus. We will not know that until it is announced by the Voice of God. At this time, we cannot even predict the year! In the same way, the fact that the fall of Babylon will require fifteen days of fulfillment, does not give the day or hour of His coming, because the seventh plague also contains other events which must also be fulfilled.

However, Jesus declared, "... when ye see all these things, know that it is near, even at the doors." Matt. 24:33. It is the privilege of God's people to unlock the secrets of prophecy so that they will not walk in darkness, but in the light of His Word. God's people obviously will need this information to encourage them as they pass through the seven last plagues and the "hour of temptation" knowing that their deliverance is near!

14. THE SIXTH AND SEVENTH PLAGUE DRAMA ILLUSTRATED

The legislation of a **UNIVERSAL DEATH DECREE**, and the span of time until it is to go into effect; the Voice of God deliverance from that decree, and the Fall of Babylon afterward, is the climax of the Great Controversy struggle as far as God's people are concerned. Revelation 17 and 18 furnish the particulars.

Revelation 17 begins this climactic struggle by describing the kings of the earth united with the beast in exultation as they have passed the Universal Death Decree. Between the time of legislation and the effective date, they "reign" together believing that when the earth will be rid of the dissenters, then God will turn away the plagues so that happiness can be restored. They reign together for **"ONE HOUR"** or fifteen literal days.

> And the ten horns which thou sawest are ten kings, which have received no kingdom as yet; but receive power as kings **ONE HOUR [fifteen days]** with the beast. These have one mind, and shall give their power and strength unto the beast. Rev. 17:12, 13.

---

1 A Biblical year, used in prophecy, consists of 360 days. See Appendix Note E.

2 Note: For a more comprehensive study of the "one hour" periods of Revelation 17 and 18 a study should be made of the timelines of Daniel 12 and this may be pursued in the book, titled *A WARNING* as advertised on the last page of this book.

TWO "ONE HOUR" PERIODS		
Legislation Date of the Universal Death Decree	Deliverance THE VOICE OF GOD **Effective Date**	
Symbolic ONE HOUR		Symbolic ONE HOUR
Fifteen Literal Days Reign of kings with the beast. Rev. 17:12, 13		Fifteen Literal Days: Kings hate her. Fall of Babylon Rev. 18:10, 17, 19

15. SEVENTH PLAGUE CONCLUDING EVENTS

> . . . and the cities of the nations fell . . .
> And every island fled away, and the mountains were not found.
> And there fell upon men a great hail out of heaven,
> every stone about the weight of a talent:
> and men blasphemed God because of the plague of the hail;
> for the plague thereof was exceeding great. Rev. 16:19-21.

The delivered immortal saints will be unharmed, while the desolating hail falls on earth upon the wicked.

> Behold, the Lord maketh the earth empty, and maketh it waste, and turneth it upside down, and scattereth abroad the inhabitants thereof. The land shall be utterly emptied, and utterly spoiled: for the Lord hath spoken this word. Isa. 24:1, 3.

> The whole earth appears like a desolate wilderness. The ruins of cities and villages destroyed by the earthquake, uprooted trees, ragged rocks thrown out by the sea or torn out of the earth itself, are scattered over its surface, while vast caverns mark the spot where the mountains have been rent from their foundations. . . . the expression "bottomless pit" represents the earth in a state of confusion and darkness . . . Prophecy teaches that it will be brought back, partially at least, to this condition. . . . "and all the cities thereof were broken down." *The Great Controversy*, p. 657-659.

THE BATTLE OF ARMAGEDDON

Gathering to Battle	Battle Alignment	Battle Action
	Universal Death Decree	
	Legislative Date ——— Effective Date	
		"Voice of God" Deliverance from the Universal Death Decree
	REIGN OF KINGS WITH THE BEAST for **"ONE HOUR" (15 days)**	**"THE FALL OF BABYLON"**
	These . . . give their power . . . unto the beast." Rev. 17:12, 13 (to enforce the Univseral Death Decree)	**"ONE HOUR" (15 days)** Rev. 18:10, 17, 19
"Gathering" to Battle. Rev. 16:14 "Running to Battle . . . for Five Months" Rev. 9:9, 10 Purpose: To gather the kings of all the earth to Legislate a Universal Death Decree		

Plague No. 6 does not describe battle action. It describes only the gathering action to battle. Neither does it describe battle alignment.
Plague No. 6 describes only that which leads up to the Legislation of a Univseral Death Decree. The battle alignment is described in Rev. 17:12, 13 and the exultation over the Decree in Rev. 11:10. Battle action does not occur until Plague No. 7 which begins with the "Voice of God."
The gathering action lasts "five months", the Reign of Kings 15 days and the Fall of Babylon 15 days. This totals 6 months (180 days). See Rev. 18:8.
How long for the first five plagues?

CHAPTER XVII

AN INTRODUCTION TO THE SEVEN TRUMPETS

We all agree that **THE BIBLE IS ITS OWN EXPOSITOR** but, in reality, we are much more apt to make up our own interpretation. Instead of permitting the seven last plagues to interpret the seven trumpets, and to let the seven trumpets furnish the missing details to the seven last plagues—thereby letting the Bible interpret itself; we have preferred to let each man generate his own interpretation of the trumpets and have ended up with views as varied as the men who devised them.

Some love war games and see the trumpets as various forms of war and military devices. Some are students of astronomy and see each trumpet as some natural disaster. Some have placed the trumpets in the past, some before the close of probation, others after. God's people will never attain unity of prophetic interpretation until they accept the Word of God as the **final word** and **its own expositor.** Not until they permit the **Bible** to interpret itself in regard to the trumpets will they see eye to eye.

> It cannot be shown that the church did, in the lifetime of Paul, reach the state of unity, knowledge, and perfection . . . The church today is almost infinitely below this state . . . not until the . . . ***last generation*** . . . [will such unity, knowledge, and perfection be achieved] by the ***last warning message*** . . . to prepare them to be translated to heaven without tasting death . . . I SP 13, 14

Some have seen the trumpets as Satan's work, but the plagues as God's revenge, placing them at different times for fulfillment, but both in the future. Others have placed the trumpets far in the past but the plagues in the future. Others are reluctant to consider a study of the trumpets assuming they have already been fulfilled, even though the prophetess is clear as to the time for their fulfillment:

> Solemn events **BEFORE US ARE YET TO TRANSPIRE. TRUMPET AFTER TRUMPET IS *TO BE* SOUNDED** [future tense], **vial after vial poured out** . . . Scenes of stupendous interest are **right upon us.**" Letter 109, 1890, Ellen G. White; 7 *Seventh-day Adventist Bible Commentary*, p. 982.

There are always some who consider prophetic expositors[1] to be more trustworthy than the inspired prophet of God.

Prophecy is the "unrolling of the scroll" in which the prophecy is understood about **the time of fulfillment**. As history has unfolded, event by event, prophecy has been viewed more and more clearly. Men must keep those prophetic Scriptures, which point to their future, in a **tentative**

---

[1] Prophetic expositors were not prophets, but common men who loved to study the prophecies and who wrote books on them, giving the popular view of their day. Examples: Sir Isaac Newton, Josiah Litch, Matthew Henry, Uriah Smith. See *The Prophetic Faith of our Fathers*, Vol I-V, p. 270, L.E. Froom, 1946.

position. Endtime events that had not yet happened, were sometimes applied to the past if they seemed to fit historical data. They did the best they could during the times in which they lived. Books written nearly a century ago should not be criteria for today. There is no substitute for an intelligent investigation of the Word in the light of ongoing endtime events. Only by keeping an open mind with study and prayer, and led by the Holy Spirit, can the prophetic expositor remain on safe ground. Clinging to the past opinions of men, is dangerous sometimes and unreliable.

What about the exposition of Uriah Smith, and Ellen G. White's references to the views held by him and other expositors in *The Great Controversy*? Are we not obligated to defend those positions as immovable truth, and set aside all other current applications? It has been a rigid allegiance to these views which has, in a great measure, held the church together in the past. These views were all supportive of Seventh-day Adventist doctrine. Must we not defend them today or see the church fragment and fall apart? Let the prophet speak to this point:

> In **every age** there is **a new development of truth**, a message of God to the people of **that generation. The old truths are all essential; NEW TRUTH IS NOT INDEPENDENT OF THE OLD, BUT AN UNFOLDING OF IT.** It is only as the old truths are understood that we can comprehend the new. . . . But it is the light which shines in the fresh unfolding of truth that glorifies the old. He who rejects or neglects the new, does not really possess the old. Christ's Object Lessons, p. 127, 128.

New truth never contradicts old truth! There is no need to destroy old truth to make way for the new! New truth or new light on prophecy concerning endtime fulfillments will not contradict the old truths on which the church was founded. New truth or new light on endtime application of prophecy must be **in addition to**, "an unfolding," with more information, supplementing old truth. Those who seek to tear down the old to make way for their new views are taking a wrong approach.

Although theologians have asserted that prophecy may not have dual applications, listen to those who wrote the *Seventh-day Adventist Bible Commentary*:

> The Scriptures abound with illustrations of prophecies having dual application . . . It was often only when Christ or the Holy Spirit "opened . . . their understanding" that men of Christian times began to "understand the scriptures" in their fullness . . . *Bible Commentary*, Vol. 1, p. 1017, 1018.

Apparently Ellen G. White recognized two fulfillments of the trumpets. She referred to Uriah Smith's application and used it freely in *The Great Controversy* as an explanation of events, some of which transpired in 1840; but also declared that these trumpets will be fulfilled in the future. The past application was valid and supportive of Adventism a century ago; and a future application, if correctly understood, will not destroy the old but continue to add information that is currently useful to the last generation!

The **manmade** "hermeneutic rule" that there are no dual applications of prophecy is simply another of Satan's devising to close off the study of Scripture and prophecy to this last generation. A "primary" application of prophecy is of ***primary importance*** to the generation for which it is most useful. It becomes a secondary application when it becomes obsolete. That does not make it wrong for those who found it useful in their day.

THE TRADITIONAL VIEW OF THE SEVEN TRUMPETS

The traditional view or application of the seven trumpets of Revelation 8, 9 and 11 is found in the book, *Daniel and the Revelation*, by Uriah Smith and the *Seventh-day Adventist Commentary*, Vol. 7. Smith's frequent references to historians and prophetic expositors of his day (See the Bibliography and footnotes), indicate that he reflected, to a certain extent, the positions of Bible students of that era. He made no claim to be a prophet nor to the prophetic gift. His views were planted in reliable historical data. His views were not always accepted as correct by other Adventists and there are records of strong disagreements between him and James White, husband of Ellen G. White. However, his book was the best they had to that date and considered to be valuable to the church at large.

Uriah Smith's application applied the first four trumpets to the barbarian invasions of Rome. This is found in Chapter XIII titled, "The Collapse of Rome." In Chapter IX titled "The Moslem World," he applied the 5th and 6th trumpets to the rise and spread of Mohammedanism. These views were previously taught by William Miller. In 1838, Josiah Litch, using this application, computed the prophetic time periods spoken of in the seven trumpets by use of the Year-day principle and predicted the fall of the Turkish power on August 11, 1840. This prediction was fulfilled at the time specified.[1] This fact was highly significant to the 1844 Advent movement because, in the providence of God, this application gave confidence in the Year-day principle which established the 2300 day-year prophecy of Dan. 8:14 to end on Oct. 22, 1844. That method of application of the seven trumpets accomplished its purpose for that day.

However, that is now long past and is of secondary importance to those who live in the closing scenes of earth's history. This generation has now more concern for the coming crisis. It is time to look closely at the fact that the prophet has declared plainly that the seven trumpets are **TO BE SOUNDED (future).**

Theologians have been employed by the church to defend it against erroneous applications of prophecy. These theologians should be recognized for the many services they have done in refuting unstable, "private interpretations" based on personal assumptions. On the other hand when scholars hide behind a "status quo" mentality, resisting all new light and current applications in which the Bible is made its own expositor, resisting the "unrolling of the scroll," they become disoriented.

Prophecies may have dual applications and are primary and secondary in nature. Not only did they have legitimate and useful application to past history, but may also be applied to endtime events which are the "grand finale." The hermeneutic principle which makes this plausible is Biblically stated:

> Now **ALL** these things happened unto them for *ensamples:* **and they are written for *OUR ADMONITION, UPON WHOM THE ENDS OF THE WORLD ARE COME***. I Cor. 10:11.

The above statement gives the last generation a special prerogative! Those who live in the endtime may use **"ALL"** that is **"written"**—*all the Scripture*, and apply it to their own day—to endtime events, where the Scripture itself or the endtime prophet declare it to be so.

This prerogative does not give permission to destroy any of the old truths on which Adventism was founded. It extends only to supplementary applications which apply to the future.

---

1 In 1840 England ruled the sea. Her ships in harbor spelled control. Her ships sailing into a nation's capital without permission indicated control of that nation—Turkey.

THE BASIC PREMISE (RATIONALE) OF THE TRADITIONAL VIEW

Before taking a new look at the seven trumpets, it is necessary to recognize the *rationale*—basic premise of Uriah Smith's traditional view. Although Smith did not make a direct statement to sum up his application, it is self-evident that it was a sequential reiteration of **Satan's use of political powers to destroy and obliterate the seat and kingdom of the Christian church.**

It must be recognized that Christianity for the first centuries centered in Rome. Smith viewed the first four trumpets as barbarian attacks on Rome. While Christianity centered in Rome, it would appear that Satan sought to wipe out its influence by the following barbarian attacks:

The First Trumpet	Alaric, The Goths	4th Century
The Second Trumpet	Genseric, The Vandals	5th Century
The Third Trumpet	Attila, The Huns	(428-468)
The Fourth Trumpet	Odoacer-Theodoric, (The Ostrogoths)	(476-793-526)

Instead of these barbarian attacks extinguishing Christianity, it gave impetus to an exodus which spread Christianity to all of Europe. Satan's attacks were therefore next directed to all Europe. About A.D. 500, Satan caused the new Islam-Mohammedan-Moslem religion to arise, like a plague of locusts out of the desert. They expanded from the Middle East in all directions, advancing over the north coast of Africa, entering Europe, not only from Turkey, but also from Spain, like two powerful pincers.

The armies of the Islamic religion would have overrun Europe had it not been for the providence of God, which raised up two great military powers in Europe to hold them back. In Austria, the powerful Hapsburgs pushed the invaders back to Constantinople and held them there. In France, the great military leader, Charles Martel, pushed them back into lower Spain. In this way, Europe was saved from the "infidel Turks" and retained its Christian identity for the next thousand years.

These efforts of Satan to destroy the Christian church are an historical background, by which this present generation can retrace the seven trumpets. Satan's pattern of destructive activity was then similar to that which he will try in the future to destroy the people of God in the time of the seven last plagues.

There is no contradiction between Smith's premise and historical application and the ENDTIME application specified by Ellen G. White. The same rationale or basic premise applies to both. Satan has, in the past, attempted to destroy God's people, and he will do so in the endtime. The endtime application is merely a reiteration of Satan's attempts, but under endtime circumstances.

> Fearful are the scenes which call forth this exclamation from the heavenly voice. The wrath of Satan increases as his time grows short, and his work of deceit and destruction will reach its culmination in the time of trouble. *The Great Controversy*, p. 623.

If prophecy which applies to the future were a danger to the true church and the people of God, there would have been no prophecy given which applies to any time after 1844. God would have left his remnant to stumble along in the dark. Plagues, trumpets, seals, and most of the book of Revelation would not have been written.

THE TRUMPETS 1-4

1. THE FUTURE APPLICATION

> The Battle of Armageddon is soon TO BE fought . . . (MS. 172, 1899) . . . the Captain of the Lord's host will stand at the head of the angels of heaven to direct the battle. Solemn events **BEFORE US ARE YET TO TRANSPIRE.** Trumpet after trumpet **IS TO BE SOUNDED, vial after vial poured out** one after another upon the inhabitants of the earth. Scenes of stupendous interest are right **UPON US**. *The Seventh-day Adventist Bible Commentary*, Vol. 7, p. 982. (Letter 109, 1890), Ellen G. White.

If the prophet said it, I believe it. The above quotation states clearly that the trumpets of Revelation are:

1. **"BEFORE US"**
2. **"YET TO TRANSPIRE"**
3. **"TO BE SOUNDED"**
4. **"RIGHT UPON US"**
5. **Connected in time with Armageddon . . . soon TO BE fought**
6. Connected in time with the seven last plagues—**future**

There is no question that the great, final, primary meaning has to do with **future events**.

Cross reference study of the Scriptures indicates that trumpets were used for a variety of circumstances: as warnings, as calls to worship, and especially to **WAR.**

> Saul now caused war to be proclaimed by the sound of the **trumpet** throughout the land, calling upon all the men of WAR . . . *Patriarchs and Prophets*, p. 617.

The first quotation above, associates the trumpets with the **BATTLE (war)** of Armageddon. Trumpets were sounded in time of war and there is an apparent affinity between the plagues and the trumpets as they are mentioned above. It is the plagues which bring to view the battle of Armageddon and reveal the final drama in the *conflict* between Christ and Satan. There is nothing in Scripture in regard to either plagues or trumpets which indicate that there is any repentance in response to these calamities, but rather that "men blasphemed God," and that many were killed.

Although it seems a noble thought that God would use calamities to turn the hearts of men to Him, thereby looking at the trumpets as warnings, there is nothing in the Scripture itself to merit such a conclusion. It is unwise to read into Scripture that which it does not say and to ignore obvious information.

A cursive reading of the seven trumpets reveals dramatic movements of vast importance which correspond to the character and drama of the plagues. The following Table of Comparisons brings this similarity of context between the plagues and trumpets to view:

2. TABLE OF COMPARISONS[1]

	The Seven Last Plagues	Rev.	The Seven Trumpets	Rev.
1.	"A noisome and grievous sore" [bad blood]	16:2	1. "hail and fire mingled with blood"	8:7
2.	"poured out his vial upon the **sea**." "it became as the **blood** of a dead man."	16:3	2. "cast into the **sea**." "the sea became **blood**."	8:8
3.	"***rivers and fountains of waters*** . . . became blood."	16:4	3. "it fell upon the ***rivers*** and ***fountains of waters***."	8:10
4.	"the **sun** . . . scorched men with fire."	16:8	4. "the **sun** was smitten."	8:12
5.	"the seat of the beast was full of **darkness**."	16:10	"A third part of them was **darkened**. The day shone not."	8:12
6.	"he gathered them together . . . **to the battle**."	16:14 16:16	5. "like unto horses prepared unto **battle**." "as the sound of chariots of many horses **running** to **battle**."	9:7
7.	"a great **voice**" "Babylon came in remembrance."	16:17 16:19	6. "*a voice*" ". . . the Euphrates [in Babylon]"	9:13 9:14
	"***voices, thunderings, lightning, earthquake***," "*hail*."	16:8 16:21	7. "***voices, lightnings thunderings, an earthquake***." "*hail*."	11:19 11:19

---

1   NOTE: The first trumpet and first plague are the only ones which do not have a direct similarity. Even in this reference to "blood" in the first trumpet, there is an inference, in that "sores" are caused by infection of the "blood," in plague No. 1.

    NOTE: The fourth trumpet includes that which pertains to the fifth plague. This gets them out of numerical comparison, but the sequence and content is still the same.

3. THE COMPLETE PICTURE IN THE RELATIONSHIP BETWEEN PLAGUES AND TRUMPETS

When plagues and trumpets are permitted to explain each other (the Bible permitted to become its own expositor) there is a marvelous relationship between the two which furnishes a very complete picture similar to a news report as follows:

THE PLAGUES EXPLAIN

WHAT	happens
WHO	participates and their actions

THE TRUMPETS EXPLAIN

WHEN	it happens and provides the timeframe
WHERE	the scope of action occurs
WHY	tells the cause and effect
HOW	the action is carried on and by what means

The trumpets supply added detail and information to the plagues making the picture complete. By the time all the questions listed above have been answered there emerges a very complete picture of future events. A chart of the alignment of the plagues and trumpets is furnished at the end of this chapter.

This clear picture of future events was not made available until the last generation should need it for the following reason:

> The future was mercifully veiled from the disciples. Had they at that time fully comprehended the two awful facts . . . they would have been overwhelmed with horror. . . . their meaning was to be unfolded **as His people should need the instruction therein** given. The prophecy which He uttered was twofold in its meaning: while foreshadowing the destruction of Jerusalem, it prefigured also the terrors of the last great day. *The Great Controversy*, p. 25.

A loving and merciful God does not overwhelm generation after generation with the horrors of trumpets and "terrors of the last great day," but has waited until necessary to impart such wisdom only to the last generation to whom it shall occur. It is significant that as prophecies open up in meaning, it is a signal that these events are very close to fulfillment.

4. LITERAL OR SYMBOLIC LANGUAGE IN THE TRUMPETS?

Uriah Smith treated the seven trumpets as if they were written in symbolic language. For example, the "star" or "mountain" or "sun" or "moon" was understood to be a symbol of certain men in conquest or in governmental positions. The "day," "year," "month," "hour," were treated as if symbolic and computed by the Year-day principle. This stretched the application of the trumpets over many centuries.

If these elements of time in the trumpets were treated as symbolic in a future application they would extend hundreds of years into the future. The reader needs to recognize that the context of the trumpets is not symbolic, but rather uses simile and is actually **literal language.** The strange descriptions are analogy or comparisons, not symbols. These similes use the terms **"like"** or **"as."** Therefore the reader should understand that he is reading a **literal context,** and any **time** element, such as the "five months" should be considered as **literal time.**

5. THE BIBLE FURNISHES THE TIMEFRAME: *WHEN* TRUMPETS WILL OCCUR
(The timeframe for the trumpets begins AFTER the close of probation.)

> And I saw seven angels which stood before God; and to them were given seven trumpets. And another angel came and stood at the altar, having a golden censer; and there was given unto him much incense, that he should offer it with the prayers of all saints upon the golden altar which was before the throne. And the smoke of the incense, which came with the prayers of the saints, ascended up before God out of the angel's hand. And the angel took the censer, and filled it with fire of the altar, and cast it into the earth: and there were voices, and thunderings, and lightnings, and an earthquake. And the seven angels which had the seven trumpets prepared themselves to sound. Rev. 8:2-6.

The *Seventh-day Adventist Commentary* gives several different views as to the meaning of the above Scripture, but the following is that which has been favored by Seventh-day Adventists:

> The picture is that of the angel adding incense to the prayers of the saints as these prayers ascend to the throne of God. The scene portrayed may be understood as symbolic [sic][1] of the ministration of Christ for His people (see Rom. 8:34; I John 2:1; cf. PP 356; GC 414, 415; EW 32, 252). Christ, as intercessor, mingles His merits with the prayers of the saints, which are thereby made acceptable with God. *Seventh-day Adventist Bible Commentary,* Vol. 7, p. 787.

The Bible is well written and gives excellent introductions to its prophetic portions. It shows Christ in the Most Holy Place interceding, but then reveals a change of great importance.

Continuing:

> And the angel took the censer, and filled it with fire. . . . Rev. 8:5.
> . . . A change suddenly comes in the scene of intercession. Once more the angel fills his censer with coals of fire, but adds no incense. [but] **Cast it into the earth** . . . Rev. 8:5.
> The meaning of this act is significant for the understanding of what follows as the trumpets are blown . . . According to the view that Seventh-day Adventists have favored, the cessation of the angel's ministry at the altar of incense is symbolic [sic] of the END OF THE MINISTRATION OF CHRIST FOR MANKIND—*the close of probation. Seventh-day Adventist Bible Commentary,* Vol. 7, p. 787

---

[1] The word "symbolic" is ill chosen. A better word would be "descriptive." The angel and the scene are not "symbolic" but simply **describe** Christ at work. The term "angel" is applied to Christ in a number of places of Scripture.

When the Bible is permitted to be its own expositor, it provides the *timeframe* for the seven trumpets. That timeframe must be viewed in **CONTEXT** and not removed from the verses before and after it. The timeframe is "sandwiched" in between trumpet verses as follows:

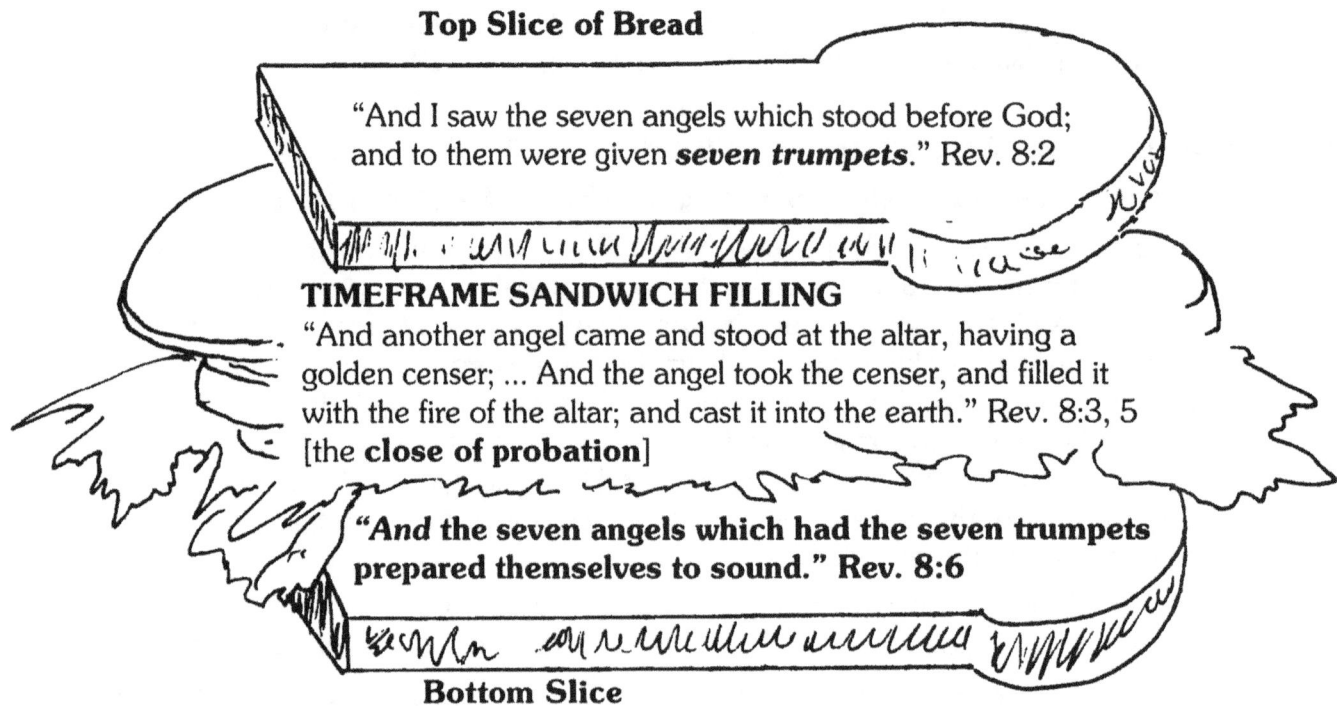

Top Slice of Bread

"And I saw the seven angels which stood before God; and to them were given *seven trumpets*." Rev. 8:2

TIMEFRAME SANDWICH FILLING

"And another angel came and stood at the altar, having a golden censer; ... And the angel took the censer, and filled it with the fire of the altar; and cast it into the earth." Rev. 8:3, 5 [the **close of probation**]

"And the seven angels which had the seven trumpets prepared themselves to sound." Rev. 8:6

Bottom Slice

The timeframe which describes the close of probation is inserted between the two introductory verses to the trumpets. The trumpet angels cannot even **"prepare"** or get ready to sound until probation has closed. Verse 8 begins with the word, "And," which assures us that this is part and parcel of the same picture. Beware of manmade arguments which would lift this timeframe out of context and confuse the timing.

The **BIBLE** supplies the timeframe of the trumpets. Ellen G. White supplies the timeframe for the plagues. They are the same! They both follow the close of probation.

THE TRUMPETS *AFTER THE CLOSE OF PROBATION*	THE PLAGUES *AFTER THE CLOSE OF PROBATION*,
I saw . . . An angel . . . reported to Jesus that his work was done, and the saints were numbered and sealed. Then I saw Jesus, who had been ministering before the ark containing the ten commandments, **throw down the censer.** He raised His hands, and with a loud voice said, "It is done."	It was impossible for the plagues to be poured out while Jesus officiated in the sanctuary; but as His work there is finished . . . there is nothing to stay the wrath of God . . . *Early Writings*, p. 280.,

Not only do plagues and trumpets rest in the same timeframe: *AFTER the close of probation*, but also John, the Revelator, who saw the vision, referred to the trumpets as "plagues." He said of the sixth angel which had the trumpet, "And the rest of the men which were not killed by **these PLAGUES** . . . repented not . . ." Rev. 9:20.[1]

The fact that they "repented not" indicates that the trumpets are not given to warn men or to bring them to repentance. The time for repentance is past—probation has closed. These trumpets are used in battle, **WAR** trumpets declaring the progress of the struggle, each step as God reveals the malignity of Satan and his destruction.

Plagues and trumpets are the two parts of one great picture and they interpret each other. Plagues explain **WHAT** happens, and **WHO** the actors are; and the Trumpets explain **WHY, WHEN, WHERE (SCOPE)** of disaster, and **HOW** (the cause and effect) the action is carried on. Only as we look at them in this way, will the picture become clear.

6. THE FIRST TRUMPET

> And the first angel sounded, and there followed hail and fire mingled with blood, and they were cast upon the earth: and the third part of trees was burnt up, and all green grass was burnt up." Rev. 8:7.

"Hail and fire."

A plague of hail and fire fell on Egypt. It affected the green herbs and trees. The "fire" is described as "lightning which ran along upon the ground."

> . . . and the Lord sent thunder and hail, and the fire ran along upon the ground; and the Lord rained hail upon the land of Egypt. So there was hail, and fire mingled with hail, very grievous . . . And the hail smote every herb of the field, and brake every tree of the field. . . . And the flax and the barley was smitten . . . Ex. 9:23, 25, 31.

Pharaoh requested that the first six plagues be taken away, but not until this plague of "fire and hail," was he caused to say . . . "I will let you go, and ye shall stay no longer." Ex. 9:28.

"Hail and fire mingled with *blood*."

The first plague does not mention "Hail and fire," nor blood. It mentions only "sores." However, it is generally understood that "sores" erupt from an infected *blood* stream.

Just as Satan brought the boils on Job, affecting his body, and also brought "fire from heaven" destroying his property, Satan will bring again the sores, destructive hail and fire.

7. THE SECOND TRUMPET

> And the second angel sounded . . . as it were a great mountain burning with fire was cast [up] into the sea:[2] and the third part of the sea became blood; and the third part of the creatures which were in the sea; and had life, died; and the third part of the ships were destroyed. Rev. 8:8, 9.

---

1 Refer to the charts on the structure and alignment of Revelation for the timeframe of the trumpets. See p. 168.

2 "***Cast*** into the sea." Some believe this disaster comes from outer space, while others see it as volcanic action. The source of the disaster is not clear in the text. But mountains do not fall from the sky. Mountains rise up and out of the earth or sea. Geophysicists are alarmed at the growing pressure under the earth's crust. They predict "an outburst . . . surpassing all recorded eruptions thus far." See U.S. Government Bulletins on volcanic activities. See *National Geographic*, Jan. 1973, "Our Changing Earth."

The second trumpet explains what causes the second plague. Literal language brings to view in the second trumpet, a volcanic eruption—"a great mountain burning with fire cast [up] into the sea"—ocean.[1] (Volcanoes come from **under** the waters).

WHERE (scope)

> And the ***third*** part of the creatures which were in the sea, and had life, died; and the ***third*** part of the ships were destroyed. Rev. 8:9.

There are three great oceans: Atlantic, Pacific, and Indian. If a great volcanic eruption were to occur in one of these it would affect **all** of the sea creatures and ships in **one** of the three oceans. Volcanic eruptions cast out poisonous fumes and gases, burning lava and cause great destruction.

Both the second plague and second trumpet declare that the sea became as blood. In the second plague it says that "every soul in the sea died," but the trumpet makes it plain that it affects a third part, or one of the three oceans. It may be that the word, "all," referred to in the second plague, means "all" in the one ocean affected. The trumpets furnish more detail. The plagues take only one chapter in Revelation, but the trumpets take up two long chapters and reveal many additional facts.

8. THE THIRD TRUMPET

> And the third angel sounded, and there fell a **great star** from heaven, burning as it were a lamp, and it fell upon the third part of the rivers, and upon the fountains of waters; And the name of the star is called Wormwood . . . and many men died of the waters, because they were made bitter. Rev. 8:10, 11.

Cause-and-effect: Whereas the third plague merely states that "the rivers and fountains of waters . . . became blood . . ." Rev. 16:4; the third trumpet explains the cause and effect. It states plainly in literal language that ". . . there fell a great star [a meteor or asteroid] burning as a lamp . . ." Rev. 8:10.

> Meteor: A transient celestial body that enters the earth's atmosphere with great velocity, incandescent with heat generated by the resistance of the air. *Webster's Dictionary*.

An endtime application will not bear a "symbolic" meaning. The time periods would extend too far into the future. A consistent literal context demands that the third trumpet be recognized as simply a **"great star"** or burning celestial body. If large enough, such an impact could create noxious debris sufficient to contaminate fresh water sources.

The result is that "many men died." In regard to the plagues, the prophetess has indicated that the first three plagues are not universal or all the inhabitants of the earth would be cut off.

9. THE FOURTH TRUMPET

> And the fourth angel sounded, and the third part of the sun was smitten, and the third part of the moon, and the third part of the stars . . . Rev. 8:12.

Cause-and-effect: The fourth plague simply states that "power was given unto him [the sun] to scorch men with fire. And men were scorched with great heat." Rev. 16:8, 9. It tells **WHAT** happens, but does not tell **WHY or HOW**. The trumpet gives added detail and says that these heavenly bodies are "***smitten***."

Satan is the "prince of the power of the air," bringing storms and devastation. What would he do with the heavenly bodies, if he were given opportunity? Perhaps the restraints will be withdrawn so that it will be demonstrated what he would do to heavenly bodies when permitted. Whether the sun and moon are actually "smitten" by a passing celestial body, or malfunction, or whether such a disaster will affect the atmosphere so that they become invisible for a period of time is in question. The "stars" may refer to the planets of our solar system. Space exploration would indicate that these are not inhabited with life as we know it here. Perhaps they will also be used as part of the great demonstration to reveal what Satan would do to heavenly bodies if given opportunity.

10. TRUMPETS AND PLAGUES RETAIN SEQUENTIAL NUMERICAL ORDER BUT NOT COMPLETE NUMERICAL ALIGNMENT.

The fourth trumpet aligns with the fifth plague. In the fourth trumpet it states:

> ... and the ... sun was smitten ... so as the third part of them was **darkened,** and the day shone not for a third part of it, and the night likewise. Rev. 8:12.

The fifth plague states:

> ... upon the seat of the beast; and his kingdom was full of **darkness** ... Rev. 16:10.

Timing: The fourth trumpet indicates the specific amount of time which this darkness will take.

> ... the day shown not for a third of it [four hours]
> ... and the night likewise [four hours]. Rev. 8:12.

A third of a 12 hour day plus a third of a 12 hour night totals **eight hours.**

When God's people see this darkness, they will know where they are in the prophetic stream of time.

SEQUENCE AND ALIGNMENT OF PLAGUES AND TRUMPETS

Plagues	1	2	3	4 ↘ ↙ 5	6	7 ↘
Trumpets	1	2	3	4	5	6 ↗ 7

Note: Plagues 4 and 5 align with Trumpet 4.
      Plague 6 aligns with Trumpet 5.
      Plague 7 aligns with Trumpet 6 and 7.

CHAPTER XVIII

THE FIFTH TRUMPET

INTRODUCTION

The fifth trumpet is aligned with and supplementary to the sixth plague. They both describe the work of evil angels. The sixth plague states plainly that ". . . they are the spirits of **devils**, working miracles, which go forth unto the kings of the earth and of the whole world, to gather them to the battle . . ." (Armageddon). The sixth plague tells **WHAT is going on,** and the fifth trumpet gives additional details describing them: **HOW MANY, HOW they work, WHO their leader is,** the **METHODS they use, HOW they look and act**, and the **TIMEFRAME—HOW LONG it will take** to accomplish their objective. It refers to their work to establish the Universal Death Decree as the **FIRST WOE.**

The sixth plague introduces the main character: "the kings of the east"—JESUS and His attendants. The fifth trumpet introduces the opposing force in the battle—Satan (Apollyon, the Destroyer) and His attendants—evil angels. This plague and trumpet bring the two opposing forces into battle alignment—Armageddon. The sixth plague introduces or supplies the name of the battle, and twice in the fifth trumpet it says that they are "running to battle."

When trumpets and plagues are viewed as one picture, they interpret each other. It is necessary to practice the hermeneutic principle: **THE BIBLE IS ITS OWN EXPOSITOR.** Then the true meaning emerges: clear, logical, and complete.

1. THE FIFTH TRUMPET IS STATED AS FOLLOWS:

And the fifth angel sounded, and I saw a star fall from heaven unto the earth: and to **him** was given the key to the bottomless pit. And **he** opened the bottomless pit; and there arose a smoke out of the pit, as the smoke of a great furnace; and the sun and the air were darkened by the reason of the smoke of the pit. And there came out of the smoke locusts upon the earth: and unto them was given power, as the scorpions of the earth have power. And it was commanded them that they should not hurt the grass of the earth, neither any green thing, neither any tree; but only those men which have not the seal of God in their foreheads. And to them it was given that they should not kill them, but that they should be tormented five months: and their torment was as the torment of a scorpion, when he striketh a man. And in those days shall men seek death, and shall not find it; and shall desire to die, and death shall flee from them. And the shapes of the locusts were like unto horses prepared unto battle; and on their heads were as it were crowns like gold, and their faces were as the faces of men. And they had hair as the hair of women, and their teeth were as the teeth of lions. And they had breastplates, as it were breastplates of iron; and the sound of their wings was as the sound of chariots of many horses running to battle. And they had tails like unto scorpions, and there were stings in their tails: and their power was to hurt men five months. And they had a king over them, which is the angel of the bottomless pit, whose name in the Hebrew tongue is Abaddon, but in the Greek tongue hath his name Apollyon. One woe is past; and, behold, there come two woes more hereafter. Rev. 9:1-12.

1. THE MAIN CHARACTERS OF THE FIFTH TRUMPET

> . . . I saw a star fall from heaven unto earth: and to **HIM** was given the key . . . Rev. 9:1.[1]

There is a difference between the "star" of the fifth trumpet and the "star" of the third trumpet. The "star" of the third trumpet is designated as "it" (Rev. 8:10); but this "star" of the fifth trumpet is identified by the pronoun **"HIM,"** obviously referring to a person. Permitting the Bible to be its own expositor, it makes very clear who this "star" is; who it was who "fell from heaven" unto the earth:

> And the great dragon was cast out, that old serpent, called the Devil, and **Satan . . . he was cast out into the earth,** and his angels were cast out with him . . . And his tail drew the third part of the stars of heaven . . . Rev. 12:9, 4.

Jesus also said, ". . . I beheld Satan as lightning **fall from heaven.**" Luke 10:18.

This "star" is a metaphor, rather than a symbol.

> Metaphor . . . a figure of speech in which a word . . . or phrase literally denoting one kind of object or idea is used in place of another to suggest a likeness or analogy between them. [Example: movie star, or one who shines brighter than his fellows . . .] *Webster's Dictionary.*

Satan, this "fallen star," is also mentioned in Isa. 14:12.

> How art thou **fallen from heaven,** O Lucifer . . . Isa. 14:12.

2. SATAN — APOLLYON — ABADDON — THE DESTROYER

> . . . a king . . . the angel of the bottomless pit, whose name in the Hebrew tongue is Abaddon, but in the Greek tongue hath his name Apollyon. Rev. 9:11. (Marginal Ref. DESTROYER).

Whereas Jehovah is the God of life and creation, Satan is known as the destroyer! Hinduism refers to Satan as "Shiva"—of the Hindu triad, representing the principle of **destruction.** See *Webster's Dictionary.*

The rationale of the plagues and trumpets, as brought forth in the introduction to this book, is that God is putting on a demonstration to give opportunity for the entire universe to see the

---

[1] Note: Much of the fifth trumpet is that of **analogy** or **comparisons, *NOT SYMBOLISM.*** For example, much of the description uses these analogous phrases: "were *like* unto," or "*as it were,*" their "faces *were as,*" "hair *as* the hair of," "teeth were *as* the teeth of," "*as it were* breastplates," "wings *as* the sound of," etc.. This is **descriptive metaphor, *not prophetic symbolism*. Therefore any time period in this passage should be treated as LITERAL TIME, specifically the *"five months"* twice mentioned.**

destructive work of Satan, when God's restraining power is removed. The fifth trumpet is a vivid description of Satan and his host of evil angels, who work under his direction; gathering the kings of the earth to the battle of Armageddon—to legislate the Universal Death Decree.

3. HOW? WITH A "KEY"

> . . . and to him [Satan] was given **the key of the bottomless pit**. And he opened the bottomless pit . . . and unto them [his evil angels] was given power . . ." Rev. 9:1-3.

This passage is best understood when interpreted by Rev. 20. If permitted, the Bible gives excellent understanding of the action of this fifth trumpet.

> And I saw an angel come down from heaven, **having the key of the bottomless pit** and a great chain in his hand. And he laid hold on the dragon, that old serpent, which is the Devil, and Satan, and bound him a thousand years, And cast him into the bottomless pit, and shut him up . . . that he should deceive the nations no more, till the thousand years should be fulfilled: and after that he must be loosed a little season. Rev. 20:1-3.

In Revelation 20 it is plain that Satan cannot work and deceive during the 1000 years, and during that time **he** is locked up in the "bottomless pit," and by a "chain of circumstances," restrained from doing his work. In the fifth plague just the **opposite** takes place. He is "given the key to the bottomless pit" and therefore has full permission to work. **The restraint is taken away in the fifth trumpet**.

A **"KEY," to the bottomless pit** can do two things. It can lock up and it can unlock! In Revelation 20 Satan is locked up; but in the fifth trumpet he is given the key and unlocks the hold of evil angels, and sends them on their way to do his work.

4. WHAT IS THE "BOTTOMLESS PIT"?

> Greek, phrear tes abussou, "pit of the bottomless [place] . . . well of the abyss." *Seventh-day Adventist Bible Commentary*, Vol 7, p. 790.

This term "bottomless pit," is used several places in Scripture (Gen. 1:2 and Rev. 20:1) to refer to a place of **darkness** and disorder. In Rev. 20 it refers to a place which shall be the abode of Satan and the evil angels for 1000 years. It is similar to the following verses:

> For if God spared not the angels that sinned, but cast them down to hell [tartarus], and delivered them into **chains of darkness**, to be reserved unto judgment . . . II Pet. 2:4.

> And the angels which kept not their first estate, but left their own habitation, he hath reserved in **everlasting chains** under **darkness** unto the judgment of the great day. Jude 6.

Therefore it would appear that the "habitation" of evil angels is that of darkness and disorder or the "abyss"—the "bottomless pit." In the 5th trumpet Satan is given the key to the "bottomless pit." He can release or let out the evil angels, which were previously restrained by God, to come out upon the earth to do their destructive work.

What is the **KEY** to the "bottomless pit"?

In Revelation 20 a picture is given which is just the reverse of that in the 5th trumpet. In Chapter 20 the "key" locks up or binds Satan so that he and his evil angels cannot work at all.

> And I saw an angel come down from heaven, having the key of the bottomless pit and a great chain in his hand. And he laid hold on the dragon, that old serpent, which is the Devil, and Satan, And bound him a thousand years, and cast him into the bottomless pit, and **shut him up** . . . Rev. 20:1-3.

In the fifth trumpet, the action is just the opposite. The "key" to the bottomless pit is given to Satan, for a period of *five months* (Rev. 9:5). Satan is permitted to open—open wide—the habitation of evil angels to release them to work without restraint. Whereas in Revelation 20, Satan cannot work at all, in the 5th trumpet he is given the key to work without restraint! No wonder it is called a "WOE." Rev. 9:12.

When the Bible is permitted to be its own expositor, letting Revelation 20 interpret Revelation 9 a clear picture emerges! Not until probation closes and restraint is withdrawn, is Satan given the key to work so that a "**cloud of darkness** covers the earth."

> And he opened the bottomless pit; and there arose **a smoke** out of the pit, as the **smoke** of a great furnace; and **the sun and the air were darkened** by reason of the smoke of the pit. Rev. 9:2.

Satan, "prince of **darkness**," takes key in hand, and opens the "pit," which is the hold of evil spirits, "reserved in everlasting chains of darkness." And they come forth, in mass, as "a smoke—[black, belching smoke of a great furnace],"—billowing out until the "sun and air are darkened by reason of the smoke of the pit." The next verse begins to describe these demons as they work:

> And there came out of the smoke locusts upon the earth . . . Rev. 9:3.[1]

5. LOCUSTS

In the sixth plague, these "unclean spirits" are likened to frogs, for their croaking, penetrating voices, agitating ". . . out of the mouth of the dragon . . . the beast . . . and the false prophet. For they are the spirits of devils, working miracles, which go forth unto the kings of the earth and of the whole world, to gather them to the battle:" Rev. 16:13, 14. These spirits of devils are likened to frogs because of their voices. In the fifth trumpet, these devils are likened to locusts, and by the term "swarm" describes their coordinated activity, and large numbers.

> And it was commanded them that they should not hurt the grass of the earth, neither any green thing, neither any tree . . . Rev. 9:4.

This trumpet is not like the first which destroyed nature. It is different. It is aggression against the people of God. If Satan could not destroy them by hail and fire, by contaminated water supplies and other natural forces, he turns to a different technique. He determines to work through the kings of the earth to set up, through legislation, a Universal Death Decree. Although these evil spirits are

---

[1] Note: Out on the prairies, the pioneers would see a "cloud" on yon horizon, which gradually appeared to blot out the sun; but as it came closer it was recognized to be a swarm of locusts, which would light upon the earth. The whirring of their wings and the crunching of their jaws proceeded night and day until every blade and leaf was gone. Women beat their dishpans, but there was no way to turn them back nor prevent them. Destruction followed their path.

permitted full freedom to work upon the kings and inhabitants of the earth; they are not allowed to touch the people of God.

> And it was commanded them that they should not hurt, but only those men which have not the seal of God in their foreheads. Rev. 9:3, 10.

> . . . and unto them [the devils likened to locusts], was given power, as the scorpions of the earth have power. . . . And they had tails like unto scorpions, and there were stings in their tails . . . Rev. 9:3, 10.

Those who have dabbled in spiritism have confessed that when brought well under the power of evil spirits, their lives have been that of torment. Not infrequently they have complained that they and their children have been pinched, choked, or clawed by evil spirits. Sleepless nights and haunted terror beset them. These evil demons go forth, to draw the world together to battle against the people of God. They are determined to set up united efforts to establish and carry out a Universal Death Decree. These evil spirits will not refrain from physical torture. "They had tails like unto scorpions, and there were stings in their tails." Any who would draw back or resist them will find themselves in utmost agony. Only those who have the Seal of God will escape.

> There shall no evil befall thee,
> neither shall any **plague** come nigh thy dwelling.
> For he shall give his angels charge over thee,
> to keep thee in all thy ways. Psalm 91:10, 11.

6. THE TIMEFRAME OF THE GATHERING ACTION

> And to them it was given that they should not kill them, but that they should be tormented *five months*: and their torment was as the torment of a scorpion, when he striketh a man . . . And they had tails like unto scorpions,[1] and there were stings in their tails: and their power was to hurt men *five months*. Rev. 9:5, 10.

After the first five plagues have fallen, the wicked will be ready to look for the cause of these judgments which have fallen on the earth. It may take several months for these first plagues to fall. Then under the sixth plague (fifth trumpet), for five months, these evil spirits will work to gather the kings of the earth together to enact the Universal Death Decree.

7. FIVE MONTHS[2]

Of *symbolic* "Babylon" it says "her plagues shall come in one [symbolic] day," or **ONE LITERAL YEAR**. Rev. 18:8. The gathering to the battle, or "running to battle," will take **FIVE MONTHS**. Rev. 9:5, 10. The "ten kings" of Revelation 17:12, 13 "reign" with the beast in setting up the

---

1. 1. "Scorpions . . . arachnids having an elongated body and a narrow segmented tail bearing a venomous sting at the tip. 2. A scourge probably studded with metal. 3. Something that incites to action like the sting of an insect." *Webster's Dictionary*.

2. Revelation is written in both literal and symbolic language. The reader needs to be conscious of changes from one to the other. For example, Revelation 16 is written in literal language until verse 12, describing literal plagues. In verse 12 it switches over to symbolic figures. Revelation 18 is symbolic with symbolic Babylon as its central figure, and the time mentioned there is symbolic time. Revelation 8 and 9 use literal language with similes and metaphors and therefore use literal time. When linking these chapters together, the symbolic sections which mention time must be translated, using the Year-day Principle, into literal time and linked with the literal passages which mention literal time.

Universal Death Decree for "one hour," or **FIFTEEN LITERAL DAYS**. After the "Voice of God" delivers God's people, the "Fall of Babylon" occurs in "one hour" or **FIFTEEN LITERAL DAYS**. The two "one hour," or fifteen day periods, total **30 days**. The five months gathering to battle total 150 days. Thirty days plus 150 days total 180 days, or half a year (six months), for plagues 6 and 7.

If the seven plagues total one **YEAR,** and plagues 6 and 7 total six months; then it is clear that the first five plagues take the first six months to occur. Prophecy is intended to give God's people light so that they will recognize these events and know exactly where they are in the stream of time.

". . . her plagues [shall] come in one day [***ONE YEAR***]" Rev. 18:8			
180 days	(5 months) 150 days	15 days	15 days,
Plagues 1-5	Plague 6	Reign of kings	Fall of Babylon,
TOTALS ONE 360 PROPHETIC DAY-YEAR			

. . . to human sight it will appear that the people of God must soon seal their testimony with their blood as did the martyrs before them. They themselves begin to fear that the Lord has left them to fall by the hand of their enemies. It is a time of fearful agony. Day and night they cry unto God for deliverance. . . . Paleness sits upon every face. Yet they cease not their earnest intercession. . . . The very delay, so painful to them, is the best answer to their petitions. As they endeavor to wait trustingly for the Lord to work they are led to exercise faith, hope, and patience, which have been too little exercised during their religious experience. Yet for the elect's sake the *time of trouble [not the timeline] will be shortened*. The Great Controversy, p. 630, 631.

It may not be wise to speculate on a "time schedule" for each plague, but enough is given, so that the people of God, can watch with knowledgeable hope as these events transpire. They can watch along the sequence and have hope, as does the traveler in following a road map, that the destination is sure.

Prophecy of future events is given because it is necessary that the people of God may have their bearings in times of stress. The loving Father has given these prophecies that the people of God may walk in the light of Scriptures even in the darkest hour. Let us thank God for loving care.

Can the wicked escape torment by suicide?

> And in those days shall men seek death, and shall not find it; and shall desire to die, and death shall flee from them. Rev. 9:6.

8. RUNNING TO BATTLE

For what purpose do the evil spirits torment men?

> And the shapes of the locusts were like unto horses **prepared unto battle** . . . and the sound of their wings was as the sound of chariots of many horses **running to battle**. Rev. 9:7, 9.

They are assuredly running to battle—". . . the battle of the great day of God Almighty . . ." "into a place called . . . Armageddon." Rev. 16:14, 16. The purpose of evil spirits in tormenting men is to force them into unity to legislate a Universal Death Decree. Plague 6 and Trumpet 5 describe this gathering action.

> And I saw the beast, and the kings of the earth, and their armies, gathered together to make war against him that sat on the horse, and against his army. Rev. 19:19.

In what other ways are these wicked demons described as they work to gather the kings of the earth and the whole world to battle against the people of God through a death decree?

1. On their heads were as it were crowns like gold[1] Rev. 9:7
2. And their faces were as the faces of men Rev. 9:7
3. And they had hair as the hair of women Rev. 9:8
4. Their teeth were as the teeth of lions Rev. 9:8
5. They had breastplates, . . . of iron Rev. 9:9

What do these descriptions or likenesses tell regarding the manner in which these demons shall work?

8.1   . . . *and on their heads were as it were crowns like gold* . . . Rev. 9:7.

The demons are portrayed with "crowns of gold," for "they are the spirits of devils . . . which go forth unto **the kings** of the earth," (Rev. 16:14). Their mission is that which deals with leadership and heads of governments.

8.2   . . . *and their faces were as the faces of men.* Rev. 9:7.

It is self-evident that these creatures are not actually men. Their faces simply appear "*as* the faces of men." Do these evil spirits assume the bodies and faces of men?

> What shall I do then with Jesus which is called Christ? Pilate asked. Again the surging multitude roared like demons. Demons themselves, **in human form**, were in the crowd. *Desire of Ages*, p. 733.

Demons, in human form, can appear "as the faces of men" in assemblies and councils, to urge for a death decree against the people of God, as they urged it against Christ in Pilate's judgment hall.

8.3   **And they had hair as the hair of women** . . . Rev. 9:8.

A woman's hair is a symbol of her "glory," or beauty.

> But if a woman have long hair, it is a glory [beauty] to her . . . I Cor. 11:15.

The evil spirits who appear as human forms will come with beauty and charm.

> The spirits of devils will go forth to the kings of the earth and to the whole world, to fasten them in deception, and urge them on to unite with Satan in his last struggle against the government of heaven. By these agencies, rulers and subjects will be alike deceived. . . . As the crowning act in the great drama of deception, Satan himself will personate Christ. . . . In different parts of the earth, Satan will manifest himself

---

1   Similes: a figure of speech [a comparison] . . . using as or like . . . *Webster's Dictionary*

among men as a majestic being of dazzling brightness, resembling the description of the Son of God given by John in the Revelation. The **glory** that surrounds him is unsurpassed by anything that mortal eyes have yet beheld. The shout of triumph rings out upon the air: "Christ has come! Christ has come! "The people prostrate themselves in adoration before him, while he lifts up his hands and pronounces a blessing upon them . . . His voice is soft and subdued, yet full of melody. . . . This is the strong, almost overmastering delusion. *The Great Controversy*, p. 624.

Satan and his evil spirits will assume a glory, showing miracles, signs and wonders that will bring the world in religious fervor to a point of fanatical determination to remove all opposition.

8.4 *. . . and their teeth were as the teeth of lions.* Rev. 9:8. (". . . and the heads of the horses were as **the heads of lions . . .** " Rev. 9:17).

Previously in verse 7, it declares that their "faces" were as those of men. Yet there is also the likeness to a "lion." There is a remarkable likeness between the face of a lion and that of a man. The "teeth" of a lion represent his cruelty and power over his prey. Despite the glory and beauty, there is a cruelty which is displayed by demons, portrayed in "lion's teeth."

8.5 **And they had breastplates, as it were the breastplates of iron** . . . Rev. 9:9

Breastplate: 1. A plate of metal covering the breast as defensive armor. *Webster's Dictionary*.

The significance of a breastplate is that it is worn **to battle**. The statement that it is of "iron," shows that these evil spirits have purpose and relentless urgency.

CHAPTER XIX

THE SIXTH TRUMPET

And the sixth angel sounded, and I heard a voice from the four horns of the golden altar which is before God, Saying to the sixth angel which had the trumpet, Loose the four angels which are bound in the great river Euphrates. And the four angels were loosed, which were prepared for an hour, and a day, and a month, and a year, for to slay the third part of men. And the number of the army of horsemen were two hundred thousand thousand: and I heard the number of them. And thus I saw the horses in the vision, and them that sat on them, having breastplates of fire, and of jacinth, and brimstone: and the heads of the horses were as the heads of lions; and out of their mouths issued fire and smoke and brimstone. By these three was the third part of men killed, by the fire, and by the smoke, and by the brimstone, which issued out of their mouths. For their power is in their mouth and in their tails: for their tails were like unto serpents, and had heads, and with them they do hurt. And the rest of the men which were not killed by these plagues yet repented not of the works of their hands, that they should not worship devils, and idols of gold, and silver, and brass, and stone, and of wood: which neither can see, nor hear, nor talk: Neither repented they of their murders, nor of their sorceries, nor of their fornication, nor of their thefts. Rev. 9:13-21.

1. WHEN: THE TIMEFRAME—"THE VOICE OF GOD"

> And the sixth angel sounded, and I heard **A VOICE** from the four horns of the golden altar which is before God . . . Rev. 9:13.

The fifth trumpet describes evil angels as they gather the kings of all nations together to legislate a Universal Death Decree. This confrontation between the wicked and the people of God is known as the **"BATTLE** of Armageddon." Just as the Universal Death Decree is to go into effect, the people of God are delivered by the **Voice of God. This Voice begins** the 7th plague and **the 6th Trumpet.** A chart of the Plagues and Trumpets, as they interpret each other is supplied at the end of this section on the Trumpets. See p. 155.

> And the sixth angel sounded, and I heard a voice from the four horns of the golden altar which is before God . . . Rev. 9:13.

In the seventh plague the Voice of God comes "out of the temple." Here in the sixth trumpet, the Voice of God comes out from a specific place in the temple (greater detail) from the golden altar. When the Voice of God declares, "It is done" the persecutions of His people are finished. As in the typical service in the earthly sanctuary, the priest came out to lay the burden of guilt on Satan (the Azazel goat), and to bless His people; so the Voice declares the "blessing" on His congregation—His people, and a curse upon the wicked. The Voice of God (Rev. 16:17) was understood to say, "It is done," to declare the day and hour of the coming of Jesus, to identify the people of God, to reiterate the covenant, and to glorify the righteous. At this point, their captivity was turned.

2. WHERE: THE SETTING—SPIRITUAL BABYLON

The curse upon the wicked is stated as follows:

> . . . a voice . . . Saying to the sixth angel which had the trumpet, **Loose the four angels which are bound in the great river Euphrates**. Rev. 9:13, 14.

The Euphrates river ran through Babylon. Literal Babylon is long gone. This is spiritual Babylon or apostate religion; all the false religions of the earth. In the 7th plague it states that after the Voice of God then:

> . . . the great city [Babylon] was divided into three parts . . . and great Babylon came in remembrance before God, to give unto her the cup of the wine of the fierceness of His wrath." Rev. 16:19.

What do the four angels represent which let loose the destructive winds? They are "bound" or **RESTRAINED** in the great symbolic "RIVER" which represents the Holy Spirit or its various works, one of which is restraint. The Holy Spirit up to this point, has not unleashed these four angels. In the sixth trumpet they are permitted to let go!

These destructive agencies have been held back all through the reign of sin and they are pictured as letting go by degrees; but under the sixth trumpet they are to be unleashed, as follows:

> The **RESTRAINING** Spirit of God is even now being withdrawn from the world. Hurricanes, storms, tempests, fire and flood, disasters by sea and land, follow each other in quick succession . . . Men cannot discern the sentinel angels **RESTRAINING** the four winds that they shall not blow until the servants of God are sealed; but when God shall bid His angels loose the winds, there will be such a scene of strife as no pen can picture. *Testimonies*, Vol. 6, p. 408.

Calamities are increasing in number and intensity, reaching a crescendo in the final fall of Babylon.

3. THE ACTION: LOOSING THE FOUR ANGELS

> And the four angels were loosed, which were prepared for an hour, and a day, and a month, and a year . . . Rev. 9:15.

The time mentioned, "an hour, and a day, and a month, and a year," is not a timeline to be added up. It refers to a particular point in time—a specific date. The Greek words indicate that this is a date appointed beforehand. The idea to be found here is that God already knows this date and it is set for a certain time so that the very hour, the very day, the very month and the very year is an "appointed time." (See the original text, p. 262)

Thousands of people have been misled by this verse by regarding it as symbolic time. Instead of recognizing this prophecy as a pre-set date or point in time, it was computed by the year-day principle.

The King James Version is not as clear on this text as many others quoted as follows: Rev. 9:15

And the four angels were loosed, which were prepared for an hour, and a day, and a month, and a year, for to slay the third part of men.   KJV

They (the four angels of destruction) had been kept in readiness for *that* year, and month and day and hour, and *now* they were turned loose to kill a third of all mankind. The Living Bible, Tyndale House, Wheaton, Ill. 1967

So the four angels were released, who had been held ready for *the* hour, *the* day, *the* month, and *the* year, to kill a third of mankind. Revised Standard Version, Thomas, Nelson, and Sons, N.Y. 1946

So the four angels were let loose, to kill a third of mankind. ***They had been held ready for this moment, for this very year and month, and day and hour.*** New English Bible, Oxford University Press 1961

. . . four angels who were waiting for *the* year, *the* month, *the* day, *the* hour, when they were to destroy a third part of mankind. Mrg. Ronald K. Knox. Burns, Oates, & Washbourne Ltd. Publisher of the Holy See. 1948

. . . the four angels were ***kept in readiness for that*** hour and day and month and year . . . were turned loose to kill one-third of mankind. Williams Bible, Concordia Publishing House, St. Louis, Mo. 1963

4. WHERE: scope

The sixth plague begins the drama described by **THIRDS or THREE**.

> And I saw **THREE** unclean spirits like frogs come out of the mouth of the **DRAGON,** and out of the mouth of the **BEAST, and out of the mouth of the FALSE PROPHET**. Rev. 16:13.

These three are: Spiritism, the Papacy, and Apostate Protestantism. They unify to enact the Universal Death Decree. When the Voice of God is heard under the seventh plague, the people of God are identified and the wicked recognize that false religion has been the cause of their downfall. At that point these three fall apart.

> And the great city [Babylon] was divided into **THREE PARTS** . . . Rev. 16:19.

The sixth plague also specifies that "the cities of the nations fell" indicating some horrendous disaster that is described in the sixth trumpet, which causes the cities to fall and a third part of men to die.

> . . . the four angels were loosed . . . for to slay a **THIRD** part of men. Rev. 9:15.

When the Bible is permitted to be its own expositor, and the plagues and trumpets allowed to interpret each other, then the picture becomes unified and understandable.

Someone will "push the button" on nuclear stockpiles and great destruction will occur, to slay a third part of men.

5. HOW: DETAILS OF THE BATTLE ALIGNMENT

> And the number of the army of the horsemen were two hundred thousand thousand: and **I HEARD THE NUMBER OF THEM**. Rev. 9:16.

The prophet distinctly heard the number of the wicked: 200 million. He also distinctly heard the number of the people of God.

> And **I HEARD THE NUMBER OF THEM WHICH WERE SEALED:** and there were sealed an hundred and forty and four thousand . . . Rev. 7:4.

As in ages past, so often the people of God have been outnumbered and defenseless. But when they cried to their God, He turned the battle to victory by causing the enemy to turn upon themselves.

> . . . for the Lord hath delivered them into the hand of Israel . . . And there was trembling in the host, in the field, and among all the people . . . a very great trembling. . . . and, behold, the multitude melted away, and they went on beating down one another. . . . every man's sword was against his fellow, and there was a very great discomfiture. I Sam. 14:12, 15, 16, 20.

When confronted by the Universal Death Decree, God's people cry "day and night for deliverance." Then the Voice of God will deliver them. The wicked then turn upon each other and the battle will be fought among the wicked destroying each other. This is described as **"THE FALL OF BABYLON"** (which follows immediately after the Voice of God).

> When the voice of God turns the captivity of His people, there is a terrible awakening of those who have lost all in the great conflict of life. . . . The people see that they have been deluded. They accuse one another of having led them to destruction . . . The multitudes are filled with fury. "We are lost!" they cry, "and you are the cause of our ruin;" and they turn upon the false shepherds. . . . Everywhere there is strife and bloodshed.
>
> "A noise shall come even to the ends of the earth; for the Lord hath a controversy with the nations, He will plead with all flesh; He will give them that are wicked to the sword." . . . The mark of deliverance has been set upon those "that sigh and that cry for all the abominations that be done." Now the angel of death goes forth, represented in Ezekiel's vision by the men with the slaughtering weapons, to whom the command is given: "Slay utterly old and young, both maids, and little children, and women: but come not near any man upon whom is the mark [seal of God]; and begin at My sanctuary." . . . "And this shall be the **PLAGUE** [or corresponding trumpet] wherewith the Lord will smite all the people that have fought against Jerusalem; Their flesh shall consume away while they stand upon their feet, and their eyes shall consume away in their holes, and their tongue shall consume away in their mouth. And it shall come to pass in that day, that a great tumult from the Lord shall be among them; and they shall lay hold every one on the hand of his neighbor" . . . In the mad strife of their own fierce passions, and by the awful outpouring of God's unmingled wrath [giving them up or over to the master they have chosen], fall the wicked inhabitants of the earth . . . *Great Controversy*, p. 654-657.

When Satan sees that he cannot touch the people of God and that they have been delivered and glorified, his pent-up rage and hatred against the human race will be demonstrated in his destruction of the wicked, as he turns on those who have sided with him. The last verses of the sixth trumpet describe the destruction of the wicked and it is referred to in Revelation 18 as the "Fall of Babylon."

> ... I will show thee the judgment of the great whore ... With whom the kings of the earth ... and the inhabitants of the earth have been made drunk ... And the ten horns which thou sawest upon the beast, these shall hate the whore, and shall make her desolate and naked, and shall eat her flesh, and burn her with fire. Rev. 17:1, 2, 16.

6. HEADS AND TAILS: CAUSE-AND-EFFECT

> For their power is in their **MOUTH**, and in their **TAILS**; for their tails were like unto serpents, and had heads, and with them they do hurt. Rev. 9:19.

This strange verse challenges the prophetic expositor! Shall he fall prey to the temptation of "private interpretation" forbidden in II Peter 1:19, 20. Shall he conjecture or assume that this is a description of some implement of war? What does the Bible say? What is the context? Is the Bible to be its own interpreter, "... line upon line ... here a little, and there a little ..." (Isa. 28:10) on this text of Rev. 9:19?

The Context. Rev. 9:19 is the **CONCLUDING** statement of the 6th trumpet description of a battle array in which a "third of men are killed" (Rev. 9:15-18). It is some kind of summary.

A larger context, involving Satan and his evil angels is given from Revelation, Chapters 12 through 20. Revelation refers to Satan with "heads" and "tail."

> ... behold a great red dragon, having seven **heads** ... And his **tail** drew the third part of the stars of heaven, and did cast them to the earth. ... neither was their place found any more in heaven. ... And the great dragon was cast out, that old serpent, called the Devil, and Satan, which deceiveth the whole world: he was cast out into the earth, and his angels were cast out with him. Rev. 12:3, 4, 8, 9.

It is the "head" which thinks up and initiates action. In Revelation 12 the "tail" reveals the *results* of that action—the evil angels were "cast out of heaven." Revelation 9:19 says, "their power is in their tails." The head initiates the agitating action and the result is "in their tails"—the destruction of the world. See Isa 9:15. **"HEADS" and "TAILS" reveal CAUSE AND EFFECT.**

Revelation 12 through 20 is a line of prophecy, including the seven last plagues, which correspond with the seven trumpets giving greater detail. The entire *context* must be the interpreter.

In the sixth plague (Rev. 16:13), evil spirits are likened to frogs which speak **"OUT OF THE MOUTH OF"** Spiritism, Catholicism, and Apostate Protestantism (the "dragon," "beast," and "false prophet") These agitate the kings of the earth to establish a Universal Death Decree, leading up to the battle (confrontation) of the wicked against the people of God—to the battle of Armageddon. However, the seventh plague is introduced by the **VOICE OF GOD**, which is their deliverance. Immediately after that there occurs the "Fall of Babylon"—the destruction of false ministers, bloodshed from one end of the earth to the other, and *"the cities of the nations fell."* **Rev. 16:19.** The sixth trumpet simply describes and gives more details as to **HOW** these cities fall. This destruction is described as "fire, smoke, brimstone." (Possibly nuclear warfare so long restrained by the four angels. At last the four angels holding back are released.)

Just as Satan with his "heads" (and mouth) deceived the angels of heaven and caused them to be cast out; so evil angels will deceive with their "mouth," and their "tails" or results will be to destroy and ruin. Just as a "third" of the angels were cast out of heaven, so a "third" of men will be killed. However, there are still some wicked left to see the second coming of Jesus.

7. TIMEFRAME REITERATED

The timeframe of the trumpets is so important that it is not only provided as the introduction to the trumpets (Rev. 8:3-7), but it is reiterated and reinforced at the close of the sixth trumpet. Rev. 8:3-7. Context places the beginning of the trumpets **AFTER** the close of probation—after the "censer is thrown down." Again in Rev. 9:20, 21 this concept is repeated.

> And the rest of the men which were not killed by these plagues yet **REPENTED NOT** of the works of their hands, that they should not worship devils, and idols of gold, and silver, and brass, and stone, and of wood: which neither can see, nor hear, nor walk: **NEITHER REPENTED** they of their murders, nor of their sorceries, nor of their fornication, nor of their thefts. Rev. 9:20, 21.

The trumpets **DO NOT LEAD MEN TO REPENTANCE. THEY ARE NOT WARNINGS.** They are trumpets of war—in the battle of Armageddon. They happen **AFTER** the close of probation. They reveal what evil angels will do when no longer restrained by the Spirit of God.

CHAPTER XX

THE SEVENTH TRUMPET

The seventh trumpet skips over to Revelation 11.

> The second woe is past; and, behold, the third woe cometh quickly. And the seventh angel sounded; and there were great voices in heaven, saying, The kingdoms of this world are become the kingdoms of our Lord, and of his Christ; and he shall reign for ever and ever. And the four and twenty elders, which sat before God on their seats, fell upon their faces, and worshipped God, Saying, We give thee thanks, O Lord God Almighty, which art, and wast, and art to come; because thou hast taken to thee thy great power, and hast reigned. And the nations were angry, and thy wrath is come, and the time of the dead, that they should be judged, and that thou shouldest give reward unto thy servants the prophets, and to the saints, and them that fear thy name, small and great; and shouldest destroy them which destroy the earth. And the temple of God was opened in heaven, and there was seen in his temple the ark of his testament: and there were lightnings, and voices, and thunderings, and an earthquake, and great hail. Rev. 11:14-19.

1. TIMEFRAME:

> **The second woe is past; and, behold, the third woe cometh quickly . . . the seventh angel sounded. Rev. 11:14, 15.**

The Three Woes	
The First Woe is	The Fifth Trumpet. It is the work of evil angels gathering the kings of the earth to battle with stings as scorpions.
The Second Woe is	The Sixth Trumpet. It is the destruction which occurs in the Fall of Babylon, when the cities of the nations fall, after the Voice of God
The Third Woe is	The Seventh Trumpet. It is voices in heaven which announce Heaven's Legislative Action.

2. *WHAT:* ACTION:

> **And the Seventh Angel sounded** . . . and there were great voices in heaven, saying, The kingdoms of this world are become the kingdoms of our Lord, and of his Christ; and he shall reign for ever and ever; Rev. 11:15.

The seventh plague (Rev. 16:18) mentions these voices, but does not indicate what they say. The seventh trumpet gives added detail telling exactly what they say. These voices declare in legislative action that the time has come for Christ to reign. They have viewed the destructive nature of Satan as he has destroyed planet earth and the wicked.

The plagues-trumpets have demonstrated beyond all doubt the wisdom and righteousness of God and His law. All accusations of Satan have been met and proven to be without cause. The restraints of the Holy Spirit have been justified in every situation. The "voices of doom" declare final judgment on wickedness and vindicate God the Father and Christ.

3. PROPHETIC FULFILLMENT

These voices proclaim the focal point of all prophetic Scripture. Daniel stated it as follows:

> And in the days of these kings shall the God of heaven set up a kingdom, which shall never be destroyed: and the kingdom shall not be left to other people, but it shall break in pieces and consume all these kingdoms, and it shall stand forever. . . . the dream is certain, and the interpretation thereof sure. Dan. 2:44, 45.

> But the saints of the most High shall take the kingdom, and possess the kingdom for ever, even for ever and ever. Dan. 7:18.

> . . . and he shall reign for ever and ever. Rev. 11:15

4. *WHO*

Who are the voices who declare these legislative actions?

> And the four and twenty elders, which sat before God on their seats, fell upon their faces, and worshipped God, Saying, We give thee thanks, O Lord God Almighty, which art, and wast, and art to come; because thou has taken to thee thy great power, and hast reigned. Rev. 11:16, 17.

The "four and twenty elders" are generally considered to be those who have been taken to heaven through translation and resurrection: Enoch (Gen. 5:24), Elijah (II Kings 2:11), Moses (Jude 9), and ". . . When he ascended up on high, he led captivity captive . . ." (Eph. 4:8)

These ". . . elders . . . ,"[1] now residents of heaven, are representatives of the human race. These are men who have led and loved Israel. They have witnessed the struggle of the great controversy between good and evil.

4.1 ". . . the four and twenty elders, which sat before God on their seats . . ." Rev. 11:16.

"Their **seats**" imply an official work. This is described in Daniel 7.

> I beheld till the **thrones** [seats] were cast down [placed] . . . the judgment was set, and the books were opened. Dan 7:9, 10.

The above quotation refers to the Investigative Judgment of the people of God. Time prophecy indicated that it began in 1844. Dan. 8:14. These four and twenty elders evidently sat before God, (the Ancient of Days Dan. 7:9), taking part in the Investigative Judgment. It is in the Investigative Judgment that the **legal right** to the kingdom is given to Christ, and it is in this judgment that the members of the kingdom are made up.

---

1   "Elders"—Enoch, Elijah, and Moses are now several thousand years old, thus known as "elders" or "old men."

> And there was given him dominion, and glory, and a kingdom, that all people, nations, and languages, should serve him: his dominion is an everlasting dominion, which shall not pass away, and his kingdom that which shall not be destroyed. Dan. 7:14.

These four and twenty elders have witnessed the mercy of God to His people in judgment. The four and twenty elders have seen the righteousness and justice, as well as mercy. They have seen the destructive and deceitful way of Satan and finally have viewed his destructive work in the seven last plagues. As they view the deliverance of the people of God, and see Jesus is finally on His way in the Second Coming to literally claim His own, they "fell on their faces," in utter acknowledgment of the wisdom and greatness of God in His marvelous methods of dealing with, and disposal of sin, in its full manifestation and exposure. They praise Almighty God and express gratitude that the struggle is over. Christ has displayed, at last, His mighty power and majesty. They say:

4.2 *"We give thee thanks, O Lord God Almighty, which art, and wast, and art to come, because thou hast taken to thee thy great power, and hast reigned." Rev. 11:17*

This declaration is that which announces the Second Coming of Jesus. The next verse gives the timely setting for His coming.

> And the nations were angry, and thy wrath is come, and the time of the dead, that they should be judged, and that thou shouldest give reward unto thy servants the prophets, and to the saints, and them that fear thy name, small and great; and shouldest destroy them which destroy the earth. Rev. 11:18.

5. SUMMARY

There are five distinct events which converge and give setting to the Second Coming of Jesus. They are (in point of time):

1. the nations **were** [past tense] angry
2. thy wrath **is** [present tense] come
3. the **time** of the dead, that they should be judged, which is the Investigative Judgment of the wicked during the 1000 years. See I Cor. 6:3.
4. reward unto . . . prophets . . . saints . . .
5. destroy them which destroy the earth

5.1 *". . . and the nations were angry . . ." Rev. 11:18.*

The sixth trumpet portrayed "smoke, fire and brimstone," which was understood to refer to war—ultimate worldwide destruction when the four angels let loose the winds of strife; when "the third part of men [will be] killed, by the fire, and by the smoke and by the brimstone." Rev. 9:18. The sixth plague says, ". . . the cities of the nations fell." Rev. 16:19. The seventh trumpet puts this action in the past tense, saying, ". . . The nations **were** angry . . ." Next is the coming of Jesus.

5.2 *"and thy wrath is come." Rev. 11:18*

> And the heaven departed as a scroll when it is rolled together; and every mountain and island were moved out of their places. And the kings of the earth, and the great men, and the rich men, and the chief captains, and the mighty men, and every

bondman, and every free man, hid themselves in the dens and in the rocks of the mountains; And said to the mountains and rocks, Fall on us, and hide us from the face of him that sitteth on the throne, and from **the wrath of the Lamb:** For **the great day of his wrath is come,** and who shall be able to stand? Rev. 6:14-17.

5.3 *The seventh trumpet gives the setting and the timing for the second coming of Jesus*. This event is well described in *The Great Controversy*:

> Soon there appears in the east a small black cloud, about half the size of a man's hand. It is the cloud which surrounds the Saviour and which seems in the distance to be shrouded in darkness . . . as it draws nearer the earth, becoming lighter and more glorious, until it is a great white cloud, its base a glory like consuming fire . . . Jesus rides forth as a mighty conqueror . . . No human pen can portray the scene; no mortal mind is adequate to conceive its splendor. . . . His countenance outshines the dazzling brightness of the noonday sun. . . . The King of kings descends upon the cloud, wrapped in flaming fire. *The Great Controversy*, p. 640, 641.

The consuming brightness of His Presence becomes to the wicked the "wrath of God," in that they, themselves, have rejected the necessary preparation. In their choice of evil, God has "given them over" to destruction, and they perish. To the question, "Who shall be able to stand?" Christ reassures the righteous, "My grace is sufficient for you." *The Great Controversy*, p. 641.

5.4 ". . . and the time of the dead, that they should be judged . . . " Rev. 11:18.

This statement gives, **"the time of,"** a specific judgment which is to begin. This cannot refer to the Investigative Judgment of the righteous, because that has already taken place. When Jesus comes, it is then time for the judgment of the **wicked** to begin. A description of the judgment of the wicked is given in Revelation 20.

> But the rest of the dead lived not again until the thousand years were finished. . . . And I saw the dead, small and great, stand before God; and the **books were opened** . . . they [the dead] were judged out of those things which were written in the books, . . . every man according to their works. . . . This is the second death. And whosoever was not found written in the book of life, was cast into the lake of fire. Rev. 20:5, 11-15.

During the millennium, those who have been saved will judge the wicked.

> Do ye not know that the saints shall judge the world? . . . Know ye not that we shall judge angels? how much more things that pertain to this life? I Cor. 6:2, 3.

5.5 ". . . and the time . . . that thou shouldest give reward unto thy servants the prophets, and to the saints, and them that fear thy name, small and great . . . " Rev. 11:18.**What is the reward which is given to the people of God? It is eternal life and eternal righteousness.**

> Amid the reeling of the earth, the flash of lightning, and the roar of thunder, the voice of the Son of God calls forth the sleeping saints. He looks upon the graves of the righteous, then, raising His hands to heaven, He cries: "Awake, awake, awake, ye that sleep in the dust, and arise!" Throughout the length and breadth of the earth the

dead shall hear that voice, and they that hear shall live. And the whole earth shall ring with the tread of the exceeding great army of every nation, kindred, tongue, and people. From the prison house of death they come, clothed with immortal glory, crying: "O death, where is thy sting? O grave, where is thy victory?" I Cor 15:55. And the living righteous and the risen saints unite their voices in a long, glad shout of victory . . . arise with the freshness and vigor of eternal youth. In the beginning, man was created in the likeness of God, not only in character, but in form and feature. Sin defaced and almost obliterated the divine image; but Christ came to restore that which had been lost. He will change our vile bodies and fashion them like unto His glorious body. The mortal, corruptible form, devoid of comeliness, once polluted with sin, becomes perfect, beautiful and immortal. All blemishes and deformities are left in the grave. Restored to the tree of life in the long-lost Eden, the redeemed will "grow up" (Mal. 4:2.) to the full stature of the race in its primeval glory. The last lingering traces of the curse of sin will be removed, and Christ's faithful ones will appear in "the beauty of the Lord our God," in mind and soul and body reflecting the perfect image of THEIR Lord. Oh, wonderful redemption! long talked of, long hoped for, contemplated with eager anticipation, but never fully understood.

The living righteous are changed "in a moment, in the twinkling of an eye." At the voice of God they were glorified; now they are made immortal and with the risen saints are caught up to meet their Lord in the air. Angels "gather together His elect from the four winds, from one end of heaven to the other." Little children are borne by holy angels to their mothers' arms. Friends long separated by death are united, nevermore to part, and with songs of gladness ascend together to the City of God. *The Great Controversy*, p. 644, 645.

The seventh trumpet is devoted to the Second Coming of Jesus and the resurrection of the righteous. The righteous are given their rewards: crowns, harps, victors' palms, and they inherit the kingdom "[and the time is come that thou], **shouldest destroy them which destroy the earth**." Rev. 11:18. Christ comes to destroy "them which destroy the earth." God is not the destroyer. To the contrary, God is the creator—the Life-giver—the Sustainer. It is Satan who is named "Apollyon—Destroyer."

The main focus of this study of the seven last plagues and the seven trumpets; the introduction to the "wrath of God," points toward the fact that these terrible judgments are not a destructive work of God, but rather a full manifestation of the destructive work of Satan and his followers. When Jesus comes, it is to destroy the destroyer's work of destruction, and all who identified with him.

What is wrong with sin? Sin is evil because it is destructive. Satan rebelled against the laws of God which are intended to preserve creation. Satan's rebellion, demonstrated on this planet, has proven beyond question, that war against the law of God results only in utter destruction. It is sin which ultimately destroys all that is living, creative, beautiful and delightful. See Rom 6:23.

> . . . because they have transgressed the laws, changed the ordinance, broken the everlasting covenant. Therefore hath the curse devoured the earth, and they that dwell therein are desolate: therefore the inhabitants of the earth are burned . . . Isa. 24:5, 6.

The whole earth appears like a desolate wilderness. The ruins of cities and villages destroyed by the earthquake, uprooted trees, ragged rocks thrown out by the sea or torn out of the earth itself, are scattered over its surface, while vast caverns mark the spot where the mountains have been rent from their foundations. *The Great Controversy*, p. 657; See Chapter 41, "The Desolation of the Earth."

And the temple of God was opened in heaven, and there was seen in his temple the ark of his testament: and there were lightnings, and voices, and thunderings and an earthquake, and great hail. Rev. 11:19.[1]

In contrast to those who "destroy the earth," by rebellion against the law of God; under the seventh trumpet, the law of God—the ark of his testament)—is EXALTED:

> The glory of the celestial city streams from the gates ajar. Then there appears against the sky a hand holding two tables of stone folded together. Says the prophet: "The heavens shall declare His righteousness: for God is judge Himself." That holy law, God's righteousness, that amid thunder and flame was proclaimed from Sinai as the guide of life, is now revealed to men as the rule of judgment. The hand opens the tables, and there are seen the precepts of the Decalogue, traced as with a pen of fire. The words are so plain that all can read them. . . .
>
> It is impossible to describe the horror and despair of those who have trampled upon God's holy requirements. The Lord gave them His law; they might have compared their characters with it and learned their defects while there was yet opportunity for repentance and reform; but in order to secure the favor of the world, they set aside its precepts and taught others to transgress. They have endeavored to compel God's people to profane His Sabbath. Now they are condemned by that law which they have despised. . . . Too late they see that the Sabbath of the fourth commandment is the seal of the living God. Too late they see the true nature of their spurious sabbath . . . They find that they have been fighting against God. *The Great Controversy*, p. 639, 640.

The above comment does not state how long the law of God is seen in the heavens. Whether this remains until the coming of Jesus is not clear.

5.6 ". . . and there were lightnings, and voices, and thunderings, and an earthquake" Rev. 11:19

This seventh trumpet corresponds with the seventh plague which states: "And there were voices, and thunders and lightnings; and there was a great earthquake . . ." Rev. 16:18.

. . . and there were lightnings, and voices . . . Rev. 11:19.

> Fierce lightnings leap from the heavens, enveloping the earth in a sheet of flame. Above the terrific roar of thunder, **voices**, mysterious and awful, **declare the doom of the wicked**. The words spoken are not comprehended by all; but they are distinctly understood by the false teachers. Those who a little before were so reckless, so boastful and defiant, so exultant in their cruelty to God's commandment-keeping people, are now overwhelmed with consternation and shuddering in fear. Their wails are heard above the sound of the elements. Demons acknowledge the deity of Christ and tremble before His power, while men are supplicating for mercy and groveling in abject terror. *The Great Controversy*, p. 638.

---

[1] Note: An earthquake may be assumed to be the direct judgment of God. However, it may be that man will initiate the earthquake. There have been a number of cautions given by scientists against testing of atomic devices, in the sea and on land. It is affecting the earth's crust and considered a danger to the earth itself.

These "voices" are not identified except to state that they are "mysterious and awful." Their message is "distinctly understood by the false teachers." These voices apparently bring terror even to the hearts of demons. The last event in the seventh trumpet, like that of the seventh plague, is **"the great hail."** ". . . every stone about the weight of a talent . . . for the plague thereof was exceeding great." Rev. 16:21.

A Correlation Chart which links the plagues and trumpets together, (permitting the Bible to be its own expositor), is on the following pages:

Notes

A CORRELATION

CLOSE OF PROBATION PLAGUES BEGIN. TRUMPETS BEGIN. Revelation 15:8; 8:3-5	PLAGUE 1 **Sores** from infected **BLOOD**. Revelation 16:2	PLAGUE 2 Ocean as **BLOOD** of a dead Man. Fish die. Revelation 16:3	PLAGUE 3 Fountains of **waters** as **BLOOD**. Revelation 16:4-7	PLAGUE 4 The **SUN** Scorches men with heat. Revelation 16:8, 9	PLAGUE 5 **DARKNESS** on the seat or kingdom of the beast. Revelation 16:10, 11
	TRUMPET 1 **BLOOD**, Hail, Fire. ⅓ of trees, All Grass Burned. Revelation 8:7	TRUMPET 2 Ocean Became as Blood ⅓ of Ships gone. Fish die. Revelation 8:8, 9	TRUMPET 3 Fountains and Rivers of **waters** bitter as Wormwood. Revelation 8:10	TRUMPET 4 The **SUN** and Moon, Stars Smitten. Revelation 8:12	TRUMPET 4 **DARKNESS** ⅓ day **DARK**, ⅓ night **DARK**, Revelation 8:12

"The Battle of Armageddon will be fought . . . the Captain of the Lord's host will stand at the head of the angels of heaven to direct the battle. Solemn events **before us are yet to transpire. Trumpet after trumpet is to be sounded, vial after vial** poured out one after another upon the inhabitants of the earth. Scenes of stupendous interest are right upon us"
The Seventh Day Adventist Bible Commentary, Vol. 7, p. 982
Letter 109, 1890. Ellen G. White

OF PLAGUES AND TRUMPETS

PLAGUE 6	PLAGUE 7			
EVIL SPIRITS gather all kings to legislate a Universal **DEATH DECREE.** Revelation 16:12-16	**VOICE OF GOD** deliverance from the **DEATH DECREE.** Revelation 16:17	Cities of the **nations fall.** Revelation 16:19	**Thunder and Lightning Earthquake.** Revelation 16:18	**VOICES of doom** from heaven **declaring sentence.** Hail. Revelation 16:18, 19
TRUMPET 5	**TRUMPET 6**			**TRUMPET 7**
EVIL SPIRITS as locusts "running to battle" to legislate the **DEATH DECREE** Revelation 9:1-11	**VOICE OF GOD** deliverance. Revelation 9:13; 11:12	**Nations [are] angry.** Revelation 11:18 Loose the **Four Angels. Jacinth. ⅓ killed.** Revelation 9:14-20	**Thunder and Lightning** **Earthquake** Law seen in the Sky. Revelation 11:12 G.C. 639	**VOICES of doom declaring sentence** on the wicked. Rewards **for the righteous. Hail.** Revelation 11:15-19
<u>**WOE No. 1**</u>	<u>**WOE No. 2**</u>			<u>**WOE No. 3**</u>

THE STRUCTURE OF REVELATION

PART I MAJOR LINES OF PROPHECY

The books of Daniel and Revelation contain not only "outlines," such as that of the plagues, trumpets and seals, but also what may be called **"MAJOR LINES OF PROPHECY."**

For example, in the book of Daniel there is but one **"MAJOR LINE OF PROPHECY."** It extends from 606 B.C. to the second coming of Christ. All four visions, or all four outlines repeat the historical events contained within that major line of prophecy which extends from 606 B.C. to the second coming of Christ. Each additional vision or outline adds detail.

The book of Revelation is more complicated. It consists of **TWO "MAJOR LINES OF PROPHECY."** The first extends from Revelation 1 through 11. The second extends from Revelation 12-22. Thus the book of Revelation may be divided exactly into two parts:—into two major lines of prophecy.

When these major lines of prophecy are viewed within their Bible stated timeframes, given "The Literal Approach," and viewed in an ENDTIME focus or perspective; it becomes obvious that a **"MAJOR LINE OF PROPHECY"** is a *chronological, sequential order of events.*

The following chapter on The Seven Seals will demonstrate this orderly arrangement.

The second "major line of prophecy" in Revelation extends from Revelation 12-22. Again, when viewed within the Bible stated timeframes, given "The Literal Approach," and viewed in an ENDTIME focus or perspective; it becomes obvious that all within that "Major Line of Prophecy" is also given in *chronological, sequential order* and *precise continuity.*[1]

Ellen G. White speaks of this Revelation 12-22 line of prophecy as follows:

> "The **LINE OF PROPHECY** in which these symbols are found **begins** with Revelation 12." *Great Controversy*, p. 438.

In Daniel there is **ONE** major line of prophecy—606 B.C. to the second coming. In Revelation there are two: the first, which is found in Rev. 1-11, covers history from the organization of the Christian Church to the Second Coming. The second spans a longer time: from Lucifer's rebellion in heaven to the restoration of all things in the New Earth. So there are just three major lines of prophecy in these two books. But the three lines all cover overlapping spans of history and are therefore related.

It is for this reason that we are counseled to study the books of Daniel and Revelation together.

RESULTS

When the Bible is permitted to be its own expositor, when the symbols are interpreted (decoded) by the Bible itself, when one timeline is aligned with another so that they are "locked" into correct historical applications; and when one timeline is permitted to interpret another (as with plagues, trumpets and seals), when the fragments are gathered up and placed in correct sequence and continuity, and given their Biblically stated timeframes, then the prophecies become clear and connected. They become distinct so that the theories, conjectures, and assumptions of men are revealed in all their disorder and confusion.

---

[1] Attention to chronological order, sequence, and continuity is basic to hermeneutic "common sense."

In the Rev. 1-11 major line of prophetic history, the sequence is perfect. This is illustrated by the following charts. Again the major line of prophetic history presented in Rev. 12-22 is in sequence, and each event follows in its order. There is a marvelous consistency and orderly arrangement which can be recognized and which assures the Bible student of correct use of Scripture.[1]

A CHART OF THE ALIGNMENT OF THE THREE MAJOR LINES OF PROPHECY OF DANIEL AND REVELATION

1. THE MAJOR LINE OF PROPHECY OF DANIEL

606 B.C. ——————————————————— STONE KINGDOM

2. THE MAJOR LINE OF PROPHECY OF REVELATION 1-11

Christian Church Organized A.D. 34 ——————————— SECOND COMING

3. THE MAJOR LINE OF PROPHECY OF REVELATION 12-22

Lucifer's Rebellion ——————————————————— THE NEW EARTH

The three major lines of prophecy cover approximately the same span of historical progression. Therefore Daniel and Revelation should be studied together:

> "The study of the Revelation directs the mind to the prophecies of Daniel, and both present most important instruction, given of God to men, concerning events to take place *at the close of this world's history.*" *Great Controversy*, p. 341.

Each major line of prophecy enhances the others with added detail. And each outline, such as those of plagues, trumpets and seals adds more details so that the picture grows as if an artist is putting

---

[1] On the other hand there are would-be expositors who freely place the fifth plague right in the middle of the 7th! Then they take many pages of explanation and quotations out of context to "prove" their theories.

They will take the 6th plague apart and insert actions which are taken from other places out of sequence and again "prove" their assumptions in the same way. They will misuse the symbolism or use oft repeated error as a stated fact. They may have a very careless approach to symbols such as a "river" and an "ocean" or "sea" assuming they are one and the same thing. This is often done in an exposition of the 6th plague which throws the entire passage out of sequence.

There are some who abuse the sequence of plagues, trumpets and seals and then use the quotations of the prophet out of context to "prove" their points. Apparently they assume that by quoting the words of a prophet they may justify their violation of hermeneutic principles and common sense.

in one stroke after another. And all of this information is given within each major line of prophecy in specific **ORDER**.

"All that God has in prophetic history specified to be fulfilled in the past has been; and all that is yet to come, **IN ITS ORDER** will be." MS 32, 1896.

When the major lines of prophecy in Revelation are aligned together it is soon evident that they are complementary and supplementary to each other. When they are thus linked, it then becomes evident that the plagues and trumpets complement and supplement each other and are part of the same picture.

These major lines of prophecy in Daniel and Revelation are presented on the next pages. They are presented with endtime events in their **ORDER—chronological time progression and sequence.** Then, the vertical dotted lines reveal how the two major lines of Revelation fit together complementing and supplementing each other.

The chapter on the Seals will provide a timeframe given by Scripture itself, which fits them exactly into their correct place.

THE CHRONOLOGICAL ORDER OF THE MAJOR LINE OF PROPHECY IN REVELATION 1-11

Rev. 1-3	Rev. 4-5	Rev. 6	Rev. 7	Rev. 8	Rev. 8-9	Rev. 10—11
7 Letters	Judgment Begins 1844	7 Seals	144,000 Sealed	Close of Probation	7 Trumpets	"Time shall be no longer" "Mystery of God finished" Kingdom Restored

7 Churches
Ephesus 100 A.D.
Smyrna 100-300
Pergamos 300-500
Thyatira 500-1800
Sardis 1800
Philadelphia 1844
Laodicea 1844-Today (Judgment Era)

1844
Rev. 4, 5
Timeframe for the 7 Seals
Investigative Judgment Begins

1844
White Horse—Everlasting gospel to the world
Red Horse—Sunday Laws remove "peace"
Black Horse—Apostasy
Pale Horse—Famine, etc.
Martyrs—Loud Cry—for retribution
144,000 sealed
Multitude comes out of Babylon

Timeframe
Close of Probation
"Censer thrown down"

7 Trumpets

Kingdom Restored

All that God has in prophetic history specified to be fulfilled in the past, has been, and all that is yet to come ***IN ITS ORDER*** will be."
Ms. 32, 1896 E. G. White

Note: The horizontal lines are given in step form to save space on the page.

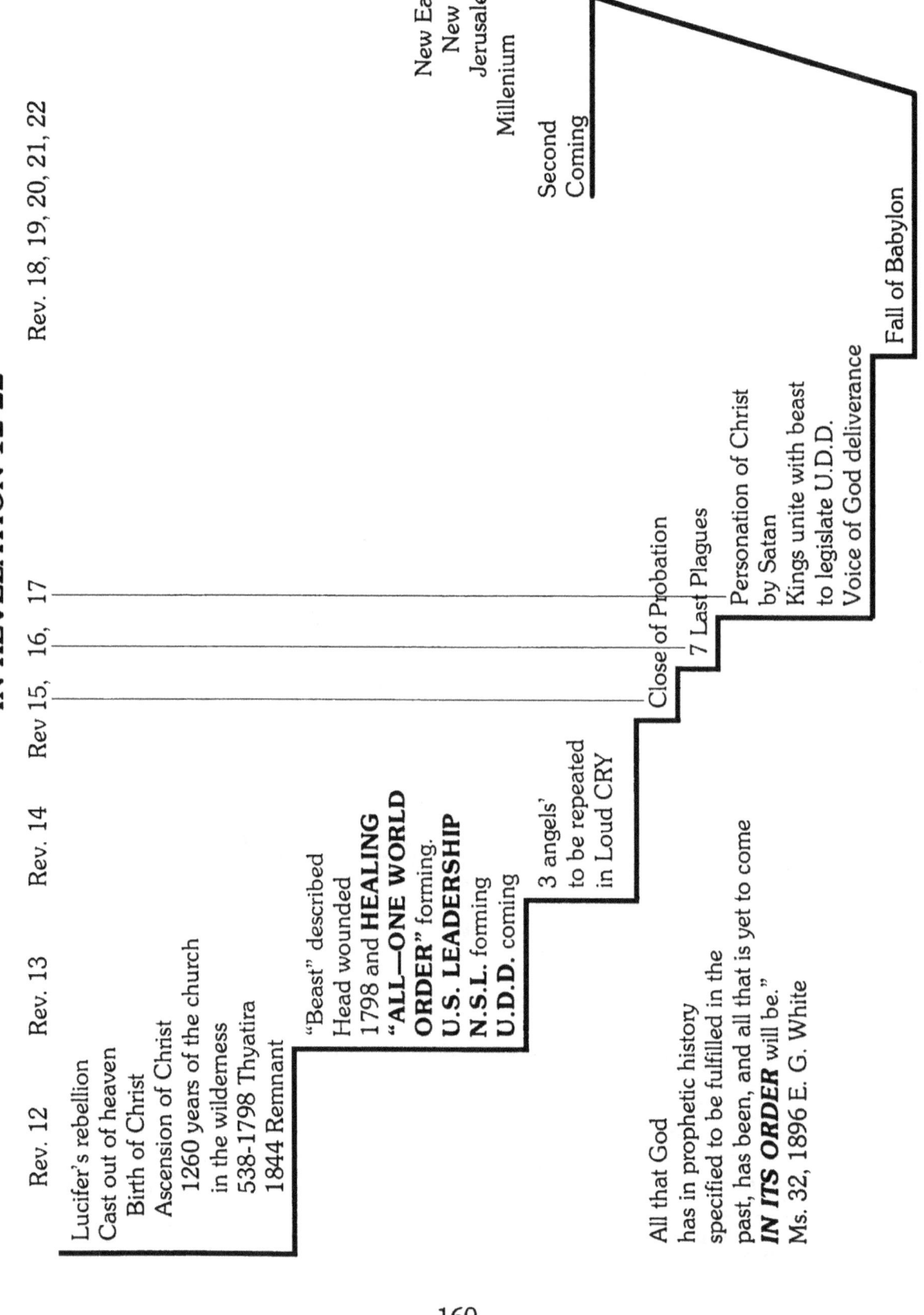

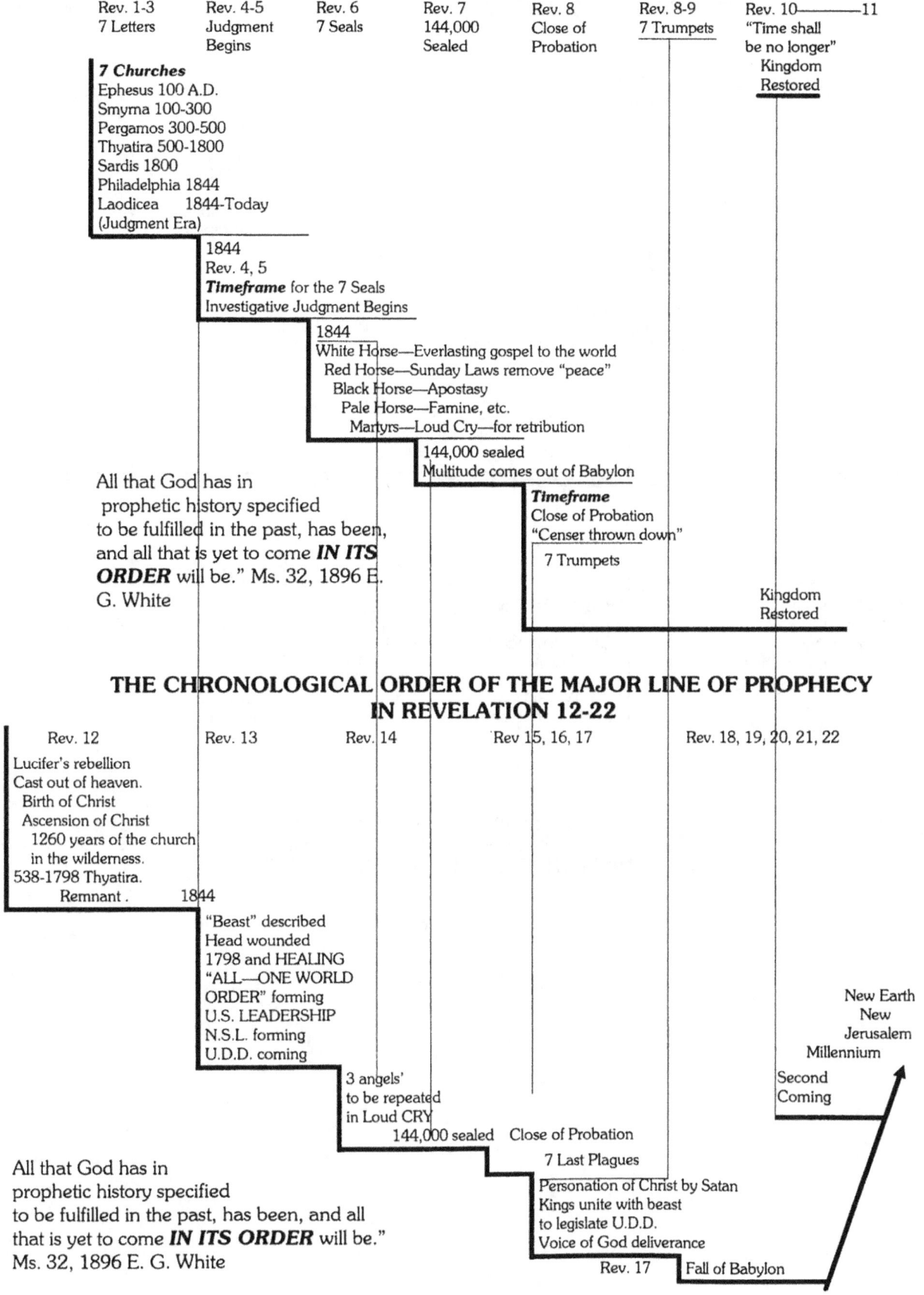

A DIAGRAM WHICH REVEALS THE SEQUENTIAL AND CHRONOLOGICAL ARRANGEMENT

MAJOR LINE 1-11

Rev. 1-3	Rev. 4-5	Rev. 6	Rev. 7	Rev. 8	Rev. 8-9
7 Letters	Judgment Scene	Seven Seals	SEALING	Close of Probation	Seven Trumpets
7 Churches			144,000		
Ephesus A.D. 100				CLOSE OF PROBATION	
Smyrna 200-300				Censer thrown down	
Pergamos 300-500				Timeframe for Trumpets to begin	
Thyatira 538-1798					
Sardis 1800					
Philadelphia 1844					
Laodicea	1844 Provides the Timeframe for Beginning the **Seven Seals** 1844 — White Horse—Today Red Horse—Sunday Laws Remove "peace from the Earth." Black Horse—Apostasy Pale Horse—Death—Hell Martyrs—Loud Cry.				

MAJOR LINE 12-22

Rev. 12	Rev. 13	Rev. 14	Rev. 15	Rev. 16
Lucifer's Rebellion Cast to this earth	"Beast" with Seven Heads	Three Angels Repeated in LOUD CRY SEALING OF 144,000		Seven Last Plagues
Birth of Christ	One—Wounded Now Healing			
Ascension of Christ	"All" worship . . .			
1260 years in the wilderness	ONE WORLD ORDER persecution to come.		CLOSE OF PROBATION No man— Mediator in temple	
538-1798 (Thyatira)				
Remnant 1844				

"All that God has in prophetic history specified to be fulfilled in the past has been, and all that is yet in the future to come IN ITS ORDER, will be." MS 32, 1896 E.G. White

OF THE TWO ALIGNING MAJOR LINES OF PROPHECY IN REVELATION

	(Rev. 9)	Rev. 10-11				
	(Trumpet 6 Four destroying angels loosed & kill 1/3 of men	"Time NO LONGER" Mystery Finished Kingdoms become Kingdom of our Lord				
	(Seal 6 Men Hide. Rocks - Mountains	Seal 7) Silence in heaven half hour. GC 641				

Rev. 17	Rev. 18	Rev. 19	Rev. 20	Rev. 21	Rev. 22
6th Plague detail. Kings unite with Beast and reign "one hour" or 15 literal days. Satan personates Christ. The world amazed to "behold" him (v. 8) 7th Plague "Voice of God" begins the "Fall of Babylon"	Fall of Babylon occurs in "one hour" (15 days)	Second Coming	1,000 YEARS Satan, sin, sinners destroyed earth melted in lake of fire	New Jerusalem descends The throne established on this earth	New Earth Eden Restored Righteousness established

AN ALIGNMENT OF THE TWO MAJOR LINES OF PROPHECY IN REVELATION

REVELATION 12-22		REVELATION 1-11	
Text	Description	Text	Description
12:3-9	Lucifer's Rebellion		
12:2-6	Christ's Birth		
12:5	Christ's Ascension	2:17	Ephesus Church
		2:8-11	Smyrna Church
		2:12-17	Pergamos Church
12:6, 13, 14	1260 Persecution	2:18-29	Thyatira Church
		3:11	Sardis Church
12:17	1844 Remnant	3:7-13	Philadelphia Church
		3:14-22	Laodicea—Judgment Hour Message
		4 and 5	Investigative Judgment Scene
13:1, 2	Beast Described		(1844→)
13:3	Beast Wounded		
13:3	Beast Healing		
13:7	Beast Persecuting	6:1-17	1844 Began the Seven Seals
14:6-13	1844 Began the Three Angel's Warning Messages		
14:1-5	144,000 Sealed	7:1-17	144,000 Sealed
15:8	CLOSE OF PROBATION	8:3-5	CLOSE OF PROBATION
16:1-21	Seven Last Plagues	8:6-13 9:1-21	Seven Trumpets
17:8	Satan Personates Christ		
17:10-13	Reign of Kings	10:7	Mystery of God Finished Time No Longer
17:16-18	Fall of Babylon		
18:5-24		11:15-19	Christ Takes the Kingdom
19:11-16	Second Coming of Christ		
20	1000 Years		
21	New Jerusalem		
22	New Earth.		

Note: The Sequence of Verses in Both Major Lines of Prophecy.
The Positive Linkage of the Close of Probation.
The Progressive, Forward Movement in both Major Lines of Prophecy from Beginning to End.

THE STRUCTURE OF REVELATION

PART II THE EIGHT VISIONS OF REVELATION

A knowledge of the structure of Revelation is vital to an understanding of the timing for the final endtime fulfillment of seals, trumpets and other important things. Not only is it necessary to recognize the two major lines of prophecy in Revelation that are written in sequence and continuity, but it is important to know the arrangement of the book according to the eight visions therein.

These eight visions provide a framework that is vital to an understanding of an endtime fulfillment of seals, trumpets and chapters 11 and 17.

The following chart was provided by the Biblical Research Institute. Although intended to be used as a defense against endtime prophetic exposition, its insight into the structure of the book is valuable. When this format is used correctly it reveals the following:

1. All eight visions begin with a *heavenly scene.*

2. That scene into the heavenly sanctuary—temple or altar, (a view of Christ or an "angel", or the inhabitants of heaven,) gives a timeframe for the *"Basic Prophetic Description"* which follows. That is, it gives the timeframe by which to begin the Seven Letters, The Seven Seals, the Seven Trumpets, The Seven Plagues, etc.

3. Before that Basic Prophetic Description is completed, there is a "pause" or *Interlude.*

4. Then after the Interlude, the Basic Prophetic Description is completed with an *Eschatological Consummation"—or* events concerning the Second Coming and close of earth's history.

It is imperative that each "heavenly scene" be correctly identified. Identification depends on what the prophet saw. For example, in the first vision, John saw *candlesticks.* Rev. 1:12. The candlesticks immediately relate to the Holy Place of the sanctuary and therefore place the ministry of Christ in that compartment. It is this timeframe that begins the Seven Letters to the churches.

The second "heavenly scene" is synonymous to the description of Daniel 7:10-13 which refers to the beginning of the Investigative Judgment when the book(s) were opened. (see Rev. 4 and 5). This scene, we know takes place within the Most Holy Place of the heavenly sanctuary and this work began in 1844. This date becomes the timeframe by which to begin the "Basic Prophetic Description"—The Seven Seals which follow, in Chapter 6.

The third "heavenly scene" reveals the "throwing down of the censer" or the close of Probation. This is the correct timeframe by which to begin the Seven Trumpets. The fourth "heavenly scene" refers to the time when Christ reigns and the kingdoms of this world are transferred to Him, thus ending the major line of prophecy of Revelation 1-11.

In resume, the Bible scholar should notice that these four heavenly visions move progressively forward, from the Holy Place beginning in 31 A.D. at the inauguration of Christ into His priestly work in that first compartment. The second scene moves into the Most Holy Place where the book(s) are opened and "the judgment was set." That action took place in 1844. The third scene again moves forward to the close of probation and the fourth brings that major line of prophecy to a close at the Second Coming of Jesus.

The most thrilling aspect of this structure is the Interlude which also moves progressively forward in time, explaining the victorious destiny of the last generation. The first interlude in Chapter 7 describes the Seal of God and the victory of the 144,000 just before the close of probation.

The second Interlude in Chapter 10 declares that the "mystery of God is finished." This term is defined by Scripture:

> . . . this mystery . . . is Christ in you, the hope of glory; . . . that we may present every man perfect in Christ Jesus. Col. 1:27, 28.

Those of the 144,000 have the Father's name (character) written in their foreheads (minds). Rev. 14:1 When this is accomplished "they will reflect the image of Jesus fully."

The third victory is seen in Revelation 11:12, at the "Voice of God" deliverance from the Universal Death Decree at which time the Law of God (the two witnesses) are seen in the sky. (See G.C. p. 639-640). This third Interlude brings that major line of prophecy (Rev. 1-11) to its victorious end, for the people of God.

This chart brings the seals and trumpets exactly into their correct places in an endtime fulfillment. It gives the reader a structured assurance that can be attained only when everything fits into its proper alignment.

Diagram 2. Paralleling Structures in Revelation's Eight Major Visions

	I	II	III	IV	V	VI	VII	VIII	
A	Victorious-Introduction Scene	Victorious-Introduction Scene	Victorious-Introduction Scene	Victorious-Introduction Scene	Victorious-Introduction Scene	Victorious-Introduction Scene	Victorious-Introduction Scene	Victorious-Introduction Scene	A
B	Basic Prophetic Description	Basic Prophetic Description	Basic Prophetic Description	Basic Prophetic Description	Basic Prophetic Description	Basic Prophetic Description	Basic Prophetic Description	Basic Prophetic Description	B
C		Interlude	Interlude	Interlude	Interlude	Interlude	Interlude		C
D		Eschatological Culmination	Eschatological Culmination	Eschatological Culmination	Eschatological Culmination	Eschatological Culmination	Eschatological Culmination		D

This diagram reveals the consistent pattern in the book of Revelation. There are eight Major Visions, each beginning with a scene in heaven, after which an historical outline is presented. There is an interlude in each outline, after which is an eschatological Culmination (events connected with the Second Coming of Jesus)

The first four visions are found in the first Major Line of Prophecy consisting of Chapters 1-11 and the last four visions are found in the last Major Line of Prophecy consisting of Chapters 12-22. The structure of the book reveals an endtime application of Seals and Trumpets. It gives correct sequence and continuity to the entire picture of the history of God's church from the First Coming to the Second Coming.

Notes

Diagram Paralleling Structures in Revelation's Eight Major Visions

THE MAJOR LINE OF PROPHECY IN REVELATION 1-11

	I	II	III	IV
A	**Heavenly-Introduction Scene** Rev. 1 Lampstand Holy Place Begin A.D. 31	**Heavenly-Introduction Scene** Rev. 4, 5 Investigative Judgment Began (1844) Most Holy Place	**Heavenly-Introduction Scene** Rev. 8:2-6 Investigative Judgment Ends "Censer thrown down" Close of Probation.	**Heavenly-Introduction Scene** Rev. 10:1-11; 11:15-17, 19 Measuring the temple—altar Kingdon is complete.
B	**Basic Prophetic Description** Rev. 2, 3 7 Letters Begin A.D. 31	**Basic Prophetic Description** Rev. 6 7 Seals Begin 1844	**Basic Prophetic Description** Rev. 8, 9 7 Trumpets (1-5) Begin after Close of Probation	**Basic Prophetic Description** Rev. 11:1-18 1260. Dan. 12 timelines Fulfilled. Law of God Attacked.
C		**Interlude** Rev. 7 144,000 Sealed	**Interlude** Rev. 10 Mystery of God Finished Christ—Formed in you	**Interlude** Rev. 11:11-13 Voice of God Law seen in the sky. Law Vindicated.
D		**Eschatalogical Culmination** Rev. 8:1 7th Seal "Silence in heaven ½ hr." Second Coming.	**Eschatalogical Culmination** Rev. 10 "Time No Longer" Literal Fulfillment 7th Trumpet.	**Eschatalogical Culmination** Rev. 11:15-19 Christ Reigns Kingdom transferred to Christ. Earthquake. Hail.

Taken from *Symposium on Revelation*, Book 1, p. 38 and 39.
See Appendix Note G.

Diagram Paralleling Structures in Revelation's Eight Major Visions

THE MAJOR LINE OF PROPHECY IN REVELATION 12-22

V	VI	VII	VII,	
Heavenly-Introduction Scene Rev. 12, 13 Woman in Sun. Dragon Beast	**Heavenly-Introduction Scene** Rev. 15 Saints Sing Song of Moses. Temple opened. No Mediator	**Heavenly-Introduction Scene** Rev. 19 Heaven Opened. Marriage Supper	**Heavenly-Introduction Scene** Rev. 21, 22 New Heavens and A New Earth	A
Basic Prophetic Description Rev. 12, 13 A.D. 31, 1260 Years Persecution (528-1798) Persecuting "beast"	**Basic Prophetic Description** Rev. 16, 17 7 Last Plagues. Reign of Kings (Rev. 17) Fall of Babylon (Rev. 18)	**Basic Prophetic Description** Rev. 19 Second Coming of Christ as KING OF KINGS.	**Basic Prophetic Description** Detailed Description and promise "I come quickly"	B
Interlude Rev. 14:6-14 Three Angels Messages Harvests. 144,000 Seal of God—Forehead 1st Harvest	**Interlude** Rev. 18:1-4 Power of Loud Cry. Final Harvest from Babylon. 2nd Harvest	**Interlude** Rev. 20 Righteous Reign as Kings (Wicked Judged) 1000 years. 3rd Harvest		C
Eschatalogical Culmination Rev. 12:17 and 13:15 Universal Death Decree. Mark of Beast. Image to Beast.	**Eschatalogical Culmination** Rev. 16:17; 18 7th Plague—Fall of Babylon.	**Eschatalogical Culmination** Rev. 21 Christ's 3rd Coming New Jerusalem comes down.		D

THE STRUCTURE OF REVELATION

PART III CHIASMS

Yes, there is such a thing as "chiasm." A chiasm is a literary pattern revealing an orderly arrangement of subject matter in the Inspired Scripture. The pattern is one in which the beginning verse of a section matches the end verse. Then the second concept matches the next to the last. Finally, in the middle of the passage, there is an "Apex" or focal point which is of superlative importance.

Example:

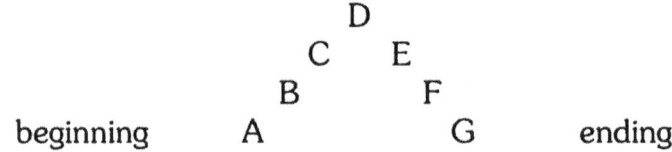

In the above chiastic structure, D becomes the Apex or focal Point of interest.

For example: The chiastic Apex of Leviticus is chapter 16 which deals with the Day of Atonement—a type of the **Investigative Judgment**. In the book of Hebrews, the Apex is chapter 9 which explains Christ's priesthood in the Most Holy Place of the heavenly sanctuary in the antitypical Day of Atonement or **Investigative Judgment**. Again in the book of Daniel the Apex is chapter 7 where Christ enters and "the books are opened and the **judgment** set." The Apex of the Song of Solomon is chapter 5 which describes the Great Disappointment of 1844 and a description of Christ in the **Investigative Judgment**.

What we need to understand is that the book of Revelation Apex is found in Chapter 15, the Close of Probation—or the ending of the **Investigative Judgment**.

However, it is equally important to recognize that there are two major lines of prophecy in the book and that each of these have chiastic structure. In each of these major lines there is an Apex. In the first line (Rev. 1-11) the Apex is formed in chapter 8:2-5 at the throwing down of the censer—close of probation. In the second line of prophecy (Rev. 12-22) the Apex is again at the close of Probation in Chapter 15.

It is also important to understand that chiastic structure can be misused, incorrectly devised, and perverted to "prove" error. The reader must be cautious. See Appendix Note G.

CHAPTER XXI

THE SEVEN SEALS

I. PAST ATTEMPTS OF PROPHETIC APPLICATIONS

Over the centuries there have been more than a hundred prophetic expositors; each was recognized for his own unique treatment of the seven seals of Revelation 6 and 7. These can be traced in the four volumes of *The Prophetic Faith of our Fathers*, by L.E. Froom. There are other views being added at the present date which contribute to a confused position.

Many prophetic expositors in the past applied the seven seals to historical periods. They divided these in different ways. Some understood that these seven seals or periods represented the entire history of man as follows:

Seal No. 1	Adam to the flood
Seal No. 2	The flood or tower of Babel to Abraham
Seal No. 3	The Hebrew Nation: Abraham to Christ
Seal No. 4	The days of Jesus and following persecutions
Seal No. 5	The 1260 years of apostasy and Papal domination
Seal No. 6	The remnant period
Seal No. 7	The last generation and Second Coming

Others assumed that it referred to seven historical periods within the Christian Church. Uriah Smith and others took this position, as follows:

Seal No. 1	The Apostolic Church
Seal No. 2	Pagan early church persecutions
Seal No. 3	Apostasy in the early centuries
Seal No. 4	Papal persecutions for 1260 years
Seal No. 5	Martyrs crying for vengeance
Seal No. 6	The wicked in terror at the Second Coming of Christ
Seal No. 7	The descent of Christ at the Second Coming

2. THE PROPHETIC APPLICATION TO THE FUTURE

Setting aside all conjectures, let the prophet speak: Ellen G. White placed the plagues, trumpets **and seals in an endtime setting with a *FUTURE APPLICATION*.** The following quotation reveals her understanding of the plagues, trumpets and seals in their relationship to each other in the future. This was written as early as 1895.

> I thought of the day when the judgment of God **WOULD BE [future tense]** poured out upon the world, when blackness and horrible darkness would clothe the heavens as **SACKCLOTH OF HAIR [quoted from Revelation 6:12—the 6th seal]**.... My imagination anticipated what it must be in that period when the Lord's mighty voice **SHALL [future tense]** give commission to His angels, "Go your ways, and pour out the **vials of the wrath of God [the seven last plagues]** upon the earth...." Revelation 6 and 7 [the seven seals] **are full of meaning**.... The seven angels stood before God to receive their commission. To them were given seven trumpets. The Lord was going forth to punish the inhabitants of the earth.... When the plagues of God shall come upon the earth hail will fall upon the wicked about the weight of a talent." *Maranatha*, p. 284, Oct. 3, Ms. 59 1895.

It is very evident from the above quotation that the prophet connected plagues, trumpet and seals together and gave them an endtime setting.

The Bible is a "web of truth" and everything in it has some bearing on everything else. There is linkage between all prophecy which projects light in all directions and on other prophecies. Plagues, trumpets, and seals are all one connected picture—one panoramic view of future events.

The one great question has to do with the point of beginning of the seven seals. If that important concept can be ascertained, whether it begins with Adam, with the Christian church or whether at some later or future time, then the meaning of the Seals should become more apparent. What does the Bible say? What is the Biblical timeframe?

3. THE BIBLICAL TIMEFRAME FOR THE SEVEN SEALS

In something as important as a timeframe—on which the whole meaning rests, please permit the Bible to be its own expositor. A Biblical timeframe immediately precedes the action. Since the seven seals are found in Chapter 6, the timeframe for their beginning would be found immediately preceding in Chapters 4 and 5. See Charts p. 159-169

At this point, Bible students should read carefully Revelation, chapters 4 and 5, to find the timeframe for the seven seals. These two chapters parallel Daniel 7:9-14, the scene of the opening of the Investigative Judgment, which began in 1844. That is the year in which the seven seals should begin, for an endtime application.

Chapters 4 and 5 of Revelation present the same scene as that viewed in Daniel 7 which is the setting for the beginning of the Investigative Judgment which began in 1844.

John and Daniel saw the same heavenly scene. They saw the heavenly courtroom, the heavenly records of men's lives as recorded in "books," or a "book." They saw Jesus was worthy and the One who could enter in before the Father to open up these records to determine the fate of men, and build His kingdom.

The following page is a comparison chart of Daniel 7 with Revelation 4 and 5.

A CHART OF COMPARISONS OF DANIEL 7:9-14 WITH REV. 4 AND 5

THE SCENE	DANIEL Chapter 7 Verses	REVELATION Chapter 4 Verses	REVELATION Chapter 5 Verses
1. A heavenly scene	9-14	1-11	1-4
2. A throne(s) were set up	9	2-6	1, 6-11
3. The Father sits on it	9	2, 3	1, 7
4. The glory of the throne	9, 10	3, 5, 6,	
5. The glory of the Father	9	3,	
6. Ten thousand times ten thousands angels	10		11
7. Jesus "came" to the Father	13		7
8. The book(s) were opened / Seals were opened (began)	10		9
9. Christ is given glory	14	11	13
10. Christ receives a kingdom	14		9
11. The saved serve Him	14		10
12. Thrones are set as for a jury	9	10	8-14

Jesus Christ is the main character in both passages of Daniel 7 and Revelation 4 and 5.

> In Revelation Christ is the "lamb, as it had been slain" Rev. 5:6-9
> In Daniel Christ is called, "one like the Son of man." Dan. 7:13

In both passages the main event is that of opening up the book(s)—The Investigative Judgment.

In both passages the date or timeframe is the beginning of the Judgment—1844.

With the opening of the book(s), the seals are opened.

> . . . thou art worthy . . . to open the seals . . . Rev. 5:9.

4. THE FOUR BEASTS AND THE TIMEFRAME FOR THE SEALS

Four beasts, which are in, about, or under God's throne are mentioned in Ezekiel, and Revelation 4 and 5. One peculiar aspect of their description is mentioned in both Ezekiel and Revelation—their **eyes**!

> . . . and their rings were **full of eyes** . . . Eze. 1:18.

> And their whole body, and their backs, and their hands, and their wings, and the wheels, were **full of eyes** round about . . . Eze. 10:12.

> And the four beasts had each of them six wings about him; and they were **full of eyes within.** . . . Rev. 4:8.

It is a well-known fact that eyes are *an extension of the brain*. It is also recognized that it is with the eyes that we see things. It is also understood that what is seen, registers in the brain. The human brain, and many other creatures' brains have the ability, not only to see, but to evaluate, assess, weigh up, synthesize, store and retrieve information or data when desired.

It would appear that these four beasts—so full of eyes, are the **recorders and memory banks** of all that has transpired in the great controversy between good and evil. With their eyes they have seen everything and are able to retrieve it as needed, especially at the time of the Investigative Judgment.

Daniel 7 and Revelation 5 mention "books" of records. ". . . the judgment was set and the books were opened." Dan. 7:10. Again, Revelation 5, speaks of a "book" which could not be opened. Today we would probably think of recorded data stored in the memory banks of a computer. The brain is the greatest "computer" ever built. What kind of computer does God use to store data? Apparently He stores information within the four living creatures—the four beasts. They see everything and have recorded it for retrieval at the time of the Investigative Judgment.

These four beasts, according to the description of Ezekiel are under God's throne and move the throne about from one place to another. The throne is above their heads. If all information is kept by these four beasts, this is God's **"confidential file," not accessible to anyone,** and cannot be tampered with until it is opened at the time of the Investigative Judgment. Revelation 5 states that no one could open the "book" until it was opened by the "Lamb, slain from the foundation of the world." The confidential file has been safely kept because God was "sitting on it."

What information and what records are kept in the book(s) of heaven? Let the prophet explain Rev. 5:1-3 as follows:

> There in his open hand lay the book, the role of the history of God's providences, the prophetic history of nations and the church: Herein was contained the divine utterances, His authority, His commandments, His laws, the whole symbolic counsel of the Eternal, and the history of all ruling powers in the nations. In the symbolic language was contained in that roll the influence of every nation, tongue, and people from the beginning of earth's history to its close. Letter 65, 1899, MS release 667.

Not just the recording of words, thoughts, and actions: but also the **influence** of each of these and of every person, as it affected the course of history.

Every aspect of Revelation 4 and 5 pertains to the great judgment of man. This judgment work began in 1844 and this date becomes vital to an understanding as to where the seals should begin, in point of time.

It is the four beasts which show all seven seals. (Rev. 6:1, 3, 5, 7, 9, 12 and 8:1) These four beasts see all and have the records of everything and are in excellent position to impart information. ***It is when the book is opened that the first seal is opened in 1844.***

> And they sung a new song, saying, Thou art worthy to take the book, **AND TO OPEN THE SEALS THEREOF** . . . Rev. 5:9.

It is also interesting to note that one of the four beasts hands the seven angels the vials of the seven last plagues (Rev. 15:7) which come at the end of the Investigative Judgment—the close of probation.

The seven seals, in an endtime application, cover the time period from the beginning of the Investigative Judgment to the Second Coming of Jesus.

5. THE FIRST SEAL

> And I saw when the Lamb opened one of the seals, and I heard, as it were the noise of thunder, one of the four beasts saying, Come and see. And I saw, and behold a **white horse**: and he that sat upon him had a bow; and a crown was given unto him: and he went forth conquering, and to conquer. Rev. 6:1, 2.

Permit the Bible to be its own expositor: What do these symbolic things mean? What does the **"horse"** represent?

> ... the Lord of hosts hath visited his flock [His people—His **church**], **the house of Judah [the remnant church],** and hath made them as his **goodly horse** in the battle. Zech. 10:3.

The **"bow"** (and arrow) is the equipment needed by a hunter (of souls). This rider is revealed, equipped for evangelism. He is engaged in missionary work. The fact that he wears a **"crown"** shows that he is in service for the King of kings and of the royal family of heaven. The statement that he goes forth conquering and to conquer shows that he is engaged in a great effort and campaign to win the lost.

Uriah Smith's understanding of the seals was based on this same Biblical interpretation of the symbolism. However, he assumed that the timeframe belonged to the first centuries of the Christian church.

Today, as we recognize the timeframe of Revelation 4 and 5 to refer to 1844, we see the true remnant engaged in a worldwide effort to give the three angels' messages to the world as predicted in Scripture. This work began shortly after 1844.

> And he said unto me, Thou must **prophesy again before many peoples, and nations, and tongues, and kings.** Rev. 10:11.

The message they were to take to all the world was referred to again in Revelation, chapter 14:

> And I saw another angel fly in the midst of heaven, having **the everlasting gospel to preach unto them that dwell on the earth, and to every nation, and kindred, and tongue, and people** ... Rev. 14:6.

The entire three angels' messages were to be taken by God's true remnant people to the ends of the earth. This is the horse and rider described in the first seal. We are still living in the time of the first seal. The remnant people still have the freedom to go forth **"conquering and to conquer." Radio and T.V. literally "fly in the midst of heaven" so that the gospel shall go to all the world, "... for a witness unto all nations; and then shall the END come."** Matt. 24:14. This understanding of the first seal becomes truly **ENDTIME** PROPHECY.

The color white represents purity. (Isa. 1:18, Rev. 19:8, 11, 14) A **white horse** in the first seal represents the purity of the Advent people—the pioneers, who were tested and tried by the Great Disappointment of 1844. After that, they were selected as God's true remnant church to take the militant position of the horse and rider going forth, "conquering and to conquer," to proclaim Present Truth as found in the three angels' messages to all the world. This work was predicted in Revelation 10:11, and described in Revelation 14:6-14.

This first seal reveals Adventism enjoying liberty, especially of the United States of America—their headquarters. In peace, freedom and prosperity for more than a century, they have taken the gospel of the three angels' messages to all the world.

But that blessing of freedom will soon be taken away and this brings us to the second seal when "peace shall be taken from the earth."

6. THE SECOND SEAL

> And when he had opened the second seal, I heard the second beast say, Come and see. And there went out another horse that was **RED:** and power was given him . . . **TO TAKE PEACE FROM THE EARTH . . . and** there was given unto him a great **SWORD**. Rev. 6:4, 5

The peace so long enjoyed by the remnant church has been guaranteed by the Constitution, which has protected the separation of church and state. But when there is a union of church and state so that in this nation there is religious legislation with attending penalties, "peace will be taken from the earth," and God's people will feel the "great sword" if they violate the laws of man. It is a sad comment that they should "kill one another." Rev. 6:4.

The specific legislation which begins this endtime scenario will be a **NATIONAL SUNDAY LAW IN THE UNITED STATES OF AMERICA**. This will be a fulfillment of Revelation 13:11 when the lamb-like beast "speaks" like a dragon. *"The 'speaking' of the nation is the action of its legislative and judicial authorities."* See The Great Controversy, p. 442. This is a fulfillment of prophecy. When this occurs, ". . . Peace [will be taken] from the earth." Rev. 6:4

All prophecy is related. It is a web of truth. The second seal is a reference to Revelation 13:11. Prophecy is interlocking and enfolds itself. Each prophecy is a part of the whole panorama.

THE ORDER AND RELATIONSHIP OF THE FIRST AND SECOND SEALS	
Seal No. 1	**Seal No. 2**
TIME: 1844	TIME: National Sunday Law
Investigative Judgment of the **DEAD** begins.	Investigative Judgment of the **LIVING** begins.
FIRST SEAL BEGINS	**SECOND SEAL BEGINS**
White Horse	Red Horse
Gospel to the world Evangelism in **Peace**-freedom	**Peace** taken from the earth.
Remnant people	Persecuted—the Sword

7. THE THIRD SEAL

> And when he had opened the third seal, I heard the third beast say, Come and see. And I beheld, and lo, a **black** horse; and he that sat on him had a pair of **balances** in his hand. And I heard a voice in the midst of the four beasts say, A measure of wheat for a penny, and three measures of barley for a penny; and see thou hurt not the oil and the wine. Rev. 6:5, 6.

The third seal has usually been applied by Sabbathkeepers to the apostasy of the third and fourth centuries. Does this third seal also have an endtime application? Listen to inspired forsight:

The same spirit is seen today that is represented in Revelation 6:6-8. [**The third and fourth seal**]. **HISTORY IS TO BE REPEATED. THAT WHICH HAS BEEN WILL BE AGAIN.** This spirit works to confuse and to perplex. Dissension will be seen in every nation, kindred, tongue, and people, and those who have not had a spirit to follow the light that God has given through his living oracles, through His appointed agencies, will become confused. Their judgment will reveal weakness. Disorder and strife and confusion will be **seen in the church.** Manuscript Release No. 1465. Letter 65, 1898. E.G. White. (Written August 25, 1898 from "Sunnyside," Cooranbong, Australia, to "Brethren [Fredrick] Griggs and Howe.")

The pioneers were quite correct applying the **black horse to apostasy in the church** in the 3rd and 4th centuries, but an application to endtime "brings it home."

While the church is going into apostasy, in the midst of the process, it is difficult to determine who is true and who is fallen. The "wheat and the tares grow together." It is dangerous to try to pull out the tares, lest the precious wheat be rooted out also. It is not necessary that God's people do the "weeding" work. The Lord Himself will do it by a turn of events. The sinners in Zion will be shaken out. That event and process will come about as the Sunday Law persecution begins.

It is persecution which will separate the church. If the symbolic "horse" represents a church in the sense of an organized unit, composed of institutions, financial structure, leadership and salaried workers, then it will be self-evident whether or not such a structure can continue to operate under its present name, without endorsing the commandments of men and denying the laws of God regarding the Seventh-day Sabbath. We are now in the "waiting and watching" time. Business as usual may continue for all who are willing to receive the mark of the beast. But the question is this, "Who will remain true to the law of God"?

The symbolic "balances" or scales in the hand of the rider who guides the horse indicate a time of judgment.[1]

The balance scales are used in the third seal in the process of selling grains which are the "Bread of life." Salvation is the bread from heaven, and in this process there appears to be a **"SELLING OUT"** of the truth. It is another statement which confirms the concept of corporate **apostasy.**

Listen to the words of the prophetess regarding future events:

> As the storm approaches, a large class who have professed faith in the third angel's message . . . abandon their position and join the ranks of the opposition. . . . Men of talent and pleasing address, who once rejoiced in the truth, employ their powers to deceive and mislead souls. They become the most bitter enemies of their former brethren. When Sabbathkeepers are brought before the courts to answer for their faith, these apostates are the most efficient agents of Satan to misrepresent and accuse them, and by false reports and insinuations to stir up the rulers against them. *The Great Controversy,* p. 608.

8. THE FOURTH SEAL

> And when he had opened the fourth seal, I heard the voice of the fourth beast say, Come and see. And I looked, and behold a pale horse: and his name that sat on him was death, and hell **[Hades—the grave] followed with him.** And power was

---

1 TEKEL: Thou art weighed in the balances, and art found wanting. Dan. 5:27.

> given unto them over the fourth part of the earth, to kill with the sword, and with hunger, and with death, and with the beasts of the earth. Rev. 6:7, 8.

A "pale" or "sick" horse is disabled. The church, when fallen in apostasy, no longer does its appointed work; then its protection and freedom, providentially sustained, is withdrawn.

The fourth seal describes that "little time of trouble" which comes before the plagues. The sword (war) and famine are predicted to cover a fourth part of the earth, which will bring death. God placed the fear of man in the beasts of the earth, the fowls of the air, and upon sea creatures after the flood. (Gen. 9:2) But as the church fails in its destiny, and falls into apostasy, the restraints of the Holy Spirit are withdrawn and the beasts of the earth contribute to the great toll of death over a fourth part of the earth. Man who has feasted on beasts, fowl, and fish will become prey to their unrestrained nature. Famine and war contribute to the general havoc let loose.

9. THE FIFTH SEAL

> And when he had opened the fifth seal, I saw under the altar the souls of them that were slain for the word of God, and for the testimony which they held; And they cried with a loud voice, saying, How long, O Lord, holy and true, dost thou not judge and avenge our blood on them that dwell on the earth? And white robes were given unto every one of them; and it was said unto them, that they should rest yet for a little season, until their fellowservants . . . should be killed as they were, should be fulfilled. Rev. 6:9-11.

The prophetess provides the setting or timeframe for this seal, as follows:

> When the fifth seal was opened, John the Revelator in vision saw beneath the altar the company that were slain for the Word of God and the testimony of Jesus Christ. **AFTER THIS came** the scenes described in the 18th of Revelation, when those that are faithful and true are **CALLED OUT OF BABYLON.** *The Seventh-day Adventist Bible Commentary,* Vol. 7, p. 968, Ms. 39, 1906.

The fifth seal refers to two groups of martyrs: past and future. It is self evident that the company "that were slain" — the martyrs referred to in this passage are those of past ages, but there is also another group of the "fellow servants [that] should be killed [future]." After they are killed, then the Revelation 18 message of the Loud Cry will be given in great power.

The previous statement places the opening of the fifth seal before the Loud Cry. The Loud Cry is the Third Angel's warning message against the "beast," his "mark," the false Sabbath.

This fifth Seal brings to view the two groups of martyrs. The first group are those of the past who cry out in Verse 10. The second group are those of verse 11 who also ". . . should be [future tense] killed . . ." (Rev. 6:11) at a later date.

The first group may extend from the martyred Abel, on down through the ages, and especially those who were martyred during the Papal Supremacy, A.D. 538-1798. The second group are those who **will be martyred** in the future under religious death penalties. These death penalties are not the same as the Universal Death Decree which occurs under the 6th plague, and from which God's people are delivered, under the 7th plague, by the Voice of God.

Martyr's blood is always "seed" for harvest. It is the martyrs that shed their blood who prepare the way for the Loud Cry final-harvest which comes out of Babylon. What does the prophetess say about all this?

> Many will be imprisoned, many will flee for their lives. . . . Many **WILL BE MARTYRS** for Christ's sake standing in defense of truth . . . *III Selected Messages*, p. 397, MS 6 1889.

The first five seals provide a panoramic view of the remnant church from 1844 until the Loud Cry has gathered in those who come out of Babylon; to the close of probation. Where and how do the first five seals fit in connection with the plagues and trumpets? The fifth seal provides this information.

The martyrs make a request, under the fifth seal, which is answered, or linked with, the first three of the plagues-trumpets. The fifth seal is a request for **VENGEANCE!**

> . . . they cried with a loud voice, saying . . . **AVENGE OUR BLOOD** . . . Rev. 6:10.

But Christ does not "avenge" until He puts on the "garments of vengeance" at the close of probation.

> Then I saw that Jesus would not leave the most holy place until every case was decided . . . not . . . until Jesus had finished His work in the most holy place, laid off His priestly attire, and **CLOTHED HIMSELF WITH GARMENTS OF VENGEANCE** . . . He will stand up, put on the garments of vengeance . . . and then the seven last plagues will be poured out. *Early Writings*, p. 36.

10. LINKAGE BETWEEN THE FIFTH SEAL, TRUMPETS 1-3, AND PLAGUES 1-3

There is linkage between the fifth seal, which cries out for vengeance; and there is vengeance meted out during the seven last plagues. The fifth seal is a request for **blood** vengeance, and the first three plague-trumpets are **blood** judgments.

THE FIFTH SEAL	PLAGUE-TRUMPETS 2, 3
And when he had opened the fifth seal, I saw under the altar the souls of them that were slain for the word of God . . . And they cried with a loud voice, saying, How long, O Lord . . . dost thou not judge and **AVENGE OUR BLOOD** . . . Rev. 6:9, 10.	And the second angel poured out his vial upon the sea; and it became as the **BLOOD** of a dead man; and every living soul died in the sea. And the third angel poured out his vial upon the rivers and fountains of waters; and they became **BLOOD.** And I heard the angel of the waters say, Thou art righteous, O Lord . . . because thou has judged thus. For they have **SHED THE BLOOD of saints and prophets,** and thou hast given them **BLOOD TO DRINK;** for they are worthy. Rev. 16:3-6.

A diagram of historical progression and linkage between the seals and the seven last plagues follows:

THE FIFTH SEAL LEADS INTO PLAGUES-TRUMPETS

THE FIFTH SEAL	PLAGUES	TRUMPETS
"And when he had opened the fifth seal, I saw under the altar the souls of them that were slain for the word of God . . . . (Verse 10) And they cried with a loud voice, saying, How Long, O Lord . . . doest thou not judge and **AVENGE OUR BLOOD** . . . . Revelation 6:10	"And the second angel poured out his vial upon the sea; and it became as the **BLOOD** of a dead man: and every living soul died in the sea. And the third angel poured out his vial upon the rivers and fountains of waters; and they became **BLOOD**. And I heard the angel of the waters say, Thou art righteous, O Lord . . . because thou hast judged thus. For they have shed the **BLOOD** of saints and prophets, and thou hast given them **BLOOD TO DRINK**; for they are worthy." Revelation 16:3-6	". . . **hail, fire, and BLOOD** . . ." Revelation 8:7 ". . . the rivers . . . fountains of waters became bitter." ". . . and the third part of the sea became **BLOOD** . . ." Revelation 8:8

THE FIRST FIVE SEALS LEAD INTO THE PLAGUES AND TRUMPETS

SEAL 1	SEAL 2	SEAL 3	SEAL 4	SEAL 5	CLOSE OF PROBATION	PLAGUES 1-3	TRUMPETS 1-3
White Horse	Red Horse	Black Horse	Pale Horse	Martyrs Loud-Cry Rev. 18			
1844 until now	NSL, USL **FUTURE**	Apostasy **FUTURE**	Famine **FUTURE**	(Past) and **FUTURE**			
Freedom to preach gospel to all the earth.	Peace from the earth, persecution	Selling out the truth, weighed-balances found wanting.	Strife, Death, Hell, grave.	Martyrs Crying out to "Avenge our BLOOD	Jesus put on garments of vengeance	Sores [Bad ......BLOOD]	Hail Fire **BLOOD**
						BLOOD Ocean	**BLOOD** Ocean
						BLOOD Rivers Waters Fountains	**BITTER** Rivers Waters Fountains

The Seven Seals, together with Plagues and Trumpets, furnish a complete historical panorama from 1844 to the Second Coming of Jesus.
The Plagues and Trumpets are inserted between Seal 5 and 6-7.

11. AN INTRODUCTION TO THE SIXTH SEAL

And I beheld when he had opened the sixth seal, and, lo, there was a great earthquake; and the sun became black as sackcloth of hair, and the moon became as blood; And the stars of heaven fell unto the earth, even as a fig tree casteth her untimely figs, when she is shaken of a mighty wind. And the heaven departed as a scroll when it is rolled together; and every mountain and island were moved out of their places. And the kings of the earth, and the great men, and the rich men, and the chief captains, and the mighty men, and every bondman, and every free man, hid themselves in the dens and in the rocks of the mountains; And said to the mountains and rocks, Fall on us, and hide us from the face of him that sitteth on the throne, and from the wrath of the Lamb. For the great day of his wrath is come; and who shall be able to stand? Rev. 6:12-17.

The full significance of the sixth seal cannot be understood until the events in Revelation, chapters 17 and 18 are made plain. The events in these chapters cannot be made plain until Plagues 6 and 7 and Trumpets 5, 6, and 7 and their alignment are understood.

It is for this reason that the book, *GETTING IT ALL TOGETHER*, gives study first to the plagues and trumpets, and then to the seven Seals. The sixth Seal occurs at the time of the seventh plague and seventh trumpet. The sixth seal is the last act of the "Fall of Babylon." The following chart is a brief review of the sequence and continuity in a correlation of plagues, trumpets, and seals.

Sequence and Continuity In a Correlation of Plagues, Trumpets, and Seals

1844	NSL, USL	APOSTASY	TROUBLE	LOUD CRY	PLAGUES 1-7 TRUMPETS 1-7	SECOND COMING
Seal 1	Seal 2	Seal 3	Seal 4	Seal 5	Seal 6	Seal 7

12. THE TIMEFRAME FOR THE SIXTH SEAL

Ellen G. White endorsed **TWO** different timeframes for the seven seals!

1. In *The Great Controversy,* p. 304-308, 333, 334, she supported an application of the sixth seal to those events which began in 1755—the Lisbon earthquake, the signs in the sun, moon, and stars, as initiating "the time of the end."

2. She also quoted from the sixth seal, giving it a future endtime application, aligning it with plagues and trumpets!

> I thought of the day when the judgments of God **WOULD BE** [future tense] poured out upon the world, when blackness and horrible darkness would clothe the heavens as **SACKCLOTH OF HAIR** [quoted from Revelation 6:12—sixth seal]. My imagination anticipated what it must be in that period when the Lord's mighty voice **SHALL** [future tense] give commission to His angels, 'go your ways, and pour out the vials of the wrath of God [the seven last plagues] upon the earth.' **REVELATION 6 and 7 [THE SEVEN SEALS]** are full of meanings.
>
> The seven angels stood before God to receive their commission. To them were given seven trumpets. The Lord was going forth to punish the inhabitants of the earth. . . . When the plagues of God shall come upon the earth. Hail will fall upon the wicked about the weight of a talent. *Maranatha,* p. 284, Ms 59 1895.
>
> The Scriptures abound with illustrations of dual applications. *The Seventh-day Adventist Commentary,* Vol. 1, p. 1017.

The sixth seal brings to view the great earthquake, signs in the sun, moon and stars which **initiate and conclude** "the time of the end."

THE SIXTH SEAL

1755		FUTURE
LISBON		
Earthquake		Earthquake
Rev. 6:12		Rev. 6:12
Sun, Moon,		Sun, Moon,
Stars	1798	Stars
		Joel 3:15, 16, 17.
		Matt. 24:29, 30.

> And I beheld when he had opened the sixth seal, and, lo, there was a great **EARTHQUAKE**; . . . Rev. 6:12.

It should be understood that "the time of the end" not only began with an earthquake but also ends with one which correlates the seven seals with the plagues and trumpets.

A CORRELATION OF SEAL 6, PLAGUE 7, AND TRUMPET 7		
SEAL 6	**PLAGUE 7**	**TRUMPET 7**
"There was a great EARTHQUAKE" Revelation 6:12	"There was a great EARTHQUAKE" Revelation 16:18	"There [was] a great EARTHQUAKE" Revelation 11:13

> And I beheld when he had opened the sixth seal, and, lo, there was a great earthquake, and **THE SUN BECAME BLACK AS SACKCLOTH OF HAIR, and the MOON BECAME BLOOD; And the STARS OF HEAVEN FELL upon the earth** . . . Rev. 6:12, 13.

Not only the earthquake, but also the signs in the sun, moon, and stars *initiated* and *conclude* "the time of the end." The book of Joel describes the remnant emerging in 1798-1844 in connection with the signs in the sun, moon and stars. Joel 2;29-31. Again, in the last chapter those same signs are repeated in connection with the actual coming of Jesus.

THE SIXTH SEAL
EARTHQUAKE AND SIGNS BEGAN AND CONCLUDE "THE TIME OF THE END"

". . . there was a great earthquake; and the sun became black . . . and the moon became as blood; And the stars of heaven fell." Rev. 6:12, 13.

"Immediately, after the tribulation of those days [1260 days of Dan. 12:7] shall the sun be darkened, and the powers of heaven shaken. And **THEN** shall appear the sign of the Son of man coming in the clouds of heaven with power and great glory." Matt. 14:19, 30.

"The sun and the moon shall be darkened, and the stars withdraw their shining. The Lord **also SHALL ROAR** out of Zion, and utter his voice from [New] Jerusalem; and the heavens and the earth shall shake." Joel 3:15, 16.

> The powers of heaven will be shaken at the voice of God. Then the **sun, moon, and stars** will be moved out of their places. They will not pass away, but be shaken by the voice of God. *Early Writings*, p. 41.

A study of the sixth seal, as it pertains to events connected with the end of time and the Second Coming of Jesus does not destroy the "waymarks" of former applications.

> In every age there is a new development of truth, a message of God to the people of that generation. The old truths are all essential; new truth is not independent of the old, but an unfolding of it. *Christ's Object Lessons*, p. 127.

It is still a fact that since 1798 we are living in "the time of the end." It is also a fact that Ellen G. White said that history will be repeated and gave seals 3, 4 and 5, as well as 6, future application.

Notes

A Correlation of Seals, Trumpets, and Plagues

Rev. 4, 5; Dan. 7 Investigative Judgment Timeframe for the Seven Seals.	SEAL 1 Rev. 6:1, 2 Rev. 14:6 Rev. 10:11 White Horse 1844-today SDA Church	SEAL 2 Rev. 6:3,4 Rev. 13:11 Rev. 13:5 Red Horse **Sunday Laws** **SDA Church** **Persecution**	SEAL 3 Rev. 6:5, 6 **Black Horse** **rider w/scales** **selling out** **Apostasy**	SEAL 4 Rev. 6:7, 8 Pale (sick) Horse **Death-Grave,** **Sword,** **Hunger,** **Beasts**	SEAL 5 Rev. 6:9-11 **Martyrs** Rev. 18:1-4 **Loud Cry** "Avenge our **BLOOD**"		
					CLOSE OF PROBATION. PLAGUES BEGIN. TRUMPETS BEGIN. Revelation 15:8; 8:3-5	**PLAGUE 1** **Sores** from infected **BLOOD.** Revelation 16:2	**PLAGUE 2** Ocean as **BLOOD** of a dead Man. Fish die. Revelation 16:3
						TRUMPET 1 **BLOOD**, Hail, Fire. ⅓ of trees, All Grass Burned. Revelation 8:7	**TRUMPET 2** Ocean as **BLOOD**, ⅓ of Ships gone. Fish die. Revelation 8:8, 9

"The Battle of Armageddon will be fought . . . the Captain of the Lord's host will stand at the head of the angels of heaven to direct the battle. Solemn events **before us are yet to transpire. Trumpet after trumpet is to be sounded, vial after vial** poured out one after another upon the inhabitants of the earth. Scenes of stupendous interest are right upon us"
  The Seventh Day Adventist Bible Commentary, Vol. 7, p. 982, Letter 109, 1890. Ellen G. White

A Correlation of Seals, Trumpets, and Plagues (continued)

								SEAL 6		SEAL 7
								Heaven's roll back as a scroll. Rev. 6:14.	Wicked hid in dens, rocks. "Hide us from the . . . Lamb" Rev. 6:15, 16.	Silence in heaven about ½ hour. Jesus is on His way to earth. Rev. 8:1.
PLAGUE 3	**PLAGUE 4**	**PLAGUE 5**	**PLAGUE 6**	**PLAGUE 7**						
Fountains of **waters** as **BLOOD**. Revelation 16:4-7	The **SUN** Scorches men with heat. Revelation 16:8, 9	**DARKNESS** on the seat or kingdom of the beast. Revelation 16:10, 11	**EVIL SPIRITS** gather all kings to legislate a Universal **DEATH DECREE**. Revelation 16:12-16	**VOICE OF GOD** deliverance from the **DEATH DECREE**. Revelation 16:17	Cities of the **nations fall**. Revelation 16:19	**Thunder and Lightning Earthquake**. Revelation 16:18	**VOICES of doom** from heaven declaring sentence. Revelation 16:18, 19			
TRUMPET 3	**TRUMPET 4**		**TRUMPET 5**	**TRUMPET 6**			**TRUMPET 7**			
Fountains and Rivers of **waters** bitter as Wormwood. Revelation 8:10	The **SUN** and Moon, Stars Smitten. Revelation 8:12	**DARKNESS** ⅓ day **DARK**, ⅓ night **DARK**, Revelation 8:12	**EVIL SPIRITS** as locusts "running to battle" to legislate the **DEATH DECREE** Revelation 9:1-11	**VOICE OF GOD** deliverance. Revelation 9:13; 11:12	**Nations [are] angry**. Revelation 11:18 Loose the **Four Angels**. Jacinth ⅓ **killed**. Revelation 9:14-20	**Thunder and Lightning** Earthquake Law seen in the Sky. Revelation 11:12 G.C. 639	**VOICES of doom** declaring sentence on the wicked. Rewards **for the righteous**. Hail. Revelation 11:15-19			
			WOE No. 1	WOE No. 2			WOE No. 3			

If seal 5 applies to a future martyrdom and the Loud Cry of the angel of Revelation 18, it is self-evident that the sixth seal which follows the 5th, extends on to those events connected with the Second Coming. It is recognized by almost everyone that the greatest part of the sixth seal is future:

> And the heaven departed as a scroll when it is rolled together; and every mountain and island were moved out of their places. And the kings of the earth, and the great men, and the rich men, and the chief captains, and the mighty men, and every bondman, and every free man hid themselves in the dens and in the rocks of the mountains; And said to the mountains and rocks, Fall on us, and hide us from the wrath of the Lamb, For the great day of his wrath is come; and who shall be able to stand? Rev. 6:14-17.

The question will arise: Are we living today under seal 1 or 6? If the Bible student cannot accept an endtime application of Plagues, Trumpets and Seals he will remain with the secondary application of the sixth seal to the 1798 era of history. If he is convinced that there is a future application that is endorsed by Ellen G. White and which is a "new development of truth for this generation" he will understand that we live under the first seal until the National Sunday Law in the United States and the Universal Sunday Law of the New World Order takes peace from the earth.

14. THE FEAST DAY TYPES AND THEIR SIGNIFICANCE TO THE SIXTH SEAL

The Bible is its own expositor. There is no need for speculation. The exact placement of events spoken of in the sixth seal may be found in Scripture through a study of the Hebrew economy.

> The whole Hebrew economy is full of instruction for us. *Review and Herald*, Feb. 4, 1902.

The Hebrew economy was a system of **TYPES** which pointed to future events.

> These types were fulfilled, not only as to the event, but as to the TIME. (Example) On the fourteenth day of the first Jewish month, the very day and month on which for fifteen long centuries the Passover lamb had been slain, Christ . . . was taken . . . crucified and slain . . . *The Great Controversy*, p. 399.

> In like manner, the **types [of feast days] which** relate to the second advent must be fulfilled **AT THE TIME POINTED OUT IN THE SYMBOLIC SERVICE.** *The Great Controversy*, p. 399, 400.

The "time pointed out" or "appointed times" are the Hebrew "mo'ed" of "mowadah." (feast days)
Definition: 4150 Hebrew and Chaldee Dictionary Strong's Concordance.
"mowadah"—"mo'ed"

> an appointment, i.e., a fixed time . . . a festival . . . an assembly. . . .
> (as appointed beforehand), solemn assembly, feast, time appointed.

The feast days of the Hebrew economy were "times appointed", set by the new moons and instructions of the Lord as "holy convocations." They were the "National Holidays" of the nation.

Modern nations enjoy their holidays. In the USA, the holidays include Independence Day—July 4, Thanksgiving, Easter, New Year's Day and Christmas, some of which are religious memorials. The Hebrew nation celebrated six **TIME EVENTS,** or feast days. We also "feast" on holidays: There is the Thanksgiving turkey 'n trimmings, and traditional meals. The Hebrews celebrated the Passover with roasted mutton, unleavened bread and an herb salad. Their autumn or harvest festivals were feasts of the fruits and vegetables, new wine and spiced juices. They were not only commemorative, but **types** of future events involving the deliverance of the people of God.

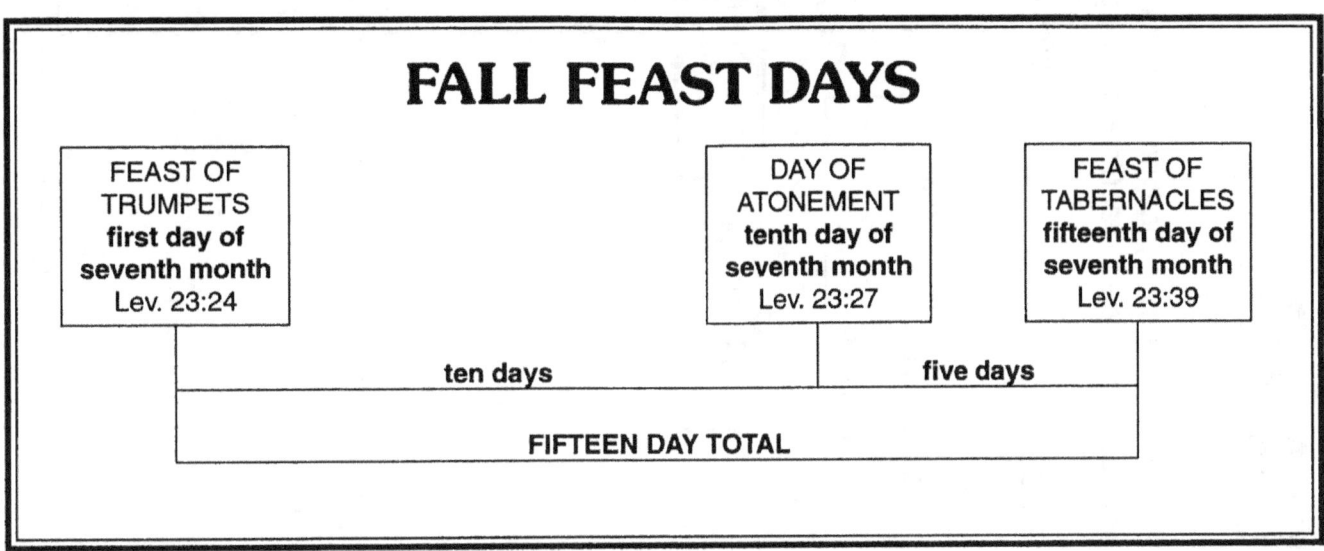

The fifteen days of the autumn Feasts "appointed times" are a type of the "timed events" which occur in the last 15 days of earth's history. They are a type of the "one hour" (literal fifteen day) period of "The Fall of Babylon." Revelation 18:10, 17, 19.

> Like the Passover, the Feast of Tabernacles was commemorative . . . not only commemorative but **TYPICAL . . . IT POINTED TO THE GREAT DAY OF FINAL INGATHERING,** when the Lord of harvest shall send forth His reapers to gather the tares together in bundles for the fire, and to gather the wheat into His garner. **AT that time the wicked will all be destroyed** [an endtime event]. Patriarchs and Prophets, p. 540, 541.

The feast days were **TYPES** of endtime events, when the "wicked will all be destroyed"—spoken of in plagues and trumpets as **"THE FALL OF BABYLON."**

The "Fall of Babylon" occurs in "one hour." Rev. 18:10, 17, 19. In the sixth seal, the wicked cry for the rocks and mountains to fall on them, to hide them from the Lamb and the "day of His wrath is come." These facts place the sixth seal within the "Fall of Babylon" and within that fifteen literal days of destruction after the Voice of God delivers His people.

> The Lord Jesus was the foundation of the whole Jewish economy. . . . Its imposing services were of divine appointment. They were designed to teach the people that **at the time appointed** One would come to whom these ceremonies pointed. Christ's Object Lessons, p. 34.

The next chart reveals the feast days as the types which give a timeframe to the events of the sixth seal.

FALL FEAST DAYS
Dan. 12 and Rev. 17:12; 18

[Spring] "types were fulfilled, not only as to the *event*, but as to the *time* . . . In like manner, the types, which relate to the second advent must be fulfilled at the time pointed out in the symbolic service." *The Great Controversy* p. 399

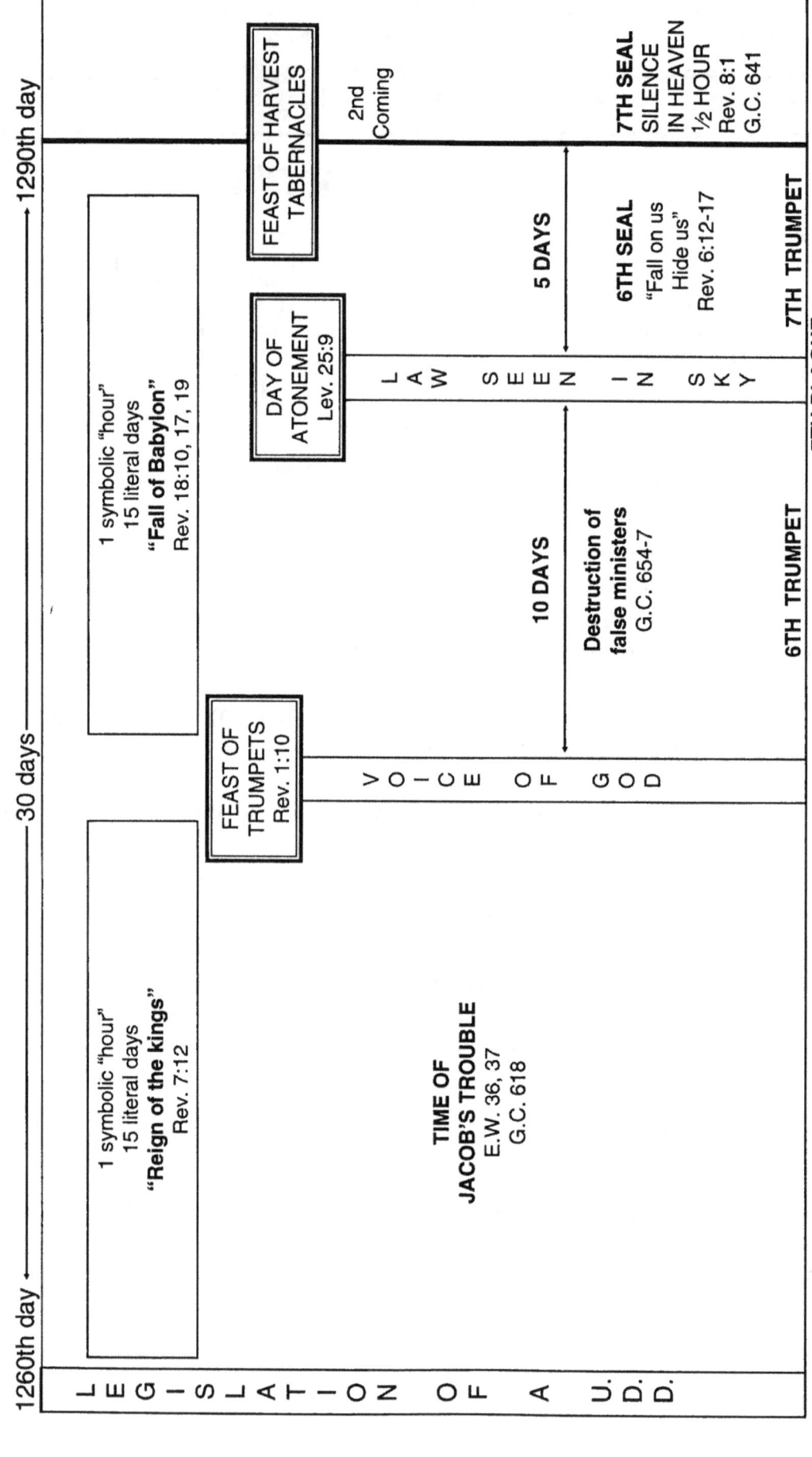

16. *SIXTH SEAL* AND THE LAW OF GOD

And the ***heaven departed as a scroll*** when it is rolled together. Rev. 6:14.

What is meant by the statement that the "heaven departed as a scroll"?

An event is mentioned by Ellen G. White which needs to be considered:

> ... ***the clouds sweep back*** ... Then there appears against the sky a hand holding **TWO TABLES OF STONE folded together**. ... The hand opens the tables, and there are seen the precepts of the ***Decalogue,*** traced as with a pen of fire. The words are so plain that all can read them. Memory is aroused, the darkness of superstition and heresy is swept from every mind, and God's ten words, brief, comprehensive, and authoritative, are presented to the view of all the inhabitants of the earth.
>
> It is impossible to describe the horror and despair of those who have trampled upon God's holy requirements. ... **NOW THEY ARE CONDEMNED BY THAT LAW** which they have despised. With awful distinctness they see that they are without excuse. ... Too late they see that the Sabbath of the fourth commandment is the seal of the living God. ... They find that they have been fighting against God. *The Great Controversy,* p. 639, 640.

There will be an effort to banish the Ten Commandments and the Bible, as was done in the French Revolution. See *The Great Controversy,* p. 265-288. See Appendix Note F. p. 266

This event is described in Rev. 11:12 where the two "witnesses"—the two tables of stone are revealed in the heavens. The Law of God will be vindicated before everyone:

> And they heard a great voice from heaven [the voice of God] saying unto them, Come up hither. And they ascended up to heaven . . . and **THEIR ENEMIES BEHELD THEM.** Rev. 11:12.

> . . . and every mountain and island were moved out of their places. Rev. 6:14.
> **(Seal 6)**

This statement aligns with the seventh plague which says:

> And every island fled away, and the mountains were not found. Rev. 16:20.
> **(Plague 7)**

When the wicked look up into the heavens, they are filled with horror and despair at the sight of that Decalogue. They distinctly see that they are without excuse. They know that all hope is gone. Their cases have been judged. They also know that Jesus is already on His way. Therefore they cry out the following:

> . . . Fall on us, and hide us from the face of him that sitteth on the throne . . . Rev. 6:16. **(Seal 6)**

17. THE SIXTH SEAL AND THE JUBILEE

When the Law of God is seen in the sky on the Day of Atonement, all the wicked realize that they are lost. Up until that time the wicked have been venting their evil, first in an attempt to put God's people to death and then to destroy the false ministers who have deceived them. They have also been destroying the earth with war. Rev. 9:14, 15. (Sixth Trumpet)

18. THE SIXTH SEAL AND THE JUBILEE . . . WHEN THE LAND SHALL REST

The earth has not **rested** under the reign of sin. Violence and bloodshed have been going on from the fall of man. But when the wicked see the Law of God in the sky, on the Day of Atonement, they know they have been judged by it and are lost. They give up in despair and cease their strivings.

The rocks (mountainous areas), dens and caves, into which God's people have retreated, at the Voice of God, are no longer inhabited by the saints. At the voice of God their faces shine so that the wicked cannot look upon them and worship at their feet. The righteous no longer remain in those dens but walk freely on the earth.

At this point, the wicked flee into those very dens and rocks so recently inhabited by God's people. They cry for the rocks and mountains to fall on them to hide them from the face of the Lamb. They know that the time for His wrath is come and their destruction is right upon them.

When the wicked cease their strivings, then—not until then, can the **"land rest."** It will continue to rest for the next 1,000 years. Ellen G. White connected the voice of God deliverance and the Jubilee, "when the land should rest;" thereby giving a timeframe for the sixth seal.

> There was one clear place of settled glory, whence came the voice of God. (Feast of Trumpets) . . . the wicked could not look upon them for the glory . . . Then (at the Day of Atonement), commenced the Jubilee. *The Great Controversy,* p. 285, 286.

> Then commenced the **JUBILEE, when the land should rest.**
> *Early Writings,* p. 34, 35. See Lev. 26:35; 25:9.

> And the kings of the earth, and the great men, and the rich men, and the chief captains, and the mighty men, and every bondman, and every free man, hid themselves in the dens and in the rocks of the mountains; And said to the mountains and rocks, **Fall on us, and hide us from the face of him that sitteth on the throne, and from the wrath of the lamb: for the great day of his wrath is come; and who shall be able to stand?** [Sixth seal] Rev. 6:15-17.

At this point Jesus is on His way and the wicked know it. The Sixth seal ends with the question, "Who shall be able to stand?" The answer is given in the seventh seal:

19. THE SEVENTH SEAL AND THE "HALF HOUR" SILENCE IN HEAVEN

> And when he had opened the seventh seal, there was **silence** in heaven about the space of half an hour. Rev. 8:1.

Ellen G. White has connected the sixth seal with the seventh seal in one descriptive paragraph of one specific scene and event. She quotes the last sentence-question of the sixth seal and then describes the action of the seventh seal which is silence in heaven about the space of half an hour. In this manner she has explained exactly the meaning of that period of silence as follows:

> Soon there appears in the east a small black cloud . . . the sign of the Son of man. . . . it is a great white cloud . . . Before His presence . . . The righteous cry with trembling "Who shall be able to stand?" [Sixth Seal; Rev. 6:17] . . . and there is a period of **AWFUL SILENCE** [Seventh Seal; Rev. 8:1]. Then the voice of Jesus is heard, saying: "My grace is sufficient for you". . . . The King of kings descends upon the cloud, wrapped in flaming fire. The heavens are rolled together as a scroll . . . every mountain and island is moved out of its place. *The Great Controversy,* p. 640-642.

20. CONCLUSION

The seven seals present, together with the plagues-trumpets, one great panorama from 1844 to the Second Coming. Seals 1-5 precede the close of probation and lead into the plagues-trumpets. Seal 6 aligns with the seventh plague and the sixth and seventh trumpets. Trumpets, seals, and plagues all come into one alignment of endtime events.

When these events of Revelation are aligned with those of Daniel 12, these prophecies all enfold and interpret each other in truth and block out error. This is *GETTING IT ALL TOGETHER*.

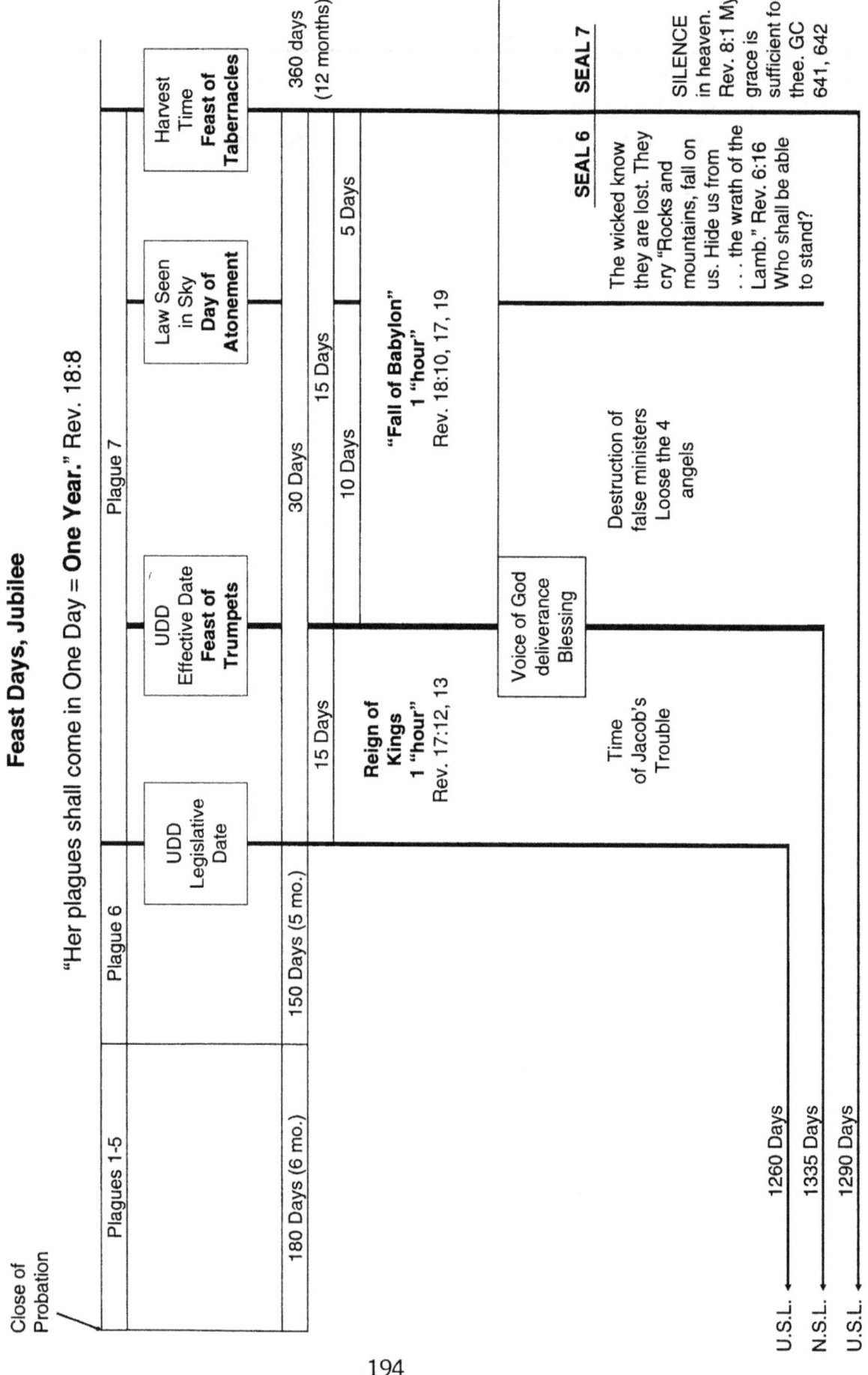

THE FEAST OF TABERNACLES

FEAST OF HARVEST

> . . . The fifteenth day of this seventh month shall be the feast of tabernacles for seven days unto the Lord. . . . (verse 34) . . . on the eighth day shall be an holy convocation unto you; (verse 36) . . . Also in the fifteenth day [the first day of the feast] . . . when ye have gathered in the fruit of the land, ye shall keep a feast unto the Lord seven days: on the first day shall be a sabbath, and on the eighth day shall be a sabbath. (verse 39) Lev. 23:34, 36, 39.

A question will arise. The Feast of Tabernacles was an eight day feast. From the first day of the Feast of Trumpets to the end of the Feast of Tabernacles was a full 23 days. Then why do we not include those eight days together with the two "one hour,"—fifteen-day periods on the chart?

The answer to that question is explained as follows:

The Feast of Tabernacles, or Feast of Harvest, was typical of the Second Coming of Jesus, when "the wicked will all be destroyed." This is the harvest of the wicked as well as the harvest of the righteous.

> In the seventh month came the Feast of Tabernacles or of ingathering. . . . the harvests had been gathered into the granaries . . . the labors of the harvest being **ENDED.** The Feast of Tabernacles . . . pointed forward to the great day of **FINAL** ingathering of the fruits of the earth . . . **AT THAT TIME the wicked will all be destroyed** . . . *Patriarchs and Prophets,* p. 540, 541.

AT THAT TIME when the wicked will all be destroyed, that will be **THE END OF EARTH'S HISTORY.** It is when Jesus comes, that the wicked will all be destroyed by the brightness of His coming and God's people will be on their way to heaven.

> We all entered the cloud together and were **SEVEN DAYS** ascending to the sea of glass, when [on the eighth day] Jesus brought the crowns and with His own right hand placed them on our heads. *Early Writings,* p. 16, 17. Maranatha p. 305.

The events regarding the history of this world cover time only to the Second Coming. The journey to heaven is not a part of earth's history. Therefore the Feast of Harvests shows only the first day on the charts. Everything after that is beyond earth's final crisis and deliverance.

A Correlation of Seals, Trumpets, and Plagues

Rev. 4, 5 Dan. 7 Investigative Judgment Time-Frame for the Seven Seals.	Seal No. 1 Rev. 6:1, 2 Rev. 14:6 Rev. 10:11 White Horse 1844-today SDA Church	Seal No. 2 Rev. 6:3,4 Rev. 13:11 Rev. 13:5 Red Horse **Sunday Laws SDA Church Persecution**	Seal No. 3 Rev. 6:5, 6 Black Horse rider with balance scales. Selling out Apostasy	Seal No. 4 Rev. 6:7, 8 Pale (sick) Horse **Death-Grave, Sword, Hunger, Beasts**	Seal No. 5 Rev. 6:9-11 **Martyrs** Rev. 18:1-4 **Loud Cry** "Avenge our **BLOOD**"		
			"little time of trouble"		Close of Probation. Plagues Begin. Rev. 8:2-5	Plague No. 1 **Sores** from infected **BLOOD**. Rev. 16:2.	Plague No. 2 Ocean as **BLOOD** of a dead man. Fish die. Rev. 16:3.
					Rev. 15:8	Trumpet No. 1 **BLOOD**, hail, fire. ⅓ of grass & trees burned. Rev 8:7.	Trumpet No. 2 Ocean as **BLOOD**, ⅓ of ships destroyed. Fish die. Rev. 8:8-9.

7 Seals   **7 Trumpets**

7 Plagues

The Sealing Work Begins
JUBILEE DELIVERANCE BEGINS
God's saints are sealed
"eternally secure"
"nevermore to be defiled"
T5 475

Day of Atonement
Investigative Judgment Ends
Jubilee Deliverance From Sin.
Dan. 9:24 fulfilled "to make an end of sins . . . to bring in everlasting righteousness" to God's people.

1844
Investigative Judgment Begins
Day of Atonement Oct. 22

Day of Atonement

A Correlation of Seals, Trumpets, and Plagues

					Seal No. 6 Heaven's roll back as a scroll. Rev. 6:14.		Wicked hid in dens, rocks. "Hide us from the . . . Lamb" Rev. 6:15, 16.	Seal No. 7 Silence in heaven about ½ hour. Jesus is on His way to earth. Rev. 8:1.
Plague No. 3 Fountains of waters as **BLOOD**. Rev. 16:4-7.	Plague No. 4 The Sun Scorches men with heat. Rev. 16:8, 9.	Plague No. 5 **Darkness** on seat-kingdom of beast. Rev 16:10, 11.	Plague No. 6 **Evil Spirits** gather all kings to legislate a Universal **Death Decree**. Rev. 16:12-16.	**Voice of God** deliverance from **Death Decree**. Rev. 16:17.	Plague No. 7			
					Cities of the nations fall. Hail. Rev. 16:19.	Thunder and Lightning. Two tables of the **Law** seen in the sky. GC 639 Earthquake. Rev. 16:18.	**Voices** of doom from heaven declaring sentence on wicked. Rev. 16:18.	
Trumpet No. 3 Fountains and Rivers of waters bitter as Wormwood. Rev. 8:8-9.	Trumpet No. 4 Sun, Moon, and Starts smitten. Rev. ⅓ darkened ⅓ day ⅓ night (8 hours) Rev. 8:12.		Trumpet No. 5 **Evil Spirits** as locusts "running to battle" to legislate the **Death Decree**. Rev. 9:1-11. WOE NO. 1	**Voice** (of God) from heaven deliverance. Rev. 11:12	Trumpet No. 6 **Nations are angry.** Rev. 11:18. WOE NO. 2	Thunder and Lightning. Earthquake. Rev. 11:12, 13.	Trumpet No. 7 **Voices** of doom declaring sentence on the wicked. Rewards for the righteous. Hail. Rev. 11:15-19. WOE NO. 3	

(Time of Trouble)	Feast of Trumpets **JUBILEE DELIVERANCE** from **THE UNIVERSAL DEATH DECREE** by **THE VOICE OF GOD.** Rev. 16:17	**DAY OF ATONEMENT** "Then commenced the Jubilee— "When the land shall rest" EW 286	**FEAST OF TABERNACLES** (7 days ascending to heaven) **JUBILEE DELIVERANCE FROM DEATH**
Her plagues shall come in one day (year). Rev. 18:8		Day of Atonement ___ 5 days to	By resurrection By translation

Jubilee Deliverances

1. From sin in the Investigative Judgment Sealing.
2. From enemies at the Voice of God.

    "the land shall rest"—the Law seen in the sky.

3. From the grave by resurrection and translation.

DANIEL 12 TIMELINES ARE THE FRAMEWORK FOR EVENTS DESCRIBED IN REVELATION

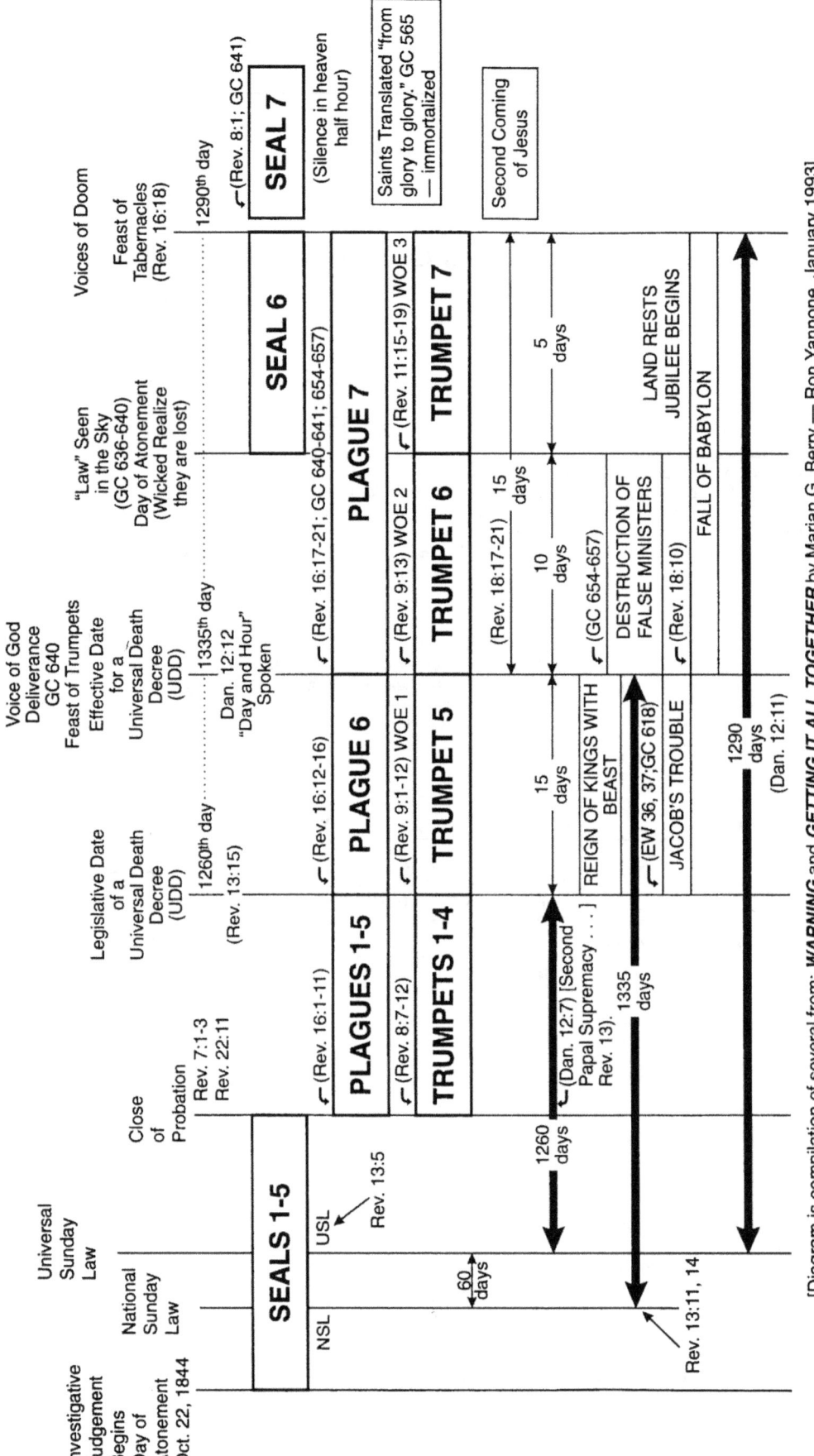

GETTING IT ALL TOGETHER

DANIEL 12 TIMELINES, PLAGUES, SEALS, AND TRUMPETS, FALL FEASTS, REVELATION 17, AND THUNDERS

With Bible and E.G. White References

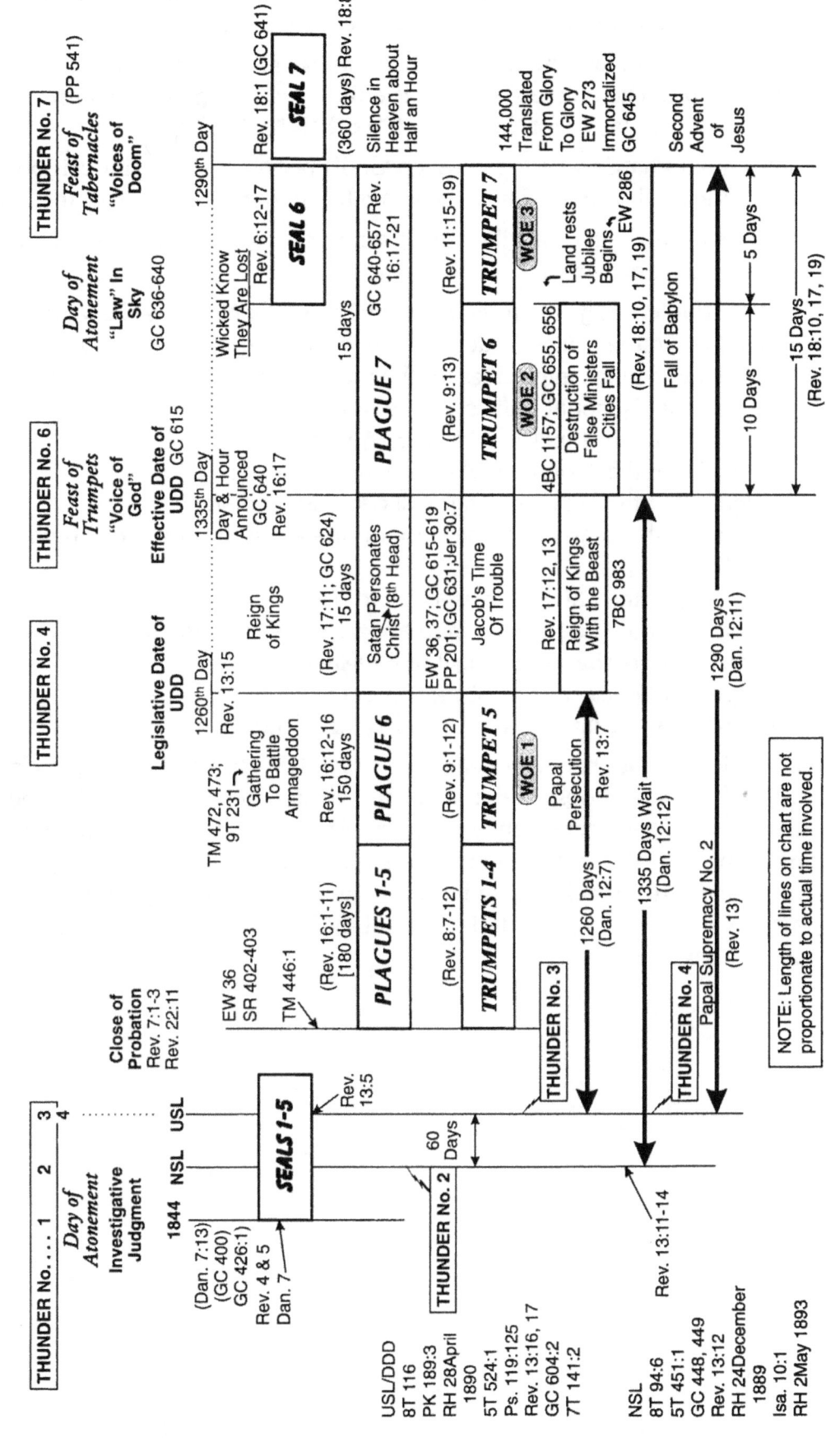

199

- **The Daniel 12 Timelines are the framework on which the events foretold in Revelation can be organized, thus forming a web of truth.**
- The National Sunday Law in the United States of America is the formation of the **image to the beast**. The Sunday law and its adherence becomes the **mark of the beast**. The decision for Sunday or for Sabbath is **THE FINAL TEST**.
- The spiritual **shaking** occurs in which God's people make their decision. They obtain the victory (the Seal of God). Thus, they pass through the judgment of the living victoriously.
- They receive the latter rain, the refreshing, to enable them to give the loud cry of the third angel to the entire world.
- The **WARNING** as given in Matthew 24:15 and Daniel 12 is the legislation of a National Sunday Law in the United States of America, and is to God's people:
  a. A signal to flee the large cities for the mountains
  b. A signal that National Ruin is soon to follow
  c. A signal that the "Final Test" is in operation
  d. A signal that the Judgment of the Living has begun
  e. A signal that the final "shaking" will occur immediately
  f. A signal of the nearness of the close of probation (first for the church and then for the world)
  g. A signal that the Latter Rain is about to begin
  h. A signal that the Loud Cry—third angel's message is to go to all the world in the power of the fourth angel of Revelation 18
  i. A signal that persecution will soon begin
  j. A signal that the timelines of Daniel 12 have begun
- Prophetic timelines begin and end with **VOICES**—legislative and judicial actions. This is a rule which can be observed in timelines which have been fulfilled in the past. The same rule can be applied consistently to the timelines of Daniel 12 which are in the future. The three timelines of Daniel stand independent of each other. When they are viewed as one unit they are **interlocking**, and give the student of prophecy an understanding of the complex actions of the very last scenes of the final conflict—final deliverance and end of evil in this world!

A Circular Correlation Chart of Interacting Endtime Events as Revealed by Plagues, Trumpets, Seals, Daniel 12 Timelines, and Major Lines of Bible Prophecy

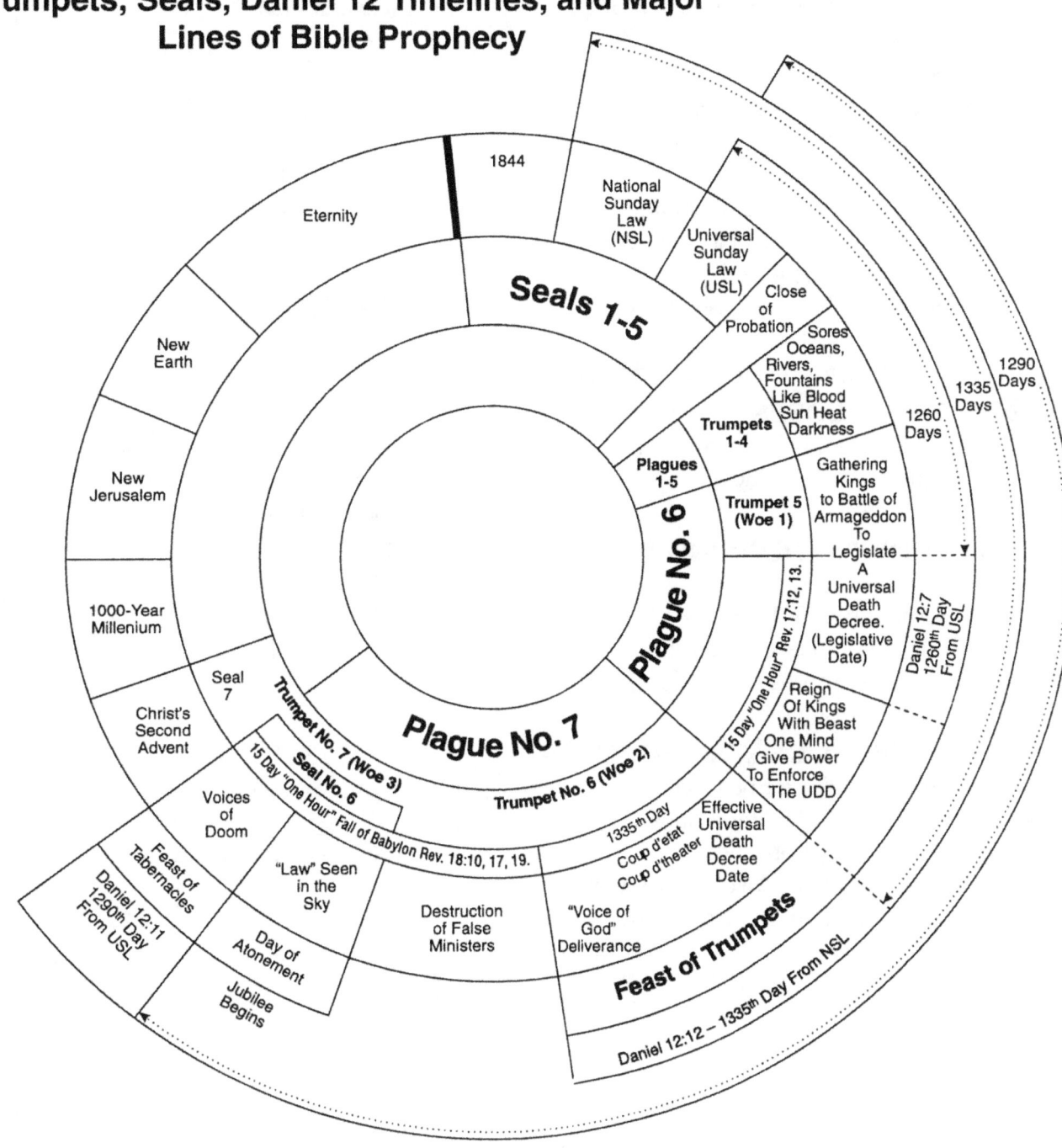

CORRELATION OF SEALS, TRUMPETS, PLAGUES, REV. 17, DANIEL 12
Provides *A SEQUENTIAL OUTLINE* **of Endtime Events From**
1844 TO CHRIST'S SECOND COMING[1]

1844 INVESTIGATIVE JUDGMENT BEGINS	(Dan. 8:14)
Seal No. 1 Begins	(Dan. 7:10; Rev. 4, 5, 6:1)
NATIONAL SUNDAY LAW (USA)	(Rev. 13:11)
Seal No. 2	(Rev. 6:4)
1335 Day Timeline Begins	(Dan. 12:12)
UNIVERSAL SUNDAY LAW	(Rev. 13:5)
1260 Day Timeline Begins	(Dan. 12:7)
1290 Day Timeline Begins	(Dan. 12:11)
"Daily" Scepter "Taken Away"	(Dan. 12:11)
PAPAL Supremacy No. 2 Begins	(Dan. 12:11)
Seal No. 3 Apostasy Follows	(Rev. 6:5,6)
Seal No. 4 Troubles follow	(Rev. 6:7,8)
Seal No. 5 Follows	
(Martyrdoms, then Loud Cry)	(Rev. 6:9-11)
PROBATION CLOSES	
Plagues Begin (Last one year)	(Rev. 18:2-8; Rev. 15:8)
Plague 1-5 (180 days)	(Rev. 16:1-11; Rev. 8:5, 10)
Trumpets 1-4	(Rev. 8:1-13)
"GATHERING"—"RUNNING TO BATTLE" TO ARMAGEDDON	
Plague No. 6	(Rev. 16:12-16)
Trumpet No. 5 (Woe 1)	(Rev. 9:1-11)
"Running to Battle five months	(Rev. 9:5, 10)
(five months is 150 days)	
to legislation date	
THE UNIVERSAL DEATH DECREE	(Rev. 13:15)
Legislation Date Ends 1260	(Dan. 12:7)
"One Hour" (15 literal days)	
Begins "Reign of Kings"	(Rev. 17:12,13)
Begins "Time of Jacob's Trouble"	
which lasts until "Voice of God"	

---

[1] Includes Fall Feast Days

THE VOICE OF GOD (Rev. 16:17)
    Effective Date of DECREE
    God's People Delivered
    Day and Hour of Christ's Coming Announced
    Everlasting Covenant Pronounced
    Special resurrection
    (Those of 3rd Angel's Message)
    Plague No. 7 begins   (Rev. 16:17)
    "One hour" Reign Ends   (Rev. 17:14)
    "One hour" Fall of Babylon Begins   (Rev. 17:14-18; Rev. 18)
    (15 literal days "Fall")
    False Ministers' destruction begins
    Trumpet No. 6 Begins Woe 2   (Rev. 9:12-21)
    Four Angels Loosed   (Rev. 9:15-21)
    Nations angry—Cities Fall
    Feast of Trumpets—10 Days Begin

TEN COMMANDMENTS SEEN IN THE SKY (Rev. 11:11,12)
    Day of Atonement Display
    Trumpet No. 7 Woe 3 "Earthquake"   (Rev. 11:13)
    Plague No. 7 "Earthquake"   (Rev. 16:18)
    Seal No. 6   "Earthquake"   (Rev. 6:12)

VOICES OF DOOM
    Feast of Tabernacles (after 5 days)
    Seal No. 7 Silence in the heavens
    Christ's Coming
    144,000 translated, General Resurrection
    Seven days Ascending to Heaven
    The Millennium

NOTE: 180 days plus 150 days plus 30 days equals 1 year. Plagues 1-5, plus 5 months, plus 30 days (15 + 15) equals 1 year which fulfills Revelation 18:8.

CHAPTER XXII

REVELATION 17—AN EXERCISE IN BIBLE SYMBOLISM

INTRODUCTION

Revelation 17 is a "wrap up" of endtime events. It is a mosaic of the symbolism from Chapter 12 through 16. It presents basically four pictures of endtime events which occur in regard to the following:

1. A view of counterfeit religion carried along and supported by Satan, himself.

2. A description of Satan's final, crowning act of deception as he personates Christ, the King of kings.

3. A picture of Satan working through the kings of the earth to legislate a Universal Death Decree and their exaltation for "one hour" or 15 literal days—until the voice of God delivers the saints.

4. An introduction to the "Fall of Babylon" which follows the voice of God deliverance. That account is continued into chapter 18.

One thing has caused confusion. John the Revelator, has gathered all the symbolism of the previous chapters into one continuous account. This means that he is first describing Satan, that great red dragon; but changes over, without notice, to the "beast" of Revelation 13. He "switches horses in the middle of the stream!"

Whereas the first symbol of Revelation 12 is that of a "red" or "scarlet" beast; the Revelation 13 beast has the body of a leopard. They do not look alike! Both the red beast and the leopard-like beast have seven heads, but they are not the same beast. Because of the fact that these beast-symbols are complicated by descriptions of heads and horns, it is very helpful to make models of them. These beasts are described in the Bible in detail, and illustrated in this chapter with pictures. Then the Bible student can visualize these beasts, their parts, heads, and horns to understand their symbolic meanings.

William Miller, so long ago, discovered the consistency of Biblical symbolism. From Genesis to Revelation it is constant in its representations. Each symbol is interpreted by Scripture itself. "Private interpretations" are forbidden. Therefore the Bible, when correctly understood, will interpret the symbols and their meanings in Revelation 17. If correctly done, they will fit in perfectly with the testimony of the plagues, trumpets and seals.

Therefore, this study will be done, verse by verse, permitting the Bible to be its own expositor. A correct Biblically interpreted understanding of Biblical prophetic symbols will preserve the Bible student from errors.

A STUDY OF SYMBOLS IN REVELATION 17

1. A SYMBOLIC *WOMAN*

The symbolic woman is introduced in Genesis 2 and 3. The literal woman from whom the symbolic woman is taken is Eve. "And Adam called his wife's name Eve because she was the **MOTHER of ALL LIVING,"** **MOTHER, not only of all who have been born here on earth, but also in the spiritual sense, a symbolic mother of all who shall have eternal life.**

The kingdom of God, in which the saved will exist forever, has a capital city, **THE NEW JERUSALEM**. The names of all the "born again" are registered there and that is why the apostle Paul said:

> . . . Jerusalem which is above is free, which is the **MOTHER of us all [both Jews and Gentiles]**. Gal. 4:26.

It is for this reason that the **WOMAN-MOTHER** symbol, which is named New Jerusalem, is understood to be the **UNIVERSAL CHURCH** of all ages. Most of her members are in the grave, she is also known as the **INVISIBLE CHURCH**.

The invisible church is **NOT** made up of members of all the other denominations which make up Babylon! This is a common error in the "New Theology."

This **WOMAN-MOTHER** is brought to view as the first symbol of that line of prophecy which extends from Revelation 12 through 22.

> And there appeared a great wonder in heaven; a woman [mother] clothed with the sun, and the moon under her feet, and upon her head a crown of twelve stars: And she being **WITH CHILD** cried travailing in **BIRTH, AND PAINED TO BE DELIVERED.** See Rev. 12: 1,2.

We are also children of this **woman-mother** because we are called her **seed**. Rev. 12:17. For this reason, Jesus is called our "Brother."

2. TWO SYMBOLIC WOMEN

In Revelation 17:1-7 **another** symbolic **WOMAN-MOTHER** of contrasting character is brought to view. The good woman of Revelation 12 is described in sharp contrast to the **bad** woman of Revelation 17. Revelation 17 is the counterpart of Revelation 12 in these two descriptions of these women. This gives the Bible student a full picture of the controversy between good and evil, between the **TRUE CHURCH and the FALSE or COUNTERFEIT CHURCH**—religions of the earth. In contrast to New Jerusalem "that great city," the bad woman symbol represents "that great city" of false and confused religions. The woman of Revelation 12 is a **UNIVERSAL CHURCH, of all ages, culminating her work in an end-time setting.**

A contrasting picture of these two women follows:

REV. 12	REV. 17
JERUSALEM	BABYLON
MOTHER OF US ALL	MOTHER OF HARLOTS

These two prophetic symbols represent two **UNIVERSAL** systems of religion. From creation to the end of time, these two symbols portray the true church and the false, or counterfeit, church.

A Table of Comparisons and Contrasts
Jerusalem - Babylon

COMPARISONS	CONTRASTS	
	Jerusalem, *the true church*	**Babylon**, *the counterfeit*
Both are represented in prophetic symbols as a **WOMAN**	Rev. 12:1-17 a **good** woman	Rev. 17:3 a **bad** woman Rev. 18
Both are represented in prophetic symbols as a **MOTHER**	Rev. 12:2 "being with child" Rev. 12:17 "her seed" Gal. 4:26 "mother of us all" Song of Songs 1:6; 6:9; 8:2, 5	Rev. 17:5 "mother of harlots"
Both women have a **name**	Gal. 4:26 "**Jerusalem**, mother of us all"	Rev. 17:5 "a name . . . **Babylon**"
Both women have **daughters**	Jer. 6:2 "I have likened the **daughter** of Zion [Jerusalem] to a . . ." Song of Songs 2:7; 3:11; 5:8, 16; 6:4, 9; 8:2	Rev. 17:5 "mother of **harlots**"
Both women hold executive positions	Rev. 12:1 ". . . upon her head a **crown** of twelve stars"	Rev. 18:7 "she saith, I sit a **queen**"
Both women are supported	Rev. 12:1 ". . . the moon under her feet" see Ps. 89:34-37 (God's covenant)	Rev. 17:1, 3, 15 "sitteth upon many waters . . . upon a scarlet coloured beast . . . peoples, and multitudes, and nations"
Both women are **clothed**	Rev. 12:1 "**clothed** with the sun" Rev. 21:2 "prepared as a bride"	Rev. 17:4 "**arrayed** in purple and scarlet colour"
Both women are **adorned**	Rev. 21:2 "as a bride **adorned** for her husband" Rev. 21:11 "her light . . . as a stone most precious" [19]	Rev. 17:4 "**decked** with gold and precious stones" Rev. 18:16
Both women are a "**city**"	Rev. 21:10 "that great **city**"	Rev. 17:18 "that great **city**"
Both women existed during the 1260 year prophetic period.	Rev. 12:6 "fled" . . . "a thousand two hundred and three score days"	Rev. 17:6 "drunken with the blood of martyrs"

A Table of Comparisons and Contrasts (continued)
Jerusalem - Babylon

COMPARISONS	CONTRASTS	
	Jerusalem, *the true church*	**Babylon**, *the counterfeit*
Both women know the prophetic beast of Revelation	Rev. 12:4, 13, 17 "the dragon stood . . . to devour her child . . . he persecuted the woman . . . was wroth . . ."	Rev. 17:3 "I saw the woman sit on the beast"
Both women deal in **merchandise**	Rev. 3:18 "I counsel thee to **buy** of me . . ." Isa. 55:1 "**buy** wine . . . and milk" Matt. 25:9 "them that **sell** and **buy**" Song of Songs 3:6 "With the powders of the **merchant**"	Rev. 18:11 "**merchants** of the earth shall weep and mourn over her" See Eze. 27; Isa. 47:15 She deals in the "souls of men" Rev. 18:13
Both women build an edifice or "**house**" (church) and invite all to enter to eat and **drink** of their doctrine	Song of Songs 8:2 "I would lead thee into my mother's **house**" 5:1 "I have drunk my wine" Pro. 9:1, 2, 5 "Wisdom hath builded her house" "she hath furnished her table." She calls "Come **eat** of my bread, and **drink of the wine** which I have mingled. . . ." "Ho, every one that thirsteth" (Isa. 55:1).	Rev. 18:3 "All nations have **drunk of the wine** of her fornication"
Both women have established a **priesthood**	Ex. 30:23-25, 29, 30 "consecrate them" "In the priest's office" "an high priest" Heb. 9 Song of Songs 4:13, 14 "anointing **spices**" Ex. 30:23-25 "an oil of holy ointment . . . an anointing oil, of principal spices"	Rev. 18:13 "**spices** and the souls of men"

3. THE GREAT DRAGON-BEAST

A symbolic snake-serpent-reptile-beast is introduced in Genesis 3. From the literal snake whom Satan possessed in the Garden of Eden, comes the symbolic snake-dragon-beast referred to from Revelation 12 through 17.

Satan is represented in these passages in three forms:

1. **A "serpent"** DECEIVER — Gen. 3
2. **A "dragon"** PERSECUTOR — Rev. 12
3. **A "beast"** PERSONATOR of the King of kings. — Rev. 17

These three symbols of Satan and his work point to the entire line of his activities. He was a **deceiver** of angels in heaven and of men, he is the great **persecutor** of God's people, and his "crowning act" brought to view in Revelation 17 is his **personation** of Christ.

The word, "beast," encompasses all these roles that Satan has taken, because, as we all know, both a serpent and a dragon are "beasts." These three roles are also significant in that they reveal his determination to take all the roles of Christ as follows:

1. A "serpent"—deceiver—forthteller—prognosticator .... **Prophet**
2. A "dragon"—persecutor—judge .... **Priest**
3. A "beast"—head of universal government........... **King**

Revelation 12 presents Satan as the "serpent-dragon,"—symbolic of him and his work.

> And there appeared another wonder in heaven; and behold a great **RED** dragon...
> And the great dragon was cast out, that old **SERPENT,** called the Devil, and Satan, which **DECEIVETH** the whole world... Rev. 12:3, 9.

The color, **RED,** identifies with the **SCARLET-colored beast of Revelation 17.** The rest of the description also identifies the Revelation 17 "beast" as Satan himself as follows:

Revelation 12	Revelation 17
"... having seven heads and ten horns... " Rev. 12:3.	"... having seven heads and ten horns." Rev. 17:3.

Chapter 17 of Revelation is a "wrap-up," a completion of the entire prophetic "mosaic," extending the picture to a description of Satan's endtime exertions. It is he who supports and carries false religion and therefore "Babylon" rides upon him.

The description of his supportive action to Babylon is pictured as follows:

Babylon rides along, not on a leopard-like beast (not the beast of Revelation 13) but "upon a ***scarlet*** colored beast, full of names of blasphemy, having seven heads and ten horns"—the great "red dragon, having seven heads" (Rev. 17:3; 12:3). "And his tail drew a third part of the stars of heaven." Rev. 12:4. And the woman was "arrayed in purple and scarlet colour, and decked with gold and precious stones and pearls, having a golden cup in her hand full of abominations and filthiness of her fornication: (verse 5) And upon her forehead was a name written, **MYSTERY, BABYLON THE GREAT, THE MOTHER OF HARLOTS AND ABOMINATIONS OF THE EARTH**: And I saw the woman drunken with the blood of the saints, and with the blood of the martyrs of Jesus . . . the beast that carrieth her, which hath the seven heads and ten horns . . . was, and is not . . . and yet is." Rev. 17:4-8.

And there came one of the seven angels which had the seven vials [the seven last plagues], and talked with me, saying unto me, Come hither; I will show unto thee the judgment [end] of the great whore [Babylon] that sitteth upon many waters[1] . . . the waters which thou sawest, where the whore sitteth, are peoples, and multitudes, and nations, and tongues. Rev. 17:1, 15.

With whom the kings of the earth have committed fornication,[2] and the inhabitants of the earth have been made drunk with the wine of her fornication. Rev. 17:2.

So he carried me away in the spirit into the wilderness: and I saw a **WOMAN [MOTHER]** sit upon a scarlet coloured **[RED] BEAST,** full[3] of names of blasphemy, [determined to usurp the titles and roles of Christ and of the Trinity], having **SEVEN HEADS AND TEN HORNS [Satan himself]**. Rev. 17:3.

And the woman [Babylon] was arrayed in purple and **SCARLET color,** and decked with gold and precious stones and pearls, having a golden cup in her hand full of abominations and filthiness of her fornication: (Rev. 17:4)

And upon her forehead was a name written, **MYSTERY, BABYLON THE GREAT [city]** the **MOTHER OF HARLOTS** and Abominations of the Earth. Rev. 17:5.

And I saw the woman drunken with the blood of the saints, and with the blood of the

---

1 How does Babylon sit on the "waters" which represent peoples and also sit on the "beast"? Babylon—false religions "sits on," or presides over, the peoples of the earth. It is Satan, however, who "carries her" inserting false doctrine and supporting her.

2 The symbol of Babylon always refers to false religions. It never refers to nations or kings. The kings commit fornication with her. The kings represent nations and kingdoms, but Babylon is "confusion" of religion.

3 Satan is red and the woman—Babylon, is arrayed in red. Isa. 1:18. A symbol for sin.

MARTYRS of Jesus [as described in the fifth seal]: and when I saw her, I wondered with great admiration [amazement]. Rev. 17:6.

And the angel said unto me, [Why] didst thou marvel? I will tell thee the mystery of the woman, and of the beast that carrieth her, which hath the seven heads and ten horns. Rev. 17:7.

Revelation 17:9-18 then explains the "mysteries" as to how this great controversy will be resolved at the very endtime crisis and deliverance. What is Satan going to do to bring all of this to an end and bring about the destruction of Babylon? This is a most exciting chapter!

4. SATAN'S "CROWNING ACT"

As the crowning act in the great drama of deception, Satan himself will personate Christ. The church has long professed to look to the Saviour's advent as the consummation of her hopes. Now the great deceiver will make it appear that Christ has come. In different parts of the earth, Satan will manifest himself among men as a majestic being of dazzling brightness, resembling the description of the Son of God given by John in the Revelation. Revelation 1:13-15. The glory that surrounds him is unsurpassed by anything that mortal eyes have yet beheld. The shout of triumph rings out upon the air: "Christ has come! Christ has come!" The people prostrate themselves in adoration before him, while he lifts up his hands and pronounces a blessing upon them, as Christ blessed His disciples when He was upon the earth. His voice is soft and subdued, yet full of melody. In gentle, compassionate tones he presents some of the same gracious, heavenly truths which the Saviour uttered; he heals the diseases of the people, and then, in his assumed character of Christ, he claims to have changed the Sabbath to Sunday, and commands all to hallow the day which he has blessed. He declares that those who persist in keeping holy the seventh day are blaspheming his name by refusing to listen to his angels sent to them with light and truth. This is the strong, almost overmastering delusion. *The Great Controversy*, p. 624.

Where is the Biblical source for this information? Revelation 17:8, 11. It is an endtime-final crisis event.

Revelation 17:8 is difficult to understand because the sentences are not complete. It says the beast—Satan, **"WAS"** and **"IS NOT"** but does not say **what** he "was" and what he "is not" now. The **Bible** must explain what Satan "was" and what he "is not."

The beast that thou sawest **WAS, and 'IS NOT'**; and shall ascend out of the bottomless pit, and go into perdition . . . Rev. 17:8.

WHAT WAS Satan? The Bible explains that he was an angel in heaven, named Lucifer—**LIGHT BEARER,** the sum of God's creative skill. He **WAS** an angel of light and glory and **VISIBLE**. Glorious in his person, he was loved by the entire heavenly host and took the highest position among all the created angels and hosts of heaven. (See Isa. 14:12-19 and Eze. 28:2-9).

How art thou fallen from heaven, O Lucifer, son of the morning! . . . thou hast said in thine heart . . . I will exalt my throne above the stars of God . . . I will sit also upon the mount of the congregation . . . I will be like the most High. Yet thou shalt be brought down to hell, to the sides of the pit. Isa. 14:12-15.

Satan **"IS NOT"** now *VISIBLE* nor glorious in our sight. We cannot even see him. Except when requested by spiritistic seance, he is not permitted now to appear to intimidate with visible glory.

The populace of the world has not chosen him as their master yet and therefore God does not give him this privilege. He cannot yet make such public appearances. But Revelation 17 explains that the day will come when he will ascend out of this obscurity.

> The beast [serpent-dragon Satan] that thou sawest was, and is not [now visible]; and shall **ASCEND OUT OF THE BOTTOMLESS PIT,** and go into perdition . . . Rev. 17:8.

The "bottomless pit" is not merely this world in a chaotic condition but also is often referred to in Scripture as the "habitation" of Satan and his fallen angels (See Rev. 9:1-2). There they are bound in "chains of darkness" and obscurity and can emerge only with God's specific permission.

Satan, the "beast" of Revelation, presents his final crowning act in the personation of Christ, coming forth in great glory and majesty. He is symbolized there as a "beast"—because he personates the KING of kings. This symbol is consistent with the Biblical interpretation of a "beast" as referring to kings as follows:

> These great beasts, which are four, are four **KINGS,** which shall arise out of the earth. Dan. 7:17.

The wicked will all be deceived by this glorious appearance of the Devil as he assumes this role of king of kings. Only God's people, who have loved Scriptural truth and accepted the gift of prophecy with love, will know that it is Satan himself:

> . . . and they that dwell on the earth shall wonder [be amazed and taken in], whose names were not written in the book of life from the foundation of the world, **WHEN THEY BEHOLD** the beast that was, and is not, and **YET IS**." Rev. 17:8.

We cannot **BEHOLD** him now. But when he personates Christ all the wicked will **BEHOLD** him. Satan "is not visible" and "yet is" very active and alive and his influence felt.

5. "AND HERE IS THE MIND WHICH HATH WISDOM" Rev. 17:9

At this point the Bible student must have the wisdom to understand that the prophecy now changes as it uses the word, "beast" from the dragon-beast of Revelation 12 to the leopard-like "beast" of Revelation 13.

At this point, John the Revelator was shown a third prophetic picture. He reveals to us how Satan, of Revelation 12, works with the "beast" of Revelation 13, and the kings of the earth, to bring about a Universal Death Decree. This is initially explained in Revelation 13:2.

> And the beast which I saw was like unto a leopard, and his feet were as the feet of a bear, and his mouth as the mouth of a lion: **AND THE DRAGON GAVE HIM HIS POWER, AND HIS SEAT, AND GREAT AUTHORITY.** Rev. 13:2.

REVELATION 17 CORRELATES WITH PLAGUES 6 AND 7

The "gathering of the kings of the earth and the whole world" by evil spirits to the Battle of Armageddon is the topic of Revelation 17:10-14.

The "Fall of Babylon," which occurs under the seventh plague, at the Voice of God is the topic of Revelation 17:15-18.

Revelation 17:10-14 simply gives additional detail, concerning the Universal Death Decree.

(A Correlation Chart follows on the next page):

A CORRELATION CHART OF AN ALIGNMENT OF REVELATION 17:10-18 WITH PLAGUES AND TRUMPETS

PLAGUE 6 TRUMPET 5	(REIGN OF KINGS WITH BEAST)	PLAGUE 7 TRUMPETS 6 & 7
Gathering of all Kings to legislate a **UNIVERSAL DEATH DECREE** Rev. 16:12-16 Rev. 9:1-11	Legislation Date of a **UNIVERSAL DEATH DECREE** → … Effective Date of a **UNIVERSAL DEATH DECREE** and VOICE OF GOD	
	Ten Horns Ten Kings "receive power" and REIGN with the leopard-like beast Rev. 17:12	**Ten Horns Ten Kings** "hate the whore, and shall make her desolate and naked, and shall eat her flesh, and burn her with fire." Rev. 17:16
	"ONE HOUR" (15 literal days)	**"ONE HOUR"** (15 literal days) Rev. 18:10, 17, 19 **THE FALL OF BABYLON** (SEALS 6 & 7)

7. THE SYMBOLISM AND SEQUENCE OF SYMBOLIC "HEADS"

A careful investigation of Biblical interpretation of heads and horns ultimately reveals that "heads" refer to *SEQUENCE* of kings or kingdoms and the "horns" to *SCOPE* of kingly power.

"Heads" in prophetic symbolism represent kingdoms.

> Thou, O king [Nebuchadnezzar] art a king of kings. . . . Thou art this **head** of gold. Dan. 2:37, 38.

A king represents his kingdom. He cannot be a king without a kingdom. A "Head" of government or the government itself, is the "head" administrative agency of the whole empire.

Revelation 17:9, 10 repeats this symbolic interpretation.

> The seven **heads are** . . . seven **kings**. Rev. 17:9, 10.

When Rev. 17:9 indicates that the seven heads are seven **mountains**, that again is a reinforcement of the idea that "heads are kings" or kingdoms, because in Daniel 2 Nebuchadnezzar saw a great **"mountain"** which was the source of the great stone **kingdom** which filled the whole earth.

The seven symbolic "heads" of the serpent-dragon-beast are **not the same** as the seven heads of the leopard-like beast.

The seven heads of the dragon-Devil reveal the entire **sequence** of his career in sin as he **attempted** seven times to establish a kingdom. These seven attempts are listed below:

8. SATAN'S SEVEN ATTEMPTS TO ESTABLISH HIS KINGDOM

HEAD NO.	ATTEMPT	TIME	ATTEMPT FRUSTRATED
1	Heaven. One third of the angels rebelled.	Before Creation	They were cast out.
2	Eden. Adam sold out his dominion. The Fall.	Creation	The Flood
3	Babel. Established as a capital of an intended world monarchy	2218 BC	Languages Confused
4	Christ. To take the King is to possess the kingdom.	AD 31	Resurrection
5	Papal Supremacy. Attempts to destroy truth and God's people.	AD 538-	1798—Pope imprisoned
6	Armageddon. A Universal Death Decree	FUTURE	The Voice of God Deliverance
7	GOG and MAGOG Attempt to take the Holy City.	End of the 1000 years	The Lake of Fire

The seven heads of the dragon-Devil reveal the sequence of his career in sin as he **attempted** seven times to establish a kingdom. Not one attempt thus far has been successful. Neither will the last two attempts succeed.

The Seven heads symbols represent a **sequence of attempts to establish the kingdom of Satan, and thereby gain this planet as his own.**

9. THE SYMBOLIC "HEADS" OF THE LEOPARD-LIKE BEAST

Again a *sequence* of *kingdoms* is revealed. This leopard-like beast is known as the "composite" beast because its description is composed of body parts which make up the four beasts of Daniel's vision in chapter 7. Daniel saw a lion, a bear and a leopard. Again, the leopard-like beast of Revelation 13 is made up of a lion's mouth, bear's feet, and a leopard-like body. These identify the first three heads:

1. Babylon
2. Medo Persia
3. Greece
4. Rome
5. Papal Rome

These heads are in sequence, and we know that the Papal Supremacy was brought to an end in 1798 by an atheistic government (ideology). Atheistic Communism spread to Eastern Europe and from there to over half of the world, persecuting God's people. It is evident by historical fulfillment, sequence, and continuity, that the sixth head referred to atheistic Communism. This is also brought to view in Daniel 11:36-45.

The seventh head of the leopard-like beast is revealed as a "New World-Order"—as yet future in Revelation 17:10.

> And there are seven kings: five are fallen, and one is [is now falling], and the other [the New World-Order with the Pope at its head] is not yet come; and when he cometh, he must continue a short space. Rev. 17:10.

This prophecy places us today between the sixth and seventh head. We have known for more than a century that we live in the time of the toes of the great image of Daniel 2. We have advanced in prophetic fulfillment so that we are just now waiting for the seventh head to emerge and become a great world empire.

Will the "New World-Order" with its Papal head become the last king? The answer is No. The prophecy does not end there.

215

> And the beast that was, and is not [Satan, himself], even he is the **eighth** [head], and is of the seven [worked through all seven to persecute God's saints], and goeth into perdition. Rev. 17:11.

Satan himself will be the last great world ruler when he personates Christ. He will then assume the role of **KING of kings.** All that he has undertaken in his rebellion here on earth has been perpetrated toward this one great goal.

10. THE EIGHT HEADS OF REVELATION 17

\multicolumn{4}{c}{THE EIGHT HEADS OF REVELATION 17}
Head No.	Empire	Date	Reference
1	Babylon	606-538 B.C.	Dan. 2:38
2	Medo-Persia	538-331 B.C.	Dan. 2:39
3	Grecia	331-168 B.C.	Dan. 2:39
4	Pagan Rome	168- A.D. 476	Dan. 2:40
5	Papal Rome	A.D. 476-538 to 1798	Dan. 7:25
6	Communism	A.D. 1798-1918 to 1989	Dan. 11:36
7	Papal Rome II (ONE WORLD ORDER)	FUTURE	Dan. 12:11
8	SATAN'S PERSONATION	END TIME	Rev. 17:11

Each emerging kingdom replaced the one before it. Satan's crowning act will occur just before the fall of Babylon under the seventh plague.

11. *THE "TEN HORNS" SYMBOL*

Anyone who has ever observed cattle or wild creatures will know that the horns of an animal determine who will be "boss" over the rest. Horns represent kings. This interpretation is taken directly from the Scripture as follows:

> And the ten horns which thou sawest are ten kings . . . Rev. 17:12.

12. *THE "TEN" SYMBOL*

Why are there **TEN** horns brought to view in Rev. 17:12?

Biblical symbols extend, not merely through prophecy but also are found in the parables. In the parable of Matthew 25, **TEN virgins** are brought to view. Five were wise and five were foolish. The **"TEN"** virgins represented **ALL who** were looking for the bridegroom to come. The number **TEN** is a symbol for **ALL.** In Revelation 17 it may be understood that these ten kings refer to *all* **the kings or governments—a "One World Order" at the end of time.** The sixth plague, which describes the same situation, states this fact very plainly as follows:

> For they are the spirits of devils, working miracles, which go forth unto the **kings of the earth and of the WHOLE WORLD,** to gather them to the battle of that great day of God Almighty [Armageddon]. Rev. 16:14.

This is the Biblical interpretation. It is not profitable to speculate that these ten refer to a certain ten countries of Europe, or ten sections of the world, or anything other than that which the Bible itself reveals: *"ALL."*

The final conflict will not be merely in Europe, nor in certain sections of the world, but will be a total conglomerate of ALL nations:

> And **ALL** that dwell upon the earth shall worship him, whose names are not written in the book of life of the Lamb slain from the foundation of the world. Rev. 13:8.

It is under the sixth plague that these ten (all) kings are gathered. It is in Revelation 17 that the picture is completed. They are gathered to legislate a Universal Death Decree against God's people. Revelation 17 adds information as to how long it will be between the legislation date and the effective date when the decree shall be enforced.

> And the ten horns which thou sawest are ten kings, which have received no kingdom as yet; but receive power as kings **ONE HOUR with the beast** [Literally 15 days]. These have one mind [are all agreed], and shall give their power and strength unto the beast [To carry out the Universal Death Decree]. Rev. 17:12, 13.

The first five plagues enrage the wicked. They think that it is the nonconformist Sabbath keepers who are preventing God's favor. The kings of the earth are all agreed at last, that it would be better to annihilate them than to continue with the plagues and the whole world perish.

Jesus explained that whatever was done to the righteous was as if it were done to Himself. Therefore the next verse says that:

> These shall make war with the Lamb [by smiting His people] and the Lamb shall overcome them: for he is Lord of lords, and King of kings: and they that are with him are called, and chosen, and faithful. Rev. 17:14.

"The Lamb overcomes them" by uttering "The Voice of God." Rev. 16:17. At that point, Babylon falls. The fall of Babylon is described in the last four verses of Revelation 17, and Chapter 18.

13. THE "FALL OF BABYLON"

> And the ten horns which thou sawest upon the beast, these shall hate the whore, and shall make her desolate and naked, and shall eat her flesh, and burn her with fire. For God hath put in their hearts to fulfill his will, and to agree, and give their kingdom unto the beast, until the words of God shall be fulfilled.
> And the woman which thou sawest is that great city, which reigneth over the kings of the earth. Rev. 17:16-18.

> ... all nations have drunk of the wine of the wrath of her fornication, and the kings of the earth have committed fornication with her ... Therefore shall her plagues come in one day, death, and mourning, and famine; and she shall be utterly burned with fire ... And the kings of the earth, who have committed fornication and lived deliciously with her, shall bewail her, and lament for her, when they shall see the smoke of her burning, Standing afar off for the fear of her torment, saying, Alas, alas, that great city **BABYLON,** that mighty city! for in **ONE HOUR**[1] is thy judgment come....
> For in **ONE HOUR** so great riches is come to naught....

---

1 Note: **"ONE HOUR"** of symbolic time represents 15 literal days.

for in **ONE HOUR is she made desolate....**
And in her was found the blood of prophets, and of saints, and of all that were slain upon the earth. Rev. 18:3, 8-10, 17, 19, 24.

THE THIRTY DAYS OF FINAL CRISIS AND DELIVERANCE

Between the 1260 and 1290 day timelines of Daniel 12, there is a 30 day difference. This 30 days describes the ascending and descending actions in the last Act of the Drama of Final Crisis and Final Deliverance of God's people.

These 30 days are divided into two 15 day periods. It is the "Voice of God" deliverance which divides the 30 days into two 15 day periods. These two 15 literal day periods are spoken of in Scripture as "one hour" of symbolic time. (One symbolic hour represents 15 literal days). These two "one hour" periods are spoken of in Revelation 17:12; and Revelation 18:10, 17, and 19.

These two 15 day periods are involved with the final Universal Death Decree; in its legislation, then in its Effective Date, the time when it is to be put into effect. On that very Effective Date, when it is to go into effect at Midnight, then the Voice of God will deliver God's people from it. The last 15 day period describes the "Fall of Babylon" which follows the "Voice of God" coup d'etat or coup d'theater. These events may all be listed as follows:

A. Legislation of a final Universal Death Decree.
B. The Exultant Reign of Kings of all the world with the Beast over the fact that they have just legislated this decree. They exult for "one hour" or 15 days. Rev. 17:12, 13 and Rev. 11:10.
C. "The time of Jacob's Trouble" is the cry for deliverance. While the wicked exult, God's people cry for deliverance.
D. The "one hour" or 15 days lasts from Legislation date to Effective Date.
E. On the Effective Date, the "Voice of God" occurs.
F. At the Voice of God, God's people are delivered.
G. God's people are glorified with light.
H. At the Voice of God, the wicked know they have been deceived.
I. the wicked cannot look at God's people.
J. the wicked worship at their feet.
K. the wicked reproach their false ministers.
L. At the Voice of God, the false ministers confess to the world.
M. The wicked turn on the false ministers and kill them.
N. False religion falls apart: At "The Fall of Babylon," Spiritism, Apostate Protestantism, and Catholicism separate.
O. The Law of God is seen in the sky. Rev. 11:12, 13; 6:14.
P. The wicked know they are lost and cases judged.
Q. The wicked hide in the caves and rocks
R. The nations are angry. Cities of the nation fall in war.
S. Voices of doom declare the fate of the wicked.
T. Jesus is seen coming in the clouds
U. There is silence in heaven. See G.C. 604.

14. CONCLUSION

> We have also a more **SURE WORD OF PROPHECY;** whereunto ye do well that ye take heed, as unto a *LIGHT* that shineth in a dark place, until the day dawn, and the daystar arise in your hearts . . . II Peter 1:19.

God has not left His people to stumble through the darkness of final crisis—the terrible plagues and trumpets, the reign of the beast power, the pressures of the "image of the beast" and passages of laws contrary to the law of God, through fines and imprisonment, and even martyrs' deaths, without the **SURETY, HOPE, COMFORT AND KNOWLEDGE** which is furnished by a correct understanding of prophecy.

Their way will be illuminated with the bright **LIGHTS** of the timelines of Daniel 12, with the information found in the correlation of plagues, trumpets, and seals.

Each fulfillment, from the passage of the National Sunday Law in the United States of America will inspire them with hope and joy. When they see all these things, they will look up with faith, knowing that their deliverance is at hand.

JESUS IS COMING TO GET US!

So likewise ye, when ye shall see all these things, know that it is near, even at the doors. Matt. 14:33.

Every prophetic utterance will have its weight—nothing will be cast aside. Each fulfillment will define exactly where God's people are in the prophetic time-clock. Hope and faith will expand to joyous expectation.

CHAPTER XXIII

THE WEB OF TRUTH SUMMARY

Permitting the Bible to define its own terms, set its own timeframes, to follow its own sequence and continuity; to permit plagues, trumpets and seals to interpret each other; to permit the symbolism to remain constant and precise, in this study, GETTING IT ALL TOGETHER, has produced a picture of God's remnant church in an unbroken line of events stretching from 1844 through the time of the plagues and trumpets; covering the final crisis, final deliverance, and on to the Second Coming of Jesus.

Prophecy is intended to provide the people of God with sufficient information so they can get their bearings as to where they are in the stream of time. It helps them to line up future events in sequence and to know what is coming next. It gives them a sense of cause and effect relationships and an insight into the great controversy struggle, and confidence in the providence of God which will see them through.

Whereas speculative and presumptive ideas imposed on prophecy leave God's people scattered and confused, floundering about in disjointed concepts, the correct methods of study bring all the prophecies into correct relationships, and shed light on what becomes cohesive and logical, thus unifying these truths into one body. The Bible, and especially the books of Daniel and Revelation, become a precious **"WEB OF TRUTH."**

This book, **GETTING IT ALL TOGETHER**, is not a new "interpretation" (decoding) of symbolism. It is more detailed, specific, and definitive. It is not a new application of past historical events, except that it permits recent events to "unroll the scroll" of fulfilled prophecy in our own day. It is not a new version of future events, other than those already outlined in scripture and by Ellen G. White.

It is unique only in that it has unified the outlines of Daniel and Revelation into one picture with a focus on endtime perspectives of final crisis and deliverance. It establishes the Holy Scriptures as a **"WEB OF TRUTH"** to glorify The Word of God.

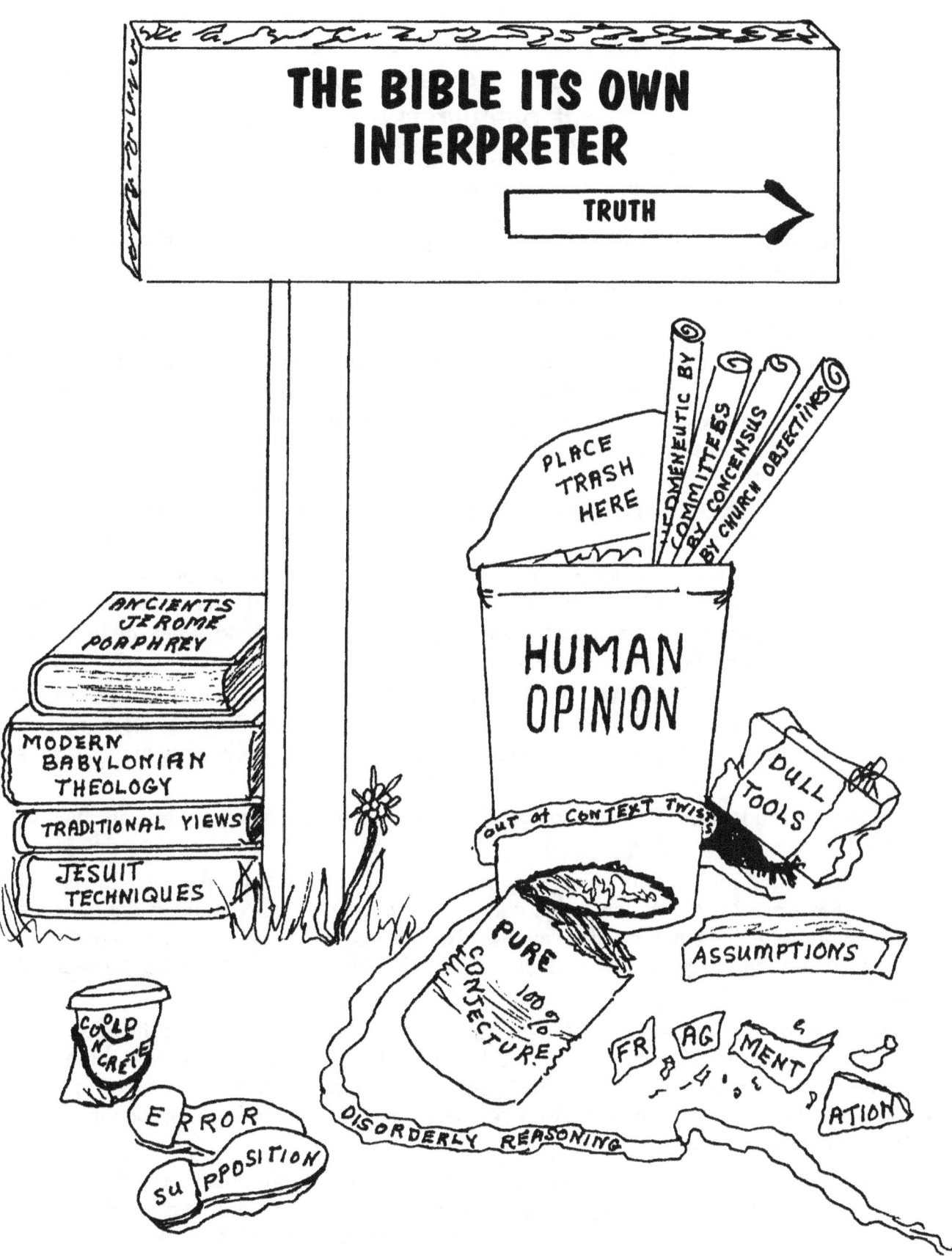

HERMENEUTICS

> **HERMENEUTIC PRINCIPLES ARE DERIVED FROM THE BIBLE**

> . . . Human teaching is shut out. There is no place for tradition, for man's theories and conclusions, or for church legislation. No laws ordained by ecclesiastical authority are included . . . *The Desire of Ages,* p. 826, 827.

True and reliable Biblical Hermeneutics are never derived from uninspired sources. They do not come from theologians or scholars, committee actions, by concensus, or by church objectives! The only safety is in the Word of God. Only as we permit the Bible to bring forth its own hermeneutic principles, to be its own expositor, to define its own terms, to decode its own symbols, to provide its own timeframes, and provide its own clues, will the links ever form one continuous chain of Truth.

The author of **GETTING IT ALL TOGETHER** has attempted to use these guidelines in dealing with the prophetic Word.

Many articles in current publications are appearing on the subject of hermeneutics. Great caution in the reading of these should be urged. There is not only apostasy in the very winds but there is also a war that is waged against the very foundation principles on which doctrines are based. If the foundations of hermeneutic principles can be shaken the entire doctrinal structure will fall.

What does the author of **GETTING IT ALL TOGETHER** recommend in an effort to assist the student in his study of the prophecies? Search and study diligently the Scripture, itself, noting the various things it says regarding your own readiness and condition of the heart, which is necessary to find Truth.

The teacher and student should always be awake to the discovery of hermeneutic principles which will facilitate progress.

The Bible specifies a multitude of concepts in regard to the hermeneutic principles: the condition of the heart and mind of the student, relationship of the scholar with God and His dependence on the Holy Spirit for enlightenment, his relationship with fellow-man, his love for, or repudiation of sin in his life and many other things, including a sanctified life of attention to what he eats, drinks and does!

But even more difficult and elusive is the fact that the student of Scripture must have an attitude which is in love with TRUTH. If his pride and love of self demands that he twist and manipulate everything to promote his own opinions and positions, in preference to an acceptance of truth, he will, by nature, use all of his talents to glorify self, sacrificing integrity and all that is connected with unbiased, objective research!

It is a fact that many minds, which appear to be exceedingly bright and productive in Biblical studies, have been so disqualified by habitual self-pride that they cannot permit the Bible to be its own expositor and they fall into the traps of "private interpretations" of Biblical symbols which are a snare to such mentality.

It is often the simple layman or child whose heart is open to instruction and who loves God supremely, who desires most of all to find the truth, who comprehends the deep things of God, prophecies, and secret things, far above and beyond that of the prideful, self-opinionated "teacher" of righteousness. It was not the Pharisees or doctors of the law who welcomed prophetic studies of Jesus, but the "common people heard him gladly." It is still so today.

How then shall we approach the Bible? One of the most important hermeneutic principles is stated below:

THE "LITERAL APPROACH"

"The language of the Bible should be explained according to its obvious [LITERAL] meaning, unless a symbol or figure is employed." *The Great Controversy*, p. 599.

"Every declaration of Scripture is to be taken in the most obvious and literal sense, except where context and well-known laws of language show that the terms are figurative, and not literal, and whatever is figurative must be explained by other portions of the Bible which are literal." *A Symposium on Biblical Hermeneutics*. G. Hyde. Statement by Don Neufield. 1974.

It is the disregard for this hermeneutic rule that has brought about the most damaging technique ever devised, against prophetic exposition: futurism and preterism.

Francisco **RIBERA** (1537-1591), Jesuit scholar and writer, introduced Futurist Counterinterpretation, against the Protestant Reformation in Europe. There was also Louis de Alcazar (1554-1613) who devised what is known as Preterism. Both of these Jesuits violated **"THE LITERAL APPROACH."** They devised a simple but very effective **JESUIT TECHNIQUE** of *interchanging literal and symbolic language.*

The European Protestant Reformers, identified Papal Rome to be the antichrist of Daniel 7. The Popes, desperate to take this accusing finger from them, commissioned Jesuit scholars to devise a method to counteract this interpretation of prophecy.

Daniel 7 is written in *symbolic language.* (Beasts, heads, horns) Therefore, the Protestant Reformers kept the 1260 timeline of Daniel 7:25 in **context,** and treated it as *symbolic* time. This identified the long reign of the Papacy as antichrist.

Ribera and Alcazar both used the Jesuit technique of interchanging *symbolic* language for *literal.* They considered the "time, times, and half a time" to be a *literal* three and a half years. It was then easy to place that three and a half years far in the future, thus taking the accusing finger off Papal Rome. Not only did they defend the Papcy but blinded Protestantism and laid the groundwork for the "gap" or rapture theory.

While Ribera placed the 1260 far into the future, called **FUTURISM,** Alcazar placed the 1260 far in the past and that is called **PRETERISM.** Either way, it took the finger off Papal Supremacy No. 1 (538-1798). By this simple technique they dissembled the Historicist prophetic interpretation of Daniel 7 and its application to Papal Rome.

What we need to understand today, is that the same Jesuit technique can be used on Daniel 12. Daniel 12 is written in *literal language* (no beasts, no heads, no horns). Therefore it is *necessary* to keep the three timelines in literal **context, so that the 1260, 1290 and 1335 are taken as LITERAL DAYS.**

If those literal 1260, 1290, and 1335 days, are treated as if they were symbolic time, that is the same Jesuit technique as that which dissembled Daniel 7. That interchanging of literal and symbolic language will produce the same results. Just as the dissembling of Daniel 7 took the accusing finger off Papal Rome (538-1798), blinding the eyes of Protestantism; in like manner that Jesuit technique on Daniel 12 takes the accusing finger off Papal Supremacy No. 2 in our near future! This is a new form of **ENDTIME PRETERISM. It blinds the eyes of Adventism to future events. Remnant people, beware!**

We need to remember that a diligent study of time prophecies which throw light upon endtime events, is not the same thing as "time setting" for the Second Coming of Jesus.

Ellen G. White has cautioned against "timesetting" for the Second Coming, but never against a study of timelines which throw light on future events. She reminded timesetters that the "prophetic time" ended in 1844, but it must always be understood that she was referring to the 2300 day prophetic timeline of Dan. 8:14. It must be recognized that the 2300 day timeline was a prophecy and therefore it was called "prophetic time." When she said that "prophetic time" ended in 1844, she was saying that *"the prophetic time LINE of 2300 day-years"* ended at that time.

When she wrote indicating that the "prophetic periods" ended in 1844, she was referring to those prophetic periods spoken of in Daniel 9 which were a part of the computation of the 2300 years. She was not referring to all time prophecy in Daniel and Revelation. We know this because she made the statement that the **"*prophetic periods of Daniel*, extending to the very eve of the great consummation (Second Coming) throw a flood of light upon events then to transpire."** Review and Herald, Sept. 25, 1883.

If there is one thing Satan hates it is a revelation of Present Truth, which is revealed in prophecy. Many statements taken out of context and misapplied are circulated to erect a barrier between the people of God and the Word of God.

Jesus said, "Search the Scriptures." John 5:39. He never said, "Leave out all prophecies dealing with time!" Neither did Ellen G. White. Beware of quotations (actually taken out of context) which instill a fear or a barrier against a study of *any* portion of the Word of God.

A study of hermeneutics is a "science." It requires the same diligent attention to research methods as does any other science. The scholar should go through the same processes: research and collection of data, organization of the data, the formulation of a thesis or premise, presentation, refinement, and closure. He should treat his subject with the same common sense, integrity, and objective, orderly attitude that would attend any other scientific research.

The teacher and student of Scripture should always be awake to the discovery of hermeneutic principles which will facilitate progress in comprehending Truth. A good teacher builds a body of knowledge in an orderly, progressive manner from simplified concepts to that which is more complex. For example: a math teacher begins the child's learning by first introducing "number concept." When that is mastered, then the child learns to add, then to subtract, then to multiply, then to divide, and then learns decimals and percentages. The process goes on until he is proficient in algebra and trigonometry, and even greater knowledge so that he can cope with the projects which need to be accomplished.

This process of learning Truth is described in Isaiah 28:9-13.

> For precept [premise] must be upon precept, precept upon precept; line upon line, line upon line; here a little, and there a little . . . Isa. 28:9-13.

This process is to continue until he can be "approved unto God, a workman that needeth not to be ashamed, rightly dividing the word of truth." II Tim. 2:15. We are commanded by Jesus to "search". John 5:39. It becomes a life-long occupation.

The one danger is that Laodicea will take the attitude toward prophetic studies, "I am rich, and increased with goods, and have need of nothing; and knowest not that thou art wretched, and miserable, and poor, and blind, and naked. . . . I counsel thee to buy of me . . . eye-salve that thou mayest see." Rev. 3:17, 18.

The hermeneutics vital to a study of the prophetic portions of Daniel and Revelation have been brought to view in the text of **GETTING IT ALL TOGETHER.** The reader may wish to review the book to list them as they are usually found in the introductions to each chapter.

Books have been written about Biblical hermeneutics. It is not necessary to repeat all of that in this Appendix section. *A Symposium on Biblical Hermeneutics,* edited by Gordon M. Hyde, prepared by the Biblical Research Institute Committee of the General Conference of Seventh-day Adventists, 1974, printed by The Review and Herald Publishing Association, Washington, D.C., is recommended. Another good source is titled, *Protestant Biblical Interpretation* by Bernard Ramm of Baker Book House, Grand Rapids, Michigan, 1970. The reader should discriminate as he reads these books, but generally many excellent explanations and helpful information can be obtained from them.

Ellen G. White's use of the Scripture and her comments on how to use the Book are valuable. They have been collected together in the book mentioned above, *A Symposium on Biblical Hermeneutics*. The topics which were addressed are as follows:

Ellen G. White's Evaluation and Use of the Bible. She wrote on the following topics:

1. Attitude toward the Bible
2. Attitude toward Truth
3. Objective Frame of Mind
4. Exacting Investigation
5. Diligence with Patience
6. The Holy Spirit's Guidance
7. Concept of the Nature of Scripture
8. The Nature of Inspiration
9. The Text and Canon of Scripture
10. Revelation is Progressive
11. The Unity of the Scripture
12. Ellen White's Biblical Hermeneutics
    A. The Historical and Cultural Setting
    B. The Cultural Background and Personal Characteristics of the Writers
    C. Word Meanings
    D. The Context
    E. The Analogy of Scripture
    F. Textual Variants

    G.   Literal meaning: Figurative Language
    H.   Modes of Using Scripture
- a. She used Direct Quotation
- b. She used Indirect Quotation
- c. Quotes conversations
- d. She used Hypothetical Conversation
- e. She used Amplification
- f. Insight. Making things clear
- g. Illustration to illustrate principles
- h. Homily. Draws lessons from Scripture
- i. Borrowing Words from Scripture to express her own ideas.
- j. Prophetic fulfillment
- k. Messianic fulfillment
- l. Extended application (Lessons for all time)

For further study of these topics see *A Symposium on Biblical Hermeneutics*. 1974. Adventist Book Centers.

Hermeneutic Principles are basically derived from the Bible itself. The author of **GETTING IT ALL TOGETHER** has no new principles to add! However, in dealing with prophetic Scripture, some guidelines are found to be helpful. As an historicist the following observations should be kept in mind:

1. Prophecy is history written in advance.
2. History may repeat itself, and thus have parallel applications.
3. History repeated may be observed in Papal Supremacy No. 1 and No. 2.
4. However, Prophecy is written in an orderly progressive forward movement, and
5. The forward progressive movement prohibits applications which throw the sequence and continuity of historical events out of order, making such applications weak and unsupportable.
6. Prophetic outlines are written in the sequential order of events predicted.
7. Major prophetic lines of prophecy maintain an orderly progressive forward movement of events in their chronological order.
8. Each additional outline provides additional detail to that which has gone before it.
9. Prophetic outlines align with, and interpret, each other.
10. The entire Bible moves from Genesis to Revelation with an overall, forward, progressive action.
11. The books of Daniel and Revelation were written, not so much for their own day, but for the last generation.
12. Daniel and Revelation interpret each other.
13. The entire Bible—"all these things" are examples; written for us (the last generation) "upon whom **the ends of the world** are come." I Cor. 10:11. This is a Biblical Hermeneutic Principle especially for the last generation.
14. Prophetic language may be either symbolic or literal.
15. Symbolic language must be interpreted by the Scripture itself.

16. Literal language may not be given symbolic meaning.[1]
17. Prophetic timelines or time must be kept in **context** with the literal or symbolic language used therein.
18. Prophetic and symbolic language when interchanged perverts prophetic interpretation.
19. Prophetic timelines must be given beginning and ending points to be of any value.
20. Prophetic timelines may not be given arbitrary beginning and ending date, but must have these derived from the Bible itself.
21. Prophetic outlines, timelines or any line of prophecy never give the day and hour of the Second Coming of Jesus.
22. Prophetic timelines or periods "throw a flood of light upon events, then to transpire," regarding final crisis and deliverance.
23. The entire Bible, with all its symbolic language is a "Web of Truth," and all interconnected.
24. Basically, prophecy outlines the rise and fall of nations and the destiny of God's people.
25. Prophecy brings the Bible student to Jesus and enlightens his mind. It shows us where we are now in the stream of time.
26. Prophetic timelines begin and end with legislative decrees.
27. Legislative action is the "speaking" Voice of government.
28. Prophetic timelines are not shortened or lengthened. Persecution has been shortened, but not the timeline.
29. Prophecy, when correctly understood, delivers God's people in every age from apostasy.
30. Correct use of prophecy unifies God's people.

---

[1] "Symbols" are not to be confused with simile, metaphore, parallels, or titles such as "the abomination that maketh desolate." A "symbol" is a "picture" or model of something such as a beast, a person, a horn, a crown, etc.

APPENDIX NOTE A

APPENDIX NOTE B

THE GREAT RED DRAGON

The "great red dragon" of Revelation represents the devil and his kingdom.

> And there appeared another wonder in heaven; and behold a great red dragon, having seven heads and ten horns, and seven crowns upon his heads. . . . the great red dragon was cast out, that old serpent, called the Devil, and Satan . . . Rev. 12:3, 9.

The devil is a "king" which seeks constantly to establish his kingdom.

> Satan's agents are constantly working under his direction to establish his authority and build up his kingdom . . . *The Great Controversy*, p. 507.

The seven heads and ten horns of the great red dragon represent a scope and sequence of his dominions.

The Bible provides its own key to prophetic symbolism. The key to the interpretation of the meaning of the heads of the dragon is given in Revelation 17:9, 10. That passage declares that the seven "heads are seven mountains." It is important to understand, however, that "mountains" are also prophetic symbolism, and must be interpreted by Biblical reference.[1] The Bible provides the key to the meaning of "mountains" in the following passage where it declares that "mountains" represent "kingdoms."

> . . . the stone that smote the image became a great **mountain** . . . the God of heaven [shall] set up a **kingdom,** which shall never be destroyed . . . Dan. 2:35, 44.

Very simply, in prophetic symbolism, a prophetic "head" is the same as a prophetic "mountain," which represents a literal kingdom.

In Revelation 17:9, 10 the concept that "heads" and "mountains" represent kingdoms is reinforced by the following verse where it reiterates that idea by repetition, saying, that:

> there are seven kings [kingdoms] . . . Rev. 17:10.

---

[1] It may require a reading of the entire chapter of Daniel 2 to get the meaning of the story to recognize that the prophetic/symbolic **mountain** in the dream of the king, was interpreted by the prophet, Daniel, to represent the **kingdom** of God, a literal (real) dominion to be established upon this earth.

This double reference is characteristic in prophetic symbolism and gives assurance of correct interpretation. It then proceeds to give the **SEQUENCE** of kingdoms (verse 10).[1]

The number "seven" would appear to give a complete sequence. The number "seven" in Scripture often implies a completed or finished work (see Gen. 2:2). Therefore, the seven heads of the great red dragon should represent the complete sequence of Satan's kingdoms or dominions.

It is not difficult to trace the seven dominions of Satan. They are as follows:

1. The dominion over fallen angels in heaven (Rev. 12).
2. The dominion over man, gained in the garden of Eden—to the flood (Gen. 3).
3. The dominion over man, re-established at Babel (Babylon) (Gen. 11).
4. The dominion over Christ, at the crucifixion (the four gospels).
5. The dominion over Christianity through the Papal Supremacy (Dan. 7:25).
6. The dominion over "all the world" at Armageddon (Rev. 16).
7. The dominion over all the wicked and evil angels at the battle of Gog and Magog.

These seven heads represent the consecutive sequence of the dominions which have been; and will be established by Satan, from the beginning of his rebellion to the last stand at the battle of Gog and Magog when he will be utterly consumed. These seven dominions will be more thoroughly considered, each in detail, in this appendix note:

THE GREAT RED DRAGON

> And there appeared another wonder in heaven; and behold a great red dragon, having seven heads and ten horns, and seven crowns upon his heads. And his tail drew a third part of the stars of heaven, and did cast them to the earth . . . And the great dragon was cast out, that old serpent, called the Devil, and Satan, which deceiveth the whole world: he was cast out into the earth, and his angels were cast out with him. Rev. 12:3, 4, 9.
>
> . . . a scarlet-colored beast, full of names of blasphemy, having seven heads and ten horns. Rev. 17:3.

DOMINION NO. 1. *Satan's Dominion Over Fallen Angels.*

Satan's first dominion was established in heaven over evil angels. This is one of the first concepts presented in Revelation 12, where the "great red dragon—Satan" is introduced:

> And his tail drew the third part of the stars of heaven, and did cast them to the earth: and the dragon . . . was cast out . . . he was cast out into the earth, and his angels were cast out with him. Rev. 12:4, 9.
>
> [Satan] . . . is a mighty general, who controls the minds of evil angels . . . *The Great Controversy*, p. 507.

---

1. The sequence of the seven heads mentioned in Revelation 17:9 refers to the heads of the composite beast of Revelation 13. However, the key to prophetic symbolism should consistently apply to prophetic symbols throughout the Scripture. The concept of "kingdoms" and the concept of sequence is therefore legitimate.

DOMINION NO. 2. *Satan's Second Dominion Established in Eden.*

By virtue of creatorship the earth belonged to God. He gave this dominion of the earth over to Adam (Gen. 1:28). When Adam, through sin, placed himself under Satan's control, he submitted the dominion of the earth into Satan's possession. "Legally," the usurper, gained dominion or rulership of the earth.[1] When Satan claimed dominion of this earth, he appeared at heavenly councils as its representative (Job 1). There he declared himself to be the "god of this world," or the "prince of this world," and protested the plan of salvation to the universe, claiming every human being to be his lawful captive. He complained bitterly when any soul was wrested from his grasp. The contest was over every human soul—whether it should be in Satan's dominion or in the kingdom of Christ.

Satan's dominion prospered so that in the days of Noah, only eight persons retained their integrity to God and entered into the ark. It was Satan's intention to blot out the people of God from the entire earth, to establish a universal dominion and thereby secure the earth for eternity.

Instead, God swept away Satan's entire dominion by a universal flood. None but God's people came forth from the ark after the flood.

DOMINION NO. 3. *Satan Re-established Dominion at Babel-Babylon.*

Satan's third attempt to establish a universal dominion began shortly after the flood in the plains of Shinar (near Mt. Arrarat where the ark had rested), at the tower of Babel.

> For a time, the descendants of Noah continued to dwell among the mountains where the ark had rested. As their numbers increased, apostasy soon led to division. Those who desired to forget their Creator, and to cast off the restraint of His law . . . journeyed to the plain of Shinar . . . Here they decided to build a city, and in it a tower . . . to found a monarchy [dominion] that should eventually embrace the whole earth. Thus their city would become the metropolis of a universal empire . . . *Patriarchs and Prophets*, p. 118, 119.

At Babel, the worship of the true God was replaced with a counterfeit system, a form of sun worship wherein the heavenly bodies were worshipped in place of the true "Sun of Righteousness." The types and symbols of true worship were misapplied; and the rites and ceremonies, originally intended to point men to the Creator/Lifegiver, were so misconstrued as to cause men to worship the sun and Satan through their conduct and evil lives.

By a confusion of languages, men were driven to all parts of the earth from Babel, and unfortunately, the Babel races carried with them false systems of worship.[2]

The land of Shinar—site of the tower of Babel—emerged at last as the great Babylonian empire which gained universal dominion in the Middle East and the then civilized world. But in a broader sense, its counterfeit religious concepts and practices were carried to all parts of the earth, permeating heathendom as well as civilized regions so that it developed into a spiritual Babylon. This influence was overpowering and universally spoken of in Scripture, and not to be swept away until the seventh plague (Rev. 16:19) and to the very coming of Jesus.

---

1 "Legally"—the dominion was redeemed or purchased back to God by the life-blood of Jesus Christ and through His death sacrifice.

2 All forms of false worship conform to remnants of Babylonian worship which are traced in Alexander Hyslop's *The Two Babylons*.

Satan's third dominion—Babylon—as an earthly empire rose and fell. It reached its climax under Satan's strategy, when it took captive God's people, the Jews (606 B.C.), with the intent and purpose that they should be obliterated, swallowed up and lost in Babylon.

DOMINION NO. 4 *"The Hour . . . of the Power of Darkness"—The Crucifixion.*

[And Jesus said] . . . this is your **hour, and the power of darkness.** (Luke 22:53).

No man could lay hold on Jesus until that "hour" (John 8:20). Jesus prayed in Gethsemane that he might be saved from that "hour" (John 12:27; 13:1, 2). When Jesus took the sinner's place; when sin was rolled upon Him; when He bore the condemnation for sin; when He submitted to Satan's cruel power and submitted to death—the penalty for sin, Satan exulted in dominion over the **Son of God**—Creator and Lifegiver.

> Angels beheld the Saviour's agony. They saw their Lord enclosed by legions of satanic forces, His nature weighed down with a shuddering, mysterious dread. *Desire of Ages*, p. 693.

> Now the tempter had come for the last fearful struggle. For this he had been preparing during the three years of Christ's ministry. Everything was at stake with him. If he failed here, his hope of mastery was lost; the kingdoms of the world would finally become Christ's; he himself would be overthrown and cast out. But if Christ could be overcome, ***the earth would become Satan's kingdom,*** and the human race would be forever in his power. With the issues of the conflict before Him, Christ's soul was filled with dread of separation from God. Satan told Him that if He became the surety for a sinful world, the separation would be eternal. He would be identified with Satan's kingdom, and would nevermore be one with God. *Desire of Ages*, p. 686, 687.

As the burden of sin came upon Jesus, the dominion of Satan engulfed Him and His life was about to be crushed out—except that an angel strengthened Him. From Gethsemane He came under Satan's dominion—the oppression of evil angels and evil men. He suffered insult and indignity. At last Satan caused Him to be put to death. His body descended down into Satan's prisonhouse—the grave. This was the fourth dominion of Satan—the short "hour"—"the power of darkness." But it was a short triumph for Satan:

> The night of the first day of the week had worn slowly away. The darkest hour, just before daybreak, had come. Christ was still a prisoner in His narrow tomb. The great stone was in its place; the Roman seal was unbroken; the Roman guards were keeping their watch. And there were unseen watchers. Hosts of evil angels were gathered about the place. Had it been possible, the prince of darkness with his apostate army would have kept forever sealed the tomb that held the Son of God. *Desire of Ages*, p. 779.

DOMINION NO. 5 *The European Papal Supremacy Over Christendom,*
A.D. 538-1798.

The fifth dominion, known as the "little horn kingdom," was established by a union of church and state, prophesied by the prophet Daniel:

> [It] made war with the saints, and prevailed against them . . . he shall speak great words against the most High, and shall wear out the saints of the most High, and think to change times and laws: and they shall be given into his hand until a time and times and the dividing of time. Dan. 7:21, 25.

Under this "little horn," the courts of the inquisition condemned and put to death innumerable martyrs.

It is important to understand that in each of Satan's dominions, his ultimate purpose is that of "murder." He rebelled against God in his first attempt and was cast out of heaven, and under each dominion his objective has been to obliterate the people of God from the earth. The intent and purpose in each of his dominions was completely demonstrated in the crucifixion of the Second Person of the Godhead—his own Creator. All who understand the true nature of this "great red dragon"—should understand this objective as it is outlined in each of the seven heads. This will give understanding to future events.

There is a strange paradox. Satan's "hour" of triumph was actually his "hour" of defeat. Christ's "hour" of defeat and death, was actually His ultimate stroke of victory. In each of Satan's dominions, as martyrs have given their lives, their hour of "defeat" was actually a victory for Christ's kingdom. Although Satan appeared to have triumphed over Christ at His crucifixion, it was the end of his influence with the universe. In each of Satan's kingdoms, his victories are ever a signal for his final destruction.

DOMINION NO. 6. *The gathering of the Whole World at Armageddon.*

> And I saw three unclean spirits . . . the spirits of devils . . . which go forth unto the kings of the earth and of the whole world, to gather them to the battle of that great day of God Almighty . . . Armageddon. Rev. 16:13, 14, 16.

The purpose of this gathering has long remained an enigma. It is, of course, to blot out the people of God. This gathering of the kings of the earth, and of the whole world to unite with the "beast," the "false prophet," and the "dragon" (Roman Catholicism, apostate Protestantism, and spiritism)—will set up a **death decree** to obliterate the people of God.

The dominions of Satan follow one pattern: he attempted to draw away all of God's subjects (angels)—but succeeded in only "one third." He gathered all but eight souls at Noah's flood. He sought the life of the Son of God. He warred against the Christian church for 1260 years during the papal reign and put to death millions. Once again, at the gathering of Armageddon, he will seek to establish his dominion with a death decree to annihilate God's people. Instead, there will be 144,000 sealed without spot or blemish.

> When the protection of human laws shall be withdrawn from those who honor the law of God, there will be, in different lands, a simultaneous movement for their destruction. As the time appointed in **the decree** draws near, the people will conspire to root out the hated sect. It will be determined to strike in one night a decisive blow . . . *The Great Controversy*, p. 635.

DOMINION NO. 7. *The Battle of Gog and Magog.*

The last attempt to unify the whole world and to wrest the earth from Christ will be after the millennium. For the last time, he will seek to establish his dominion over the whole world to take the Holy City.

> And when the thousand years are expired, Satan shall be loosed out of his prison, And shall go out to deceive the nations which are in the four quarters of the earth, Gog and Magog, to gather them together to battle: the number of whom is as the sand of the sea. And they went up on the breadth of the earth, and compassed the camp of the saints about, and the beloved city: and fire came down from God out of heaven and devoured them. Rev. 20:7-9.

The last dominion is no more successful than any which preceded it. Nevertheless, each attempt—signified as a "head"—has provided a graphic prophetic picture of Satan's mighty attempts and rebellion against the government of God.

> But the judgment shall sit, and they shall take away his dominion, to consume and to destroy it unto the end. And the kingdom and dominion, and the greatness of the kingdom under the whole heaven, shall be given to the people of the saints of the most High, whose kingdom is an everlasting kingdom, and all dominions shall serve and obey him. Hitherto is the end of the matter . . . Dan. 7:26-28.

The Ten Horns and Seven Crowns

The seven crowns simply appear to reinforce the concept of kingdoms—kingly reign and establishment of dominions by Satan. (Kings wear a crown.)

The ten horns refer to the universal scope of power in that Satan has used the state governments universally to accomplish his purposes.

APPENDIX NOTE C

THE COMPOSITE BEAST OF REVELATION 13 AND 14

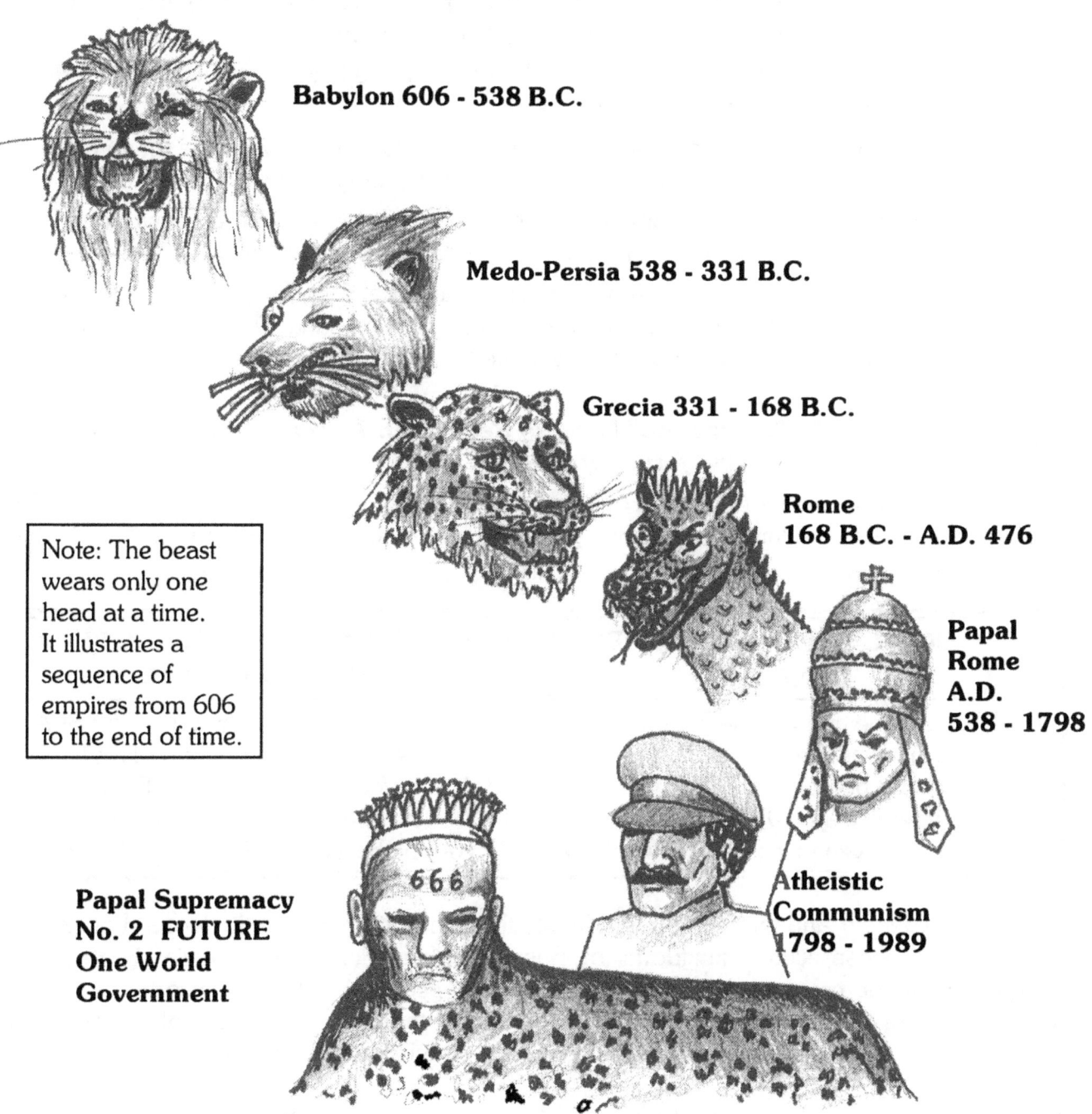

And I stood upon the sand of the sea, and saw a beast rise up out of the sea, having seven heads and ten horns, and upon his horns ten crowns, and upon his heads the name of blasphemy.

And the beast which I saw was like unto a leopard, and his feet were as the feet of a bear, and his mouth as the mouth of a lion: and the dragon gave him his power, and his seat, and great authority.

And I saw one of his heads as it were wounded to death; and his deadly wound was healed: and all the world wondered after the beast.

And they worshipped the dragon which gave power unto the beast: and they worshipped the beast, saying, Who is like unto the beast? who is able to make war with him?

And there was given unto him a mouth speaking great things and blasphemies; and power was given unto him to continue forty and two months.

And he opened his mouth in blasphemy against God, to blaspheme his name, and his tabernacle, and them that dwell in heaven.

And it was given unto him to make war with the saints, and to overcome them: and power was given him over all kindreds, and tongues, and nations.

And all that dwell upon the earth shall worship him, whose names are not written in the book of life of the Lamb slain from the foundation of the world. Rev. 13:1-8.

And the third angel followed them, saying with a loud voice, if any man worship the beast and his image, and receive his mark in his forehead, or in his hand, The same shall drink of the wine of the wrath of God, which is poured out without mixture . . . Rev. 14:9-10.

PREMISE NO. 1. *The "composite" beast of Revelation 13 represents the emergence, history and future of ROME.*

The composite description of the beast of Revelation 13 reiterates the prophetic symbols of Daniel 7. They represented the three universal empires that preceded the Roman empire out of which it was formed.

CORRELATION OF DANIEL AND REVELATION ON THE "BEAST"	
DANIEL 7	**REVELATION 13**
7:3 Beasts came up from the SEA.	13:1 I saw a beast rise up out of the SEA.
7:4 The first was like a LION.	13:2 His mouth as the mouth of a LION.[1]
7:5 A second beast like a BEAR.	13:2 His feet as the feet of a BEAR.
7:6 Another like a LEOPARD.	13:2 The beast . . . like unto a LEOPARD.
7:11 Beast . . . given to the BURNING FLAME.	20:10 The beast (in THE LAKE OF FIRE).

Historical evidence[1] and the Scriptures[2] identify the lion, the bear, and the leopard as prophetic symbols of the consecutive kingdoms of Babylon, Medo-Persia and Grecia. Each of these conquering kingdoms, not only consumed the territory geographically, but absorbed the cultures and religions of the conquered empires. In this sense, the composite beast of Revelation was formed, culminating in the fourth universal kingdom—the Roman Empire, or ROME.[3]

---

1 The winged lion, representing Babylon, is on display at the Art Museum in New York City and may be seen in many history books. Archeological evidence is also abundant with proof that the symbols of the lion, the bear, and the leopard represented these nations. One needs only to consult the public library to verify this information.

2 The Bible identifies the bear to represent Medo-Persia (Dan. 5:31). The leopard is identified as the third kingdom (Dan. 8:20, 21).

3 The transition of power from Grecia to Rome is described in most history books used in high schools. It is commonly noted that the Grecian culture was absorbed by the Romans.

The composite beast of Revelation 13:1-10 represents the universal kingdoms of the **OLD WORLD,** culminating in the establishment of the dominion with its capital in the city of **ROME**. The beast of Revelation 13:11-18 represents the **NEW WORLD**—the **UNITED STATES OF AMERICA.**

It would appear that the apostle John simply picked up the prophetic symbolism of Daniel 7, aligning the "composite" beast of Revelation 13 with that of Daniel's "indescribable" beast of Dan. 7. Both of them had "ten horns." The fourth beast of Daniel, which was a prophetic symbol of the Roman Empire, is linked to the "composite" beast seen by John, continuing the description where Daniel left off, giving sufficient detail to establish beyond doubt the identity of the composite beast as **ROME**. There it proceeds with advanced information pertaining to the final crises, and the leading role ROME shall take in the future.

It must ever be understood, however, that the throne of ROME was relinquished by the Caesars to the Popes and that ROME, in the conclusion of the prophecy of the composite beast therefore, refers specifically to **PAPAL ROME,** the fifth head. 538-1798.

> In [Revelation] chapter 13 (verses 1-10) is described another beast, "like unto a leopard," to which the dragon gave "his power, and his seat, and great authority." This symbol, as most Protestants have believed, represents the papacy, which succeeded to the power and seat and authority once held by the ancient Roman empire. Of the leopard like beast it is declared: "There was given unto him a mouth speaking great things and blasphemies. . . . And he opened his mouth in blasphemy against God, to blaspheme His name, and His tabernacle, and them that dwell in heaven. And it was given unto him to make war with the saints, and to overcome them: and power was given him over all kindreds, and tongues, and nations." This prophecy, which is nearly identical with the description of the little horn of Daniel 7, unquestionably points to the papacy. *The Great Controversy,* p. 439.

PREMISE NO. 2. *The seven heads of the composite beast of Revelation 13 represent a complete[1] sequence[2] of the past, present and future dominions of the Old World which had, in the past, and will have in the future, determination to annihilate the people of God.*

The number 7 indicates completeness . . . *The Acts of the Apostles,* p. 585.

The Biblical interpretation of the seven heads is given in Revelation 17:9, 10. Verse 9 identifies the seven heads as seven "mountains." However, both "heads" and "mountains" are synonymous prophetic symbols. One must find the prophetic interpretation of "mountains." This is given in

---

1   ***"Complete"*** sequence. The seven heads refer to a complete history, or complete sequence, of the kingdoms of the Old World, which has been recorded by historians from the time of the descendants of Noah and extends to the second coming of Jesus. The number ***seven*** (heads) represents completeness or a finished work. (See Gen. 2:1, 2.) The seven day week is a complete unit, instituted by the Creator at creation. It is a fundamental premise or key to prophetic symbolism. The seven heads represent a complete composite picture of historical drama of the Old World as it has and will affect the people of God.

2   ***"Sequence."*** The sequence of the heads is in contrast to the ***scope*** of the ten horns. In both the prophecy of the ten horns of Daniel 7 and the ten horns of Revelation 17 (ten kings), these reign "together with" the beast. All emerged together and thus represent scope rather than sequence. Good history books provide both scope and sequence. Prophecy, which is history in advance, should consistently do the same.

Daniel 2, which indicates that a prophetic "mountain" in prophecy represents a literal kingdom or dominion.[1]

> ... the stone that smote the image became a great **mountain,** and filled the whole earth.... the God of heaven set up a **kingdom,** which shall never be destroyed ... Dan. 2:35, 44.

Revelation 17:9 states plainly that the "seven heads are seven mountains [kingdoms]," "and there are seven kings [kingdoms]." This double reference ensures the correctness of the symbolic interpretation. It then proceeds to give the SEQUENCE of these seven kingdoms:

> ... five are fallen [past], ... and one is [present], and the other is not yet come [future] ... Rev. 17:10.

\multicolumn{4}{c}{**SEQUENCE AND CONTINUITY OF THE SEVEN HEADS OF THE BEAST OF REVELATION 13**}			
Head No.	**Empire-Kingdom**	**Date**	**Reference**
1	Babylon	606-538 B.C.	Dan. 2
2	Medo-Persia	538-331	Dan. 5, 6
3	Grecia	331-168	Dan. 7
4	Rome (pagan)	168-A.D. 476	Dan. 7-11
5	Rome (Papal Supremacy No. 1)	538-1798	Dan. 7-11
6	Atheistic Communism	1798-(1918)[2] 1989[3]	Dan. 11 Rev. 11
7	Rome (Papal Supremacy No. 2)	Future	Dan. 11,12 Rev. 13-20

Note: Visual models probably can never do justice to the concepts portrayed. However, in an attempt to produce such a model, many of the features, otherwise unnoticed are brought to attention and the prophecy is better understood. A visual model is also an excellent medium of communication. This beast of composite structure is undoubtedly one of the most challenging of all the prophetic symbols mentioned in the Holy Scripture. (See picture on p. 235).

PREMISE NO. 3. *The first three of the seven heads (sequential kingdoms) should align with the composite parts of the beast.*

The Bible does not leave loose ends so that the expositor must pull ideas out of his imagination or set up a "private interpretation." The prophecy gives sufficient information within itself to identify the first three heads specifically. They should represent Babylon, Medo-Persia and Grecia. These

---

1 The assumption that the "mountains" refer to literal hills is dubious as many cities are built on hills—depending on the city limits.

2 1798—Fall of Papal Supremacy No. 1.

3 1918—Bolshevik Revolution established Communism until the 1989 Fall of Communism.

first three heads should be portrayed therefore as the head of a lion, the head of a bear, and the head of a leopard. These heads will then correspond to the "mouth of a lion" (which logically would be inserted into a lion's head), "the feet of a bear," and the "body of a leopard."

The fourth head represents the Pagan Roman Empire which Daniel described as a "terrible" beast with ten horns. The Rome—Dragon of Rev. 13:2.

The prophecy and description of Revelation 13:3 states that ". . . one of its heads was wounded to death . . ." This represents the Papacy wounded in 1798, and one of the heads on the composite beast is that of a pope with Papal crown. This is the fifth head, overcome by atheism.

The six heads of the composite beast are therefore identified. The seventh head is "not yet come" but is of the OLD WORLD. If the beast represents Empires in the OLD WORLD (Europe and the Middle East), then all seven heads must also be in the Old World. The seventh head represents an Old World Empire (in Europe), and refers to Papal Supremacy No. 2—yet to come. See Rev. 13. It extends its relationship to the kings of the earth and the whole world (horns) with whom it accomplishes its final designs. Revelation 13 also states that it has a number, 666. See Rev. 13:18. This head is "not yet come"—future, and it is "a man," the Pope of Rome. Revelation 13.

PREMISE NO. 4. *The First Head Represents Babylon.*

Shortly after Noah's flood, his descendants built the tower of Babel in rebellion against God. They disregarded His rainbow covenant promise; instituting instead a counterfeit religion. They used the symbols of true worship, but applied them to the figures of sun-worship. Gen. 11:1-9. From Babel, Babylon is first in its rebellion and inherent enmity against God and against His people. In 606 B.C. Babylon swallowed up Israel. Were it not for the Providential deliverance of God in the decrees to return to rebuild Jerusalem, the people of God would have been absorbed and obliterated. Judah would have been as the "ten lost tribes of Israel."

It is basic to an understanding of the beast and its heads, that its **nature** is that of a **persecuting** power. The secular kingdoms become a representative and tool of Satan himself, whose continuing objective is to gain universal dominion of this world, and to **destroy** the people of God, and the kingdom of Christ. This concept is plainly stated in the description of the beast:

> . . . And the beast which I saw was like unto a ***leopard,*** and his feet were as the feet of a ***bear,*** and his mouth as the mouth of a ***lion:*** and ***the dragon gave him his power, and his seat, and great authority. . . . it was given unto him to make WAR with the saints***. Rev. 13:2, 7.

Not merely to the papacy, has the dragon given his "power, and seat, and great authority," but also to the kingdoms represented as the leopard, bear, and lion. In these nations, as well as the papacy, it was his purpose to "**make war** with the saints."

This composite beast is a "mosaic" of Old World kingdoms to whom Satan gives power with one objective—to destroy and annihilate God's people. Satan sought to destroy Israel through the Babylonian captivity.

The emphasis is on the ***"mouth"*** of the lion. A "mouth" was also in the "little horn" of Daniel 7. A "mouth" represents doctrines or teaching. The doctrines of Babel were, unfortunately, disseminated to the whole world, as evidenced in the unified symbolism and concepts of sun worship, as observed today in all parts of the world. The tower of Babel is reproduced in the pyramids of Egypt, Central, and South America. The worship of "bel" (Ba-**bel**) has even been found recently in ancient structures in the United States.[1]

Although the Babylonian empire was overcome by the Medo-Persians, the religious concepts of its form of worship live on in the "mouth of a lion." The complete reproduction of the Babylon in the forms of the worship carried on by the papacy is fully documented.[2]

"Babylon" first in structure (Tower of Babel), and in universal empire, is also last in spiritual influence; so that spiritual "Babylon" is the last to be overcome in the seventh plague. Rev. 16:19.

Therefore, this first head representing Babylon with its lion's open mouth—(was first) on the composite beast, reigning over God's people 606 to 538 B.C.

There is a "cup" in the hand of Babylon. Revelation 17 and 18. The contents of her cup is that mixture of truth and error on which the nations of the earth are intoxicated. In that cup is also the blood of martyrs. The destructive mouth of the lion and the blood in the cup are both eloquent in revealing the true nature of Babylon—past and future—a basic element in the nature of the composite beast, bent upon the destruction of God's people.

PREMISE NO. 5. *The second head should be that of a bear to represent the second kingdom, Medo-Persia.*

> . . . his feet were as the feet of a bear . . . Rev. 13:2.

A bear's feet are fashioned in a peculiar manner with strong paws and long nails to perform a destructive work. He rips apart logs, claws open doors and shutters on houses and there is hardly a container which can withstand his powerful feet.

Under the reign of Medo-Persia, in the days of Ahasuerus, who reigned ". . . from India unto Ethiopia over a hundred and twenty seven provinces . . ." (Esther 1:1), a death decree was devised by an enemy of the people of God. Under the instigation of Haman, the legislation was passed to destroy all of the people of God on a certain date.

> Then were the king's scribes called on the thirteenth day of the first month, and there was written according to all that Haman had commanded unto the king's lieutenants, and to the governors that were over every province, and to the rulers of every people of every province according to the writing thereof, and to every people after their language; in the name of king Ahasuerus was it written, and sealed with the king's ring. And the letters were sent by posts into all the king's provinces, to destroy, to kill, and to cause to perish, all Jews, both young and old, little children and women, in one day . . . and to take the spoil of them for a prey. The copy of the writing for a commandment to be given in every province was published unto all people, that they should be ready against that day. Esther 3:12-14.

The bear's head on the composite beast, representing Medo-Persia, 538-331 B.C. in its **Universal Death Decree,** is akin to that of the seventh head, activated by the same dragon, the devil, in a union of church and state, to annihilate the people of God.

---

[1] *Reader's Digest.* 1977 February "Who Discovered America First?"

[2] *The Two Babylons* - Hyslop

PREMISE NO. 6. *The third head of the leopard represents Grecia. 331-168 B.C.*

The markings of a leopard's body are subtle camouflage, difficult to see even in the direct sunlight as he glides fleetingly from cover to cover. The subtle forces of Grecian civilization have been one of the dragon's most successful and effective weapons against the Truth, the plan of salvation and Christ's kingdom.

The enchantment of the theater—now reflected in cinema and television, art and literature, has intoxicated and stupefied millions of souls and threatens Christ's true church. The sophisticated arts of logic, the mingling of myths with Bible truth, have appealed to the intellectuals and have laid foundation for false education, evolutionary theory, false science, and erroneous theological assumptions; woven into a fabric as complicated as the leopard's spotted pattern gliding by. The inhabitants of the world are assailed by a colorful kaleidoscope of sensual imagery and inundated by a flood of flotsam from the press, intended to overcome the world with a potion, brewed of a plant with its roots in Grecian culture, to crowd out and deny the saving Truth.

This "body of the leopard," and head of a leopard, formed a foundation for the teachings of the papacy, extracted directly from Roman culture, which in turn, was borrowed from the Greeks. This culture in its varied forms is still a large part of the entertainment and education of the present generation. Greece attempted to obliterate the religion of the Jews.

PREMISE NO. 7. *The fourth head represents the fourth universal kingdom, The Roman Empire. 168 B.C. - A.D. 476.*

Again, the Jews, the people of God were captured and brought under Roman rule. Jerusalem fell permanently in A.D. 70 After this, the dispersion of the Jews followed. It was Satan's plan to destroy the covenant people. It was Herod, under Roman rule, which sought to put to death the newborn Christ child. It was Roman soldiers who nailed the Prince of Life to the cross. If the dragon could have destroyed the King of kings, the subjects of His kingdom would have all been destroyed together.

PREMISE NO. 8. *The fifth head represents the European Papal Supremacy No. 1 (538-1798).*

Under the European Papal Supremacy A.D. 538-1798, through the courts of Inquisition, and in a union of church and state; the papacy was responsible for millions of martyrs' deaths. For over a millennium, "the dragon persecuted the woman," seeking to destroy the people of God from the face of the earth.

> "Power was given unto him to continue forty and two months." And, says the prophet, "I saw one of his heads as it were wounded to death." And again: "He that leadeth into captivity shall go into captivity: he that killeth with the sword must be killed with the sword." The forty and two months are the same as the "time and times and the dividing of time," three years and half, or 1260 days, of Daniel 7—the time during which the papal power was to oppress God's people. This period, as stated in preceding chapters, began with the supremacy of the papacy, A.D. 538, and terminated in 1798. At that time the pope was made captive by the French army, the papal power received its deadly wound, and the prediction was fulfilled, "he that leadeth into captivity shall go into captivity." *The Great Controversy*, p. 439.

PREMISE NO. 9 *The sixth head represents the **ATHEISTIC** IDEOLOGY—*
COMMUNIST REGIME, 1798-1989.

The heads, which represent a **SEQUENCE** of empires, also reveals a certain **CONTINUITY**. For example, as Babylon was losing strength, Medo-Persia was rising to take its place. The "scepter of power" was passed hand to hand from one to the next. Therefore, to establish the identity of the sixth head, it is necessary to look at the power which took away the scepter from Papal Supremacy No. 1 in 1798. In that year, the Pope was taken prisoner by a French general under the ***atheistic*** government of France. It was atheism which emboldened France to resist the political power of the Roman Catholic system. Atheism did not die but continued to prosper in many lines, so that the theory of evolution and revolt against religion became the order of the day. Atheistic ideology became the backbone of the new Communist revolution which had pushed into Russia.

By 1918, the Bolshevik revolution overturned religious power. It became stronger and spread rapidly, developing an "iron curtain," in its attempt to become a world empire. At one point it became dominant on more than half the world's surface. The western nations entered into a life-struggle. It persecuted millions of people and martyred thousands. Not until 1989 was there evidence that Communism was falling. It was undermined by the Popes of Rome. We are now living between the sixth and seventh head!

PREMISE NO. 10 *The seventh head—yet future—is Papal Supremacy No. 2—*
a "New World-Order": Papal power in the Old World which will
legislate a Universal Death Decree.

The sequence of the seven heads of the beast is declared:

> ... the other is not yet come; and when he cometh, he must continue a short space. Rev. 17:10.

Revelation 17 refers also to the union of church and state:

> And the ten horns ... are ten kings ... which have received no kingdom as yet; but receive power as kings one hour with [the seventh head of] the beast. Rev. 17:12.

It is probably not an injustice to the meaning of verse 12 to insert the words (seventh head) as that concept is qualified back in verses 11 and 12. The seventh head (the last in the sequence) representing that **final phase** of **Papal power,** will reign together with the "ten kings" or as it says in Revelation 16—the "kings of the earth and of the whole world"—a universal union of church and state, the seventh empire.

> These [the kings, gather together under the sixth plague to legislate against the people of God and these] have one mind, and shall give their power and strength unto the beast. ... These shall make war with the Lamb [through the persecution of His people] ... Rev. 17:13, 14.

PREMISE NO. 11 *The composite beast of Revelation 13 is the central figure of the*
Third Angel's Message warning and is vital to the Loud Cry and
Latter Rain in the finishing of God's work on earth.

This composite beast of Revelation 13, representing the Roman Papacy, is the "beast" against which the third angel of Revelation gives warning. Before the people of God are able to give a meaningful explanation of this prophetic symbol, they must be able to identify, not only the beast, but each of its parts in a simple, logical manner. A complete identification of the beast, and ***all of its seven heads,*** is essential to a valid presentation of the message of the third angel. It is fundamental to an understanding of the final crisis and preparation for the Seal of God, and an avoidance of the "mark of the beast."

This composite beast of Revelation 13 provides a comprehensive historical view of the rise and fall of empires, with a pointed focus on the issues of closing events and the role of God's people.

Note: Other great empires existed before Babylon, but Daniel did not reiterate past events. He started from his own day and revealed the **future**.

APPENDIX NOTE D

317 HELPFUL QUESTIONS

Are you understanding what you are reading in GETTING IT ALL TOGETHER? If you can answer these questions, you have grasped the concepts and with God's blessing, present it to others.

The page numbers will help you to locate elusive answers.

Chapter Number	Question Number	Question	Page
Intro.	1	Of what significance is crisis and deliverance in the book of Daniel to you?	v, xv
1	2	What is required of the last generation regarding lifestyle?	1
2	3	Of what historical significance is the image of Daniel 2?	3
	4	In Daniel 2, with what crisis was Daniel confronted?	3
	5	Who are the "wise men" through all of earth's history?	3
	6	What is the "resource" in extremity? See Dan. 2:17, 19.	3
	7	What is the parallel between Nebuchadnezzar falling down and worshipping Daniel and the wicked at the "Voice of God?" See Dan. 2:46	3
3	8	What common displeasure is revealed in Nebuchadnezzar and Satan?	4
	9	Name the different metals in the image of Daniel 2.,	
		Name the empire or kingdom which each metal represented.,	
	10	What is the parallel between Dan. 3:3 and Rev. 16:12-16?	4
	11	What is the parallel between the three Hebrew worthies in Daniel 3 and God's people at the end of time?	5
	12	What is the parallel between the three Hebrew worthies just prior to the fiery furnace ordeal and Christ's Calvary experience? And for God's people at the time of the Universal Death Decree?	6
4	14	Of whom was Nebuchadnezzar a type?	4
	15	What is the parallel between Nebuchadnezzar's banishment and Satan's experience during the millennium?	8
	16	What is the connection between Dan. 4:25 and Rev. 20?	8
	17	What is the parallel between Nebuchadnezzar after his illness and Satan after the 1000 years?	8

Chapter Number	Question Number	Question	Page
5	18	What dramatic announcement was made to king Belshazzar?	8
	19	What parallel exists between the events of Daniel 5 and the final events connected with Satan's kingdom?	10
	20	To what do the Scriptures liken a "vessel"?	10
	21	How does Revelation describe the "Fall of Babylon"?	10
	22	During what plague will judgment fall on Babylon? See Rev. 16:17,	
	23	Like Nebuchadnezzar, who does Belshazzar represent?	10
	24	What does "the handwriting on the wall" represent?	11
	25	What is the parallel between the interpretation of "TEKEL" and the first angel's message of Rev. 14:6, 7?	11
	26	Why was Belshazzar judged guilty?	11
	27	What is your impression of the term "numbered" in judgment?,	
	28	What did the term, "MENE" announce? See Rev. 14:8, Dan. 5:26, 30.	11
	29	What brought about the fall of ancient Babylon?	11
	30	What is the parallel between the military strategy of Darius and the strategy of the Son of God in executing the final fall of spiritual Babylon? See Rev. 16:14.	11
	31	What two plagues describe the final fall of spiritual Babylon? See Rev. 16:14-19,	
	32	What does a "symbolic **RIVER**" represent?	11
	33	What is the connection between the Latter Rain and the Loud Cry warning?	12
	34	What happens to a river when the rain ceases?	11
	35	Is the Holy Spirit withdrawn plague by plague?	12
	36	Who are the characters in the sixth plague drama?	13
	37	In what way does the "drying up of the river Euphrates" prepare the way for the Second Coming of Jesus?	13
	38	Who are the three unclean spirits of Revelation 16:13?	13
	39	What does the symbolic number 3 signify regarding Babylon?	14

Chapter Number	Question Number	Question	Page
	40	What is there about frogs which fit into the picture of Rev. 16:13?	14
	41	Who is the symbolic dragon of Rev. 12; 13:3? Through what agencies does he work?	15
	42	Who is the beast in Rev. 13:1, 2? Rev. 16:13?	15
	43	Who is the false prophet of Rev. 16:13?	15
	44	For what do the three evil spirits agitate in Rev. 16:13?	14
	45	What kind of union must occur before religion can bring about death sentences on those who resist?	15
	46	How extensive will the union of church and state be to bring about a Universal Death Decree? See Rev. 16:14, Rev. 13:15.	17
	47	What is the parallel between Belshazzar's feast and the gathering action under the sixth plague?	18
	48	Who are the "kings of the east?"	13
	49	Is the action in Rev. 16:16 one of division or gathering?	18
	50	What term is used to describe the collusion of the kings of the earth with religion (Babylon)? See Rev. 14:8.,	
	51	What does "one hour" symbolic time represent in literal time?	65
	52	What does the word, "Armageddon" mean?	19
	53	Do the sixth and seventh plagues represent any confrontation? Between whom?	19
	54	What is the parallel between the writing on the wall at Belshazzar's feast and the three angel's messages given in the Loud Cry?	11
	55	What actually delivers God's people from the Universal Death Decree? See Rev. 16:17.	20
	56	What brings about the "Fall of Babylon?" See Rev. 16:17.	20
6	58	What similarity of character did Daniel possess (Dan. 6:4) to that of those who are living (Rev. 14:5) at the time of the Universal Death Decree?	21
	59	What is the purpose of the Day of Atonement in regard to Dan. 9:24? List the four great objectives.	21

Chapter Number	Question Number	Question	Page
	60	Compare the assembling of the "presidents and princes" to the gathering of the kings at the end of time. See Rev. 16:14	21
	61	What was Daniel's response to gathering crisis?	22
	62	What will be the corresponding response by the 144,000 to the passing of a Universal Death Decree?	22
	63	What is the parallel between Daniel's being thrown into a lions' den and the 144,000 in the time of Jacob's trouble?	23
	64	By what means were the lions' mouths shut?	22
	65	What parallel fate befalls Daniel's enemies and the enemies of the 144,000?	23
	66	What encouragement awaits God's people as they enter into final conflict? See Dan. 12:12	23
7	67	What theme runs through the entire book of Daniel?	25
	68	List the seven accounts in the book of Daniel where persecution is met with Providential deliverance?	25-26
	69	What do the beasts represent in Daniel 7? (According to the Biblical decoding or interpreting of it) See Dan. 7:17	26
	70	What does the "little horn" represent?	27
	71	What are the Biblical descriptions of the "little horn" Papacy?	27
	72	How long did Daniel see Papal Supremacy No. 1 to reign? See Daniel 7:25	27
	73	Against whom are God's people to give a warning message at the end of earth's history? See Rev. 14:9-11	27
	74	How was Daniel's question as to what would bring this beast or "little horn" power to its end, answered? See Dan. 8:14	28
	75	What kind of judgment occurs when the "books are opened?"	28
	76	What is the outcome of the "Investigative Judgment?"	28
	77	How did Daniel know how to begin counting the 2300 days? See Dan. 9:24 . . . to begin counting from what point?	32
	78	What is the difference between the Investigative Judgment and the judgment of Rev. 20:12? Who are affected in each?,	

Chapter Number	Question Number	Question	Page
8	79	Daniel 8 repeats the vision of the rise and fall of empires. But what quickly caught his attention? See Dan. 8:9-12,	
	80	What did Daniel hear? Dan. 8:13,	
	81	What did the two saints in conversation ask? Dan. 8:13,	
	82	What did Daniel hear as the answer to the question? See Dan. 8:14,	
	83	To what does a symbolic day equate? See Num. 14:35, Eze. 4:6,	
	84	How will the beast be affected by the 2300 prophecy? See Dan. 7:26,	
	85	What is the terrible thing the beast is always doing? Rev. 13:7,	
9	86	What two "deliverances" are brought to view in Daniel 9?	30
	87	Why was Daniel so distressed? (Dan. 8:27)	30
	88	What was Daniel's recourse to such distress? Dan. 9:3-20,	
	89	In what way are the concerns of Daniel, our concerns today?	31
	90	What was to happen to the nation of Israel?	32
	91	With what event does one begin to count the "seventy weeks?"	32
	92	How long did it take for the Jews to rebuild Jerusalem?	32
	93	Would the Messiah be born and when would He come?	32
	94	When the Messiah should die, what would happen to the sacrificial system?	32
	95	Did the Messiah die for His own sins or yours?	32
	96	Why would the Jews no longer be the chosen people after 34 A.D.?	32
	97	Would God reject them, or was it their own action?	33
	98	After Jerusalem was rebuilt, would it stand forever? See Dan. 9:26	33
	99	Does Rome (Pagan and Papal) continue to the end of time? See Dan. 8:25; 11:45	33
	100	Is there any way to avoid conflict with the beast? Dan. 9:27	33
	101	What will finally bring the "Little horn" power to an end?	33

Chapter Number	Question Number	Question	Page
	102	From what date does one compute the 2300 Year-days?	34
	103	How long is it from 457 B.C. to A.D. 1844?,	
	104	If the Investigative Judgment refers only to God's professed people, how then can it bring the "little horn" to its end?	34
	105	How does the "cleansing of the sanctuary" actually affect the record of sins in the minds of God's people? Dan. 9:24	34
	106	Can the records of heaven be cleansed without a corresponding work in the minds of God's living remnant? See G.C. 425, 240	34
	107	How does the "end of sins" in God's people bring the little horn power to its end? See Rev. 7:1-4; 14:1-5	34
	108	Does the Investigative Judgment completed bring the history of this world to a close? Dan. 9:23, 24	35
	109	Is this vision sure of fulfillment? Dan. 10:1	35
	110	What will Jesus have accomplished by the time He has completed the Investigative Judgment?	110
	111	What was the burden of Daniel's prayer? Dan. 9:5, 6, 8, 11, 13, 16	35
	112	What is the parallel between Daniel's prayer and the church today?	35
	113	How does the subject of deliverance arise from a study of the Investigative Judgment? Delivered from what?	35
10	114	When Daniel found himself in the presence of God, what was his physical and spiritual reaction?	38
	115	How long from Daniel's fasting and prayer until the Lord heard and answered?	37
	116	What will attend the Latter Rain? See Joel 2:12, 13	38
	117	When tempted to be discouraged with our weakness, what encouragement comes from Daniel 10:10, 12, 16, 18, 19. 5T 472-476	39
11	118	Is Daniel 11 tracing the rise and fall of nations as it was given in Dan. 2, 7, and 8? Or rise and fall of kings?	40
	119	Is Daniel 11 more detailed than chapter 2, 7, and 8? Is Daniel 11 adding detail to Chapters 2, 7, and 8?	40
	120	Uriah Smith's application of Dan. 11 is helpful up to what verse?	41

Chapter Number	Question Number	Question	Page
	121	Why does Uriah Smith's application become weak after that?	41
	122	To whom do the titles, "King of the South," and "King of the North" apply in Daniel 11:5-14?	42
	123	From what geographical center were these kings identified?	42
	124	To what great empire in the Old World does Daniel 11:35-39 point?	44
11	125	In 606 B.C. who was "the king of the north?" Why? When Syria was taken, who became "the king of the north?" When Pagan Rome handed the scepter to Papal Rome, who then? Who is the "King of the north" today?	45
	126	In reference to the progressive, forward movement of prophecy, and the chronological progression of verses, does Daniel 11: verses 35 and 40 phrase, "the time of the end," both refer to 1798? Why so or why not?	46
	127	Who was "the king of the south" in 606 B.C.? Who is the "king of the south" today?	47
	128	List the seven empires spoken of in Daniel 11. How do these correspond to the seven heads of Rev. 13:1-3?	58
12	129	List the seven heads in the book of Revelation.	57
	130	Is Daniel 12 written in literal or symbolic language? List the symbols if possible.	61
	131	Was "2300 days" a prophecy? Was it "prophetic time?" Was it a "prophetic time line?" Did that "prophetic time line" end in 1844? Did all prophecy which deals with time end in 1844?	63
	132	Does any prophetic timeline establish a date for the Second Coming of Jesus? Do the three timelines in Daniel 12 establish a date for the Second Coming? Do these timelines throw a "flood of light on **events** regarding endtime?	62
	133	What is the difference between an "interpretation" and an "application" of prophecy?,	
	134	What will happen to the "holy people" (God's people) during the 1260 days of Daniel 12:7? Explain what that means.	63
	135	If the 1260 days of Daniel 12:7 is written in the context of literal language, are they literal days?,	

Chapter Number	Question Number	Question	Page
	136	Does Daniel 12:7 say the same thing as found in Rev. 13:7? Do they both describe "persecution?" Past? Future?	63
	137	Will there be a "Papal Supremacy No. 2?" Rev. 13:14-17.	64
	138	How do the timelines begin? See Dan. 9:24. How therefore should a future 1260 days begin?,	
	139	Why would the 1260 days and 1290 days both begin together? (Can a persecution take place without a persecutor?),	
	140	Where in Scripture is there an explanation of the 30 day difference between the 1260 and 1290 days? See Rev. 17:12, 13 and Rev. 18:10, 17, 19.,	
	141	Is that day 30 difference the "last act" of the drama of earth's history? Is it important to understand it?	65
	142	At what point within those 30 days does God deliver His people from a Universal Death Decree?	66
	143	Is the midnight "Voice of God" deliverance from the Universal Death Decree the same event as the Second Coming of Jesus?	66
	144	How many literal days is computed by the Year-day Principle from the "One Hour" periods of Revelation 17 and 18?	67
	146	What pronouncement is made by the "Voice of God?" Day and Hour of the Second Coming? Everlasting Covenant? Persecution finished for God's people? A Blessing?"	69
	147	What ends the 1335 days of Daniel 12:12?	69
	148	What begins the final confrontation of the three timelines of Daniel 12?	69
	149	What is the signal for God's people to flee the large cities?	70
	150	What is the "Voice of a nation?" How does it apply?	77
	151	Define "Prophecy." "Prophecy is merely what?,	
12	152	How do the "Voices" of the Seven Thunders of Revelation 10 correspond to the "Voices" which begin and end the timelines of Daniel 12?	77, 78
	153	Date these. Papal Supremacy No. 1? Papal Supremacy No. 2?	57

Chapter Number	Question Number	Question	Page
	154	Is history—the "stream of time" a sequence of happenings? Is a prophetic outline also a sequence of predicted events? If this sequence is broken in prophetic applications, what does that do to the entire process?	xvii
	155	Is an alignment of all four visions of Daniel necessary? Why?	xvii
	156	What is the first rule in decoding or "interpreting" Scripture? (prophetic symbols) II Pet. 1:20,	
	157	How then can prophetic symbols be decoded? See Isa. 28:10-14,	
13	158	Where in Revelation is the "Wrath of God" cited?	88
13	159	Is the "Wrath of God" a change in God's character? See James 1:17	88
	160	What is the Bible definition of the "Wrath of God?" See Rom. 1:18, 21, 24, 26, 28.	88
	161	In the plagues, what does God control? What does Satan control?	89
	162	How are the restraints on Satan explained by Job? See Job 1:6-22	90
	163	What accusations has Satan made against God's restraints on him? In heaven? On earth?	90
	164	What protects God's people when the wicked are given over to the "entire control" of Satan? See Rev. 7 and 14:1.	91
14	165	What do the first five plagues affect?	94
	166	What is the beginning timeframe for the seven last plagues?	92
	167	Are the first five plagues universal? Why?	93
	168	What is God demonstrating in the plagues?	90
	169	In what way is the Close of Probation connected with the Seven Last Plagues?	92
	170	What do the second and third plague affect?	94
	171	What is the effect of the fourth plague?	95
	172	What does the fifth plague affect?	95
15	173	Is the sixth plague written in literal or symbolic language?	97

Chapter Number	Question Number	Question	Page
	174	Is it consistent to regard the "river Euphrates" as symbolic?	97
	175	What do "waters" represent? What does a symbolic "river" represent? See John 7:38, 39.	97
	176	Who was the best interpreter of Biblical symbols? John 7:39	100
	177	What is meant by the "drying up" of the symbolic "river?"	100
	178	Identify the three unclean spirits of Rev. 16:13.	102
	179	What does the phrase "out of the mouth of" signify?	103
	180	What is the conflict in the battle of Armageddon?	104
	181	What action leads up to the seventh plague?	107
	182	Does the symbolic "river" and the three unclean spirits relate to spiritual Babylon? How?	105
	183	In what way is the "Voice of God" the "coup d'etat" of history?	108
	184	What does the "Voice of God" glorify?	109
	185	What characterizes the people of God at the "Voice of God?	110
	186	What is the timeframe for the "Voice of God" deliverance?	110
	187	What will the Universal Death Decree specify?	110
	188	Name at least ten things which occur at the "Voice of God."	112-114
	189	What causes the "Fall of Babylon?"	115
	190	Who makes up the "fabric" of Babylon	116
	191	How long do the plagues last? See Rev. 18:8. Is the context literal or symbolic? Is the day symbolic? Is the "day" Rev. 18:8 symbolic or literal?,	
	192	Is the time required for the seven last plagues to fall the same amount of time required for "The Fall of Babylon?"	116
	193	Does the knowledge of the fact that the seven last plagues require one year of time, give the date, day and hour of the Second Coming of Jesus? Is it wrong to know?	116
	194	Can you identify the beginning and ending actions of the two "one hour" periods? At least try!	117

Chapter Number	Question Number	Question	Page
17	195	Are trumpets future? Are they connected to the plagues in any way?	120
	196	What were trumpets used for in Israel and other nations?	124
	197	Can the seven last plagues and the seven trumpets be aligned?	125
	198	What do the plagues tell us or explain?	126
	199	What additional or supplementary information comes in the trumpets?	126
	200	Are the trumpets written in literal or symbolic language?	126
	201	When do the trumpets begin? After what?	127
	202	What is meant by a "timeframe sandwich?"	128
	203	How could "blood" spoken of in the first trumpet be related to "sores" in the first plague?	129
	204	How does "fire from heaven" in the first trumpet relate to the "fire" spoken of by Job, which destroyed his property?	129
	205	Who brings such fire down?	129
	206	What "cause" is given for the second plague?	130
	207	Are the effects of these trumpet-plagues universal?	130
	208	What Bible text gives the third trumpet?	130
	209	What "cause" is given for this third trumpet-plague?	130
	210	What other name could be given a "great star from heaven?"	130
	211	What "cause" is given for the fourth plague in Trumpet No. 4?	130
	212	How does Trumpet No. 4 coincide with Plagues 4 and 5?	131
18	213	How shall the Trumpets be applied? Who has the right?	131
	214	Who becomes very active under the sixth plague, gathering kings?	132
	215	What similar individual or spirits are active in the fifth trumpet?	132
	216	The Sixth Plague aligns with which trumpet?	132
	217	Which trumpet is the first woe?	133
	218	What or who are emerging as the "smoke of a great furnace"? in Trumpet No. 5? Why would this be a "woe"?	166

Chapter Number	Question Number	Question	Page
	219	Who is the main character or "king" described in Trumpet No. 5?	133
	220	Is the language of the fifth Trumpet that of symbolism or analogies?	133
	221	What is handed to the "fallen star" in Trumpet No. 5?	134
	222	What does the "key" do regarding those shut up in the bottomless pit?	134
	223	What is the "bottomless pit?" See II Pet. 2:4 and Jude 6	134
	224	When is the "bottomless pit" locked up again? See Rev. 20	134
	225	What will protect God's people when the devils are loosed from the "bottomless pit?" See Rev. 9:4,	
	226	How long are the evil spirits "running to battle" under the fifth trumpet?	136
	227	How long are the unclean spirits "gathering to battle" under the sixth plague?	136
	228	To what battle are they "running" or "gathering" and for what purpose?	138
	229	What do the evil spirits do to the kings and the people to line them up against the people of God?	136
	230	How can anyone escape such torment? Suicide? The Seal of God? Rev. 9:4-6	
	231	Under the fifth trumpet, is the work of evil exerted on nature or upon men bringing them into line?	135
	232	Discuss each of the following and the significance: a) "On their heads were . . . crowns like gold." Rev. 9:7 b) "And their faces were as the faces of men." Rev. 9:7 c) "And they had hair as the hair of women." Rev. 9:8 d) "Their teeth were as the teeth of lions." Rev. 9:8, 17 e) "They had breastplates . . . of iron." Rev. 9:9	138
	237	How many woes follow this fifth trumpet? To which trumpets do they pertain? Rev. 9:12	146, 155
	238	What linkage between plagues and trumpets is found in Rev. 16:17 and Rev. 9:13? Which plague? Which trumpet?	155

Chapter Number	Question Number	Question	Page
19	239	At the "Voice of God" what is stated regarding the trials of God's people? Rev. 16:17.,	
	240	Where are the "four angels (which held back the winds of strife) when they are loosed under the sixth trumpet?	141
	241	Where is the Euphrates? How does this link with Plague No. 6? and Plague No. 7?	141
	242	How definite is the time when these angels will be loosed?	142
	243	How many are lined up against God's people?	142
	244	In what way is the Voice of God and the "Fall of Babylon" connected? Rev. 16:17; Rev. 9:15. Discuss this.	143
	245	What do "mouth" and "tail" represent? Beginning and ending action? What begins the Universal Death Decree? Agitation? What ends the great controversy?	144
	246	What kind of destruction occurs under the sixth trumpet?	144
	247	Is that destruction before or after the "Voice of God?" If the "Fall of Babylon" pertains to religious ministers and false religion, who are destroyed in the sixth trumpet?	144
	248	Which woe happens under the sixth trumpet? See Rev. 11:14, 15,	
20	249	If the sixth trumpet aligns with the seventh plague, what great event follows? Rev. 11:15	146
	250	What happens under the third woe—seventh trumpet? See Rev. 11:14-19. How does that also align with plague No. 7?	147
	251	Revelation is structured on the basis of two major lines of Prophecy. Which chapters are included in the first major line? Which chapters are included in the second?	156
21	252	What does Ellen G. White declare the seals to refer to? Past? Future?	171
	253	What parallel exists between Daniel 7 and Revelation 4 and 5? How does this explain when the seals should begin?	173
	254	What role do the four beasts of Revelation 4-6 have to the seven seals and the Investigative Judgment?	173
	255	What about the seven seals is connected with the history of God's people?	174

Chapter Number	Question Number	Question	Page
	256	What is the Biblical interpretation of a symbolic "horse?"	175
	257	What does a symbolic "bow" and "crown" represent?	175
	258	Under what seal is the church functioning now?	175
	259	What does the symbolic color "white" signify?	175
	260	What does the symbolic color "red" signify? Especially when connected with a symbolic "sword?"	176
	261	What event in the near future will remove freedom to do God's work as it has been done in the past and bring persecution and bloodshed?	176
	262	As the church reacts to persecution and takes a stand, what will be the result in many lives? See Rev. 6:5, 6	177
	263	What does the symbolic color "black" represent? (See Song of Solomon 1:5, 6. What does the "sun" have to do with it?	177
	264	What do the symbolic "balances" have to do with the destiny of the church? What is being "sold out?" What is made of wheat and barley? What does bread symbolize spiritually?	177
	265	When men reject Truth, what is removed from them? Name the results listed under the fourth seal.	178
	266	What two major events are related to the fifth seal? See Rev. 18:1-4 and 14:9-12 and verse 18, 19. 7 B.C. 968.	182
	267	What message is given just prior to the close of probation?,	
	268	Why did E.G. White reveal that the fifth seal occurs just before the Close of Probation and why have we not seen it until now? What is the "unrolling of the scroll" and when does it happen?	179
	269	When the fifth seal refers to TWO groups of martyrs, does this fact make allowance for a past and a future application?,	
	270	What do the martyrs under the fifth seal cry out for?	179
	271	What linkage is there between the fifth seal cry for avenging their blood and the opening of the plague-trumpet sequence?	179
	272	Which seal, with its earthquake and signs in the sun, moon and stars, spans "the time of the end"—1798 to the future?	179

Chapter Number	Question Number	Question	Page
21	273	Construct a chart depicting the following items: a) Universal Death Decree Legislative Date b) Universal Death Decree Effective Date c) The Seventh Plague d) The sixth trumpet e) The seventh trumpet f) The sixth seal Can we know the calendar date of these items or do we simply understand the sequence and linkage here?	182
	274	Why are the Levitical feast days important to our understanding of endtime events? Were they commemorative or typical? What is the purpose of a type?	188
	275	What do the seventh plague, seventh trumpet and sixth seal have in common? See Rev. 16:18; 11:19; 6:12	184
	276	What other signs are given which link Joel 3:15, 16 as well as Matt. 24:29, 30 to the sixth seal of Rev. 6:13?	184
	277	What is the connection between the sixth seal and the Jubilee?	190
	278	What do the wicked see that causes them to retreat to the dens of the earth, to cease their troubling, and allow the "land to rest"?	192
	279	When the heavens depart as a scroll, what is revealed to the wicked? What then do they know?	192
22	280	What four graphic pictures are revealed in Rev. 17?	204
	281	What does a symbolic "woman" represent in Scripture?	205
	282	What is the name of the "Universal Church" of all ages? Gal. 4:26	205
	283	When did the Universal Church begin? Where are the names of all her residents kept?	205
	284	Who is the exact opposite of this Universal Church? Name?	205
	285	Is Babylon also a Universal System of all false religions? Or does she just refer to the Papacy?	206
	286	What is the connection between the serpent of Gen. 3, the dragon of Rev. 12 and the scarlet beast of Revelation 17?	209
	287	In Revelation 17:1-7, is Babylon riding on the beast of Rev. 12 or the serpent-beast of Rev. 12 or the beast of Rev. 13? How do you know. See Rev. 17:3.	209

Chapter Number	Question Number	Question	Page
	288	In Revelation 17:8, what does the word "behold" imply? What is Satan's crowning act? See G.C. p. 624.	211
	289	How long has Satan been invisible? When will he become visible? Is he the beast that was (visible), is not now (visible) but will become visible when he personates Christ and the wicked behold him?	211
	290	What does it mean that he "ascends out of the bottomless pit?" See Rev. 17:8 and 9:1, 2.	212
	291	Is a serpent a "beast?" Is a dragon a "beast?" What office or role does a "beast" assume? See Dan. 7:17	212
	292	In what way is Rev. 17:9 a pivotal text? What shift is being made regarding beasts?	212
	293	List the empires of the seven heads of the beast of Rev. 13. Who is the eighth head in this sequence? When does this eighth reign as KING OF KINGS? With whom does he reign? How long do they reign? See Rev. 17:11-13.	235
	294	When Satan and the kings of the whole earth reign together what are they trying to accomplish? See Rev. 13:15,	
	295	Why does Satan need the kings of the earth to give their power and strength to him? To accomplish what?,	
	296	In what way are the seven heads of the red dragon different from the seven heads of the beast of Rev. 13? See Appendix B.	229
	297	What does a symbolic "horn" represent?	217
	298	Why would symbolic horns have symbolic "crowns" on them?	220
	299	What good is prophecy? See II Pet. 1:19 and Matt. 14:33,	
	300	Why do we say that the Bible is a "Web of Truth?"	220
	301	What does a symbolic number "ten" represent? See Matt. 25	217
	302	Under which plague are the "ten kings" reigning?	217
	303	What are the ten kings gathered attempting to accomplish?	217
	304	What is meant by the "Old World?" Where is it geographically?,	
	305	Under what symbol is the "New World" given? See Rev. 13:11,	
	306	Therefore, could the USA be one of the leopard like beast's heads?,	

Chapter Number	Question Number	Question	Page
	307	Who is the symbolic Lamb of Revelation?,	
	308	How many symbolic "beasts" are brought to view in Revelation? See Rev. 5:13; 12:3; 13:2; 13:11,	
	309	By what means does the Lamb overcome the "beast?" Rev. 12:11. Who are his armies? Rev. 14:105; 7:14; Eph. 6:13-17.,	
	310	What is the only reliable source of Hermeneutic Principles?	222
	312	By what Jesuit technique was Daniel 7:25 turned into futurism?	223
	313	By what Jesuit technique is Daniel 12 now to become Endtime Preterism?	223
	314	Of what importance is "The Literal Approach?"	223
	315	Of what importance is sequence, continuity and alignment?,	
	316	What is the place of prophecy in Christian experience?	224
	317	How many endtime hermeneutic principles are you aware of?,	

APPENDIX NOTE E

EQUATING 1260 DAYS, 42 MONTHS, AND 3½ TIMES

The period of "a thousand two hundred and three score days" is variously referred to in the scriptures. It appears in three forms:

As 1260 days in Revelation 12:6.

As 42 months in Revelation 11:2 and 13:5.

As 3½ times in Daniel 7:25; 12:7, and Revelation 12:14.

These all refer to the same period and can easily be calculated. A time is a year, as is evident from Daniel 11:13, marginal reading. A year has twelve months, and a Biblical month contains thirty days. Thus we have the following:

```
1 year of 12 months at 30 days     =   360 days
3½ years, or times, of 360 days    =  1260 days
42 months of 30 days               =  1260 days
```

A year made up of 12 months will readily be conceded, but that the month has 30 days needs to be demonstrated. This can readily be seen by referring to the record of the flood in Genesis 7 and 8. There we learn the following:

1. That the flood came on the seventeenth day of the second month. (Genesis 7:11)
2. That the waters subsided on the seventeenth day of the seventh month. (Genesis 8:4)
3. That the flood continued for five months from the second to the seventh month.

Reference to Genesis 7:24 reveals the fact that "the waters prevailed upon the earth a hundred and fifty days." Our calculation showed five months. This text mentions 150 days; hence we have five months equaling 150 days, or 30 days to a month.

Thus we have a definite measure for calculating the prophetic periods, bearing in mind that in prophecy a day is equal to a year. *Daniel and the Revelation,* p. 533, by Uriah Smith, 1944 edition.

Note: Revelation 9:15

Most translators of the New Testament have correctly stated this destruction of the "third part of men" as taking place on this specific point of time. Let us note one or two.

> They (the four angels of destruction) had been kept in readiness for that year and month and day and hour, and now they were turned loose to kill a third of all mankind. LB.

> So the four angels were released who had been held ready for the hour, the day, the month and the year, to kill a third of mankind. RSV.

> So the four angels were let loose to kill a third of mankind. They had been held ready for this moment, for this very year and month and day and hour. NEB.

> These four angels had been put there ready for this hour of this day of this month of this year, and now were released to destroy a third of the human race. JB.

But the King James Version does not clearly state that this is a specific point of time when the unsealed will be destroyed.

> And the four angels were loosed, which were prepared for an hour, and a day and a month and a year, for to slay the third part of men. KJV.

Thousands of people have been misled by this translation, to regard this as a prophetic timeline. They have applied the Year-day principle instead of recognizing this prophecy as the point of time when sudden destruction falls on those who have not availed themselves of the provisions of grace.

> And when the sixth angel sounded, I heard a voice that came from the four corners of the golden altar which stands in the presence of God. It said to the sixth angel, as he stood there with his trumpet, Release the four angels who are imprisoned by the great river, the river Euphrates. So these were released, four angels who were waiting for the year, the month, the day, the hour, when they were to destroy a third part of mankind. And the muster of the armies that followed them on horseback. . . . Mrg. Ronald D. Knox Translation.

> Then the sixth angel blew his trumpet, and I heard a voice from the corners of the altar of gold that was before God say to the sixth angel who had the trumpet: "Turn loose the four angels that are bound at the river Euphrates." Then the four angels that were kept in readiness for that hour and day and month and year were turned loose to kill one-third of mankind. The number of the armies of the horsemen was two hundred million; I heard their number. In my vision . . . Rev. 9:13-17.

THE SEVEN ANGELS' MESSAGES OF REVELATION

Content

FIRST Angel's Message
1833-1844

Everlasting gospel
Fear God. Give glory to Him
THE HOUR OF HIS JUDGMENT IS COME.
(Investigative Judgment began in 1844 for the DEAD)
Worship the Creator:—
(Remember the 7th-day SABBATH)
Receive the SEAL of God.

SECOND Angel's Message
Began summer of 1844

"Babylon is fallen"
"all nations have..."
"not yet complete"
G.C. 389

THIRD Angel's Message
1845—

If any man worship
1. The BEAST—(Papal Rome)
2. His IMAGE (Apostate Protestantism)
3. or receive His MARK (Sunday—the false sabbath)
4. He will receive the wrath of God (seven last plagues)
He will have the MARK OF THE BEAST
5. FIRE & Brimstone

FOURTH Angel's Message

"Babylon is fallen"
"**ALL NATIONS**..."
"earth lightened with the Glory of God..."

"Come out of her, my people" by "another voice" [the Sixth Angel]

(Fourth Angel "unites with the Third Angel and gives power")

"LOUD CRY"
FIFTH Angel's Message
and Reaping Action
from the temple

"THE TIME IS COME..."
(Investigative Judgment of the LIVING is come)

First Harvest: **Barley**
First Fruits—144,000

SIXTH Angel's Message
and Reaping Action
from the temple

"earth was reaped"

Second Harvest **Wheat**
Babylon is reaped.

"LOUD CRY"
SEVENTH Angel's Message
and Reaping Action
from the altar

4. Receives the wrath of God (seven last plagues)

Third Harvest: **Grapes**
The wicked are reaped destroyed Joel 3:13-16

TIME SETTING

References
Rev. 14:6,7,8,9-12

Rev. 18:1-4
G.C. p. 604
Sunday Law Legislation.
THE FINAL TEST Points to the future

Rev. 14:14-20
"The SHARP SICKLE"
The Closing of the Judgment Scene.

A LINEAR CHART OF THE SEVEN ANGEL'S

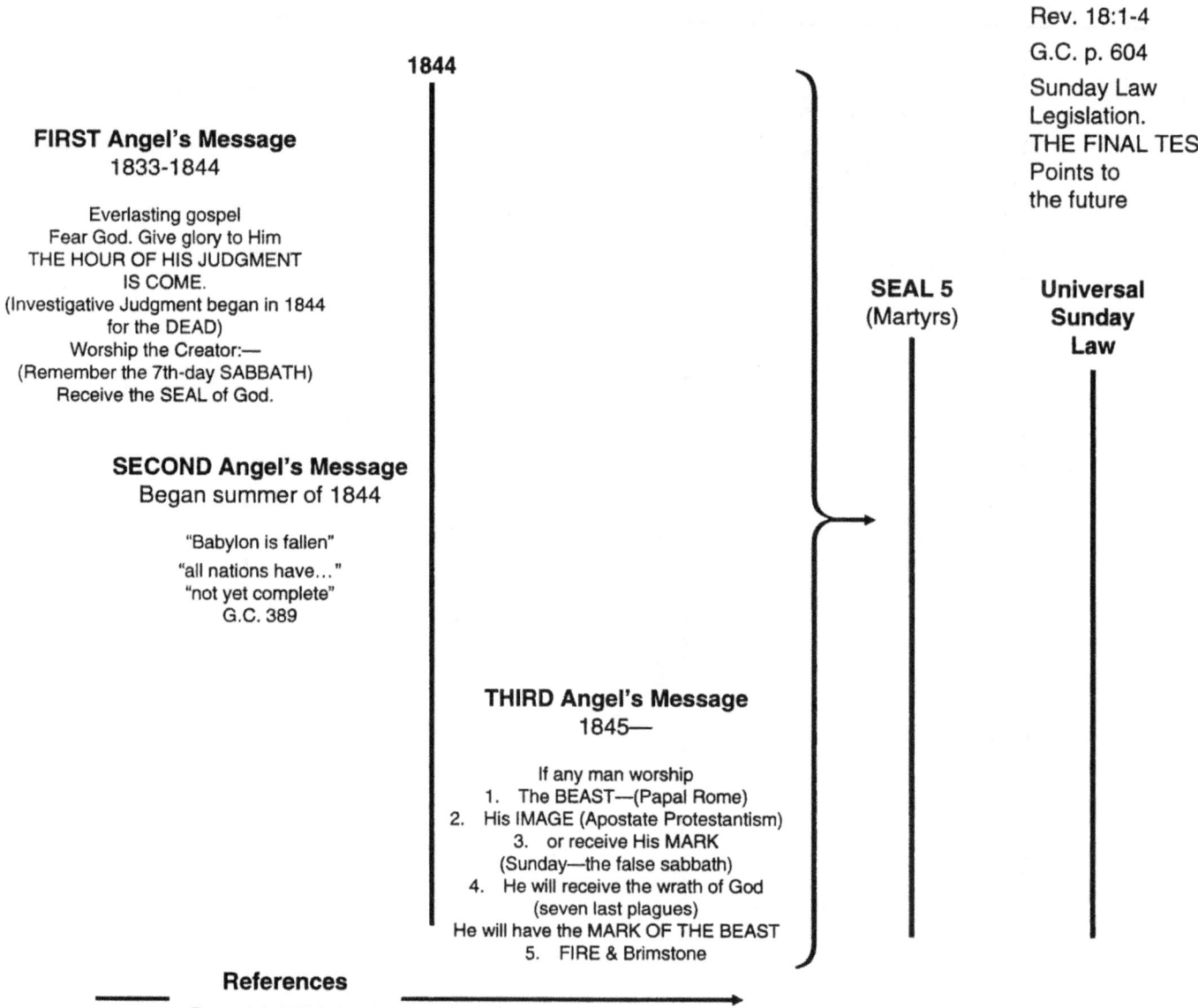

MESSAGES OF REVELATION 14 & 18

FOURTH Angel's Message

"Babylon is fallen"
"**ALL** NATIONS…"
"earth lightened with the
Glory of God…"

"Come out of her, my people"
by "another voice"
[the Sixth Angel]

Fourth Angel "unites with the
Third Angel and gives power"

"LOUD CRY"
FIFTH Angel's Message
and Reaping Action
from the temple

"THE TIME IS COME…"
(Investigative Judgment
of the LIVING is come)
First Harvest: **Barley**
First Fruits—144,000

SIXTH Angel's Message
and Reaping Action
from the temple

"earth was reaped"

Second Harvest **Wheat**
Babylon is reaped.

CLOSE OF PROBATION

"LOUD CRY"
SEVENTH Angel's Message
and Reaping Action
from the altar

4. Receives the wrath of God
(seven last plagues)

Third Harvest: **Grapes**
The wicked are reaped destroyed Joel 3:13-16

Rev. 14:14-20
"The SHARP SICKLE"
The Closing of the Judgment Scene.

← Angels 5, 6, 7 →

APPENDIX NOTE F

REVELATION 11

Revelation 11 has, in the past, been understood to refer to the French Revolution. (See *The Great Controversy*, Chapter 15, titled "The Bible and the French Revolution." p. 265-288).

> In the sixteenth century the Reformation, presenting an open **Bible** to the people, had sought admission to all the countries of Europe. Some nations welcomed it with gladness, as a messenger of Heaven. In other lands the papacy succeeded to a great extent in preventing its entrance; and the light of Bible knowledge, with its elevating influences, was almost wholly excluded. In one country, though the light found entrance, it was not comprehended by the darkness. For centuries, truth and error struggled for the mastery. At last the evil triumphed, and the truth of Heaven was thrust out. "This is the condemnation, that light is come into the world, and men loved darkness rather than light." John 3:19. The nation was left to reap the results of the course which she had chosen. The restraint of God's Spirit was removed from a people that had despised the gift of His grace. Evil was permitted to come to maturity. And all the world saw the fruit of willful rejection of the light.
>
> The **war against the Bible**, carried forward for so many centuries in France, culminated in the scenes of the Revolution. That terrible outbreaking was but the legitimate result of Rome's **suppression of the Scriptures**. (See Appendix.) It presented the most striking illustration which the world has ever witnessed of the working out of the papal policy—an illustration of the results to which for more than a thousand years the teaching of the Roman Church had been tending.
>
> The suppression of the Scriptures during the period of papal supremacy was foretold by the prophets; and the Revelator points also to the terrible results that were to accrue especially to France from the domination of the "man of sin." *The Great Controversy,* p. 265, 266.

The Prophetic-Historical Outline and its 1260 day timeline of Revelation 11:2-13 were applied by the pioneers of Adventism as follows:

> Said the angel of the Lord: "The holy city shall they tread underfoot forty and two months. And I will give power unto **My two witnesses**, and they shall prophesy a thousand two hundred and threescore days, clothed in sackcloth. . . . And when they shall have finished their testimony, the beast that ascendeth out of the bottomless pit shall make war against them, and shall overcome them, and kill them. And their dead bodies shall lie in the street of the great city, which spiritually is called Sodom and Egypt, where also our Lord was crucified. . . . And they that dwell upon the earth shall rejoice over them, and make merry, and shall send gifts one to another; because these two prophets tormented them that dwelt on the earth. And after three days and a half the Spirit of life from God entered into them, and they stood upon their feet; and great fear fell upon them which saw them." Revelation 11:2-11.
>
> The periods here mentioned—"forty and two months," and "a thousand two hundred and threescore days"—are the same, alike representing the time in which the church of Christ was to suffer oppression from Rome. The 1260 years of papal

supremacy began in A.D. 538, and would therefore terminate in 1798. *The Great Controversy*, p. 266.

The reader is strongly urged to read the entire Chapter 15 of *The Great Controversy* to absorb that **valid** application. But he should also note the following statement which refers to an endtime similar situation:

> . . . what is to prevent the world from becoming a second Sodom? At the same time anarchy is seeking to sweep away all law, not only divine, but human. The centralizing of wealth and power; the vast combinations for the enriching of the few at the expense of the many; the combinations of the poorer classes for the defense of their interests and claims; the spirit of unrest, of riot and bloodshed; the world-wide dissemination of the same teachings that led to the French Revolution,—**all are tending to involve the whole world in a struggle similar to that which convulsed France.** *Education* p. 288.

The question is this? If the French Revolution is described in Revelation 11, can that same description be applied in **detail** to the scenes and historical events which will occur at the end of the world? What inspired counsel can we get regarding this matter?

> Let all who would understand the meaning of these things read the eleventh chapter of Revelation. **READ EVERY VERSE** and learn [about] things that are **YET TO TAKE PLACE IN THE CITIES**. Read also the scenes portrayed in the eighteenth chapter of the same book [Revelation 18]. Letter 158, May 10, 1906. (Written to Dr. Kress and his wife with a Heading: Rev. 11 and 18 Portray Things That **WILL TAKE PLACE IN THE CITIES**.)

It is time to give Revelation a second look to find the endtime application. The following questions need to be answered:

1. What does Revelation 11 have to do with the Revelation 18 message of the **LOUD CRY,** and the endtime **"ONE HOUR" FALL OF BABYLON?**

2. Will the timeline of the 1260 days or 42 months of Revelation 11 fit into an endtime application of future events?

3. How Does Revelation 11 fit together with the Daniel 12:7-13 timelines of the 1260, 1290, and 1335 literal days?

4. How does Revelation 11 fit on the "grid" formed by the intersecting alignment of the two major lines of prophecy in Revelation and the eight major visions?

5. Will there be, in the final crisis, a "war against the Bible or Law of God" similar to that carried on in the French Revolution?

6. If so, how then, and when will the Law of God be glorified so that "all their enemies " will behold them? (Rev. 11:12)

7. Does Revelation 11, when given an endtime fulfillment, actually "throw a flood of light on events then to transpire"?

To answer these questions, it is important to follow the counsel of the prophet and examine Revelation 11 **VERSE BY VERSE** to discover what it is that will take place in our cities at the end of time.

A VERSE BY VERSE STUDY OF REVELATION 11

THE TIMEFRAME

Chapter 10 provides the timeframe for Chapter 11.

> And he said unto me, Thou must prophesy again before many peoples, and nations, and tongues, and kings. Rev. 10:11.

This verse describes the commission given to the Advent people to give the three angels' messages which will swell into the **LOUD CRY**. While the Loud Cry is going on, the Investigative Judgment is closing. Revelation 11 begins with a "measuring" or investigation of "them that worship." The dead are not worshiping! Therefore, this is a description of the **JUDGMENT OF THE LIVING**.

God's people are "living stones" which make up the "temple." (See I Pet. 2:5) Will these "stones" fit into place? The people of God are also measured by the Law of God of which Jesus was a living example. The "altar" signifies the sacrificial aspects of Christ and those of His followers: This is spoken of in Revelation 11:1.

> And there was given me a reed like unto a rod; and the angel stood, saying, Rise, and measure the temple of God, and the altar, and them that worship therein. But the court which is without the temple leave out, and measure it not; for it is given unto the Gentiles; . . . Rev. 11:1, 2.

"The Gentiles" [or heathen] will be judged during the millennium. Verses 2 and 3 then refer to a period of 1260 days or 42 months under which the Investigative Judgment will close.

> . . . and the holy city [God's people] shall they tread under foot **forty and two months** . . . my two witnesses, . . . shall prophesy **a thousand two hundred and threescore days** in sackcloth. Rev. 11:2, 3.

This same period is spoken of in Daniel 12:7 and Revelation 13 as follows:

> . . . it shall be for **a time, times, and an half:** and when he shall have accomplished to scatter [persecute] the power of the holy people, all these things shall be finished. Dan. 12:7.

> . . . and his deadly wound was healed: . . . and power was given him to continue **forty and two months** . . . And it was given him to make war with the saints, and to overcome them: and power was given him over all kindreds, and tongues, and nations. Rev. 13:3, 5, 7.

Revelation 11 describes the closing up of the Investigative Judgment—the Judgment of the Living. All this occurs at the time of the 1260 literal days of persecution, at which time, the people of God will receive the Seal of God and the wicked receive the Mark of the Beast as a result of the Loud Cry of the Third Angel of Revelation 14 and 18.

THE TWO WITNESSES

There is much speculation and conjecture as to the identity of these two witnesses of Revelation 11:3-12. Some believe that they represent Moses and Elijah or John the Baptist. Can we permit an inspired prophet to make the interpretation? Can we permit the endtime prophet, Ellen G. White, to interpret the writings of prophets who wrote the Scripture just as we permit the Bible to be its own expositor? What did the prophet say about the "two witnesses"?

The prophetess said:

> The two witnesses represent the Scriptures of the **OLD AND NEW TESTAMENT.** Both are important testimonies to the origin and perpetuity of **THE LAW OF GOD.** *The Great Controversy*, p. 267.

In like manner, the identity of the "two olive trees" and the "two candlesticks," as they relate to the Scriptures, is explained as follows:

> "These are the two olive trees, and the two candlesticks standing before the God of the earth." "Thy word," said the psalmist, "is a **lamp unto my feet, and a light unto my path." Revelation 11:4; Psalm 119:105.** The two witnesses represent the Scriptures of the Old and New Testament. Both are important testimonies to the origin and perpetuity of the law of God. *The Great Controversy* p. 267.

Olive trees produce olive oil. This oil was used in the "candlesticks" to give light. The oil symbol represents the Holy Spirit which accompanies a study of the Scripture to produce light and truth.

The entire Chapter 15 of *The Great Controversy*, which comments on Revelation 11, is titled **THE BIBLE AND THE FRENCH REVOLUTION.** The Bible or the "Two Witnesses" are the main characters of this chapter. This chapter cannot be understood, in a past application or in an endtime fulfillment until the identity of these "two witnesses" is securely in place. There was war against the Bible during the French Revolution and there will be war again at the end of the final crisis against the Bible or Word of God and the Law of God. The entire controversy between good and evil is over the Law of God.

THE TWO WITNESSES SPEAK

> And if any man will hurt them, fire procedeth out of their mouth, and devoureth their enemies: and if any man will hurt them, he must in this manner be killed. Rev. 11:5.

The verse above simply explains that the fate of the wicked will be the lake of fire described in Revelation 20.

> These have power to shut heaven, that it rain not in the days of their prophecy: and have power over waters to turn them to blood, and to smite the earth with all plagues, as often as they will. Rev. 11:6.

The verse above declares the inevitable fulfillment of the prophetic Word of God. Whatever is predicted **will take place.** (See I Kings 17:1; 18:45; Ex. 7-11 and Rev. 16)

WAR AGAINST THE TWO WITNESSES

> And when they shall have finished their testimony, the beast that ascendeth out of the bottomless pit shall **make war against them, and shall overcome them, and kill them.** Rev. 11:7.

In France, during the Revolution and Reign of Terror, a war was waged against God and His holy word. The worship of the Deity was abolished by the National Assembly, Bibles were collected and publicly burned with every possible manifestation of scorn. The law of God was trampled under foot. The institutions of the Bible were abolished. The weekly rest day was set aside, and in its stead every tenth day was devoted to reveling and blasphemy, Baptism and the Communion were prohibited. (See *The Great Controversy* p. 274) We need to remember that "the world-wide dissemination of the same teachings that led to the French Revolution,—all are tending to involve the **whole world** in a struggle similar to that which convulsed France. This war against God, His Word, and His law will be repeated in the last act of the great drama of prophetic fulfillment of Revelation 11.

THE BEAST OF THE BOTTOMLESS PIT

Past applications presented "the beast that ascendeth out of the bottomless pit" to refer primarily to Satan, and his power.

> . . . here is brought to view a new manifestation of Satanic power. *The Great Controversy* p. 269.

This new manifestation of Satanic power, spoken of during the French Revolution, was atheism. (See The *Great Controversy* p. 269) But in an endtime fulfillment of Revelation 11, what "new manifestation of Satanic power" will occur? Let the prophet describe it:

SATAN WILL PERSONATE CHRIST

> As the crowning act in the great drama of deception Satan will personate Christ . . . The teachings of this false christ are not in accordance with **Scriptures**. His blessing is pronounced upon the worshipers of the beast and his image, the very class upon whom the **Bible** declares that God's wrath shall be poured out . . . only those who have been diligent students of the **Scriptures** and who have received the love of the truth will be shielded from the powerful delusion that takes the world captive. *The Great Controversy* p. 624-625.

"The beast that ascendeth out of the bottomless pit"—Satan, in his personation of Christ, is also described in Revelation 17:8.

> The beast that thou sawest was, and is not; and shall **ascend out of the bottomless pit,** and go into perdition: and they that dwell on the earth shall wonder [be amazed], whose names were not written in the book of life from the foundation of the world, **WHEN THEY BEHOLD** [a visible manifestation of] the beast that was, and is not, and yet is. Rev. 17:8.

It is when Satan becomes visible in great glory, claiming to be Christ, that he wars against the Word of God and the Law of God, declaring that he has changed its institutions—the Sabbath, and nullifies the Word and the Law.

Revelation 17 makes clear the fact that when the kings of the earth gather to legislate a Universal Death Decree against the people of God, Satan will reign over them as the **EIGHTH HEAD.**

> And the ten horns which thou sawest are ten kings [all the kings of the earth. [See Rev. 16:14], which have received no kingdom as yet, but receive power as kings one hour with the beast. These have one mind, and shall give their power and strength to the beast . . . And the beast that was, and is not, even he is the eighth [head to rule over them] Rev. 17:12, 13 and 11.

Although Satan will appear at other times, this "crowning act" places him as the **eighth head,** which presides over the kings of the earth in that "one hour" reign in which the Universal Death Decree is passed. Not only will Satan, through these kings, seek to destroy the people of God, but he will also make war against the Bible—a constant rebuke to wickedness. Revelation 11 describes that final action or war against the Law of God in verse 7:

> . . . the beast that ascendeth out of the bottomless pit shall make war against them [the two witnesses—the Scriptures], and shall overcome them, and kill them. And their dead bodies shall lie in the street of the great city, which spiritually is called Sodom and Egypt, where also our Lord was crucified. Rev. 11:7, 8.

Let the prophetess identify "the great city, which spiritually is called Sodom and Egypt, where also our Lord was crucified."

> "The great city" in whose streets the witnesses are slain, and where their dead bodies lie, is "spiritually" Egypt. Of all nations presented in Bible history, Egypt most boldly denied the existence of the living God and resisted His commands. No monarch ever ventured upon more open and highhanded rebellion against the authority of Heaven than did the king of Egypt. When the message was brought him by Moses, in the name of the Lord, Pharaoh proudly answered: "Who is Jehovah, that I should hearken unto His voice to let Israel go? I know not Jehovah, and moreover I will not let Israel go." Exodus 5:2, A.R.V. This is atheism, and the nation represented by Egypt would give voice to a similar denial of the claims of the living God and would manifest a like spirit of unbelief and defiance. "The great city" is also compared, "spiritually," to Sodom. The corruption of Sodom in breaking the law of God was especially manifested in licentiousness. And this sin was also to be a pre-eminent characteristic of the nation that should fulfill the specifications of this scripture. *The Great Controversy*, p. 269.

The French nation and French Revolution was but a shadow of the condition of the entire world at the close of earth's history. The corruptions of Sodom sweep over society and prepare the way for the final conflagration. A Godless and lawless society enable Satan to make war on the Word and Law of God. When he does this, the reaction of wicked men is described as follows:

> And they that dwell upon the earth shall rejoice over them [the two witnesses, that they have been "killed."] and make merry, and shall send gifts one to another; because these two prophets tormented them that dwelt on the earth. Rev. 11:10.

The "two prophets" also represent the prophetic Word of God or the two Tables of Stone by which men are judged.

THE THREE AND AN HALF DAYS

> And they of the people and kindreds and tongues and nations shall see their dead bodies **THREE DAYS AND AN HALF,** and shall not suffer their dead bodies to be put in graves. Rev. 11:9.

Although action is taken to destroy the Law and Word of God, the people of earth do not "allow their dead bodies to be put in graves" for the simple reason that it is such a great event that it is all they can talk about!

THE LAW OF GOD WILL BE SEEN IN THE HEAVENS

> And after three days and an half the Spirit of life from God entered into them, and they stood upon their feet; and great fear fell upon them which saw them. And they heard a great voice from heaven saying unto them, Come up hither. And **they ascended up to heaven in a cloud, and their enemies beheld them.** Rev. 11:11, 12.

Let the prophetess describe this action, in which the Decalogue-The Ten Commandments will be seen in the heavens so that "their enemies beheld them."

> While these words of holy trust ascend to God, the clouds sweep back, and the starry heavens are seen, unspeakably glorious in contrast with the black and angry firmament on either side. The glory of the celestial city streams from the gates ajar. Then there appears against the sky a hand holding **two tables of stone** folded together. Says the prophet: "The heavens shall declare His righteousness: for God is judge Himself." Psalm 50:6. That holy law, God's righteousness, that amid thunder and flame was proclaimed from Sinai as the guide of life, is now revealed to men as the rule of judgment. The hand opens the tables, and there are seen the precepts of **the Decalogue**, traced as with a pen of fire. The words are so plain that all can read them. Memory is aroused, the darkness of superstition and heresy is swept from every mind, and God's ten words, brief, comprehensive, and authoritative, are presented to the view of all the inhabitants of the earth.
>
> It is impossible to describe the horror and despair of those who have trampled upon God's holy requirements. The Lord gave them His law; they might have compared their characters with it and learned their defects while there was yet opportunity for repentance and reform; but in order to secure the favor of the world, they set aside its precepts and taught others to transgress. They have endeavored to compel God's people to profane His Sabbath. Now they are condemned by that law which they have despised. With awful distinctness they see that they are without excuse. They chose whom they would serve and worship. "Then shall ye return, and discern between the righteous and the wicked, between him that serveth God and him that serveth Him not." Malachi 3:18. *The Great Controversy*, p. 639, 640.

And they ascended up to heaven in a cloud; and their enemies beheld them. Rev. 11:12.

> The enemies of God's law, from the ministers down to the least among them, have a new conception of truth and duty. Too late they see that the Sabbath of the fourth commandment is the seal of the living God. Too late they see the true nature of their spurious sabbath and the sandy foundation upon which they have been building. They find that they have been fighting against God. Religious teachers have led souls to perdition while professing to guide them to the gates of Paradise. Not until the day of final accounts will it be known how great is the responsibility of men in holy office and how terrible are the results of their unfaithfulness. Only in eternity can we rightly estimate the loss of a single soul. Fearful will be the doom of him to whom God shall say: Depart, thou wicked servant. *The Great Controversy*, p. 640.

THE TIMEFRAME FOR THE THREE DAYS AND AN HALF

On the same page *(The Great Controversy* p. 640) where the Decalogue is seen in the heavens, the Voice of God, which delivers the saints from the Universal Death Decree is mentioned. The question is this: How does the Voice of God connect with the vindication of the Law in the heavens? Is it before or after the Voice of God? Where does the three days and an half between legislation against the Law of God and its appearance in the heavens fit into the drama?

At this point, it is important to look closely at the words of the prophet for some clue regarding this timeframe of events. It is these "prophetic periods"—the 1260, 1290, 1335 days and the "three days and an half" which "throw a flood of light on events then to transpire." What help will come from the words of Ellen G. White?

> In like manner the types which relate to the second coming must be fulfilled **AT THE TIME POINTED OUT IN THE SYMBOLIC SERVICE.** *The Great Controversy* p. 299.

"The symbolic service" mentioned in the quotation above is referring to the autumn feast days of Israel; The Feast of Trumpets, The Day of Atonement, and The Feast of Tabernacles. How do the "three days and an half" fit into this grid?

It should be remembered that the prophet merged Revelation 11 with Revelation 18—"The Fall of Babylon" which occurs in "one hour" or the last literal 15 days of earth's history. See p. .267

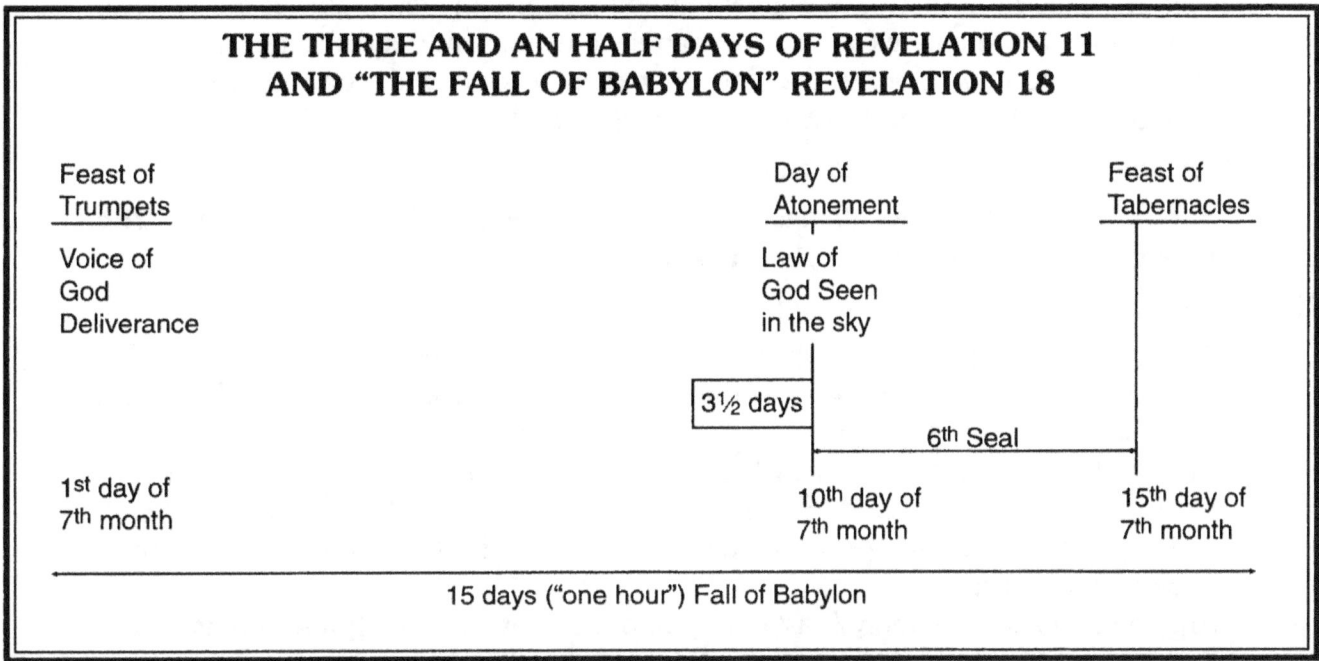

How appropriate that the Law of God should be seen in the sky on the Day of Atonement! All through the antitypical Day of Atonement or Investigative Judgment, men have been judged by that law.

Apparently, three and an half days before the Day of Atonement, legislative action will be taken, as it was in France, against the Law of God. After the Decalogue is seen in the sky, the wicked, in horror, carry out the action of the sixth seal.

> And I beheld when he had opened the sixth seal, and, lo, there was a great earthquake, and the sun became black as sackcloth of hair, and the moon became as blood: And the stars of heaven fell unto the earth, even as a fig tree casteth her untimely figs, when she is shaken of a mighty wind. And **the heaven departed as a scroll when it is rolled together;** [so that the Law of God is seen up there], and every mountain and island were moved out of their place. And the kings of the earth, and the great men, and the rich men, and the chief captains, and the mighty men, and every bondman, and every free man, **hid themselves in the dens and**

in the rocks of the mountains. And said to the mountains and rocks, Fall on us and hide us from the face of him that sitteth on the throne, and from the wrath of the Lamb. For the great day of his wrath is come and who shall be able to stand?

Revelation 11 with its "three and an half days" is given that we may know exactly where we stand in the stream of time, Each fulfillment will sustain faith in God and in His Word.

REVELATION 11 AND TRUMPETS 6 AND 7

Revelation 11 is linked with the 6th and 7th trumpets. This places the fulfillment of Revelation 11 in an endtime setting. Past applications were approved of God for their day in past history, but their primary fulfillment is at the end of time. The events of Revelation 11 are linked to the trumpets as follows:

> And the same hour there was a great earthquake, and the tenth part of the city fell, and in the earthquake were slain of men seven thousand: and the remnant were affrighted, and gave glory to the God of heaven. The second woe [6th trumpet] is past; and behold, the third woe [7th trumpet] cometh quickly. Rev. 11:13, 14.

In Revelation 10, the prediction was made:

> But in the days of the seventh angel [7th trumpet] when he shall begin to sound, **the mystery of God should be finished. Rev. 10:7**

Revelation 11 then describes that seventh angel or seventh trumpet action:

> And the seventh angel sounded; and there were great voices in heaven, saying, The kingdoms of this world are become the kingdom of our Lord, and of his Christ; and he shall reign for ever and ever.
> And the four and twenty elders, which sat before God on their seats, fell upon their faces, and worshipped God, Saying, We give thee thanks, O Lord God Almighty, which art, and wast, and art to come; because thou hast taken to thee, thy great power, and hast reigned.
> And the nations were angry [past tense], and thy wrath is come [present tense], and the time of the dead, that they should be judged, [future tense] and that thou shouldst give reward unto thy servants the prophets, and to the saints, and them that fear thy name, small and great; and shouldst destroy them which destroy the earth. Rev. 11: 15-18.

If any have doubted, up to this point, that Revelation 11 has an endtime application, verses 15-18 should settle the matter.

The last verse of Revelation 11 is a victorious scene and vindication of the Law of God before the whole earth:

> And the temple of God was opened in heaven, and there was seen in his temple the ark of his testament: and there were lightnings, and voices, and thunderings, and an earthquake, and great hail. Rev. 11:19.

The "great hail" refers to the last act of the seventh plague.

This reference to the "great hail" removes it from an 1844 setting and places it right before the coming of Jesus. Past applications were a "shadow" only, of that which is to occur at the end of this world's history. The primary fulfillment occurs under the seventh trumpet-seventh plague and seventh seal!

When God's temple in heaven is opened, what a triumphant time that will be for all who have been faithful and true! In the temple will be seen the ark of the testament in which were placed the two tables of stone, on which are written God's law. These tables of stone will be brought forth from their hiding place, and on them will be seen the Ten Commandments engraved by the finger of God. These tables of stone now lying in the ark of the testament will be a convincing testimony to the truth and binding claims of God's law. Letter 47, 1902 (See *Seventh-day Adventist Commentary,* Vol 7, p. 962)

APPENDIX NOTE G

COMMENTS ON SYMPOSIUM ON REVELATION, Bk I, II

SYMPOSIUM ON REVELATION—Book I and II, authored by members of the Daniel and Revelation Committee of the Biblical Research Institute, published by the General Conference of Seventh-day Adventists, Silver Springs, MD 20904.

The reader should understand that the Biblical Research Institute was formerly called "The Literature Defense Committee." It continues under new name to make a defense against that which is considered aberrant from correct positions of theology.

SYMPOSIUM ON REVELATION—Book I and II is a defense against endtime prophetic applications. The reader should understand that. Although there is much valuable information in these two books, there is an argument, persistent and sustained to dissemble all endtime applications such as those presented in *GETTING IT ALL TOGETHER IN DANIEL AND REVELATION.*

Although both publications give consideration to Biblical hermeneutic, exegetical studies, the structure of Revelation, the eight visions of the book, the writings of Ellen G. White, and the contents of Revelation, it is soon evident that all of this is widely divergent in approach.

The reader, if seeking to study both publications, should make an effort to compare (contrast) basic and fundamental points of view to assess either of the books; and of course, select that which he considers best.

A chart revealing the "Basic Differences" in approach and conclusion has been prepared to assist the reader to locate and assess points of interest.

We all need to remember that it is easier to state an error than to refute it. An error may be as short as three words: "Black is white" but to refute it may require a scientific explanation of vibrations, illustrations and books written to encompass the subject. It is better to state truth and let error manipulate itself into destruction, but that all takes time and in this age, time is at a premium. Satan would deceive and for this reason, truth and error need to be placed in sharp contrast. Therefore the following chart has been prepared to save the reader time and energy so that he may just check out what he needs.

BASIC DIFFERENCES

GETTING IT ALL TOGETHER	SYMPOSIUM ON REVELATION
Definition of Exegesis An exhaustive cross-reference of all Scripture and the prophetic utterances of Ellen G. White. Isa. 28:9-13.	***Definition of Exegesis*** Using the tools of scholarly expertise to determine "what the author had in mind."—The author's intent. See Bk I, p. 77; *The New Catholic Encyclopedia* Vol. 5, p. 707 McGraw Hill. 1978.
Use of Ellen G. White's Writings Acceptance of the prophetess's clear statements to mean exactly what they say.	*Use of Ellen G. White's Writings* Ellen G. White's statements may be "Nonexpositional", "incorporational", "didactic", "extentional", "nontechnical", "pastoral". See Bk I, p. 146-161. Her tiredness accounts for her confusion. See Appendix Bk I, p. 369
Hermeneutic Source Scripture. Prophets.	*Hermeneutic Source* List of Church Objectives. See *Journal of Adventist Theology.* Committee Action. Theological Declaration.
STRUCTURE Revelation is divided in two. It is divided at chapter 12. See G.C. p. 438 (The two sections align with each other)	STRUCTURE Revelation is divided at chapter 15. Bk I, p. 30 There is no alignment between the two sections. Revelation is linear.
Chiastic Structure There are three chiastic patterns. There is chiastic pattern in chapters 1-11 and another in chapters 12-22. There is also chiastic pattern in 1-22.	Chiastic Structure There are several chiastic patterns. Chiastic pattern divides the book at Chapter 15
The Eight Visions 1. All eight visions begin with an heavenly scene of sanctuary significance. The lampstand of Ch. 1 reveals the Holy Place.	The Eight Visions 1. All eight visions begin with a heavenly scene except the first which is an earthly scene of Jesus among the churches.
2. Chapters 4, 5 align with Dan. 7 and refer to the Most Holy Place of the Investigative Judgment and 1844	2. Chapters 4, 5 are a song of of praise at the inauguration of Christ in 31 A.D.
3. Chapter 8 "throwing down the censer" refers to the Close of Probation. See E.W. p. 279, 280	3. Chapter 8 "throwing down the censer" refers to Christ's continuing ministry. Bk I, p. 188

GETTING IT ALL TOGETHER	SYMPOSIUM ON REVELATION
Eight Visions continued 4. Chapter 8 The ark of the covenant seen in the sky at the Voice of God. See G.C. p. 639 (in the context of Rev. 11:15-19 endtime events of Christ's taking the kingdom).	*Eight Visions Continued* 4. Chapter 8. The ark of the covenant dated 1844. Beginning the Investigative Judgment.
5. Chapter 12 Begins a new line of prophecy (G.C. 438) with Satan's rebellion, the birth of Christ, the 1260 years and continues to endtime remnant persecution (See Rev. 12:17	5. Chapter 12. Follows Chapter 11 Investigative Judgment Scene with the 1260 year period.
6. Chapter 14. Three Angels Chapter 15. Close of Probation	6. Chapter 14. Three Angels Chapter 15. Close of Probation
7. Chapter 19. Second Coming	7. Chapter 19. Second Coming
8. Chapters 21, 22. New Jerusalem	8. Chapters 21, 22. New Jerusalem.
CONCLUSION Two aligning major lines of prophecy place Seals, Trumpets and Plagues in an endtime framework.	*CONCLUSION* Seals, Trumpets are "recapitulations" of the 7 letters of chapters 2-3.
The structure and the heavenly scenes provide the timeframe for the basic prophetic outlines to begin. Correct identification of the first five heavenly scenes moves seals and trumpets into endtime settings.	The structure and the heavenly scenes provide the timeframe for the basic prophetic outlines to begin. "Backing up" the heavenly scenes without recognition of the two major lines of prophecy, prevents endtime application of seals and trumpets.
An endtime view of the seven seals reveals a black horse or apostasy in the church yet future.	A Uriah Smith view of the seals prevents any application which would predict apostasy in an endtime setting.
Specific Definitions of: "Future Applications" as different from "Futurism," explaining it as a Jesuit technique which switches symbolic and literal language and a violation of "The Literal Approach" hermeneutic principle.	No definitions of: "Future Applications" as different from "Futurism," thereby confusing the two, labeling Future Applications as "Futurism."
Recognition of Dual Application See *The Seventh-day Adventist Bible Commentary,* Vol. 1 p. 1017.	No recognition of Dual Applications Bk I, 154, 155.

GETTING IT ALL TOGETHER	**SYMPOSIUM ON REVELATION**
Dual Application defined as two applications of one verse.	Dual Applications implied to be two applications by two different persons such as one application by Uriah Smith and another expositor today.
"The Historicist School of Prophetic Exposition" defined by hermeneutic principles.	"Historic" Adventism defined by the personal views of Uriah Smith or other pioneers of Adventism.
The timelines of Daniel 12 applied to the future.	The timelines of Daniel 12 applied to the medieval era.
An attitude to expect "a new development of truth to each generation." COL 127	A position to defend past exposition fearful that new positions will tear down the foundations.
A search for linkage between Daniel and Revelation and endtime *significance*.	A modern exegesis (modern definition) of determining what the author had in mind.
A linkage between Dan. 11 and Rev. 13 "beast with seven heads" Seven heads represent 7 empires significant to the people of God.	Various theories denied. Then the author says, "No alternative interpretation has been suggested." Book II p. 205
The angel of Rev. 10 of the seven thunders links with Dan. 12 timelines, placing them in the future in reference to time. Rev. 10:7 context which declares that the "mystery of God should be finished,—endtime. Literally then, time will be no *longer*.	The angel of Revelation 10 of the seven thunders links with Dan. 12 timelines placing them in the medieval era in reference to time. Bk I, p. 28-321

APPENDIX NOTE H

LETTER TO JOHN ON "FUTURISM"

8-14-1993

Brother John Barrows
1414 Gray Rd.
Cumerlana, Me. 04021

Dear Brother John:

In reply to your inquiry of 8-11-93, in which you requested some definitions, I suggest that you use this letter if you are to meet with your friends to discuss the issues involved.

DEFINITIONS

1. "Future Application" 2. "Futurism"

1. *"Future Application"*

Any prophecy which is applied to the future by a prophetic expositor, is a "future application."

Examples:

1. The millennium or 1,000 year prophecy pertains to the future. When you apply it to the future, you are making a "future application."

2. The seven last plagues are future in their fulfillment. When we teach that they are future events we are making a "future application."

3. The Second Coming of Jesus is a future event. When you say that it is future, you are making a "future application."

4. Any prophecy, whether it be an event in a prophetic outline or a timeline or whatever it is, if you say it pertains to a future event which will fulfill that prophecy, you are making a "future application.

2. *"FUTURISM"*

"Futurism" rests on a specific *Jesuit technique,* devised in the sixteenth century and propagated by Francisco Ribera (1593); and *"Preterism,"* which also rests on the same *Jesuit technique.* was propagated by Loui de Alcazar (1614).

THE JESUIT TECHNIQUE WHICH INITIATED BOTH "FUTURISM" and "PRETERISM"

First, it is necessary to understand the *objective or goal* of Futurism and Preterism. In the sixteenth century in Europe, the European Reformers, such as Martin Luther, used the prophecies of Daniel 7 to identify the antichrist or "little horn" as **Papal Rome.** The European Reformers split the Papal power, taking almost all of northern Europe away from Rome, forming the Protestant

Reformation. Rome trembled. They were losing great sums of revenue. The Popes desired to find someone who could refute the "little horn" identification of the antichrist and come up with a new interpretation of Daniel 7. It was their **objective** to take the finger of accusation off of Papal Rome so that no one would identify the Papal power as the antichrist.

Ribera and Alcazar accomplished this perversion of prophetic exposition by the following technique:

1. They **interchanged the symbolic and literal language** of prophecy.

    Example: Daniel 7 is written in symbolic language. Daniel 7 has a symbolic **context** of "beasts," "heads," "horns," the "little horn." Daniel 7, in connection with the symbolic "little horn," also mentions a timeline of "time, times, and dividing of time" (1260 days.) In harmony with those symbolic beasts, those "days" should also be considered **SYMBOLIC TIME.** Using the "Year-Day Principle", those symbolic "days" should be considered as 1260 **LITERAL YEARS.**

    Ribera and Alcazar both ignored the symbolic language, and symbolic context and treated Daniel 7:25 as if it were literal and treated the 1260 "days" as if they were **literal time.** They taught that the 1260 "days" were literal days, or a **literal three and a half years.**

2. Ribera put that three and a half years in the distant future.

    THAT IS FUTURISM. He also taught that during that three and a half years, the antichrist would reign but that we do not know who he will be. This is the way they met their goal or **objective of taking the finger of accusation off Papal Rome.**

3. Alcazar put that three and a half years is the distant past. **THAT IS PRETERISM. He taught that the "little horn"** was not Papal Rome, but rather, the early persecutions of Christians by the Jews paralleling the former persecutions of the Jews by Antiochus for three and a half years.

SUMMARY: "Futurism" and "Preterism" both exist primarily to take the finger of accusation off Papal Rome. Their theology is based **ON AN INTERCHANGE OF SYMBOLIC AND LITERAL LANGUAGE OF PROPHETIC TIME.**

Protestantism followed in the footsteps of "Futurism" and thereby built upon it the "gap theory", placing the 70th week of Daniel 9:24-27 with its three and a half year periods at the end of time, and endorsed the **"RAPTURE."** Almost all of Protestantism has fallen into this trap and Seventh-day Adventists stand nearly alone in their historicist position of handling symbolic and literal Scripture with integrity.

Adventism has the advantage of a prophetess, who gave us the hermeneutic principle as to how we shall approach the Bible. Her statement is called **"THE LITERAL APPROACH."**

> "The language of the Bible should be explained according to its most obvious [literal] sense unless a symbol or figure is employed." The *Great Controversy* p. 599

As long as we use this hermeneutic principle, we will be on safe ground in regard to Daniel 7, and **also Daniel 12**

DANIEL 12
THE 1260, 1290 and 1335
timelines

We need to recognize the fact that Daniel 12 is not written in the symbolic language as that of Daniel 7. **DANIEL 12 is WRITTEN IN LITERAL LANGUAGE.**

There are no symbolic "beasts," "heads," "horns," or "little horn." It is written in literal language and the timelines of 1260, 1290, and 1335 "days" should be held in literal context and considered to be **LITERAL DAYS.**

The context of Daniel 12 is written regarding the **"END"**. (See Dan. 12:4,6 "when all these things shall be finished," verse 7, 8,9,13.) It refers to the "end" of all things,—not to "the time of the end" (1798 or 1844.) In 1798 and 1844 "all these things were *not finished.*"

In Daniel 12, those **LITERAL DAYS,** of 1260, 1290 and 1335 refer to the same power as that of Daniel 7, *Papal Rome*. Daniel 7, with its 1260 day-years, describes the medieval reign of the Papacy from 538-1798; while Daniel 12 describes a future Papal Supremacy and Daniel 12:7 describes a future persecution of God's "holy people." Daniel 12:11 timelines tells how long that Papal Supremacy No. 2 will reign. The 1335 days limit the time that God's people will be in the time of trouble and final crisis until they are delivered by the Voice of God.

Daniel 7:25 reveals the 1260 day-years of Papal Supremacy No. 1 when it reigned over Europe, but Daniel 12 reveals the 1260, 1290 literal days of Papal Supremacy No. 2 in the future. This is not futurism, it is merely a Future Application of what is coming in our very near future.

ENDTIME PRETERISM

When anyone, Seventh-day Adventists included, **INTERCHANGES THE LITERAL LANGUAGE** of Daniel 12, treating it as if those are *symbolic* times (1260, 1290, 1335) *he is using a Jesuit technique,* just as surely as did Ribera and Alcazar on Daniel 7.

When the prophetic expositor switches the literal time of Daniel 12 over to symbolic time, and places it far back in the medieval era he is creating a new form of **ENDTIME PRETERISM.**

In manipulating the Scripture in this way, he is again taking the finger of accusation off of Papal Rome as it is now emerging as the last great world empire (Head No. 7 of Rev. 13) in which "all the world will wonder after the beast." (verse 3) and he will have "power over all kindreds, and tongues, and nations."—a "New World Order," or head of "A ONE WORLD GOVERNMENT."

This "endtime Preterism" is Satan's effort to mute the Third Angel's Warning Message against the beast. Modern theologians, whether in the Seventh-day Adventist Church or in the independent ministries need to do a quick turn-around or face embarrassment and accusations of subversion of truth.

Those who are now inadvertently or consciously confusing legitimate "Future Applications" of Daniel 12 with "Futurism." need to take a second look and "wise up."

TIME SETTING

The statements of Ellen G. White regarding "timesetting" are made in regard to setting a time or date for the Second Coming of Jesus. Many have done this in the past and some are still doing so.

We need to understand clearly that the timelines of Daniel 12 do not set a date for the Second Coming—not the day nor the hour, not the month, nor year. They do not set a date for the Close of Probation, the Latter Rain or any other such thing, not even for the Sunday Laws. Then what are they for?

> ". . . the prophetic periods of Daniel, extending down to the very eve of the great consummation, **throw a flood of light on EVENTS, then to transpire.**" R&H Sept 25, 1883.

We need this **"FLOOD OF LIGHT"** on events (not the second coming). The timelines of Daniel 12 put these events in their order, and are the very framework on which to place events spoken of in Revelation! These timelines bring clarity and order to a study of future events.

The "prophetic periods" which ended in 1844 were those which are contained in the 2300 day-year prophecy of Daniel 8:14. There were a number of "prophetic periods" that rested within that 2300-day-years such as the 70 weeks, one week, etc, etc, and they were all ended by 1844 including the 2300 itself.

Whereas Ellen G. White spoke of the 2300 day-years Prophetic periods as ending in 1844, she spoke of other "prophetic periods" in the book of Daniel which "extend to the very eve of of the great consummation." She was not contradicting herself. We need great care when we read these statements that we understand to what she was referring when she used "Prophetic periods" in different ways.

The "prophetic time" which ended in 1844 was again the prophetic time or prophetic timeline of the 2300 days. The 2300 days were indeed "prophecy" or "prophetic time." But when she made that statement she was referring only to the 2300 days, not to all time prophecy of the Scripture. We need to use the same integrity when using her writings as when we use the Bible itself, not taking things out of context.

It is true that the Third Angel's Message is not "hung on time." Certainly not hung on time or dates for the coming of Jesus. All should agree on that. When her writings are taken in their original context, and correctly understood, they will not conflict with Scripture, nor the light breaking on Daniel 12 which points to the future Papal Supremacy.

You will want to get the book, **GETTING IT ALL TOGETHER IN DANIEL AND REVELATION** which will give about 250 pages of explanations of all these things in careful detail.

Prophecy is a "light in a dark place." II Pet. 1:21. When the world sinks into "impenetrable darkness" God's people will carry the torch of prophecy to light the way all the way to the kingdom. We will need it to carry us through the time of trouble and the seven last plagues!

In regard to your other questions: David Koresh thought he had some light on the Seven Seals of Revelation. I have no idea what he had in mind. He may just have been stalling for time.

I do not know what David Koresh taught about the seven trumpets.

The SDA pioneers viewed the seals and trumpets as "recapitulations" of the seven letters of Revelation 1-3. I have no fault to find with their understandings because what they had to offer was supportive to the message they had to give at that time.

We do not need to tear down the pioneer positions on prophecy because, they like prophetic expositors in all past centuries, were still groping to find meaning. However, today, we need to look for meaning that is more in harmony with the later statements made by the prophetess which place seals and trumpets in an endtime setting.

At Glacier View Conference, which dealt with the Desmond Ford controversy, the SDA theologians made a "rule" that prophecy may not have dual applications. The SDA scholarly theologians of the BRI have just published the book, **SYMPOSIUM ON REVELATION** Book 1 and Book II, advertised in your Sabbath School Quarterly this quarter. They bring up many arguments that there can be only one application of seals and trumpets as put forth by Uriah Smith. His personal views or applications are confused with "historic Adventism" which rests on hermeneutic principles rather than personal views of any expositors.

The Seventh-day Adventist Bible Commentary, Vol. 1 p. 1017, states that "The Bible abounds in dual applications."! It continues for three pages to give examples. Ellen G. White explained that Matt. 24 is a dual prophecy and that it refers to the destruction of Jerusalem and the end of the world.

I believe that there are dual applications of the seals, and trumpets and especially that which gives them endtime significance.

Sincerely,

Marian G. Berry

Marian G. Berry

APPENDIX NOTE I

SOME THOUGHTS ON TIMESETTING

Please do not be intimidated by oft repeated error which will separate you from a study of the Word of God concerning prophecies of Daniel and Revelation which deal with time.

Ellen G. White did **NOT** say that there would be no more study of time prophecy after 1844. She did **NOT** say that **ALL** prophecy ended in 1844. She did **NOT** say that **ALL** "prophetic time" ended in 1844. She did **NOT** say that **ALL** the "prophetic periods" ended in 1844. She did **NOT** say that the Year-day Principle ended in 1844. No? Then what did she say?

1. *"Prophetic time."* The 2300 day-year prophecy of Daniel 8:14 is prophetic. It deals with time. Therefore it is "prophetic time." It is a "prophetic time[line]." When Ellen G. White referred to the 2300 day timeline she abbreviated it to simply call it "prophetic time." The context of her statements must be considered. Those statements so often quoted from *The Seventh-day Adventist Bible Commentary,* Vol. 7 p. 971 where she says that "prophetic time" ended in 1844 apply only to the 2300 day-year prophecy, **NOT** to **ALL** the other prophecies dealing with time in Scripture.

2. *"Prophetic periods."* Referring to the same 2300 day-year prophecy of Daniel 8:14, she said that the "prophetic periods" ended in 1844. What "prophetic periods" was she talking about? Within the 2300 "prophetic time" line there are a number of "prophetic periods." There is the 70 week "prophetic period." There are the 62 weeks, the 69 weeks, the one week, two three and a half week "prophetic periods" and the 2300 itself. First-day Adventists were manipulating these "prophetic periods," adding one to another and changing beginning dates in attempts to set a date for the coming of Jesus. She explained that all of these "prophetic periods" including the 2300 itself had ended by 1844. She was **NOT** referring to **ALL** the prophetic periods mentioned in the Bible.

3. *Contradictions.* Did Ellen G. White contradict herself? When she made what appears to be contradictory statements, she was speaking of two different things. Look at the example below:

". . . there should be time no longer (Rev. 10:5,6). This message announces the end of the prophetic *periods."* . . . *1844 . . .* *II Selected Messages 108*	"The *prophetic periods* of Daniel, extending to the very eve of the great consummation, throw a flood of light on events then to transpire." *Review and Herald,* Sept 25, 1883

The quotation on the left is referring to the 2300 day-year prophecy of Daniel 8:14, but on the right she refers to other "prophetic periods" of Daniel.

Look at the full quotation again:

> In the Scripture are Present Truths that relate especially to **our own time.** To the period **just prior to the appearing of the Son of man,** the prophecies of Scripture point, and their warning and threatenings preeminently apply. The **PROPHETIC PERIODS** of Daniel, **EXTENDING TO THE VERY EVE OF THE GREAT CONSUMMATION,** throw a flood of light on **events then to transpire.** The book of Revelation is also replete with warnings and instruction for

the **LAST GENERATION** . . . None need be unprepared for the day of God.
Review and Herald, Sept. 25, 1883

"The great consummation" is the Second Coming of Jesus. The "very eve of the great consummation" is the night before! The "prophetic periods" of Daniel 7 and 8 do not reach the "very eve of the great consummation." They reached only to 1798 and 1844. The only other periods which, when given correct application, are the 1260, 1290 and 1335 literal day timelines of Daniel 12.

Ellen G. White did not say that the "prophetic periods of Daniel" (12) would tell us the the day and hour of the Second Coming. She said that they would "throw a flood of light on **events** then to transpire." She was right when she said that there would be no more definite tracing of the time (to find the day and hour of the Second Coming of Jesus.) There is no time prophecy of Scripture which gives the date or timesetting for the coming of Jesus. The third angel's message is not hung on time. We are not to know the time for the outpouring of the latter rain or the close of probation. These exact dates are not given. The purpose of prophetic timelines is to "throw a flood of light on **events** then to transpire."

Fanatical speculation is quite different from a study of Scripture. Setting dates for the coming of Jesus is quite different from a study of the timelines of Daniel 12. A "future application" of these timelines is quite different from "Futurism" which twists symbolic and literal language to place an **UNIDENTIFIED** antichrist in the future. A genuine study of Daniel 12 will bring to view the "beast" of Revelation 13 and identify him as the same power as that referred to in Daniel 7 as the "little horn"—The Papacy. A genuine study of the of "prophetic periods" expands the Third Angel's Message. It does not mute it.

It is also necessary to distinguish that which was said by Ellen G. White and that which was said by other people. For example:

> Seventh-day Adventists have generally understood . . . the "time" to be prophetic time . . . the 2300 days of Daniel 8:14. **After this there is to be no further message bearing on definite time. No time prophecy extends beyond 1844.** *The Seventh-day Adventist Bible Commentary,* Vol. 7, p. 798

Ellen White did not say this. Other writers assumed it.

Unfortunately, the writers of the *The Seventh-day Adventist Bible Commentary* lifted statements from their historical and circumstantial context. This, obviously, confused them and has done the same for others ever since. We need to take great care when the writings of uninspired persons are mixed in with those of the prophet.

We need to keep a "level head" in the study of the writings of Ellen G. White to treat them with the same integrity that we use in a study of Scripture. The paradox, so often used by Jesus, which appears to be contradictory is actually, when understood, a means of opening the mind with light and truth.

For example, Ellen G. White wrote that we cannot, by using types, symbols, or any other device, set a date or time for the coming of Jesus. This is in harmony with Matt. 24:36 "of that day and hour knoweth no man (no man makes known). Yet, she wrote:

> These types were fulfilled, not only as to the event, but as to the **time** . . . In like manner the types, which relate to the second coming must be fulfilled, **AT THE TIME POINTED OUT IN THE SYMBOLIC SERVICE.**
> *The Great Controversy,* p. 399

It is imperative that the Bible student balance out all of these things. The Hebrew economy is full of instruction for us. The timelines of **ALL** Scripture are for our learning and in "every age there is a new development of truth." COL 127. Let no erroneous quotations stand in the way of a study of the Word of God and an open mind in the investigation of truth. If there were portions of the Word of God which we should not understand, the Lord would not have put them in there!

There is nothing sacred regarding the applications made by previous expositors, such as Uriah Smith. He and others wrote many things helpful in regard to prophetic exposition, but they were not inspired prophets and it is not our duty to hold their opinions as sacred. A study of prophecy which is correct will expand and reinforce the waymarks and foundations of our faith.

"Timesetting" or date setting for the latter rain, the close of probation for individuals or for the church, or for the coming of Jesus is wrong. A study of prophetic periods which throw a flood of light on events then to transpire, or reveals time relationships is right. Be assured that a study of the timelines of Daniel 12 will not be an exercise of timesetting or date setting.

APPENDIX NOTE J

THE HEWIT STATEMENT (See p. 62)

The "Hewit Statement," though ambiguous, is often used as "proof" that the 1335 days of Daniel 12 were fulfilled in the past, and may not receive an endtime application. However, by 1893, the same prophet placed the 1335 days in a future setting. Both statements are quoted below:

> Brother Hewit from Dead River was there. He came with a message to the effect that the destruction of the wicked and the sleep of the dead was an abomination within a shut door that a woman, Jezebel, a prophetess had brought in and he believed that I was that woman Jezebel. We told him of some of his errors in the past, that the 1335 days were ENDED and numerous errors of his. It had but little effect. His darkness was felt upon the meeting and it dragged.
>
> I felt that I must say a few words. In the name of Jesus, I got up and in about five minutes the meeting changed. Everyone felt it at the same instant. Every countenance was lighted up. The presence of God filled the place. Brother Hewit dropped upon his knees and began to cry and pray. I was taken off in vision and saw much that I cannot write. It had a great effect upon Brother Hewit. He confessed it was of God and was humbled in the dust. He has been writing ever since that meeting and is now writing from the same table renouncing all his errors that he has advanced. I believe God is bringing him up and he is calculated to do good, if God moves through him.— Letter 28, 1850, p. 3. ("To the Church in Bro. Hastings" House," November 7, 1850.)—*Manuscript Releases Volume Six*, p. 251-252
>
> This is the sanctification to which those attain whose love of God's law increases as the contempt of transgressors increases. There is need for this increased confidence in the law, for fraud, violence, and crime are rapidly increasing. Men show their hatred of God by fighting against His law which He has pronounced "holy and just and good." Liquor saloons are established in every city. These are death traps, and those who establish them, seeking to accumulate gain at the cost of poverty, misery, and woe, provoke the Lord of hosts to their destruction.
>
> God gives to all a period of probation but men can reach a point where they can expect from God nothing but *indignation and punishment. This time is not just now, but it is fast approaching. The nations will advance from one degree of sinfulness to another. The children, educated and trained in transgression, will add to the evil entailed on them by parents* who have no fear of God in their hearts.
>
> Already the judgments of God have begun to fall upon the world in various calamities, that men may repent and be converted to truth and righteousness. But *the candle of those who harden their hearts in iniquity will be put out by the Lord. They have lived only for themselves, and death must come to them.*
>
> *When the limit of grace is reached, God will give His command for the destruction of the transgressor. He will arise in His Almighty character as a God above all gods, and those who have worked against Him* in league with the great rebel, *will be treated in accordance with their works.*

In his vision of the last days Daniel inquired, "O my Lord, what shall be the end of these things? And he said, Go thy way, Daniel: for the words are closed up and sealed till the time of the end. Many shall be purified, and made white, and tried; but the wicked shall do wickedly: and none of the wicked shall understand; but the wise shall understand. . . . *Blessed is he that waiteth, and cometh to the thousand three hundred and five and thirty days.* But go thou thy way till the end be: for thou shalt rest, and stand in thy lot at the end of the days" [Dan. 12:8-13]. Daniel has been standing in his lot since the seal was removed and the light of truth has been shining upon his visions. He stands in his lot, bearing the testimony which was to be understood at the end of the days.

"And at that time shall Michael stand up, the great prince which standeth for the children of thy people: and there shall be a time of trouble, such as never was since there was a nation even to that same time: and at that time thy people shall be delivered, every one that shall be found written in the book. And many of them that sleep in the dust of the earth shall awake, some to everlasting life, and some to shame and everlasting contempt. And they that be wise shall shine as the brightness of the firmament; and they that turn many to righteousness as the stars for ever and ever. But thou, O Daniel, shut up the words, and seal the book, even to the time of the end: many shall run to and fro, and knowledge shall be increased"[Dan. 12:1-4].—Manuscript 50, 1893, September, 1893. (MR 900.33)—*Sermons and Talks Volume One,* p. 225-226

The following translations make clear the endtime application of the 1335 days of Daniel 12:

How blessed is he who keeps waiting and attains the 1335 days.
New American Standard Bible

Blessed is the one who waits for and reaches the end of the 1335th day.
New International Version

Blessed are those who wait and remain until the 1335th day!
The Living Bible

APPENDIX NOTE K

THE "ONE HOUR" PERIOD OF REV. 17:12 (See p. 71)

The "*one hour*" periods of Rev 17:12 and 18:10, 17, 19 do not refer to an "indefinite brief space of time." Out of seventeen versions and translations of the Bible, only one paraphrase refers to it as a brief space of time. The Greek Diaglot Interlinear reads as follows:

> ἐξουσίαν ὡς βασιλεῖς μίαν ὥραν λαμβάνουσι
> authority as kings one hour they receive
>
> 12 And the ‡TEN Horns which thou sawest are Ten Kings, who have not †[yet] received a Kingdom; but they receive Authority, as Kings, One Hour with the BEAST.

Strong's Exhaustive Concordance also gives the meaning of this passage as "one" and "hour," in connection with Revelation 17:12 and 18:10, 17, and 19, as follows:

> Re 3: 3 shalt not know what h' I will come "
> 10 keep thee from the h' of temptation."
> 8: 1 about the space of half an h'. 2256
> 9:15 prepared for an h', and a day, and 5610
> 11:13 same h' was there a great "
> 14: 7 for the h' of his judgment is come: "
> 17:12 power as kings one h' with the "
> 18:10 for in one h' is thy judgment come."
> 17 in one h' so great riches is come "
> 19 for in one h' is she made desolate. "

"**HOUR**" The Greek word ὥρα, hora, number 5610, has the meaning of a literal hour. Other figurative meanings may be given to it. The scholars who have translated the Bible have almost unanimously selected the literal "hour" in preference to figurative meanings. See *Strong's Greek Dictionary of the New Testament*.

> 5610. ὥρα hōra, ho'-rah; appar. a prim. word; an "*hour*" (lit. or fig.):—day, hour, instant, season, × short, [even-] tide, (high) time.

"**HOUR**" The Hebrew word סָפַר, caphar, (pronounced saw far') number 5608 (taken from 5610) carries an intrinsic meaning of "to declare" or "to tell forth" (a **DECREE** published abroad) or to "inscribe" (a writing or DECREE) and to **CELEBRATE**. These meanings contain the very essence of the action taking place during the "one hour" of Rev. 17:12 when the "ten kings" exalt or celebrate over the fact that they have legislated a Universal Death Decree to destroy the people of God. See *Strong's Hebrew and Chaldee Dictionary* as follows:

> 5608. סָפַר çâphar, saw-far'; a prim. root; prop. to score with a mark as a tally or record, i.e. (by impl.) to inscribe, and also to enumerate; intens. to recount, i.e. celebrate:—commune, (ac-) count, declare, number, + penknife, reckon, scribe, shew forth, speak, talk, tell (out), writer.
>
> 5609. סְפַר çephar (Chald.), sef-ar'; from a root corresp. to 5608; a book:—book, roll.
>
> 5610. סְפָר çephâr, sef-awr'; from 5608; a census:—numbering.

The word, "**ONE**", in connection with Revelation 17:12 and 18:10, 17, 19 is also to be investigated in *Strong's Exhaustive Concordance*. It is listed as word number 3391.

```
17:  1 there came o' of the seven angels    "
    10 five are fallen, and o' is, and the   "
    12 as kings o' hour with the beast.    3391
    13 These have o' mind, and shall give    "
18:  8 shall her plagues come in o' day,     "
    10 in o' hour is thy judgment come.     "
    17 in o' hour so great riches is come   "
    19 for in o' hour is she made desolate.
21:  9 unto me o' of the seven angels      1520
    21 every several gate was of o' pearl:   "
```

The Greek word μία, mia, (pronounced mee-ah), word number 3391, is taken from word 1520, which refers to a primitive number, that is, **"ONE."** It also has the meaning of "first." See *Strong's Greek Dictionary of the New Testament* as follows:

```
3391. μία mia, mee'-ah; irreg. fem. of 1520; one
or first:—a (certain), + agree, first, one, × other.
```

The Hebrew word יֶרַח, yerach, (pronounced yeh-rekh'), word number 3391, refers to a **LUNATION,** or **MONTH.** The two "one hour" periods of 15 literal days each make up one month or 30 days of final crisis and deliverance. First, the kings reign or celebrate the legislation of The Universal Death Decree, but on the effective date, the Voice of God delivers the people of God. The voice of God also reveals the identity of Babylon and for the next 15 literal days (one hour) the kings destroy those who deceived them, which is "The Fall of Babylon." Rev. 18:10, 17, 19.

The Feast of Trumpets is the *first* day of the seventh month, and according to the types of the Hebrew economy, the day for the Voice of God deliverance from the Universal Death Decree. See Strong's Hebrew and Chaldee Dictionary as follows:

```
3391. יֶרַח yerach, yeh'-rakh; from an unused
      root of uncert. signif.; a lunation, i.e.
month:—month, moon.
3392. יֶרַח Yerach, yeh'-rakh; the same as 3391;
      Jerach, an Arabian patriarch:—Jerah.
3393. יְרַח yᵉrach (Chald.), yeh-rakh'; corresp. to
      3391; a month:—month.
3394. יָרֵחַ yârêach, yaw-ray'-akh; from the
      same as 3391; the moon:—moon.
```

Index

A
Acknowledgments, xii
Action: Loosing the Four Angels of Destruction, 141
Action: To Unify Babylon for Armageddon, 99
Acts 1:7, 8 Ye Shall Receive Power to Know Times, 76
Agitating for Legislation of the Universal death Decree, 102
Alignment of Two Major Lines of Prophecy in Revelation, 164
Applications, Past, 171
Armageddon, 19
Atheism Reigns three and an half days, 271
Avenge our Blood Request Leads into the Plague-Trumpet Blood Judgments, 179

B
Babylon Falls After the Voice of God, 115
Babylon, Fall of—Rev. 17, 217
Battle Alignment: 144,000 Vs. 200 million, 142
Beast Represents the Papacy, 101
Bible and Law of God is legislated away, 271
Bible is its own Expositor, 83
Bible Its Own Interpreter, 87
Bible Its Own Interpreter Cartoon, 221
Biblical Definitions Vs. Human Conjecture, 88
Biblical Timeframe to Begin the Seven Seals, 172
Buying-Selling Decree: Dan. 11:43: Rev. 13:16, 17, 52

C
Cartoon: The Bible Its Own Interpreter, 221
Characters of the Drama, 99
Characters of the Sixth Plague Drama, The, 13
Chart
    Aligning, Interlocking Structure of Prophecy, 85
    Alignment of Plagues and Trumpets, 131
    Alignment of Rev. 1-11 and 12-22, 161
    Ascending and Descending Action of Final Crisis and Deliverance, 68
    Basic Differences Between Getting All Together book and Symposium Books I and II, 277
    Battle of Armageddon: Gathering Action, Battle Alignment, Battle Action, 119
    Chronological Order of Revelation 1-11, 159
    Chronological Order of Revelation 12-22, 160
    Circular Correlation Chart of Seals, Trumpets, and Plagues, Timelines of Daniel 12, 201
    Comparison of Dan. 7 with Rev. 4 and 5, 173
    Correlation of An Alignment of Revelation 17:10-18 With Plagues and Trumpets, 213
    Correlation of Plagues and Trumpets, 154
    Correlation of Seal 6, Plague 7, Trumpet 7, 184
    Correlation of Seals, Trumpets and Plagues, 186
    Correlation of Seals, Trumpets and Plagues Aligned with Day of Atonement 1844 to End, 196
    Daniel 12 Timelines—The Framework for Events Described in Revelation, 198
    Earthquake and Signs Begin and End "The Time of the End", 184
    Eight Heads of Revelation 17, 216
    Fall Feast Days, 189
    Fall Feast Days—Dan. 12 and 17:12, 190
    Fifth Seal Leads into the Plagues-Trumpets, 180
    Final Timelines of Daniel 12 with Added Detail, 74
    Final Timelines of Daniel 12:5-13, 73
    First Five Seals Lead Into the Plagues and Trumpets, 181
    Gathering Action, 105
    Getting It All Together with References, 199
    Last Year of Earth's History, 194

National Sunday Law USA begins the 1335 days, 70
Order and Relationship of Seals 1 and 2, 176
Satan's Seven Attempts to Establish His Kingdom, 214
Seal 6, Plague 7, Trumpet 7 Correlation, 184
Sequence and Continuity in Correlation of Plagues, Trumpets and Seals, 182
Sequence and Continuity of Daniel 11 Historical Fulfillment, The, 58
Seven Heads of the Beast, 235
Seven Heads of the Leopard-Beast, 215
Seven Thunder "Voices" of Revelation Identified, 78
Ten kings (all) Reign wit the Beast "one hour", 213
Thirteen Hundred Thirty Five Day Wait for the "Blessing", 69
Three Major Lines in Daniel and Revelation, 157
Two "one hour" Periods, 118
Voice of God Deliverance, 67
Charts, Diagrams, and Illustrations List, vii
Chiasms, 170
Christ Revealed as the Redeemer and Deliverer, 39
Common Sense Guidelines in Prophetic Studies, 226
Complete Story: Who, What, When, Where, Why, How, 126
Composite Beast of Revelation 13 and 14 Correlation of Daniel 7 with Revelation 13, 235
Composite Beast of Revelation 13, The, 49
Content of the Book opened—Rev. 5, 174
Correlation of Daniel 11 and Revelation 13, A, 48
Counting timelines does not set dates, 62

D

Daniel 11:35 "The Time of the End—1798", 43
Daniel 11:35 Papal Supremacy Ends—1798, 43
Daniel 11:36-40 The Rise of Atheistic-Communism, 44
Daniel 11:40, Papacy Rises and Enters Israel, The, 48
Daniel 12:4-13 Refers to the "Utmost End" of time., 63
Daniel 12:5-12 is an Epilogue, 61
Daniel 12:5-13 Applies to the Third Angel's Message, 64
Daniel 12:5-13 Final Timelines Chart, 73
Daniel 12:5-13 is Written in Literal Language, 61
Daniel 12:5-13 Refers to Papal Supremacy No. 2—Future, 63
Daniel 12:5-13 Uses no Symbols, 61
Daniel and the Final Deliverance (Introduction), xiii
Daniel's Questions and Gabriel's Answers, 32
Death Decree and the Deliverance, A, 3
Deliverance by the "Faith of Jesus", 4
Deliverance by the Voice of God Under the Seventh Plague, 21
Deliverance from Human Weakness, 37
Deliverance from the King of Babylon, 8
Deliverance from the King of the North, 40
Deliverance from the Little Horn Power, 25
Deliverance In the Timelines of Daniel 12, 60
Deliverance of Israel as a Nation and the Deliverance of Spiritual Israel from Sin, The, 30
Deliverer and Redeemer, Christ Revealed as, 39
Diagram
  Eight Visions of Revelation, 166
  Eight Visions of Revelation, Detailed, 168
  Forward Movement of Datable Time, Alignment, Sequence and Continuity of the outlines in the Book of Daniel, The, 40
  Sequence and Order of the Two Major Lines of Prophecy in Revelation, 162
Dragon Represents Satan in many forms of worship, 100
Drama of the Sixth Plague, The, 13

E

Effective Date:—a Time Appointed, 110

Eight Visions of Revelation, 165
1844—Opens the Books, 174
Ellen G. White's Use of the Bible, 225
Equating 1260 days, 42 Months, and 3 1/2 Times, 261
Evil angels appear as men in glory and beauty, 138
Evil angels come as a plague of locusts to devour, 135
Evil angels deal in cruelty and force running to battle to legislate a Universal Death Decree, 139
Evil angels emerge as smoke from a furnace, 135
Evil angels gather the kings of the earth to battle, 138
Evil angels run to battle five months, 136
Evil angels sting the wicked like scorpions, 136

F

Fall of Babylon After the Voice of God, 115
Fall of Babylon and the Seventh Plague, The, 10
Fall of Babylon—Rev. 17, 217
False Prophet Represents Apostate Protestantism, 101
Feast of Tabernacles—The Wicked Destroyed, 195
Fifth Trumpet, 132
Five Months: Evil angels run to battle, 136
Four Beasts—Recorders and Retrievers, 173
Four Symbolic Pictures of Revelation 17, 204
Future Application, 171
Future Fulfillment of Seven Trumpets, 120
Futurism-Preterism and "The Literal Approach", 223

G

Geographical Identification Map Orientation, 42
God Controls the Plagues. Satan Controls the Wicked, 89
God will deliver His people at Midnight, 66
Great Red Dragon in Detail, 229

H

Heads and Tails: Cause and Effect, 144
Hermeneutic Principle: "Context is King" to define what is symbolic and what is literal, 116
Hermeneutic Principles and the Structure of Revelation, 84
Hermeneutic principles are derived from the Bibl, 222
Hermeneutics—Historicist "School" Vs. Human Opinion, 86
Historicist "School" Hermeneutics Vs. Human Opinion, 86
How Long Until the Deliverance?, 29
Human Conjecture Vs. Biblical Definitions, 88

I

Illustration
    Composite Beast of Revelation 13 with Its Seven Heads, The, 55
    Prophetic Clock, The, vi
    Timeframe Sandwich, 128
INTRODUCTION TO THE SEVEN TRUMPETS, 120
Introduction: "King of the North," "King of the South", 42
Introduction: Daniel and the Final Deliverance, xiii
IStruggle For World Domination, The, 41

K

"King of the North" is Papal Rome—shifts of title, 45
"King of the South"—"Egypt"—Atheistic Communism, 47
"King of the South" Identified, 47
Kings of the Earth and of the Whole World, The, and the Beast, 18

L

Law condemns the wicked, 274
Law of God and Bible legislated away, 271
Law of God Will Be Seen in the Sky, 271
Letter to John On "Futurism", 280
Linkage (Praface), x
List
    Events during the Thirty Days of Final Crisis and Deliverance, 218
    Premises Pertaining to the Final Timeline of Daniel 12:5-13, 72

Seals, Trumpets, Plagues, Rev. 17 Events and Dan. 12 Picture from 1844 to Second Coming, 202
Voice of God Events, 112
"Literal Approach" and Preterism-Futurism, 223
Literal Approach Hermeneutic, The, 62

M

Major Lines of Prophecy, 156
Midnight Deliverance, 110

N

National Sovereignty—the Scepter of Power, Seat and Authority will be taken away from the Nations and given to the Future Papal Supremacy One World Order, 64
New World Order, Papacy Head of, 48
No Timelines Give Day and Hour for the Second Coming, 62
Nuclear War: Smoke, Jacinth, Brimstone, 142

O

Objective of the 2300, 34
"One hour" Fall of Babylon Occurs Between the Voice of God and the Second Coming, 67
"Out of the Mouth of" Signifies Verbal Agitation, 101

P

Papacy Became the Fifth Empire, The, 43
Papacy Rises and Enters Israel, The, Daniel 11:40, 48
Papal Head of the New World Order, 48
Papal Supremacy Ends—1798, Daniel 11:35, 43
Papal Supremacy No. 2 Will Be Established by a Universal Sunday Law, 64
Past Applications, 171
Persecution is climaxed in the Universal Death Decree, 66
Plague 4 Affects the Sun, 95
Plague 5—Supernatural Darkness, 95
Plagues 1-5, 92
Plagues 2 and 3 Affect Water and Weather Systems, 94
Plagues Begin After the Close of Probation-Timeframe, 92
Pope in Jerusalem, 53
Power to Know Times—Acts 1:7, 8, 76
Preface: Linkage, x
Premises, Summary of, 96
Preparing the Way—The Gathering Action, 100
Preset Date Rev. 9:15, 142
Preterism-Futurism and "The Literal Approach", 223
Prince of the Covenant Broken A.D. 31, 43
Prophecy is Linear—Moving Forward in Sequential Order, 84
Prophecy Is Simply History Written in Advance, 84
Prophetic Clock, The (illustration), vi
Prophetic periods "throw . . . light on events", 60
"Prophetic Periods of Daniel" Quotation, 60
Psalm 91, 106

R

Rationale: Restraints Removed to Illustrate two Demonstrations: Good and Evil, 89
Redeemer and Deliverer, Christ Revealed as, 39
Religious Liberties Taken Away, 64
Rev. 8:5 Established Trumpet Timeframe, 127
Rev. 9:15, A Pre-set date, 262
Revelation 11, 266
Revelation 11 describes events of Trumpets 6 and 7, also Seal 6, 274
Revelation 17—A Wrap-up of Symbolism in Revelation, 204
Rewards and Retribution, 146
Righteous Glorified at the Voice of God, 109
Rise of Atheistic-Communism, The, Daniel 11:36-40, 44
"River" Symbol—Represents the Holy Spirit, 98
Rome Became the Fourth World Empire, 42

S

Safety in the Seal of God, 91
Sanctified Life, The, 1
Satan gave the beast "power, seat, authority", 212
Satan Given the Key to Unleash evil spirits, 134

Satan Personates Christ, 212
Satan Personates Christ—they will Behold him, 270
Satan supporting and carrying Babylon, 210
Satan Wars Against the Two Witnesses, 269
Satan's Arguments Against Restraint and Law, 90
Satan's Crowning Act, 211
Satan: The Main Character and his evil spirits, 133
Satan: The Serpent-Dragon-Beast with seven heads, 209
Scope of Action of the Plagues, 93
Scope of Action: One Third of Men Killed, 142
Seal 1 opened 1844 The Gospel to all the world, 174
Seal 2 Opened with Sunday Legislation, 176
Seal 3 Apostasy, Selling out of truth. Weighed and found wanting, 176
Seal 4 Death, sword, hunger, beasts of the earth, 177
Seal 5 Martyrs—Rev. 18 Loud Cry and Harvest, 178
Seal 6 and the Jubilee, 191
Seal 6 and the Law of God Seen in the Heavens, 191
Seal 7 and the Half Hour Silence in Heaven, 192
Second Coming of Jesus, 146
Sequence of Plagues, 94
Sequence of Seven Heads, 214
Sequence of Seven Heads Revealed by Dan. 7, 48
Setting: Babylon, 97
Setting: Legislation of a Universal Death Decree, 107
Setting: Spiritual Babylon, 141
Seven Angels' Messages of Rev. 14 and 18, 263
Seven Deliverances in the Book of Daniel, The, 25
Seven Heads Represent Seven Empires, 48
Seven Heads, Sequence of Revealed by Dan. 7, 48
Seven Seals, 171

Seven Thunder Voices Identified by the Daniel 12:5-13 Timeline Voices, 78
Seven Thunders—Rev. 10:4 in Relation to Time, 76
Seven Trumpets—Future Fulfillment of, 120
Seven Trumpets—Traditional Views of, 122
Seventh Head Represents A "One World Government" Under Papal Control, 51
Seventh Plague Deliverance, 107
Seventh Trumpet, 146
Sixth Empire Established, The, 45
Sixth Head Represented Atheistic Communism, 51
SIXTH PLAGUE GATHERING ACTION TO ARMAGEDDON, THE, 97
Sixth Trumpet, 140
Some Thoughts on Timesetting, 285
Structure and Drama of Plagues 6 and 7, 107
Structure of Daniel, The, xvii
Structure of Revelation: Major Lines of Prophecy, 156
Struggle Between the Papacy and Communism, The, 47
Suggestions For Use of This Program, 288
Summary of Daniel 11, 55
Summary of Premises, 96
Babylon Falls in "one hour"—15 days, 116
Symbolic Service types fulfilled at the Second Coming, 188
Symbolic Woman Symbols, 205
Symposium on Revelation Book I and Book II Analysis, 276

T

Table
   Comparisons and Contrasts of Jerusalem and Babylon, 207
   Thunder Sequence, Timeline Identification, Event, and Scripture Reference, 79
Table of Comparisons: Seven Plagues With Seven Trumpets, 125
Table of Contents, iv
"The Time of the End—1798," Daniel 11:35, 43
THE WARNING book Order Page, 81

There will be a Future 1260 Literal Days of Persecution, 63
Thirty Day Difference Between the 1260 Days and the 1290 Days Is Explained In Revelation 17 and 18, 65
Three Deliverances, The, 110
Three Evil Spirits in Action, 100
317 Helpful Questions, 244
Three Unclean Spirits, The, 14
Three Woes, 146
Three-Fold Union, The, 15
Timeframe For the Sixth Seal—an Earthquake, 183
Timeframe Reiterated, 145
Timeframe: Investigative Judgment, 1844, 173
Timeframe: Judgment of the Living, 268
Timeframe: The Voice of God Begins It, 140
Timeframe: When the land shall rest, 192
Traditional Views of the Seven Trumpets, 122
Triumph of John Paul II: Life Magazine, 228
Trumpet, 126
Trumpet 1 and 2, 129
Trumpet 3 and 4, 130
Trumpet 5, 132
Trumpet 6, 140
Trumpet 7, 146
Trumpet Language: Symbolic or Literal, 126
Trumpet Timeframe Established by Rev. 8:5, 127
Trumpets 1-4—Future Application, 124
Twelve Hundred Ninety "days" Limit the Reign of Papal Supremacy—Future, 65
1260 Ends, 268
Twelve Hundred Sixty Literal "days" and the 1290 "days" Begin Simultaneously, 65
Twelve Hundred Sixty Literal Days of Persecution, 63
Two "One Hour" Periods of Revelation 17 and 18 Reveal the Ascending and Descending Action of the 6th and 7th Plagues—Arm, 66
Two Symbolic Women Picture, 206
Two Witnesses—Old and New Testament, 266

U

Union of Church and State, The, 17
Universal Death Decree Goes Into Effect at Midnight, 66
Universal Death Decree, The, 16, 21
USA-NSL is a Warning to Leave the Large Cities, 70

V

Value of Prophecy, The, v
Voice of God Declares Day and Hour, 108
Voice of God Deliverance, 108
Voice of God Deliverance, The, 23
Voice of God Delivers God's People, 66
Voice of God is not Second Coming, 66
Voice of God Pronounces the Everlasting Covenant, 109
Voices of Doom on Babylon, 151

W

Web of Truth Summary, 220
White, Ellen G—her use of the Bible, 225
Wicked cry for rocks and mountains to fall on them—Sixth Seal Language, 274
Witnesses, Two—Old and New Testament, 266
Witnesses, Two—Satan wars against, 269
Woes, Three, 146
Women, Two Symbolic Picture, 206
Wrath of God, The, 88

We invite you to view the complete
selection of titles we publish at:
www.TEACHServices.com

We encourage you to write us
with your thoughts about this,
or any other book we publish at:
info@TEACHServices.com

TEACH Services' titles may be purchased in
bulk quantities for educational, fund-raising,
business, or promotional use.
bulksales@TEACHServices.com

Finally, if you are interested in seeing
your own book in print, please contact us at:
publishing@TEACHServices.com

We are happy to review your manuscript at no charge.

www.ingramcontent.com/pod-product-compliance
Lightning Source LLC
Chambersburg PA
CBHW080725230426
43665CB00020B/2625